THE FIX

SOCCER AND ORGANIZED CRIME

DECLAN HILL

McCLELLAND & STEWART

Cloth edition published 2008
Paperback edition published 2010

Library and Archives Canada Cataloguing in Publication

Hill, Declan
    The fix : soccer and organized crime / Declan Hill.

Includes bibliographical references and index.
ISBN 978-0-7710-4139-6

    1. Soccer – Corrupt practices. 2. Organized crime. I. Title.

GV943.H45 2010   796.334   C2009-905218-0

We acknowledge the financial support of the Government of Canada through the Book Publishing Industry Development Program and that of the Government of Ontario through the Ontario Media Development Corporation's Ontario Book Initiative. We further acknowledge the support of the Canada Council for the Arts and the Ontario Arts Council for our publishing program.

Published simultaneously in the United States of America by McClelland & Stewart Ltd., P.O. Box 1030, Plattsburgh, New York 12901

Library of Congress Control Number: 2009935656

Typeset in Minion by M&S, Toronto
Printed and bound in Canada

McClelland and Stewart
a division of Random House of Canada Limited
One Toronto Street
Toronto, Ontario
M5C 2V6
www.mcclelland.com

4 5   14 13

Praise for THE FIX by DECLAN HILL

Winner of the 2009 Play the Game Award

"*The Fix* is a ground-breaking piece of investigative journalism of a kind almost never seen in sport. It contains the necessary mix of love for its subject and ice-cold analysis to function as an effective remedy against an illness that threatens to eradicate sport as we know it."
— Jens Sejer Andersen, Director of Play the Game,
an international conference and website for sports debate

"[This book] is one that any lover of soccer really should not ignore."
— *Fox Sports*

"A book I cannot recommend highly enough."
— Lawrence Donegan, *The Guardian*

"Excellent book! Top research, clean prose, beautifully paced."
— *Financial Times*

"Sensational. . . . fascinating reading." — *Winnipeg Free Press*

"A wake-up call for those in authority in football, and a call to arms for all of us who love the 'the beautiful game.'"
— Steven Powell, Director of Policy & Campaigns,
Football Supporters' Federation (England & Wales)

"*The Fix* is only the second football book, after Jennings's *Foul*, worthy of sharing the shelf with Yallop's *How They Stole The Game*. This book has me reaching into the depths of my own memory for any unappreciated signs of its existence in the world I was proudly a part of for so long. Declan Hill, many may fear, has produced an account of major significance."
— Shaka Hislop, ESPN soccer commentator and
former English Premier League and World Cup goalkeeper

". . . written with elegance and verve. Declan Hill has announced himself on the world stage with nothing less than a total triumph. No one who reads this will ever watch a match the same way."
— Joe McGinniss (author of *Selling the Presidency*
and *The Miracle of Castel di Sangro*)

2015

Love Jaimee

Have a great birthday!

Love Sydney !!

To Mum, for teaching "never give up"
even when my team was losing 8-0.

CONTENTS

NOTE ABOUT LANGUAGE

The cultural gap between Europe and North America is never bigger than when discussing the world's most popular sport. To Europeans, the sport is football and there is no other possible word. To North Americans, football is what men with shoulder pads, tight pants, and helmets play and the other sport is called soccer. In this book, I have tried to be consistent and call the sport soccer wherever possible. However, there are certain proper names – European Football Associations, FIFA, UEFA, etc. – where the word *football* is necessary. I have also not changed the interview excerpts: if a person used *football* or *soccer* I have kept the original usages. I have included certain words that are part of the universal language and lore of soccer. Most North Americans play soccer games or matches on either a field or a pitch. I hope the reader will understand when I use both.

PREFACE TO THE PAPERBACK EDITION

> This story is about the battle between good and evil that is at
> the heart of international soccer.
> *Emmanuel Petit, World Cup–winning French midfielder.*

It begins with a murder. Actually, it begins with two gruesome, bloody murders. On August 9, 2008, in the northern English town of Newcastle, the bodies of Kevin Zhen Xing Yang, a good-looking, friendly Chinese graduate student, and his girlfriend, Cici Xi Zhou, were discovered in a small flat near the city centre. Yang and Zhou had not simply been killed but tortured for hours before their deaths: his throat was slashed, her head smashed in three places. The police were mystified. The couple seemed to be popular. They had lots of friends and no apparent enemies. The case seemed unsolvable, until the police discovered Yang's real career. He was not, as he had told immigration authorities, a graduate student, but part of an international gambling ring. Yang's job was to organize other young Chinese living in the UK to monitor British soccer games for the multi-billion-dollar illegal Asian gambling market. They would go to the stadiums, watch the games, and provide live commentary on their mobile phones back to Asia. It was a clear, simple and very well-rewarded task, but somewhere, some how, Yang decided to betray his employers.

When the mob decides to kill, what they do with their victims' bodies sends a clear signal to the rest of the world. Most people disappear, ending up in anonymous cement holes or piles of acid-made dust dumped into a harbour. But for traitors and betrayers there must be a public demonstration of the power of the mob. Yang and Zhou got made into a message. Their mutilated bodies were symbols of what happens to those who betray a powerful, criminal industry.

English police caught a man who had been at the house. He had blood on his clothes and Yang's watch and computer. His defense was that he was simply renting a room in their apartment. He had been forced to open the door to the murderers and was tied up, terrified, in the bathroom while the torture and murders were going on. Despite this story, he was convicted and sentenced to thirty-three years in jail, but no one, not the police, not the judge, not the victims' families thought he was the brains behind the killings nor that he had acted alone. The judge said at the trial that he thought the defendant was too frightened to reveal who the other killers had been. To announce this finding, the English police held a public press conference. It was largely ignored in their own country and in the rest of Europe. However, it was broadcast live to China. There, an estimated *five hundred million* people tuned in to watch the event, or five times the number who watched the 2008 Super Bowl.

Kevin Yang, Cici Zhou, and their murderers are part of an international revolution. A global phenomenon of gambling and match-fixing that is transforming societies and destroying sports around the world. Many of the leagues in Asia, where it started, and Eastern Europe, have effectively collapsed because of this corruption. Now, the fixers are coming to Western Europe and North America and they are fixing hundreds of games.

A reader might be thinking, "Say what!? A multi-billion-dollar illegal gambling market? Five hundred million people watching what? Hundreds of fixed matches? This is too much!" I would not blame you if you did think that. When I began my research seven years ago, I knew little of this industry or its power. I was extraordinarily skeptical. This book is a record of what I discovered. It will explain to you how the industry functions and why the fixers have been so successful. You will read about hundreds of fixed matches in dozens of different countries around the world. You will read about pistol whippings, kidnappings, and murders. You will read about the good men who have tried to fight against this tide of corruption and how they have often been marginalized, sacked, imprisoned, or killed.

In short, you will read about the two greatest scandals in world sports today. You will read that there is a gang of fixers linked to organized criminals who have fixed some matches at the biggest sports tournaments in the world.

There has been a major European police investigation motivated, in part, by the first edition of *The Fix* and the controversy generated by the book. The investigation was launched by the organized crime team of the Federal Police in Bochum, Germany. The detectives listened to thousands of hours of covertly recorded telephone conversations. They placed dozens of people under surveillance and worked around the clock to try to uncover the true extent of the fixing network. After more than a year of this work, at exactly 6:24 a.m., on a cold November morning in 2009, hundreds of policemen across Europe moved in and arrested dozens of suspects. Over the next few days, they announced the preliminary findings of their work: two hundred suspicious matches across nine countries, and one hundred different players, referees, coaches, league officials, and gangsters were suspected of being involved. Over the ensuing weeks, the number of suspicious games and players involved climbed. It was a new type of globalized corruption that stretched across countries and continents: a fixer living in Germany, allegedly controlling players living in Switzerland, Turkey or Greece, defrauding the illegal gambling markets in Hong Kong and Malaysia with the help of assistants in London and Holland.

The games under suspicion range from matches in the prestigious Champions League down to youth-level games played by adolescents in local parks. Even the hapless Canadian national team was unwittingly involved. In November 2009, a few weeks before the arrests were made, the Canadians had lost 3-0 to a weak Macedonian team. It was not that the Canadians had lost to such pitiful opposition that aroused the suspicions of the investigators, but that the match had featured four penalties. Four penalties is a lot for a soccer match; most games do not even feature one. Stranger still was that on the Asian illegal gambling market, someone had placed a very large bet on there being at least three goals and the exact number of penalties awarded. When news of the "irregular betting patterns" on the number of goals and penalties emerged, UEFA, the organization that runs European soccer, decided to both investigate and suspend the referee.

This book introduces you to some of the key fixers and shows you how they operate. You will read in Chapter 8 about a fixer from China who in 2004 moved to Belgium. He was helped by a local Sicilian businessman and he fixed dozens of games over the next year in the Belgian top division. You will read in Chapter 11 about the depth of corruption in the Turkish league, how both players and club officials there were involved in numerous cases of match-fixing. In Chapter 12, you will read about the Sapina brothers, two Croatians living in Germany, who fixed a number of matches in the German leagues. In Chapter 14, you will read about William Lim, a Malaysian-Chinese, who in 2007 was convicted of fixing games in Austria. From Chapter 16 on, you will meet Lee Chin, a gangster-fixer living in Bangkok, who claims to have fixed dozens of high-level matches.

Here is the headline: they are – according to the German police investigation – connected. Most of them know each other and phoned each other regularly. According to the prosecution report, and this has been untested in court, Sapina's good friend and business partner was a fellow-Croat living in Nuremburg who was heard on secret surveillance tape talking about William Lim as "his good friend." They even phoned Lim in his secret hideout in Europe. There is other evidence of the linkages between these convicted fixers. For example, in Lim's copious police files and phone records, marked VNR ST/1528209/2005, there is a sheet of paper with the Belgian fixer's phone number and the name of a well-known fixed match written on it. I want to stress that this is not a well-ordered criminal conspiracy. They do not have a strict hierarchy and clear structure. There is no Capo or boss of bosses ordering the rest of them around. It is simply a group of criminals doing what they do: sometimes colluding, sometimes competing with each other, but always looking for the next chance to profit by fixing a soccer game.

Here is a second headline, and this strangely has not yet motivated a major police investigation: a similar gang of fixers has been operating at every single major international soccer tournament for at least the last twenty years. As you will read in this book, their record has been confirmed by dozens of different players, coaches, and senior sporting officials. These fixers have been present at the Under-17 World Cup, the Under-20 World Cup, the Olympic soccer tournament, the Women's World Cup, and the Men's World Cups. I believe they have successfully fixed matches at a very high level of international soccer.

When *The Fix* was first published in September 2008, there was a big push-back against my findings. Much of that push-back was innocent. Many fans simply did not want to know bad news. It is like a patient hearing from a doctor that they have cancer. It is easier, in some cases, to deny reality than to admit what is actually going on. Now that the European police investigation is confirming much of what is written in this book, some fans are proceeding from denial to resignation, without going through combat. They are saying things like, "Well, it is only the small games in small leagues from small countries that are involved." This is the attitude of the deliberately blind. It also avoids the question, What happens in five years? Star players do not emerge fully grown from the ground. Many players on big teams in the big leagues come from the very teams and leagues that have now been shown to be corrupt.

Nor, if you are reading this book in North America, should you be too smug. It may all sound exotic and quaint, but this new form of sports corruption will come here. The amount of money in the Asian gambling market is simply too large not to start flooding into North American sports, even down to a very low-level. It is already here in a small way. I have spoken to a number of professionals in the Major League Soccer (MLS). They told me of other players working for gamblers – not fixing but just providing them with information, who was injured, who was getting on the bus, who was going to play well. This is where it starts. It is what is known as "a gateway crime," and it means that in a few years, unless something is done to stop it, North America will have its own fixing scandals based on this new network of corruption.

Strangely the attitude of deliberate ignorance does not stop with ordinary soccer fans; the push-back goes all the way to many top-level soccer officials. This is why I wrote earlier of the two greatest scandals in the sports world today. The first scandal is that gangs of criminals have been so successful at destroying so many soccer leagues and tournaments. The second scandal is that many sports officials, in charge of running those tournaments, have known of the presence of these fixers and chosen to take very little effective action against them. I am not saying that all games in all leagues should be suspected, nor am I saying that all sports officials are corrupt or have chosen to be complicit with corruption. The world of international sports organizations is a house with many rooms: most people in most of those rooms are hard-working, honest, decent people. However, many officials simply do not want to know what is really going on.

This may seem extraordinary to a reader. Surely, everyone connected would want to do everything possible to stop corruption? However, some of the very top officials, the ones in charge of leading the organizations, have some very odd backgrounds. There is, for example, Grigori Surkis. In 1995, he was the president of Dynamo Kiev, the top team in the Ukraine at the time. Dynamo was thrown out of the Champions League, when some of its officials tried to bribe the Spanish referee for an upcoming game with fur coats. Two of Dynamo's administrators were banned for life from the sport: Vasiliy Babiychuk, the general secretary of Dynamo, and Igor Surkis, Grigori's brother and a board member of the club. A number of UEFA officials told me that after they made this decision they had to receive police protection from who they thought were the Ukrainian mafia, presumably unconnected with the club. A few months later, UEFA changed its decision and Dynamo Kiev was allowed back into the competition the next year and the bans against Igor Surkis and Babiychuk were overturned. Igor Surkis has subsequently become president of Dynamo Kiev. However, in 2004, Grigori Surkis was officially banned from entering the United States for corruption and falsifying election results. Surkis claimed in an Ukrainian newspaper that the American charges "do not correspond with reality." Certainly, they have not hindered his rise in the Ukraine where he is now both a politician and President of the Ukrainian Football Federation. Nor have they hindered him in the world of inter-national soccer, for also in 2004, he was appointed to sit on the Executive Committee of UEFA – the board that runs the organization that runs all of European soccer.

Another football association, another room. Since the publication of this book I have been asked by a number of European soccer officials to consult for their organizations. At best, the officials want to discuss how to put in place measures to stop match-corruption. There are lots of ways to do this – more women and professional referees, better pen-sions and education benefits for players, an integrity unit in each soccer association made up of ex-policemen. All of these things are relatively easy to do and many soccer officials are often ready and willing to listen to the ideas.

However, at worst, the officials actually want to know who my sources are and how to get hold of them. Last year, I had a meeting with two prominent European soccer officials in a café that was one of those types of meetings. We spoke at length, and I told them that, like all good researchers, I would never reveal my sources. It is a principle of trust. One of the executives is a very honest and decent man. His colleague, who is from a European area renowned for organized crime, had a dif-ferent attitude towards corruption than his colleague. He said, "Maybe the best way to deal with corruption is to bury it. Deny it exists. If too many people start to doubt the sport, what can we do?"

At one point, the first executive excused himself and went to the bathroom. When he was gone, the second executive leaned across the table and said, "You spoke about trust at the beginning of our conversation. Well it also works the other way. In my home city I have lots of friends, of the type that you know. If you fuck us over, they will fuck you over, you understand?" There was a slight pause and then he laughed. I said, "Oh really? Well maybe your people should speak to my people." And then we both laughed. When the other executive came back neither of us said a word about this conversation and they left soon afterwards.

A final note. You will understand that the research for this book has been dangerous. For that reason I have held back certain names, dates, and other information. After the publication, I placed complete files with two different lawyers in two different countries. I gave them specific instructions, if anything were to happen to me, that they should release *all* the details. I did this for my family and for my own protection. I hope you will never read those files. I hope that this book will do. I hope it will be enough to change the sport for good, forever.

THE BIRDS OF PREY

July 17, 1994, was a hot, sunny Californian day. In the Rose Bowl, Pasadena, over 90,000 spectators had jammed themselves in to watch the final of the World Cup. On the field, the Italian and Brazilian national teams would fight it out for soccer supremacy, and a worldwide television audience estimated at more than two billion people watched them. Meanwhile, in the VIP section sat the cream of international society. Pelé, the man who had been the world's best and most popular player, mingled among celebrities and political leaders such as Al Gore and Henry Kissinger. But in the box sat someone with a more controversial background – Anzor Kikalishvili. A U.S. Congressional inquiry and the Federal Bureau of Investigation (FBI) would both name him as one of the top mobsters of Russian organized crime. He had been a communist government functionary, but after the collapse of the Soviet Union, he became the president of an organization: the 21st Century Association. The 21st Century Association had bad luck with its presidents. Its last chief executive had been killed by a sniper's bullet. The one before that had been murdered in a mafia shoot-out. 21st Century was reputed to offer protection (or "krisha") to the other Russian "mafiyas" who offered krisha to the rest of the country. A month after the World Cup Final, an FBI investigation – attempting to stop Kikalishvili's steady incursion into Florida – had wiretapped him threatening to skin a Florida couple like animals. None of the FBI investigators doubted his threats.

Anzor Kikalishvili probably felt quite comfortable with some of the other guests in the section that afternoon. At the centre of the box was João

Havelange, then head of the Fédération Internationale de Football Association (FIFA). He had been named in 1994 by a Brazilian district attorney for his connections with "the country's most notorious capo," one Castor de Andrade, the head of an illegal gambling network estimated at $2.6 billion. A man who also had, according to Brazilian law enforcement, connections with top Colombian drug gangs. Near to him sat Vyacheslav Koloskov, then president of the Russian Football Union, an organization plagued by the problem of mafiya contract killings. Juan José Bellini, the president of the Colombian Football Federation, was not there. He could not make it that afternoon: one of the players on the Colombian team had been gunned down soon after returning from the World Cup. A year later, Bellini would be convicted of "illegal enrichment" and money laundering for the Cali cartel. FIFA is the world organization that runs soccer. All of these men were either members of FIFA or were guests at the biggest showcase of soccer in the world.

I met Anzor Kikalishvili in a Georgian restaurant in Moscow in the winter of 1999. He told me the story of how he had enjoyed watching the 1994 World Cup Final and how he loved sports, particularly soccer. I was there as an associate producer on a television documentary for the Canadian Broadcasting Corporation (CBC) that was later broadcast for the American program Frontline. Since the 1994 World Cup, Kikalishvili had been banned from entering the United States, and he wanted to impress us as a reasonable and civilized man. He took us for dinner at a tiny restaurant. It was, like a lot of Moscow at the time, slightly surreal. The front section of the restaurant was full of English construction workers who had been flown into Moscow to work on a building project. Why one would fly English workers into Russia, a country with high unemployment and low wages, was never explained. They were drinking pints of lager and rapidly getting drunk. Behind their section was a narrow hallway that led to an expensive restaurant. It was beautifully decorated and served exquisite Georgian food. Kikalishvili arrived late; his armour-plated 4 x 4 mounting the pavement and stopping three feet from the restaurant door. A very large, muscular guard in a designer suit stood in front of the door. Two more men were in the tiny hallway. I know this because when I got up to go outside and check on our driver, they would not let me leave without a nod from Kikalishvili. There were no other exits from the room. The food was excellent, the wine plentiful, and Kikalishvili a very good host. However, Kikalishvili's security precautions were probably a good idea. A few weeks after our visit, his offices near the Kremlin were blown up in a bomb attack. Kikalishvili was unhurt, which is more than can be said for the heavily damaged building.

The research for the television documentary was interesting. The program was based on the revelations of a freelance journalist, Robert Friedman, who had shown the connections between Russian mobsters and players in the National Hockey League. He had also had a contract put on him by some of the same Russian mobsters. Although one U.S. Senate investigator estimated that more than 80 per cent of hockey players were paying protection money to mobsters, the connections were often deeper: they were about friendships, business, or political ambitions. Pavel Bure, for example, was a great hockey player, but also a kind of male Anna Kournikova, a high-profile pin-up boy who enjoyed wide popularity on both sides of the Atlantic. He was, as well, Anzor Kikalishvili's political protégé, and when we visited Moscow, there were posters across the city of the two men together, campaigning for the 21st Century Association. Other major hockey players were helping mobsters with their immigration requirements or their business activities or just hanging out as friends.

What stunned me was that so few people actually seemed to mind the presence of so many organized crime figures in a sport. I went to interview a top Russian player, one of the most influential players in the league. He had been linked to mobsters by sources at the FBI. As I was leaving to meet him, one of my bosses came out of his office and spoke to me about the meeting. He did not want to know the player's views on the mafia or the possibility of games being fixed or even some of his potential connections. Rather, my boss asked me to inquire about his play in a recent play-off game. I was struck by this incident. Here was a seasoned, cynical journalist who knew the essential structure of the story, but even he was dazzled by the thought of meeting, albeit indirectly, a top player. It made me realize the power and ability of sports players to airbrush the images of even the most unsavory characters. After the investigation, I worked on other organized crime stories. But as I did so, I could not help my mind turning over the question: if a relatively low-profile sport like hockey could sanitize mobsters, would the same be true for international soccer?

I was raised in England, so soccer was my sport. I love the game with a love and desire that is almost unexplainable except to other lovers. My first experience came in one of those moments that change your life. I was in primary school and a gang of classmates came up to me and asked which team I liked better, Arsenal or Liverpool? I was six. I had heard of neither team, but I thought that Arsenal was such a ridiculous name that they must be the weaker, underdog team, so I chose them. It was a decision, casually made, that has been impossible to alter. I read once of a soccer fan who said, "You can be a lousy father, you can divorce your wife, you can move countries, but you can never change your soccer team." So it has proven with me. For most of my childhood and adult years, I loathed everything about Arsenal. Their style was unpardonably ugly. They delighted in kicking great lumps out of their opponents and then kicking the ball far down the pitch. They had no technique, no skill, and no verve. Worse, I discovered that, unlike a genuine underdog team, they were rich. They could have played with panache and flair. But instead under a range of different managers they played as thugs. Not much good it did me. Like a man in love with a faithless woman, I discovered I was powerless to change a decision of my heart. Years were spent, until the arrival of Arsène Wenger, watching Arsenal kick, thump, and intimidate their way to victory.

I also played for years, but I was never a particularly good player. Every season I would play superbly for about half an hour. In that half an hour, I would fly across the pitch. Whatever skills, stamina, speed I had would all unite in one brief moment of injury-free bliss. The memories of those half-hours would keep me warm in the winter. They would keep me playing in dozens of games, when I did nothing of note. They would keep me turning up at the start of new seasons ready to enjoy my half-hour of soccer heaven. So I do not have racks of medals or trophies. But I do have good memories and great friends given to me by the beautiful game. It is for those memories and loves that I decided to use my investigative skills to give back something to the game that has given me so much.

It is easier to write a book with the weight of a large institution behind you than as a freelance writer. So I enrolled as a doctoral student at the University of Oxford. It was a place I had dreamed of going for most of my life. It is glorious: full of interesting history, superb buildings, and great resources. My first year there was, probably, the happiest of my life. However, it was not a complete dream, and I have a great dislike of those books about Oxford whose authors describe it all as glamour, glory, and glittering prizes. There are plenty of little people in the big buildings there. But I do owe the university a large debt of gratitude. The teachers, tutors, and supervisors, for the most part, did something almost unknown in the academic world: they left me alone. They made it clear that they were ready to chat if I needed any help, but then they figuratively nodded at the books and all the resources of the university and told me to get on with it.

My college, Green, was a scholar's dream: a small, protective enclave full of fascinating people. It even has an eighteenth-century observatory at its centre, surrounded by a garden perpetually in bloom. I loved my life there. I joined Green's rowing team. One of my teammates spoke eighteen languages (no, I didn't believe him either, until I heard him speak them all); another was a graduate student/computer hacker/CEO of a computer company that had invented a new form of Internet money (no, I don't know when he slept either); another one has graduated to running six-day marathons in the Sahara Desert; and the rest were simply medical students or Fulbright Scholars. I ended my time at the university working with the type of man that I thought had disappeared with the death of David Niven or Rex Harrison – a true English gentleman. His name is Anthony Heath. He was the chairman of the Sociology Department. We would meet in his book-lined office and our discussions of the work were usually conducted over cups of tea, but Heath's beautifully gentle manner hides a tough, rigorous mind and an athlete's past. He has done a range of interesting work, from exploring class and education in the U.K. to designing political surveys in current-day Iraq. He guided me through the difficulties of completing a doctorate at Oxford, and I will forever be grateful to him for his graciousness and intelligence.

But I did not work simply as an academic. I also used the skills that I had developed as an investigative journalist. I interviewed people who had been involved in the game. It may seem odd, but very few journalists have tried to speak to people inside soccer about the presence of organized crime in the game. This is partly to do with the role of sports journalists. Sports journalists are often intelligent, hard-working, principled people. However, they have a job to do, and that job is to report on the results of not one particular game but on every single game, week after week, season after season. This means that they depend on the club or league officials to get them access to the matches and players. It means that if they discover something scandalous, they have to weigh up an odd dilemma: do I reveal the scandal and thereby potentially lose my access, or do I keep quiet and keep my job easy? For me, there was no dilemma. I did not care about the results of the game. I was not interested in securing long-term access to players. I just wanted to understand the truth of what was going on inside the sport. Ironically, people were often very interested in speaking to me, because no one had contacted them before and they desperately wanted to speak out about the corruption in the sport.

At first, I was interested in the general issue of organized crime in soccer. I was particularly fascinated with the concept of image laundering, where a previously unknown gangster takes over a prominent club or links himself with a famous player and begins to transform himself from a "controversial businessman" to a "colourful businessman" to, when his team or player wins the championship, a "member of the establishment." The most successful proponent of this skill was Joseph Kennedy, who had gone from a bootlegging scumbag supplying the mob with liquor in the midst of Prohibition in one generation to being the father of the president of the United States in the next. However, events overtook me. Some of the top *teams in Europe were bought up by people so corrupt that you would hesitate to have your wife, son, or wallet within a hundred yards of them. Yet no one seemed to have stopped them.*

However, I began to become interested in the subject of match-fixing. It was, in the words of one worried tennis executive I spoke to, "the ultimate threat to the credibility of the sport."

I visited some of the world's most famous soccer stadiums, teams, and games to see organized criminals in action. I investigated leagues where Chinese triads have fixed more than 80 per cent of the games; and I found that top international referees often get offered, and accept, "female bribes" before they arbitrate some of the biggest games in soccer.

When I first started giving lectures at Oxford, people were surprised to hear about the connections between organized crime and sport. I gave presentations at international conferences. I said publicly, and at some risk to myself because my research was not finished, that European sport leagues were facing a tsunami of match-fixing by Asian criminals. Few people wanted to believe it. Even fewer people seemed to want to do anything about it. It was mostly, as I will show, out of incompetence and racist ignorance. It was also because the factors that have given rise to this new wave of fixing are unprecedented and have never really been seen or studied before. But it was in small part because of a phenomenon that was recognized more than eighty years ago. It was supposed to have occurred during the scandal surrounding the trial of baseball's Chicago White Sox. The team threw the 1919 World Series with the help of mobster Arnold Rothstein. One of their players was the clean-cut star "Shoeless" Joe Jackson. As Jackson came up to the courthouse, a little boy was supposed to have elbowed his way through the crowd, gazed up at his hero with big, clear, innocent eyes, and said, "Say it ain't so, Joe. Just say it ain't so." The little boy represents the faith that we embody in our sporting heroes. We do not want to believe that human frailty lurks within them. We do not want to believe that they, who can do what we cannot, would stoop to sully themselves. We do not want to believe, when so much in our lives is so corrupt, that the garden of innocence that is supposed to be sport could also be corrupt.

In my journey I did find real heroes: people who have attempted to clean up the world's "beautiful game." They have, for the most part, been marginalized, stamped on, or silenced. Their stories are littered throughout this book: failed journalists, dead referees, ignored players. I will also introduce you to some of the fixers, criminals, and con men who corrupt the sport. Whenever possible I have tried to allow the criminals to speak for themselves, using verbatim transcripts of either their interviews or covertly recorded conversations. The work has, at times, been difficult and dangerous. For that reason, in some places in the text, I have changed the locations of the interviews and the names of both the innocent and the guilty. (The first time that I introduce someone whose name has been changed, I will place an asterisk beside it in the text.) I have done that to protect myself and my interview subjects from all the dangers that a reader can imagine.

I have also tried to show the results of my research at the university. Woven through the journey, I try to explain how soccer players and referees actually perform in fixed games, the structure and mechanics of illegal gambling syndicates, why relatively rich and high-status athletes would fix games, why club officials decide to try to bribe the opposition, how clubs go about doing it, how they get referees "on their side" and how, I believe, Asian gambling fixers have successfully entered the game and fixed top international matches. I found that many of these underlying criminal mechanics are not only found in soccer. Really, the methods, manners, and motivations of the fixers could work for almost any other team sport, be it hockey, basketball, or baseball. Consequently, I have put in examples from other sports to show the similarities. Understand how gambling fixers work to corrupt a soccer game and you will understand how they move into a basketball league, a cricket tournament, or a tennis match (all places, by the way, that criminal fixers have moved into).

My views on soccer have changed. I still love the Saturday-morning game between amateurs: the camaraderie and the fresh smell of grass. But the professional game leaves me cold. I hope you will understand why after reading the book. I think you may never look at sport in the same way again.

ASIA
THE STORM CLOUDS

PROLOGUE

Raul Hernandez (*) was at one time one of the most promising young players in the world. I interviewed him in Singapore on the night of a Champions League game. European games start at two or three o'clock in the morning Singapore time, so after the interview we sat up long into the night to watch the match. In the interview and conversation, Hernandez seemed very honest. He had spoken about his problems adapting to a lifestyle of fame and status. He had become a drug addict, got divorced, and eventually dropped out of the game. But now with his parents' help, he had turned his life around. Hernandez remarried, became a publicly professed Christian, and re-entered soccer.

He told me he had taken part in fixed matches where his team's manager or owner had bribed players on the opposing team. But he claimed he had never taken a bribe or had anything to do with gambling in his life.

The next day we met for coffee. He had been playing for his club and had received no salary. The owner had simply refused to pay him.

But he had a surprise for me.

As we drank our coffees and chatted about the game the night before, he leaned forward and said, "You know a lot of these fixers, don't you?"

"Well, I have interviewed some of them, yes," I replied.

"Give me one of their phone numbers."

"What?"

"Give me one of their phone numbers," he repeated. "Look, I haven't been paid in four months. I have a wife. I have commitments. I could make a lot of money this way."

1

THE CONQUEST OF THE LOCUSTS

He was a great guy. He took me into "table talks" with the
Tiger Generals. That is a rank in the triads. They would sit
down and pull out their knives and screwdrivers, put them
on the table and then it was, "Okay, let's talk." There were men
behind us, armed bodyguards, and we would just wait. This
was all the ritual of the table talk. It depended on the invitation. If the invite said, "Between 7:00 and 7:30," it meant
"there was still room for talk." If it said, "7:30 exactly," it
meant "you are going to fight."

On October 2, 2004, Yang Zuwu, the manager of the Chinese team
Beijing Hyundai, did something odd. In the eighty-fourth minute of a
game in front of thousands of fans at the Wulihe Stadium in Shenyang,
he ordered his team to walk off the field. The referee had just called a
penalty against his team. However, several even odder things followed
Yang's command. Not only did his entire team obey him, but as the
players sat in their dressing room, Yang stood outside and announced
that his team was refusing to take part in the rest of the match or in any
more matches in the Chinese Super League.

Yang was no ordinary head of an ordinary team that could be dismissed for mere petulance. Beijing Hyundai was one of the richest teams
in the league, sponsored by the Korean car company. Yang Zuwu, a

veteran of more than forty years of Chinese soccer, declared that the league was too full of "faked matches, black whistles, illegal betting on games, and other ugly phenomena." All these factors had become so blatant that it was, in his view, impossible to play honestly in the league. Yang received support from other top clubs. One official, Xu Ming, the owner of the Dalian Shide football club and the most powerful private investor in the sport, came out publicly with his support, saying that another group of teams was also considering pulling out of the Chinese league because the corruption was so bad.

At first, the Chinese Football Association (CFA) refused to listen. It was all too embarrassing. They had only established the new league six months before Yang's pull out. The idea had been to establish an elite, professionally run league that could help catapult Chinese soccer to the top of the world game. Each team that wanted to participate in the league had to have a capitalization of tens of millions of dollars. A prominent Asian soccer official who had visited one of the Chinese clubs described it in awestruck tones:

> I visited one club that had twelve practice pitches: an Olympic stan-
> dard stadium, fitness centre, community centre. There were dormito-
> ries, housing complexes. It was incredible, like something out of the
> days of Mao.

Now, with Mr. Yang's very public protest, only six months after its incep-
tion, the Chinese Super League, with all its hundreds of millions of dollars, had effectively collapsed.

It really should not have come as a surprise to anyone connected with Chinese soccer. For years before the founding of the Super League, the Chinese Football Association had heard about the stories of corruption that swirled around their sport. The Chinese national team had taken part in the 2002 World Cup; they had not scored a goal and it was alleged in Chinese newspapers that they had thrown their games in return for gambling payoffs. The players and officials all denied it, claiming that they would never betray their country; however, many newspapers remained skeptical. But the big scandal that might have led to a cleansing of the game was the Black Whistles Affair. It broke in 2001, when Song Weiping, a construction magnate turned soccer club owner, went public with his complaints about corruption. He made hundreds of millions as a property developer and sponsored his city's second division soccer team. Then Song publicly threatened to give up soccer for the kinder, gentler world of the construction business because the sport was so corrupt and he was tired of paying bribes to referees. Song even provided documents and a list of referees who took bribes – "most of them," he alleged. A sports newspaper, *Qiu Bao*, took up the investigation and discovered that the corruption might have spread further, right into the Chinese Football Association. One team alleged that they had paid 800,000 RMB (Chinese renminbi, roughly US$100,000) to an official of that organization – alternately described by commentators as "non-descript" to "radioactive – everything they touch seems to shrivel and die" – to appoint referees favourable to their team.

The Chinese Football Association responded to this situation by declaring an amnesty and no public exposure for any corrupt referee who came forward. Gong Jianping, the chief referee of the association and a FIFA-ranked international referee, promptly took them up on their offer. Just as promptly, the Chinese authorities broke their word and arrested him. His trial featured accounts of sex bribes for referees and card games with high-ranking Chinese Football Association officials. An ambitious referee, it was alleged, was supposed to play cards for high stakes with the CFA officials, then lose the game, so that the officials would receive his money. In return, the referee would receive the plum international games to referee. The only way the average referee could afford to play in the card games was to accept bribes. For his apparent honesty, Gong Jianping received the "lenient sentence" of ten years in a hard labour camp. He died soon afterwards. Since then, no other referee has taken up the Chinese Football Association's offer of an amnesty.

This was the state of affairs that Sepp Blatter, the president of FIFA, flew into in the summer of 2004. At first, he seemed curiously unaware of the corruption in Chinese soccer. He gave a speech in which he did not mention corruption. Rather, he talked about top European clubs sending their young players to Asia to give them more experience. Blatter seemed ignorant of the nature of the "experience" that the rising stars of the game may have begun to learn, but he did not remain ignorant for long.

On July 17, 2004, Blatter and other FIFA officials along with senior officials of the Chinese Football Association visited the Beijing Workers' Stadium to see the opening of the Asian Cup. Someone probably thought that a ceremony in one of the most repressive countries in the world, held a few kilometres from Tiananmen Square, would present no controversy or problems. But that is to underestimate the power of soccer. When the unpopular deputy secretary-general of the Chinese Football Association tried to address the stadium, the furious crowd shouted him down. They screamed insults at all the Chinese Football Association officials. When the head of the Asian wing of FIFA stood up, they insulted him too. Then someone *really* made a mistake. Thinking that no one would dare jeer the president of FIFA, authorities let Blatter go ahead with his planned speech. The crowd booed him. The whole thing became an international diplomatic incident. What really shocked the Chinese was that FIFA officials, whose idea of a heated discussion is normally about as spicy as fizzy water, held a press conference after the game, and said publicly, "You don't deserve to hold the Olympics, if this is how you treat your guests."

The horde of locusts that destroyed the credibility of the Chinese Super League has devoured soccer across Asia. Five players on Hong Kong's 1998 World Cup team were caught fixing a qualifying match against Thailand. The players were convicted after the Hong Kong anti-corruption squad busted a $50 million illegal gambling syndicate with connections in Malaysia, Singapore, and Thailand. In Indonesia, a prominent soccer official came forward and spoke about the existence of a "referees' mafia." In Vietnam, the notorious mafia chief Nam Cam was put in front of a firing squad June 3, 2004. The reason for his execution was partly his widespread fixing of soccer games. He was so successful that he fixed many of the Vietnamese soccer league and national team matches. He even fixed matches featuring the Hanoi police team. His death did not end the fixing.

These Asian fixers kept me up at night. As I travelled the continent researching their activities, I was nervous. I heard stories of their terrifying reach almost everywhere I went. Each night before I went to bed, I would carefully unscrew the lightbulb in my hotel room, rearrange the furniture, and put my bed in a different position. I calculated that if anyone came into the room, they would enter in one of two ways: either barge straight in, switch the light on, and shoot me or creep in slowly in the dark and kill me while I was still asleep. Either way, I thought I had about five seconds to alter their strategy and throw them off balance. If the door was barricaded with a dresser, if they could not switch the light on, or if they tripped over something while searching for the bed, it changed the odds in my favour just a little. Goodness knows what I could have done after that. The fixers are not known for their gentility. The legends of their violence hang over the world of Asian sport. I received countless warnings to stay away from them. They are spoken of in whispers by frightened players and sports officials. Bruce Grobbelaar, the goalkeeper with the English team Liverpool who allegedly took money from an Asian gambling syndicate, once told a friend about the dangers of crossing the "Mr. Bigs" of this world:

> Because then you're fucking him around, and he won't like it, and he'll tell his Short Man . . . and then you get the chop and then you better watch it. You better get a bulletproof fucking vest, then . . . That's how fucking big it is . . . This is how fucking dangerous it is . . . When you're playing with fucking dangerous men, it's fucking dangerous.

Grobbelaar is not alone in his fear. In Malaysia and Singapore, there are stories of gang attacks, a poisonous cobra being put in a player's car, and of a goalkeeper dying in a "mysterious" car accident. One defender told the police about how he was forced into fixing a game:

> It was during training time. Two Chinese men, maybe five feet six inches, thirty years old, came up to me and congratulated me. They said they knew Mike and Jimmy [two Singaporean match-fixers]. They were Jimmy's men. They had just met some of the other players. They asked me to co-operate with a fix against Singapore. I refused. I left. The two Chinese followed me and forced me to stop. One of them took out a Rambo-style knife and threatened to kill me and my wife if I did not agree to help them.

A coach who had worked in Asian leagues told me how his players were approached by gambling match-fixers.

> There is no nice chat, no long-term relationship stuff. They just ring up the players and say, "You do it or else." They will phone the players and say, "We want this game to be 2-0 spread. You win. Or you lose." If the player tells them to fuck off, they say, "We know where your sister goes to school" or "where your granny shops."

These are not isolated incidents. In the last fifteen years, soccer leagues across the continent have effectively been sabotaged by match-fixing. But the first, the biggest, and the most public fiasco was in Malaysia and Singapore in the early 1990s. It was there that I decided to begin my research.

In 1989, the Malaysian and Singapore Football Associations established a new professional league. The idea, as with the Chinese league fifteen years later, was to catapult their national teams into international prominence by having a well-established, well-run domestic league. The two federal governments helped with funding. There were new, modern stadiums built. There was a lucrative television contract that ensured that the league was seen by millions of people. Teams were allowed to import foreign stars to improve the quality of the play. The league was popular, with some matches attracting over fifty thousand fans.

It became a complete disaster.

The conventional story is that as interest in the league grew, so did the number of people betting on the results of the games. The fixers moved in. They understood there was an enormous amount of money to be made fleecing the betting public if they could fix the results. By the time the authorities finally cracked down on the league in 1994, over 80 per cent of the games were thought to have been fixed, and the fixers had spread their attention to matches around the world, purportedly trying to fix English Premier League matches. However, the real story about the collapse of the Malaysian and Singaporean soccer league has not been told before.

Every story needs a hero and this one has two: Lazarus Rokk and Johnson Fernandez. In the early 1990s, they were two hard-working sports journalists writing for the sister papers the *Malay Mail* and the *New Straits Times*. They were not investigative journalists, simply two guys who liked their soccer. I interviewed a wide range of journalists on the Malay Peninsula, and some of them are quite open about helping criminals or players fix games. One even told me exactly how he helped out:

> I worked a couple of times for the bookies. They asked me to speak to some of the players. So during the practice I said [to the player], "Lim (*) asks, Okay?" And the player replied, "Okay." That was it. No more. They had their agreement. They were just confirming it.

This journalistic culture of sleaze is part of what made doing the research so tense. I knew that some of the journalists I interviewed worked as middlemen for the gangs. In a way, the more honest ones were the ones who told me that they helped the fixers. What I did not know was if, or when, other, more complicit people that I interviewed were going to tell their criminal friends to pay me a visit in the middle of the night.

Rokk and Fernandez are not like that. They are two decent men, now in their early fifties, who remain traumatized years after these events. Their suspicions of the widespread fixing began soon after the end of the professional league's first season. Fernandez was summoned to his editor's office. There was a "well-dressed gentleman" from the Malaysian Anti-Corruption Agency (ACA) who wanted to talk to him. The ACA man had come to Fernandez because of his knowledge about sport, and he started asking Fernandez questions about the possible involvement of some members of one of the Malay Royal Families in some of the fixing.

There is a huge difference between what journalists think they know and what they can legally print in their newspapers. The official investigation into one of the Malaysian Royal Families, perhaps deliberately, went nowhere. So at first Fernandez and Rokk were not able to get the evidence to write full stories.

> For years, we had been trying to get the state FAs and the Malay Football Association to start probing into match-fixing in the country. But they didn't take us too seriously. They didn't think it was serious enough. So we decided to go in ourselves . . . after we dug further, whatever we knew and whatever we saw was only the tip of the iceberg. Our probing became a little bit more intense, and we discovered a whole lot more maggots in soccer.

They got their break when they discovered a source who worked with the fixing gangs. He brought a whole new perspective to the investigation. He would tell them *before* the games what the final score would be. Their source was a big, tough Brickfields gangster. Brickfields is the working-class area, mainly Indian, around the Kuala Lumpur central train station. Malaysia is not a particularly dangerous country for street crime, but Brickfields is not the kind of place you want to wander around at night. Rokk and Fernandez's source was the King of Brickfields. He showed them a whole new side to life and sports. Rokk even remembers him bringing them to meetings with the triads:

> He was a great guy. He took me into "table talks" with the Tiger Generals. That is a rank in the triads. They would sit down and pull out their knives and screwdrivers, put them on the table and then it was, "Okay, let's talk." There were men behind us, armed bodyguards, and we would just wait. This was all the ritual of the table talk. It depended on the invitation. If the invite said, "Between 7:00 and 7:30," it meant "there was still room for talk." If it said, "7:30 exactly," it meant "you are going to fight."

With the help of their underworld source and others, the two journalists discovered how the fixing in the league was organized. Fernandez and Rokk laid it out for me, and I was able to corroborate the fixers' strategies with the players, policemen, and the fixers themselves. First off, here is how the fixers and players use networks to co-operate with one another. For a start, most gambling fixers don't actually meet directly with the players. Rather, they use what are known as "runners." Fernandez explained to me who they were:

> They use former players. They are known to officials and players. They don't create suspicion. They just look as if they are interested in the fate of their former team. It is often that they [the fixers] use former players.

This type of runner is perfect for a fixer. Whereas an outsider will not get past security, a former player with a big reputation can easily get access to any team event or into their hotel. They can walk into a player's room without any questions being asked. The players trust them. They can also speak to the fixers, as they are not being watched by team security. They are the connectors between the illegal gambling world and a potentially corrupt soccer team. However, those runners, as former players, obviously, cannot fix the games themselves. They need someone directly on the team.

Scott Ollerenshaw never fixed a game in his life, but he taught me the next stage of fixing. He was a star forward in the Malaysian League in the 1990s. Ollerenshaw played around the world, from his early days with the Sydney Olympic of New South Wales, to Walsall in the English third division, to an international match against the great Brazilian national team, starring Romário, in front of tens of thousands of screaming fans. However, nothing prepared Ollerenshaw for what he faced while playing in Asia.

> There were rumours all the time, but basically half the team was on the fix and the other half of the team was out there trying as hard as they could.

Now that he is no longer playing, Ollerenshaw is a lovely, amiable man. But he was one tough player: a fiery redhead with a quick temper. After one game, some of his corrupt teammates tried to break his legs because he threatened to beat them up for fixing a game. But he knows now how they operated.

> What happened with our mob was that there was a ringleader. And the bookie would contact him and say, "You're playing such and such a team, we are desperate for you to lose the game. Here is $50,000, how you distribute is up to you." So then he would know that there were five or six corrupt guys on the team and he would go up to five of them and say, "Okay, here is four or five thousand for you after the game. I will pay you cash if you help me lose the game." He was basically like a project manager. He would get the money, make sure the job was done right, and then distribute the money.

This project manager must be an influential player. South African cricket captain Hansie Cronje fixed international matches; the infamous fixing of baseball's 1919 World Series by the Chicago White Sox was led by their star players; and when Liverpool and Manchester United decided to fix a game in 1915, the scam was led by their top players. Many people are surprised when they hear that the very best athletes would be the project managers of a fix. It is *because* those players are stars that fixers really want to work with them. Star players have the influence and prestige on the team that means that few of the other players will say no to them. They are able to build a corrupt network and culture on the team far more easily than any other player.

However, a fixing project manager in a team sport, no matter how good, needs a network on the team. He needs at least three to five other players to help fix the match. With fewer players, they *might* succeed, but the result is not guaranteed. In soccer fixes, normally five to seven players are enlisted, but the absolute minimum, say the fixers and players, are: the goalkeeper, a defender, and a striker.

Most of the time, however, corrupt players don't want all their teammates in on the fix partly because they don't want to share the money, and partly because it makes it more difficult for the spectators to see what is going on. One Singaporean player who had fixed games told me that people judge the performance of the team as a whole, rather than as a collection of individuals. Not having the whole team taking part in the fix actually aids the corrupt players. If there are six players throwing the game, but five desperately trying to win, the onlookers are less likely to figure out that a fix is taking place – or even which particular players are taking part in the fix.

But how, if this fixing network is in place, do the corrupt players actually play in the fix? The Malaysians and Singaporeans were to teach me that as well.

2

"WHAT THE HELL DO YOU THINK YOU'RE DOING?"

It was ridiculous mistakes that a professional footballer
shouldn't make. Things like missing tackles, clearing the ball
by tapping it five yards straight to the striker five yards from
the goal. Or playing a stupid offside. That was probably the
best one. You go charging up the field to play an offside and
the forward goes charging through.

The Malaysian police have all kinds of ways of making prisoners talk.
They are not big on being nice to prisoners. The interrogation culture
came of age in the middle of a bloody communist insurgency, when
thousands of people were killed and tens of thousands imprisoned.
The Malays learned from their British colonial governors and then they
came to surpass their teachers. Amnesty International reports that the
Malaysian police have refined torture to an art form: "Detainees have
been assaulted, forced to strip, deprived of sleep, food and water, told
that their families would be harmed, and subjected to prolonged aggressive interrogation to force confessions or obtain information." Rank is
no protection. Anwar Ibrahim, the former deputy prime minister, who
in the late 1990s was silly enough to speak out against the then-prime
minister, was put in a police cell for months. He appeared in court with
a black eye and bruises; he had been beaten up by a senior police officer.

At his trial, another police officer, the former head of the Intelligence Services, testified about the common practice of "turning over" prisoners for political purposes.

I made friends with some of those policemen. They became interested in my work and they offered to help. It is always odd being friends with torturers. There is something about them: some indefinable thing that marks them out. In southeastern Turkey, during the 2003 war in Iraq, I met several men like that. One of them, a former high-ranking officer in the Turkish military intelligence, became as close to a friend as possible. He helped arrange a covert meeting with Syrian drug dealers to see if they could smuggle me into northern Iraq. Throughout the negotiations he was extremely kind and hospitable. Despite being a wealthy man, he shared the long overnight bus journeys that were the only means of travel my freelance journalist budget could cover. He invited me to family parties and social get-togethers. He was urbane, cosmopolitan, and friendly. But I remember seeing him at a reception at the Ankara Hilton; it was for the opening of a television program claiming that the Armenian genocide never happened. Holding his wineglass by the stem, he looked across at someone as if calculating how much pain the person could take. For all his urbanity, for all his culture, this was a man who had stood beside the chair or the hook or whatever godforsaken instrument of torture, had nodded and increased the pain. Torturing another human being produces a bruise on the soul that rots from the inside out, and no matter how the torturers try to hide, you can always sniff them out.

The contacts in the Malaysian police were like the Turkish intelligence officer: friendly, generous, and helpful. But they all had that odd coldness at the heart of their laughter that comes from the power of being able to place other humans in pain. They also had a treasure trove of documents about match-fixing. In 1994 and 1995, when Johnson Fernandez, Lazarus Rokk, and other journalists had written too many stories about match-fixing in the Malaysian League to ignore, the police moved in. They called it Operation Bola. In a series of nationwide raids, they arrested more than 150 soccer players and coaches. Under legislation dating back to the colonial era, the police kept the players in prison for a number of days or weeks and then exiled over twenty of them to different parts of the country. Oddly, none of the players ever went on trial. So in the files of the Royal Malaysian Police, there was a horde of confessions by these players that had never been examined by anyone outside the police force. They invited me look at some of these documents.

On a hot spring day in Kuala Lumpur, with the temperature in the nineties and me sweltering in a woollen suit, I went to their headquarters. Say the words *Kuala Lumpur* and it may conjure up images of palm trees, exotic buildings, and flowing rivers under tropical moonlight or a glorious sunset. Go there for one day and you discover that the city used to look like that, but now it has been invaded by that Californian pastiche architecture that has conquered the rest of the world: buildings that look as if they were made by opening a packet and adding water; pale, anemic shopping malls split open by multi-lane highways; and long passages of neon lights marked by gas stations that hurry you from nowhere to nowhere.

The Royal Malaysian Police Headquarters is another instant noodle of a building. It is built on the edge of the remains of Kuala Lumpur's city park: imagine a desecrated Hyde or Central Park, with six-lane highways whizzing around it. My identification was checked three times before I could enter. And there, in an anonymous office room, a source pulled out the files of the arrested players and we read them. Together those pages gave a picture of an incredible network of crime. The players spoke of games fixed to an extraordinary level, of criminals threatening players and giving them covert payoffs, of alleged ties with some of Malaysia's top politicians and businessmen. They also show some remarkable stories of courage and fortitude; of lonely coaches beset by corruption who desperately appealed and motivated their corrupt players to play honestly. It is a wonderful resource, with the materials for several novels.

One story will do.

Rafiq Saad (*) had been one of the best players in the Malaysian League. But that didn't do him much good in 1994 when he was alone in a prison cell with a group of policemen who *really* wanted him to talk.

It must have been tough for him. The officer conducting the interrogation writes in the secret report that Saad started the first day as "unco-operative." But it goes on to say, prosaically, that on the second day Saad became much more "co-operative." He certainly did. Alone in a cell with those Malaysian police officers and their enthusiastic methods for ensuring co-operation, he sang like a canary.

Saad is not his real name, but we know everything about him. We know his salary. We know how, as a project manager, he organized players on his team to fix matches. We know which teams he played for. We know some of the games he helped fix and how much he got paid for doing so. And we know how he fixed those games. Because at some point in one of those long, arduous conversations, the interrogating officer began to get curious: How exactly did players fix matches? What methods did they use? How could they carry them out successfully?

Those are good questions because it is genuinely difficult to fix a soccer match. There are twenty-two players, the referee, two linesman, and various coaches to take into account. Each of them could swing the game one way or another. There is the crowd often ready to scream at a player if he makes an honest mistake, let alone deliberately sabotages his own team. There are ways of doing it really badly. For example, the entire Genoa and Venezia teams arranged a match between them in the spring of 2005 and they almost managed to screw it up. The arrangement was that Genoa would win and get promoted to Italy's top division, Serie A, and Venezia would get a lot of money. But in the second half, the Venezia manager got a call from the Genoa coach, "What the hell do you think you're doing? Your player scored a goal!?" he screamed.

"I know, I know," replied the Venetian. "The players are crazy! They scored a goal by mistake!"

To the Genoa's team great relief, Venezia did manage to let them score and the game ended, as arranged, in a victory for Genoa so they could advance to Serie A. Well, they would have done, if the whole arrangement had not been caught on tape by Italian magistrates investigating the team officials.

Different era, same league, same problem. In his autobiography, *In the Mud with the Soccer God*, the 1970s Italian forward Carlo Petrini described the problem he and his Bologna teammates had when they arranged a fix against Juventus in a Serie A match. The plan was that both teams would draw the match 0-0. Great. Except in the fifty-fifth minute, someone on the Juventus team actually shot at the Bologna goal! It had been snowing, so the Bologna goalkeeper could not hold the ball, and it slipped past him into the net. 1-0 Juventus. The Bologna team was furious. There was, according to Petrini, almost a fight between the two teams in the middle of the pitch. However, a Juventus midfielder calmed them when he called out, "Don't worry, lads, we'll score an equalizer for you." Ten minutes later, there was a corner kick against Juventus and one of their team rose magnificently in the air to head it into his own net. The game ended 1-1, and everyone went away happy, except the fans, who were so enraged with the game that they pelted the players with snowballs.

At the international level, there were the same problems delivering a fixed match in Singapore in 1986. The Merlion Cup was an international tournament featuring Indonesia, Malaysia, China, North Korea, Singapore, and Canada. An outsider may have thought that of all those teams, the one least likely to accept a bribe would be the relatively rich Canadians. However, on the Canadian team, a group of players had arranged with some gambling fixers to lose the semi-final to North Korea. One of those players was furious with Paul James, a defender whom he thought was in on the fix, playing honestly. "What the hell do you think you're doing?" he screamed at James for passing so well that the Canadians almost scored a goal. However, all went well in the end for the fixing Canadians, and the Koreans were allowed to win 2-0.

If a player who is fixing a match wants to avoid all the craziness of the Venezia game or the problems of the Canadians, how does he play? There are essentially three problems for the player in a fixed match: how do you deliver the promised result, how do you make sure that no one guesses that you are fixing the match, and how do you play badly enough to lose but not jeopardize your place on the team?

Those were the questions that the Malaysian police officers asked Rafiq Saad in his long, dark night in the police cell. And in his confession he includes a two-page list of all the different tactics that the players in each position can use.

GOALKEEPERS

Goalkeepers are obviously key to guaranteeing a good fix. According to Rafiq Saad, the key strategies for the goalkeeper are the exact reverse of how to play well in goal: for example, a goalie should leave his area as much as possible: "On a breakaway, the goalie will deliberately leave the goal and play so far up that the goal is clear."

This is a key tactic: if a corrupt defender can ensure that an opposing forward is running on to the net alone, an honest goalkeeper could still do a lot to stop a goal by playing the angles of the net. A corrupt goalkeeper, however, will immediately rush out of his net and allow the forward to step around him and score. The goalkeeper, of course, flails wildly about and curses as if he honestly missed the play. It is almost impossible for a bystander to judge if the goalkeeper has made the mistake deliberately.

A Finnish player who fixed games in his country's Premier League in 2004 helped to describe how a corrupt goalkeeper will roam out of the penalty area in a fixed match:

> . . . [The goalie] comes outside the penalty area to collect a pass but he comes up against a forward. The forward now has an easy job to put the ball in the goal . . . Team A scores again. Team B loses in big numbers, just as people expected.

A good fixing goalkeeper doesn't have to act like an idiot; he doesn't have to wander around on the other side of the goal. Saad talks about a goalkeeper "putting himself in the wrong position." This can be by standing one metre away from where he should be. As the forward shoots, it allows the keeper to throw himself bravely but vainly, as the ball whistles past his outstretched hands.

Another tactic goalkeepers use allows them to seemingly innocently misplay the ball: "Goalkeeper drops the ball: he could catch it, but he just pats it away."

This strategy is the most obvious and it is, of course, the exact opposite of what every childhood coach tells their young student: "Catch, smother the ball with your body." By pushing the ball out into the area, or dropping it, the fixing goalie can cause all kinds of problems for his teammates. One player remembered one incident clearly:

> There was one game, and the other team had a corner. I was on the goalpost. I was defending. And the corner came in. And it was floating. It wasn't played with any pace. I was standing right beside the goalkeeper. And it was like something in slow motion. The goalie went up, caught the ball, and then dropped it right at the feet of their player who scored. And I was so frustrated that I went up and pushed him. I was boiling. And I shouted "You fucker! I know what you were doing!" And he said, "Oh come on . . ." And you know they act all innocent. But I was convinced I knew what was going on.

You need to get defenders onside for a successful fix because one mistake by them can so easily lead to a goal. In a 1960 exposé, the *Daily Mail* revealed one nasty tactic: the Suicide Pass. "The ball is placed by a defender too far away for the goalkeeper to clear it or gather it, but near enough to the opposing forward for him to nip in and score a gift goal . . . Every soccer fan has seen this happen, but sometimes it is not an accident," they reported that "a famous goalkeeper" told them.

Rafiq Saad's strategies are more commonplace:

- *The left back and right back will not assist the sweeper when he is being attacked.*
- *The sweeper will not assist the left or right back when they are being attacked.*
- *The defence will not play all out and will purposely allow the attackers to get by us.*

Like the goalkeeper dropping the ball or patting it loose in a crowded penalty area, these tactics are the exact opposite of what every soccer coach has taught young players to do since the ball was first invented. One Singaporean player told me:

It was ridiculous mistakes that a professional footballer shouldn't make. Things like missing tackles, clearing the ball by tapping it five yards straight to the striker five yards from the goal. Or playing a stupid offside. That was probably the best one. You go charging up the field to play an offside and the forward goes charging through.

FORWARDS

It is, of course, no use signing up your defence and goalkeeper to fix a game if your star forward is knocking in goals. If the forwards score too many goals, the fix becomes very obvious. So the fixers have all kinds of strategies for the forwards to follow.

- *Keep the ball for a long time, to allow the opponents to take away the ball.*
- *Dribble the ball straight at the opponent, allowing them to take away the ball.*
- *Miss goal opportunities by either kicking directly at the keeper or missing the goal altogether.*

Almost one hundred years ago in 1915, Fred Pagnam was a young Liverpool forward. His teammates subscribed to the Rafiq Saad school of match-fixing. Pagnam was one of the few players on his squad that decided not to throw a game against Manchester United. The game was at the end of the season, Liverpool had nothing to play for, and Manchester United was struggling against relegation. The First World War was on and in a few months most of the players would be in the army, so many of them decided to rig the match to give Manchester the points and themselves a little more cash. Pagnam was told on the way to the match by his corrupt teammates to follow the same kind of instructions that Saad would give: at all times lose the ball and if you are in front of the goal – miss.

Pagnam testified later that near the end of the game he even took a shot on the United goal, hit the crossbar, and then one of his corrupt teammates asked him what he damn well meant. After that, they made sure he never got another chance to score.

Because they usually do not play right in front of a goal, midfielders do not have as direct an influence on the game as goalkeepers, defenders, and forwards. However, they have an important job to do: controlling the fix. To lose a game against a strong team that really wants to win is not particularly hard, but for a strong team to lose credibly against a weak team is actually very difficult. Give the ball to an incompetent but honest team and there is no telling what they will do. They can even make such stupid mistakes that the fixing team will have to score.

So controlling the game for fixers is a complicated and important task. One fixer that I spoke to described having to coach his teams to lose by holding on to the ball for a few seconds, then passing backward, each corrupt player does the same thing, nothing is obvious, but in the fixer's words, the corrupt players "buy time."

In recent years, this skill of controlling is becoming increasingly important, as fixers are asking the players not only to lose the game, but also to change their game depending on the time of the match. Here is why. Almost any punter can bet on a team to win or lose, but the really skilful fixer wants to make the maximum amount of money. They can do this by winning bets that have far higher odds than just win/loss, such as predicting total goals scored in the match or when those goals will be scored.

Rafiq Saad described a similar series of movements for corrupt midfield players:

- *The midfielder will keep the ball for a long time to allow the other team to take it away.*
- *The midfielder will interrupt the system of playing by passing the ball back to the defence.*
- *The midfielder will make a pass that is 50-50, so that the opponents will get the ball.*
- *The midfielder will keep the ball in his own area and will not allow the ball to get open.*

Reading Rafiq Saad's confession was interesting, but I really wanted to know if what he was claiming about playing in a fixed match was true. After all, who knows what people will say when they're strapped up in the hands of torturers? I know if I had been in the clutches of a Malaysian police officer, I would have been offering them my MasterCard, Visa, and anything else to let me go within about five minutes. I wanted to know if there were any special indications that could predict a fixed match by the way it was played. So I devised a way to test Saad's confession to find out if he was telling the truth.

EXPERTS IN VERBAL BULLSHIT

It is all the verbal bullshit before a game; they shout lots of stuff, "Come on, come on!" Then during the game it is just little tiny things like just mistiming a sliding tackle or letting a guy go through. These guys became experts in making it look like they were out there giving blood to their team. Coming in after the games and throwing themselves on the floor and screaming.

In all the legends that surround fixing in Asia, there is none more powerful than the disappearance of Michael Vana. It happened one day in 1994, but Singaporean soccer fans of a certain age still talk as if it were yesterday. There are always these mysteries that seem to haunt a nation's collective imagination: the United States has Amelia Earhart, England has Lord Lucan, and Singapore has Michael Vana.

Vana was a star. One of the best players to ever tread on a Singapore soccer field, he was a Czech player who had all the talent to be one of the best in the world but never quite made it in Europe. He went to Singapore and there, in a league of much lower quality, set it alight. One of his old coaches in Singapore remembers him as "the best player I have ever coached. He had it all. He was an amazing player."

According to the Singapore authorities, Michael Vana also fixed matches.

On the night of August 12, 1994, just before Vana's Singapore team would win the league championship, the police moved in. They arrested Vana claiming that he had earned hundreds of thousands of dollars fixing matches. Vana was due to stand trial the following month. He showed up in court September 14, 1994, and posted bail of $500,000. He left the room and disappeared. Vanished. Vamoosed. This is not as facetious as it sounds. Singapore is an island. Living there is like taking part in a social experiment designed in a science-fiction novel. Its law enforcement is famous for its ferocity. Miscreants that chew gum or litter can be heavily fined. Hooligans are flogged. Drug dealers are killed. At the time, there was just one bridge to the Asian mainland. One passenger airport. One train line. The way in and out of the island is carefully checked. One day, Vana was on bail being monitored by the police in Singapore; the next day, he was discovered watching a soccer match in Prague, free as a bird, denying he had ever taken a bribe and with no intentions of ever returning to Singapore. How did he get there? How did he get out of Fortress Singapore? There are all kinds of tales told in Singapore bars as the night winds down and the alcohol mounts up. Vana was smuggled out in the personal limousine of a wayward, heavy-gambling Malaysian Royal Prince. Vana went out by boat to Indonesia. Then Vana took a flight back to Europe. He didn't realize it, but the plane stopped at Singapore. Terrified, he spent three hours hiding in a cubicle in a men's room of the Singapore airport. Whatever the truth of the stories, no one except Vana really knows how the greatest disappearing act in Singapore's recent history was accomplished.

His former coach described the most blatant method of controlling a match that he saw Michael Vana employ during a game against a much weaker team:

> I think the one that capped it was, we were doing very well . . . [and] the betting was that we would win by more than three [goals]. But we were missing goals from two yards out. In fact, there is one incident that I clearly remember when one of our players was in with their goal

at his mercy when Vana ran across him, took the ball off him and passed it off to the right wing!

Usually, Vana and the other fixing players are not as obvious. They have to have other skills aside from soccer. A fixing player has to be a great actor. It is no use just playing badly; the player also has to pretend to be trying hard. Jackie "Mr. TV" Pallo was a popular British wrestler for three decades. Tall, good-looking, and utterly extravagant, he became famous as a "baddie" whose job was to torment the "blue eyes" (wrestlers who played heroic roles) and the audience. However, at the height of his career, he was excluded from a lucrative television contract. Accordingly, he wrote a tell-all autobiography called *You Grunt, I'll Groan*. Pallo claimed the entire British version of wrestling was a fraud. Most of the "savage bouts" that thrilled the audience were actually scripted to decide who would win. In chapters called "The Six Commandments" or "The Office Hold," Pallo even described in detail some of the fixes in wrestling and how they are performed. However, the thing that Pallo emphasized was the skill of "dying" at the end of the other wrestler's fake moves:

> . . . it is important for fighters to respond to one another's moves . . . if I'd just dropped a man on his head with a fucking great bang, I'd expect him to roll around on the deck for some seconds, clutching his nut as if in agony. This is called "dying" to the other man's move, or "selling" his move.

It is the same in a crooked soccer match: the corrupt player needs to "sell" the fix. As each move is sold in wrestling as a genuine, pain-causing manoeuvre, each match-fixing soccer player must do the same thing. They must act off the field as if the idea of fixing is the last thing in their minds. Scott Ollerenshaw played on a Malaysian team where police eventually discovered that some of his teammates were involved in fixing games. He claims before their arrests that even though he knew something corrupt was going on, he could not be sure which players were taking part.

> It is all the verbal bullshit before a game; they shout lots of stuff, "Come on, come on!" Then during the game it is just little tiny things like just mistiming a sliding tackle or letting a guy go through. These guys became experts in making it look like they were out there giving blood to their team. Coming in after the games and throwing themselves on the floor and screaming.

It is professional suicide for a player ever to admit to fixing or not trying as hard as he could. Acting as if they are ready to give everything for their team plays on a clear and certain advantage corrupt players do have in fixing a game: few people, even trained coaches, can actually tell if they are really fixing the game. If carried out with subtlety, the Rafiq Saad guidelines can appear to be the simple mistakes of an otherwise hard-working player. This became a problem for the Singaporean police when they were trying to investigate the issue. One officer said, "Football is very subjective. So people can have a bad game, just because they are playing badly. Even if they are bribed . . . Who can tell?" This subjectivity is not only a difficulty for the police: it became an issue while I was researching this book. I witnessed a top international match that I think was fixed. Fixers told me that it would be fixed, they predicted the right score, but how was I to know for certain whether a match was fixed? Were there special features that could show a fixed match? I wanted to find out.

Nuffield College was founded by the British carmaker Lord Nuffield, who in the years before his death gave an enormous sum of his money to found a new Oxford college and a foundation that would be based on the principal of "helping humanity." What he got was a college full of social scientists. During the term, the sociologists would meet in a cramped room every Wednesday at five o'clock for seminars. These meetings of the almost-living were dreadful affairs that would gladden the heart of any anthropologist looking for strange rituals of exotic tribes. Frequently, some poor lecturer from an outside university would be invited to present his or her work. The lecturer would, presumably, think it was an opportunity to share ideas and research with the bigwigs of Oxford. The actual purpose was to provide meat for an academic shark frenzy. He or she would stand in the middle of the small room. Faculty would be around the first row. By an unspoken and never broken decree, they had to ask the first set of questions. They would sit with their legs tightly crossed, frowns tightly affixed, toes, frequently untrimmed, waggling out from their sandals. Behind them would sit, packed in like galley slaves, the graduate students, all wearing their most unctuous expressions, ready to agree or disagree with the speaker depending on what their supervisors thought. The visiting academic would finish. There would be a silence while various mental knives were sharpened. And then one of the front row would speak out in a long, lazy drawl, and say something like:

> That was all very *interesting*. But have you actually ever *read* the work of Sebastian and myself on the British Family Survey? I think you'll find it very *helpful*. (*Modest smirk from Sebastian at this point. The "questions," usually long negative comments on the speaker's research, would go on.*) "It seems to me, looking at your data, that you have made the mistake, the rather elementary mistake I might add, of confusing correlation with causation . . ." (*Translation: You're a bloody idiot.*)

When I got back to this world, after months of talking with fixers, corrupt players, and police in Asia, I decided I wanted to test whether Rafiq Saad and the other players were lying. I wanted to see if there was a way of knowing if, and when, a game had been fixed. It got me thinking: at the university I was surrounded by smart, bright people who understood statistics. I needed to drop *my* intellectual snobbery. Yes, Nuffield Seminars were dreary affairs, blighted with personal politics, but so were many journalists' story meetings that I had attended. Surely there must be a way of testing this idea of *underperforming* to achieve a successful fix, using some of the methods discussed in the seminars.

There is a rising new field, investigative economics, that became an inspiration for me. Investigative economics is where economists finally do something they have largely never done before: study the real world. Many orthodox economists deliberately exclude social factors when constructing their models. They find them too distracting. They search for intellectual holy grails, like the "perfect market" or an "equilibrium point." It is the reason why you have to be educated for a long time to be as stupid as some economists. It is the reason why in the midst of the Irish potato famine or the Great Depression or any of the other economic calamities that have befallen our societies, there are always some economists to be found saying things such as, "wide-scale relief to the starving millions is bad because it would depress the market." In the last few years, thankfully, that is changing. In particular, there have been a number of excellent studies on corruption in sports.

The American academics Justin Trogdon and Beck Taylor showed in their 2002 study that during certain seasons in the National Basketball Association, some weak teams would deliberately lose games at the end of the season to get better recruits for the next year. Charles Moul and John Nye of Washington University examined the Soviet chess system and revealed that there had been widespread collusion between Soviet players in international chess tournaments between 1946 and 1964 to help one another reach Grand Master status. And the great American economist Steven Levitt and his colleague Mark Duggan showed a similar pattern of corrupt collusion in Japanese sumo wrestling.

I did a series of similar experiments, with the help of a couple of statistical colleagues. I collected a sample of more than 130 soccer matches that were known beyond legal doubt to have been fixed and I compared them to a control group of presumed honestly played matches. I wanted to see if there were any patterns that made fixed games different from honestly played games.

I studied the confessions and interviews of the corrupt players and noticed one clear phenomenon: for the most part, players did not talk about *committing* a crime to fix a match, it was always *omitting* to do something. It's a bit like Catholic theology. For the believers, there are two types of sins: omission and commission. Sins of commission are misdemeanours that come from actually doing something: "my neighbour's house is on fire because I set it alight." Sins of omission are the misdemeanours that come from not doing something that one should do: "my neighbour's house is on fire and I did not phone the fire brigade."

The first thing I realized was that it is impossible to measure *sins of omission* that a player or a referee may have committed in fixing a match. Television pundits, referees, and millions of fans all may argue that a player should have done better in making a tackle or passing a ball, but really, their judgment remains subjective. The only tests that I could do were on the *sins of commission* or the events that had occurred in games that could be quantified and measured in an objective manner. Three events suggested themselves: penalty kicks, own goals, and red cards (when a referee sends a player off the field for a foul with no replacement allowed). It seems reasonable to expect that there would be more of these events in a fixed game than in an honestly played match. For example, a source at the Union of European Football Associations (UEFA) had told me:

> There is a specific referee that we are investigating. He is betting on himself on the gambling market: when he gives out a yellow card [a warning given by a referee], to which team, etc. He did this in the qualifying rounds of the European Championship [a Europe-wide national team tournament]. I won't give you his name. I have to wait for him to be charged, but let's say that he is an Eastern European referee.

After spending months compiling the database, I finally began to run the numbers and discovered some interesting results.

PENALTY KICKS

What I discovered was that if players were fixing, there was no significant rise in the number of penalties. In other words, Rafiq Saad had largely been telling the truth. If a player wanted to give away a goal, he would not cut down an opposition player but simply let him get past without trying to stop him. Presumably, this is because to give up a penalty draws undue attention to the fixing player. By just screwing up in small ways, a player doesn't get the coach screaming at him or the crowd throwing things. The unavailing slip, the attempt to get the ball, the mistimed tackle, all accompanied with Pallo's "selling of the fix" grunts and groans, are as effective in accomplishing the fix and less conspicuous.

Crooked referees, however, do use penalties to deliver fixed matches. When a referee had been bribed to fix a game, penalties were twice as likely as when a game was being honestly played.

OWN GOALS

The one seemingly obvious phenomenon that the Rafiq Saad does not mention is own goals. One might think that would be the most common way for a player to fix a match: knock a goal into his own net, hang his head in public shame, and then go pick up the payment the next day. For example, Vlado Kasalo, a Croatian international playing in the German Bundesliga in 1991, was arrested after scoring two own goals to help pay off his gambling debts.

However, one of the Asian fixers that I spoke to said he *hated* own goals. He declaimed against a Vietnamese gambling ring who had fixed their national team to lose in the Southeast Asian (SEA) Games in December 2005. "They don't know what they are doing . . . but they were stupid. Scored an own goal almost, very stupid [sic]. Too obvious."

My research showed that own goals are scored in about 10 per cent of the normal games, and in just under 20 per cent of fixed matches. This means it is a significant rise, but it shows *only* that *certain* players may score own goals to help the fix. In other words, own goals are not a consistent tool used to corrupt matches, as penalties are with referees. Again, I think this falls within Rafiq Saad territory and "sins of omission"; scoring an own goal is simply too obvious for most people taking part in a fix.

RED CARDS

One might think that getting thrown out of the game would be a perfect way for a dishonest player to help corrupt a match: shout abuse at the referee, storm off the field, and the other team wins with a one-player advantage. It also seems a perfect tool for a dishonest referee: removing the star player from the team that the referee is trying to make lose would surely aid the fix.

However, the research showed that red cards are *not* a tool used in a statistically significant way by either corrupt players or dishonest referees in fixing matches. Again, Saad was right; it is better for a dishonest player to be on the field than off. Actually dishonest players seem to have *fewer* red cards in fixed matches than players do in honestly played matches. I think the numbers indicate that dishonest players are either not trying hard enough to warrant a red card or that they are deliberately trying *not* to get sent off the field. Presumably, being on the field to aid the fix is better.

The statistical analysis seems to support Saad's confession. With penalties, own goals, and red cards, there are no statistically significant increases when the data is analyzed for corrupt players. So is there a way of recognizing a fixed match? Are there definite patterns that distinguish a dishonestly played match from a regular match?

I believe there might be. In other work, I was able to show that there is a statistically significant difference between the total number of goals scored in fixed matches compared to honestly played matches. Matches that are fixed have, on average, 20 per cent more goals scored than do honest matches. But the key to recognizing potential dishonest patterns is to examine *when* the goals are scored in the games.

One of the many myths that surround match-fixing is that play in the late stages of a match – last-minute penalties and late goals – secures the fix. The inference is that the referee or corrupt players wait until the last few minutes of the game – controlling the ball – and then score late in the game to achieve the desired result.

An excerpt from Joe McGinniss's book *The Miracle of Castel di Sangro* suggests the opposite. McGinniss, the American journalist who wrote *The Selling of the President,* fell in love with soccer late in life. He spent a season following an Italian Serie B (second division) team, Castel di Sangro, sharing its triumphs and heartbreaks. It is a story, beautifully and lyrically told, of love's bitter disillusionment, for in the final game of the season, McGinniss witnessed first-hand a fix between his beloved Castel di Sangro and a team from Bari. He heard the corrupt players discuss the timing of the goals in the following way:

A player said, "The first [goal] must come immediately. Even before the people take their seats. That way it is not noticed so much. And then two more, as they develop, but all in the first half."

"And in the second?"

A player laughed. "In the second we all lie down and take a nap."

"But this will not look bad?" a younger player asked, sounding worried.

Another laughed. "Look bad to whom? . . . Do not worry. No one pays attention at these times. Everyone looks the other way. Only be careful never to shoot at the Bari goal tomorrow. That would be a mistake."

This method of scoring early and then players "taking a nap" is certainly what seemed to have happened in the "shoddy accomodation" between the Austrian and West German teams in the 1982 World Cup. Both teams would progress to the second round if West Germany won the game 1-0. The Germans scored in the first eleven minutes, and the rest of the match was an exercise in the manner of the Castel di Sangro players.

However, there is another theory: that a match-fixing performance is also, at least partly, opportunity based. In other words, finely laid plans are all very well in theory, but in the reality of a game, players simply have to take the opportunity to fix when it comes. The Italian players hint at this when they describe the second and third goals coming "as they develop."

So I analyzed the database specifically looking at the time of goals. What I discovered was surprising. There is a difference between when goals are scored in fixed and honest matches. In fixed matches, the number of goals scored goes up in the first ten minutes and goes *down* in the last ten minutes. This finding runs completely contrary to popular wisdom and the idea of a rush of last-minute goals. What I realized is that those games with a run of late goals were actually marked by failure. People were aware that a fix was going on because the teams were so desperate to score and were rushing to score in the last ten minutes. In most successfully fixed matches, the fix was achieved long before the final ten minutes. In fact, the players and referee would try to arrange them as early in the game as possible. This is the reason why there are so many goals in the first ten minutes of fixed games.

However, there was an important point missing in the research in Asia. I was beginning to understand the role of the players in the fix, but the deeper my research progressed, the more I realized I was missing how the top sports officials were and were not dealing with the scandal.

4

MISSING THE BIG BOYS

They arrested a lot of the players. But they definitely missed a lot of the big boys. A lot of the big boys. And there was no doubt those guys were involved in fixing. And those guys are still involved in football in some capacity in coaching or whatever. But they definitely missed some of the big boys.

The best piece of advice I received when doing my research came from an English professor living in Asia. We met late one night at a food court in central Kuala Lumpur. I had just arrived and he took me out for a meal and shared his thoughts on the country. We ate in one of those Asian outdoor food courts that provide, dollar for dollar, the best food in the world. There was everything, from the wonderful coconut taste of nasi lemak to Singapore noodles to spicy Szechuan chicken, to Indian masala dolsa and mango lassi. Even late at night, it was very hot and near each table fans sprayed out fine jets of water. In the hustle and bustle around us were a dozen different cultures meeting and eating. There were Tamil families with the women in brightly coloured saris; groups of Malay office workers in glaring pink T-shirts; and at another table sat a group of glamorous but tough-looking Russian prostitutes with improbably blond hair, impossibly high heels, and faces so sharp you could cut cheese with them.

At the end of our meal, after I told the professor my research topic, he leaned forward and said, "If you want to find out anything in this place, don't look like an investigative journalist. Be polite. Dress well. But look innocent and don't ask direct questions."

The more I worked and travelled, the more I realized how right he had been and the more I realized how little of "the truth" had actually been told publicly. For example, one of the things that had always puzzled me was that when the Malaysian and Singaporean police finally moved in, they arrested an enormous number of players, a few bookies, and one or two coaches, but that was it. Surely, I thought, some sports official at a higher level must have known what was going on? This chapter is not about the players but about the officials of the Asian soccer world – what did they know about the match-fixing?

Much of the conventional wisdom about the cleanup of Malaysian and Singapore soccer is wrong: match-fixing had not suddenly arisen with the advent of the professional league; it had long been a part of the established culture in Malaysian soccer. Even several of the senior soccer officials who were running the league admitted that they actually took part in fixed matches themselves when they played the game. Farok Ali (*) was both a player during the 1960s and a soccer official. He told me quite openly about his participation in match-fixing as a player: "There was nothing obvious. Some of the senior players would tell us the difference should be in the goal difference. In other words, don't win by three goals, just win by a couple of goals less."

I interviewed some of the players who had played in the league in the 1990s. They were all reasonably forthright about what they thought may have gone on:

Question: Was the [team] management ever involved in the fixing?
Answer: Yes, sometimes the management gets involved. They start
             to get involved in fixing. You think 40K in 90 minutes is
             not tempting? Sometime the owners will tell me, "Look,
             I bet 40 K on 8 ball [the owners had bet $40,000 that

there would be 8 goals scored in the game] . . ." You ask
the other players they will tell you this.

A player who had been in the dressing room with many of the match-fixing players said:

> They arrested a lot of the players. But they definitely missed a lot of the
> big boys. A lot of the big boys. And there was no doubt those guys were
> involved in fixing. And those guys are still involved in football in some
> capacity in coaching or whatever. But they definitely missed some of
> the big boys. I would say that who has been involved is just the icing
> on the cake . . .

Johnson Fernandez discovered similar stories with the help of his under-world sources in 1993 and wrote a series of explosive articles, one of which was entitled, "How do you pin down a 'fix'? Officials are into the racket, too." He wrote: "It has been learnt now that players aren't the only ones fixing matches. Officials have got into the act, too. Some of them unscrupulous, some of them going for wins and throwing matches that aren't detrimental to their team's chances of a title or a place in the Malaysia Cup."

Peter Velappan is one of the top Asian soccer officials. He was the general secretary of the Asian Football Confederation (AFC) and continues as an influential executive. The AFC is the Asian branch of FIFA. FIFA pretty much runs everything in world soccer and the AFC runs soccer in Asia. But even Velappan in 1993 was quoted by Fernandez as saying about match-fixing: "They [the soccer officials] are sweeping it under the carpet. I have not come across any FA in this region who have faced the problem squarely."

I visited Velappan in the AFC's headquarters in Kuala Lumpur to see what he thinks now. Velappan is a clean-cut looking man, but he is very tired. Tired because he has spent a lifetime fighting the match-fixing that plagues Asian soccer leagues. He has had direct experiences with corruption: "In West Asia [the Middle East for Europeans] I once picked up a newspaper. It had been slipped under my hotel room door. There was $10,000 under the paper." He immediately returned the money to the man who was trying to bribe him. Velappan calls match-fixing "the ghost" because it is so difficult to see or clamp down on. Despite his experience, he claims that although there was enormous amounts of match-fixing in Asian soccer, it has died down as the various soccer associations have now "got it under control." For the record, he is the only person that I spoke to in Asia who said something like that; all the other sports officials at least privately still claimed that it was a huge problem for them.

After we spoke, I wandered about the AFC headquarters for a couple of days. It is a nice, comfortable place with a large stream filled with fish just outside the entrance hall. I found most of the AFC officials to be extremely kind and diligent. I learned that there were 46 national associations, 29,000 clubs, and more than 105 million players in more than 100,000 teams in Asia. I learned that there were more than 716,000 referees in the AFC zone. I learned that in 1981, one of Saddam Hussein's henchmen had beaten up one of those referees because he had officiated a game in Baghdad that Kuwait had won. The bruised and beaten referee was driven hurriedly to the airport and put bleeding on a plane out of the country. And I spoke to an official who told me the following story of when he was an international referee:

It was in an international tournament in West Asia. The match was between X and Y, but if Y lost, a third team would go through. So fifteen minutes before the match, "the big man" who was connected to the third team came into the referee's dressing room where I was changing. He was very blunt. There was no beating around the bush. He just said, "So what do you want, cash or cheque?"

I said, "What?"

He said, "Cash or cheque?"

"I don't understand."

"I can have the money delivered to your hotel..."

I was very embarrassed I didn't know what to say ... I was shocked. Then a few minutes later the big man came back; he talked to the assistant referees in Arabic. I speak a little Arabic and I could understand that he was ordering them out of the room.

When they were out of the dressing room, he turned and said to me, "Ten thousand dollars."

I said, "No, I want to do good match [sic]."

"I want you to do good match too [sic]," he said. "I just want one penalty. One penalty for X. That's all. Ten thousand dollars cash."

"No," I said and left the dressing room. I was very upset ... There is a ceremony where both teams line up with the linesmen and they wait until the referee comes out. Well, I didn't wait, I just walked onto the field ..."

I will not name the official. He seemed like a good, honest man, someone who was genuinely shocked by the bribe attempt and wants to do his best for the world's game. Moreover, the AFC does not seem like the kind of organization that tolerates a lot of openness or revelations from its junior administrators. As we talked in the armchairs of the entrance lobby, Mohamed bin Hammam, the Qatari president of the AFC, drove up in a dark limousine. The man I was speaking to became agitated. "The president is coming. The president is coming," he said. I was bewildered. I thought that the president of some Asian country was coming into the room. The official, seemingly frightened, stood up as bin Hammam walked into the lobby twenty yards away. Bin Hammam paid very little attention to us, or to any of the other AFC officials who all stood at attention. He nodded affably at the room, smiled, waved, and walked into an elevator. Only after he did so, did anyone in the room relax.

Here is the problem for Peter Velappan and all the AFC administrators who are not corrupt: the Big Man that the official spoke of was, he says, a senior executive in the Asian soccer world. Part of his bribe attempt was, after the money was turned down, to claim to have influence on the selection of referees for international tournaments. The referee was promised that if he helped the Big Man's team into the next round, the referee could expect to work high-profile international matches.

The Big Man is not alone. Even at the most innocent level, there is a kind of strange cognitive dissonance about corruption that infects many Asian sporting officials. Most of them are hard-working, dedicated individuals who genuinely want to see their sport grow. But some simply did not get it. One official I interviewed, who seemed honest and deeply committed to helping clean up the corruption, gave a long, insightful interview. But at its end, I asked, "How much does it cost to fix a soccer game?"

He replied, "I really don't know. But hold on a moment. I have a friend who does this kind of thing all the time. Let me phone him and ask him."

He punched in his speed-dial. His friend answered.

"Hello? Yes, I am here with a fellow from Oxford. How much does it cost to fix a soccer match nowadays? No, no. It's all off the record. No problem. What's that? About ten thousand Malaysian ringgit. Right. No, no. See you next week. Thanks."

He switched off the phone and turned to me.

"My friend tells me that when he and his bookie friends fix a game here, it costs about ten thousand Malaysian ringgit."

If that particular official were an exception, then the anecdote could be described as an aberration, but in other interviews I discovered other officials who had similar conflicts. On my first research trip to the area, I met another of Asia's top sports officials. At the most prestigious sports club in the city, we talked about the anti-corruption efforts needed to clean up the game. As the interview continued, we sat on the balcony, watching a game of cricket. He drank Scotch and water. I drank a pot of tea. I was talking about a Singaporean soccer match that I had seen the night before.

"The game was great: 4-2. And all four goals by one team in the last twenty minutes. It was a fantastic effort! A never-say-die attitude from the players that I loved watching!"

He looked at me incredulously. "You want to see more matches like that?" he asked. "You should stay around! You think that game was played honestly? One team scored all their goals in the second half! Ha ha! If you like games like that, this is the place for you. Never-say-die attitude! Oh dear." He laughed uproariously into his drink at my naïveté. A businessman came up to the table.

"Hey, Wing (*), meet this fellow. He thinks that Singaporean soccer players are very honest. He thinks they never give up!"

The businessman began to laugh too. He nodded at me politely, though, and then handed the sports official a brown envelope. The official opened it, took out the bank notes that were inside, checked them, and then said, "Thanks. Come and join us for a drink."

"No, I can't. I have some more meetings like this one."

They both laughed. Then the businessman left and the sports official continued to tell me about all the corruption in the soccer leagues.

However, if there is complicity and corruption among high-level Asian sports officials, it is nothing to the connections between the most powerful people in their society and the criminal organizations.

In 1882, a British colonial official W.A. Pickering was concerned about the effects of gaming houses in Singapore. They were more than a hundred of them in the city at that time, established and run by Chinese organized crime groups or triads. Pickering set up a commission to investigate the activities of one group, the "Ghee Hok Secret Society," who ran a number of the gambling establishments. A few months later, a carpenter by the name of Chua Ah Siok went into Pickering's office under the guise of presenting a petition. Instead, he threw an axe into Pickering's forehead. It is a warning that echoes through the ages for anyone who messes with the power of these groups. If influential sporting officials are helping with the fixes on one side, on the other side, even more powerful people aid the criminal organizations that run the gambling industry that surrounds the fixing.

The purported division that is supposed to exist in the West between organized crime and "respectable" society does not exist in Asia. (It is not clear that it actually exists in the West, but that is another story.) Kuala Lumpur, Malaysia's capital, for example, was founded by two rival triad operations. They only allowed the British government into the area as a form of neutral referee, to settle a series of mining disputes between the triads. In Imperial China, much of the political opposition to the Manchu rule and the colonial domination came from triads. Asian organized crime is immensely powerful precisely because it is so embedded in society.

At the heads of these groups are quite literally the heads of society or "respectable," legitimate businessmen. These "Mr. Bigs" may not always be involved in the day-to-day running of the groups, but they do provide the triads with political protection and influence. At the lower levels, they can provide the protection that will keep the police from interfering too often or demanding too much in bribes. At the higher levels, they can even influence government decisions. Mr. Bigs can provide this protection because, if the rumours are true, who they are is a hair-raising proposition for anyone interested in Asian civil society: cabinet ministers, very prominent businessmen, men who drive Rolls Royces and own swathes of real estate property. One source I spoke to was quite phlegmatic about the relationship between organized crime and politicians. He told me, "You won't understand Malaysia if you look at the government. The government is the shadow of the mafia. It is the mafia that controls everything and then the government is their shadow."

His views are echoed by Bertil Lintner, a long-time correspondent with the *Far Eastern Economic Review*, who wrote:

Success in politics and business in Asia depends on powerful contacts, who are often above the law and adept at bending it. It is contacts rather than the courts which serve as arbiter; who you know, not how many lawyers you employ, which decides the outcome of difficult business undertakings and political careers. The same factors decide how successful you will be as an extortionist, a pimp or a pirate.

Lintner also wrote the excellent book *Blood Brothers* about these wide-ranging connections in Asia between politics, business, and crime. There is one job description he could have added to the last sentence – illegal gambling bookmaker.

Joe Saumarez-Smith, a London-based gambling consultant, was once asked to come out to Thailand to do some work for one of the heads of an Asian gambling syndicate. He laughingly told me of his experience:

> They are "illegal." I mean, the guy in Thailand. When I got off the plane there was a police officer at the airport with my name on a board. And when he saw me, I thought, Oh no! What is happening? He took me straight through customs and my luggage had been put to the front of the plane and we are escorted into the centre of Bangkok by a three police car cavalcade. We go to the bookmaker's office and have a nice meeting and go out to his shop and restaurant and there is a chief of police coming to dinner with us. If that is not the message "I've got protection," I don't know what is!

The question is, *why* would these powerful individuals be so interested in helping and protecting organized crime groups and bookies? The answer is that it is because all those people are involved in an industry so vast, so massive, that it dwarfs almost all others in Asia.

5

KEEPING THE SYSTEM TURNING

I do remember that one of the police officers, one of the lead guys in the investigation, we caught him meeting with one of the bookies that we were trying to investigate. We put a tail on him and I got a call on my phone from people who were tailing him. He was meeting with the Chinese bookie we were investigating in a hotel in Klang.

I was on an obscure little dock on a tidal inlet in Batam, the Indonesian island just south of Singapore. The scene was a sleepy one: palm trees, little bamboo groves, the early morning sun casting a golden light over the wooden dock. Then the gambling boat from Singapore came in. Casino gambling was, until very recently, illegal in Singapore. If Singaporeans wanted to gamble, they had do it on a ship in international waters. However, for various legal reasons, the gamblers had to stop in Indonesia and then transfer to another boat to take them out to the ship. The gambling boat was a very small cruiser that looked like the ocean-going version of a Mini. But like the circus performance in which innumerable clowns pour out of a tiny car, from out of this boat came a stream of gamblers. Forty seemed too many to fit into the boat, but first sixty, then eighty, then a hundred, then finally more than a hundred and twenty people came pouring out of the boat, walked over the dock, and

54

boarded another tiny boat that puttered back out of the inlet to one of the large gambling ships.

The scene is repeated frequently across Asia. In casinos in the jungles of Burma to the wastelands of North Korea, millions of people are gambling. In 2006, Macau "officially" surpassed Las Vegas as the gambling capital of the world. "Officially" because the illegal amount of money washing through that city has always been far more than any official count. The Asian gambling world is like the American porn industry. It is a vast, well-connected structure of indeterminate legal status that has connections with both organized crime and legitimate companies generating enormous amounts of money. In the same way that the porn industry is financially larger than many regular entertainment industries, so the Asian gambling industry is far larger than many regular, well-established industries. But because much of the industry is officially illegal, it is, like the porn industry, difficult to measure. However, a recent study for the American journal *Foreign Policy* estimated that the entire Asian gambling industry, both legal and illegal, at US$450 billion a year. In comparison, the Asian pharmaceutical industry is worth roughly US$106 billion a year. It is difficult to know how accurate that figure is or how much of it is spent on sports gambling. However, a Harvard School of Government Affairs study (2002) estimated that the amount of money put on illegal sports bets on just one league, the English Premier League, for just one year – 2001 – in just one Asian country (Hong Kong) at US$2.5 billion. The estimated figure for the illegal sports betting market in Singapore is roughly the same, so when the range of other countries that share gambling organizations – Indonesia, China, Vietnam, Thailand, and Malaysia – are factored into the estimate, then the size of the illegal Asian sports gambling is in the tens of billions of dollars.

These financial estimates may seem incredible, except for the following politically incorrect, but utterly truthful, fact: lots and lots of Chinese people love to gamble. Actually, that is not strictly accurate. The truth is:

lots of Chinese people really, really, really, really, really, really love to gamble.

This is not a covert boast of cultural superiority. All cultures choose their own form of pleasure. In Western societies, lots of people drink far too much. Alcoholism and alcoholic dependency is so common that few people even notice it. In the same way that it is almost impossible to go bankrupt selling alcohol to Westerners, it is almost impossible to overestimate the Chinese propensity for gambling. Go to most Chinese social or family gatherings and people will be gambling in the same way other cultures will play charades or Scrabble.

This love of gambling has a long history in the continent. In 1868, the British colonial lieutenant-governor of Malacca, a province of Malaysia, despairingly wrote of the efforts of his tiny police force to control gambling:

> A passion for gambling pervades all classes of the Chinese, it may be said to be the national pastime, and the only results of our efforts to make it criminal is a through demoralization of the Police who extort large amounts as hush money from the players and then become their confederates and scouts.

The quote can serve as an exact and accurate prophecy about the next 140 years of Malaysian police efforts against gambling.

There are about two dozen international-level bookies who are at the head of national gambling syndicates across Asia. One of their business associates told me that they don't like the term *bookies*; they prefer *super-agents*, and the people who work for them are *agents*. This is because bookmaking is still illegal in most Asian countries, so the term *bookies* attracts too much unwanted attention. But they really are bookies and they are based in Hong Kong, Bangkok, Johor Bahru (a small city just across the Malay Peninsula from Singapore), Taiwan, and Jakarta. Most of them are ethnically Chinese, meaning they consider themselves Chinese, even though they were born and raised in other countries. They have very strong interconnections in that they compete and co-operate with one another every day. They will balance their accounts by laying off bets with one another. (Figure 5.1 shows the rough structure of the Asian gambling industry.) There are a couple of caveats to this diagram. It is not an exact anatomical chart. A lab skeleton tells you that the foot bone is attached to the ankle bone and the ankle bone is attached to the shin bone. A structure of the skeleton of the American mob would tell you that the foot soldiers report to the capos who report to the dons: and the *consiglieri* are elder statesmen and advisers to the dons of each of the families. The Asian gambling world is not quite so precise.

Inspector Lee Chung (*) gave me that warning. He is, I suspect, a bent cop, one of the "demoralized police," warned of by the lieutenant-governor 140 years ago who has become a "confederate and scout" of the gambling operations. I don't have any proof to support that accusation. It is just a feeling. He is a high-ranking officer in the Royal Malaysian Police. We met in my hotel room, as he did not want to be seen meeting me in public. Before we talked or even shook hands, he searched the room for hidden video cameras and frisked my shirt and suit for listening devices. However, it was not those actions that made me think he was on the take, but his clear, deep, and very obvious passion for gambling, the very "criminal" action he was supposed to be clamping down on. He talked enthusiastically for more than an hour on the successful, long-term strategy for betting on soccer that he uses. For the record, one of his strategies is: "Always take the favourite: Chelsea, Manchester United, Arsenal. They rarely lose; the bookies will try to make you forget it, but don't. I could show you the places to gamble." Then he would remember and correct himself hurriedly and say, "Where my friends gamble. My friends gamble." He did, however, have a number of good points about illegal gambling in his country. "Very loosely knitted organization," he said. "Lots of small-timers. Just like direct selling or marketing. One line. One partner. Thousands of small bookies."

Figure 5.1 Structure of Illegal Asian Bookmaking Syndicate

"Mr. Big" Overworld
A prominent politician or businessman

Triad Underworld
Provides the muscle to collect debts or provides protection from other groups

National Level Bookies

CAPITALIZATION AND PROTECTION LEVEL

- -

(Line of police arrests: above this line few people have been arrested)

LOCAL GAMBLING LEVEL

Regional Bookies in Counting Centres

The Runners
Each runner has between 15 to 100 clients. Supplies them with Internet technology, collects money from losing bets, and pays off winning bets.

The Punters
Millions of bettors, wagering on European and local football leagues, four-digit lotteries, horse racing, etc. Placing bets in person on slips of paper, over the phone, or more often now through the Internet.

What he is speaking of are the bottom rungs of the illegal gambling ladder. Here, there are literally millions of punters. They place their bets with runners for local bookies. These local runners are small fry. They have the same name as the runners who work for the fixers to corrupt the games. This is because they literally do the same thing: they *run* back and forth for the bookies. Again, there are thousands of them; they work for different organizations or bookies. They compete, collude, and co-operate with one another, depending on the bets or the event.

Steve and Don (*) are examples of the people at the lower levels of the gambling market. They are two pleasant Chinese guys living in Johor Bahru. I met them a number of times, and they gave me tutorials both on how to gamble and how the system works. We would usually meet at Don's house, which looks like a suburban house anywhere: a low-slung brick house with a little lawn in front of it. Inside his living room he has a giant satellite TV screen and leather chairs where we could watch the European soccer matches as they came in live in the middle of the night. The walls are covered with framed bank notes from around the world. Don runs a small casino in Indonesia. Steve is a shipping executive, although he claims that his brother-in-law runs an illegal bookmaking operation in Georgetown, a city in northern Malaysia.

Together they look a little like an Asian Laurel and Hardy. Don is chubby, perpetually in jeans, perpetually on the hunt for the next business scheme, perpetually with an affable grin on his face. Steve is the slim puritan of the pair: lips tight as he moralizes about gambling. They share two great loves: betting and cooking. Incongruously, in the midst of discussing illegal gambling syndicates, they would break off to give one another recipe tips. The conversations went something like:

Don:	You took Liverpool, two ball [Liverpool to win the game by two goals]! Why? You crazy?
Steve:	No way, la. You don't know what you're talking about. Rafa, he knows what he is doing. Take the odds, la.

Don:	Bullshit! Fowler. He is too old, just fucking around. Go under. Eat ball. Hey, I have a great menu for you! Fish satay with deep-fried mushrooms.
Steve:	You told me about that last week – didn't work.
Don:	That's because you weren't using right kind of mushrooms. Fucking idiot! Shiitake. Shiitake. Not ordinary shit mushrooms. You heat the pan, then garlic, then mushrooms.
Steve:	You didn't say that!

When I first met them, Don was bemoaning his luck over an English Premier League match the night before. He had bet the total goal line. The higher and more unlikely the score, the more money you stand to win if correct. Don had bet on Fulham to beat Norwich with a total score in the game of four goals (3-1, 4-0). The actual result was that Fulham beat Norwich 6-0. If they had kept the score down, Don would have made twenty-three times the money on his bet. As it was, he had lost it all.

The things that can be bet on in the Asian gambling syndicates are a testimony to the human imagination: four-digit number rackets, horse races, cockfights, boxing matches, basketball games, Formula One racing, hockey competitions, cricket tournaments, pre-Olympic events. In soccer alone you can bet on which team will win, by how much, who scores first, who scores last, who will get the first yellow card, who will get a red card, how many yellow cards will be shown, when the first goal will be scored, when the last goal will be scored, the total number of goals, how many headers there will be in the match, how many offsides, corners, and free kicks. The most popular structure of bet, however, is the Asian Handicap, which is like the North American idea of the point spread, where the favourite to win in the gambling market has to win the match by a certain number of goals. So if I bet on a really strong team to beat a weaker team by "two ball," it means that the strong team must score at least two goals more than the other team: if it loses, draws, or wins by only one goal, it is counted as a loss in gambling terms.

These bets are a subject of obsessive interest across Asia. A gambler can bet on just about any soccer league in the world – from the Chinese Super League, to the English Premier League, to the Scottish youth leagues where the players are students or part-time amateurs. I once had a long and fascinating conversation with a supplier for one of the major triad operations in Kuala Lumpur. He was an expert on betting patterns in the Icelandic Football League. I did not know that Iceland had a soccer league before our conversation, but we sat in the cocktail bar of a five-star hotel drinking coffee and beer, discussing the fortunes of various teams in places such as Reykjavik and Akranes. He reckoned that the Icelandic league was so small that it must be honest. "After all they are Scandinavian. Like Vikings. Very honest. Very blonde, la. No fixes."

Don and Steve, like the beer supplier, would often stay up most nights betting live on European soccer matches. It used to all be done by phone calls or word of mouth, but Steve and others told me that in the last few years technology has begun to change the methods of the gambling syndicates. "Internet and pagers have replaced the phone. When we talked, we would say ten sen, which would mean a hundred RM (Malaysian ringgit, or $30), or one RM, which means a thousand RM ($300). Now you get an Internet CD from the bookie. He wants to know your business address and phone, and your home address and phone, and your credit card info, everything possible . . . the technology was from India, but the gang is Hongkies [from Hong Kong] and Malays. The Hongkies came in three years ago and they agreed to split up the market."

There are runners who take Don and Steve's payouts to the local bookies. These bookies may have a territory of a large neighbourhood or small town. At this level in Singapore or Malaysia, it is quite possible for a runner to be of an ethnicity other than Chinese, but as one rises up in the hierarchy, the opportunities for non-Chinese people dries up.

Above the local bookies are the regional representatives who have counting centres where the total bets of the region are calculated and compiled. The local bookies pay into these centres. They are usually nondescript houses in quiet neighbourhoods with little traffic.

Steve and Don took me to one small counting centre in Johor Bahru. It was just above a car-repair shop and from the outside, it looked perfectly normal. Inside, it looks like a small office, with rows of computers and telephones. In all counting centres, there is supposed to be one button that they can push to erase all confidential files and bets in case of a police raid. But Steve told me that these raids were mostly theatrical performances designed to make the police officers, such as Inspector Lee, look good and not trouble the gambling syndicates too much. "Occasionally the bookies will give the police a house to raid. Just for show, la. Keep the system turning. Not make anyone look too bad."

Malaysia is not alone in this type of corruption. I wanted to get some perspective on Asian organized crime and illegal gambling, so when I returned to Oxford, I contacted Joe Pistone. Pistone is one of the heroes of the North American anti-mafia fight. For six years, he worked as an undercover agent using the name Donnie Brasco and managed to infiltrate one of the five big New York crime families – the Bonannos. In his eventual court testimony, he helped convict more than one hundred mobsters. Few people know the inside world of the American mob as well as Pistone. We spoke about his experiences when he was running an illegal bookmaking operation.

> We were paying off police officers, sure. Look, gambling doesn't exist without payoffs. It's not something that you can hide, you know what I mean? Because you have to go somewhere to place your bets, and the bookie has to be somewhere. You know, he's got to be hanging out on a corner or in a bar or in a restaurant. So unfortunately that happens, yeah.

I began to tell him about the Malaysian police making staged raids on gambling houses, but he stopped me before I could finish my sentence.

Right, and they make a bust. I mean, that happens here in the States too. They make a bust and they arrest some nobodies, so it looks like they're doing something. I mean, that's the old game, that's not something new. . . . It keeps the newspapers happy, it keeps the people happy, you know, the citizens happy, that, you know, the police are doing something. Somebody gets arrested. You know, somebody of no consequence. And they make sure that there's not that much money there at the time. I mean, that's not a new game. That game's been around forever.

The kind of shadow puppet theatre of fake police raids is also common in the world of Asian illegal gambling syndicates. In 1995, after the scale of the Malaysian and Singaporean match-fixing was revealed, the Royal Malaysian Police moved in. They arrested more than 150 people connected to the league: players, coaches, even a regional bookie. It was, according to one author, "the biggest and most thorough inquiry in the history of the professional game." If this is true, the game is in a very bad way, for the investigation was, according to some of its own top police investigators, deeply flawed. I met one officer in the food court of a shopping mall on the outskirts of Ipoh, a provincial town in northern Malaysia. The story he told, amidst the mundane setting of plastic tables and disposable cups, was incongruously fascinating. It was the lieu-tenant-governor's warning of squalid police corruption and betrayal to the gambling syndicates made real more than a century after he wrote his original warning.

The officer told me: "I do remember that one of the police officers, one of the lead guys in the investigation, we caught him meeting with one of the bookies that we were trying to investigate. We put a tail on him and I got a call on my phone from people who were tailing him. He was meeting with the Chinese bookie we were investigating in a hotel in Klang."

I asked him whether they had arrested their colleague. He replied: "No, it would have been too embarrassing. He was a triad expert. I think

I know how he got his expertise, so we took him down a rank and let him resign."

The stories of high-level corruption in the Malaysian police may sound incredible to an outsider, but on one of my stays there, there was a government-appointed inquiry, that released yet another report into police corruption. They had discovered that some of the traffic units were making so much money from shaking down motorists that they were auctioning off the post to the highest bidder within the force. If an officer wanted a high-level position, it was alleged, he or she had to pay to work in the unit.

However, apart from financial security, there are two other phenomena that keep the illegal gambling structure in place and ensure that the theatre of enforcement goes on: they are called "trust" and "a serious reprimand."

6

THE MOB, TRUST, AND SERIOUS REPRIMANDS

I mean there are a lot of things that come into consideration.
But mostly I would say that you're going to be bullied or hit
or beaten up. They are going to smash you up. You're probably in the stages for a serious reprimand.

There was something rotten in the Petaling Street Market. At first, it
looked like a bustling, crowded market full of independent traders. My
hotel was just near the market in central Kuala Lumpur's Chinatown
and I would see the area getting busy just after sunset. In the darkness,
there were approximately three hundred and fifty market stalls jammed
into four city blocks. Each seller was crammed next to his neighbour. It
looked like a highly competitive place. There were stalls selling counterfeit perfumes, shoes, and designer clothes for a range of different prices
to bemused tourists from a dozen different countries. The air was full of
the sounds of bargaining, the imploring shouts of the sellers and the
smell of durian, the Malaysian fruit which gives off an odour of garbage
and rotting cheese. When I first came to the city I worried that in a few
years the market would disappear, like much of the city, under concrete
and tarmac. It seemed a long way from its original function, a place providing for the needs of the local Chinese community, and now it was full
of stalls catering to sun-soaked tourists.

It was the DVD sellers who gave me the first indication that there was something different happening there. In the midst of the confusion, there would always be young men wandering around carrying stacks of pirated DVDs under one arm. Oddly, for all the number of sellers, their prices were relatively consistent. The DVDs were always listed at ten Malaysian ringgit a disc (approximately $2.50). No matter how much bargaining a tourist was willing to do, that price would not change. It seemed odd in such a highly competitive atmosphere. However, after a few months of wandering around the market talking to the stall owners and the DVD sellers. I discovered that there was actually only one "Mr. Big" (their term) who controlled all the DVD sellers. All the DVDs sold in the market were owned by him, and the appearance of a highly competitive market was an illusion. Actually, the longer I stayed there, the more I realized that few people in Kuala Lumpur even shopped at the market. Most Malaysians went to air-conditioned shopping malls: "Better selection, cheaper too, la," my friends would tell me. I realized that the Petaling Street Market was not kept open *despite* the tourists who went there, but in large part *because* of the tourists. We were being given the experience we expected: "exotic Asia" – hot, cramped, and crowded, and not the one that actually existed.

Then I noticed the burnt-out stalls: half a dozen in each row, burned to the ground, their ashy wreckage untouched in the middle of the seeming chaos. The owners of other stalls looked embarrassed and shrugged their shoulders when I asked them how so many stalls could catch fire when ones that were in between them all stayed intact.

Finally, I took a couple of friendly shop owners who I had done business with to one side, nodded to the burnt-out wreckage and said that universal word, "Mafia?"

They nodded grimly. "Yes, yes, mafia."

The illegal Asian gambling syndicates are a little like the Petaling Street Market: there is an illusion of a highly competitive system. However, what actually exists is a very carefully controlled structure, owned and financed by a relatively small, select group of men, and to make their market work, they need two things: trust and violence.

Having problems with your gambling debts? Can't pay? Won't pay! Don't worry. The Asian gambling boys will soon be around to visit you. At first, they will be quite nice as Steve told me earnestly. "You can go to them and say, 'I'm sorry. I cannot pay all the money. I will pay you a thousand now and then week from now. I will pay but I need time. . . .' They will give you time. They will shut you down from playing until you pay, but they are not bad."

His description is accurate if a gambler has the wherewithal and intelligence to go to his bookies and tell them about minor debts and, conveniently, has a brother-in-law who, like Steve, is a major operative. However, for the normal punters with big debts, the local bookies will call in the muscle. They will stage an escalating series of retributions up to major burglary raids, where they steal everything, burn the house, and possibly chop up the bad-faith bettors. The newspaper columns of Singapore feature the occasional stories of innocent citizens being mysteriously attacked by gangsters or disappearing for "no apparent reason."

There is, in reality, a very good reason for the disappearances. The gamblers are promoting trust. It may seem odd, but along with money and protection, this multibillion-dollar industry relies on one other major sociological phenomenon – trust. Amid the murders, house raids, and muggings, there is a pattern.

Academic Partha Dasgupta once described the need for people *to trust* in the enforcement arm of organized crime. The credibility of organized crime consists of their ability to make use of what he calls "credible levels of force." It works both to deter other criminals and persuade ordinary citizens to co-operate with the gangs. In burning up stalls in street markets, poking people's eyeballs out, or chopping up persistently non-paying gamblers, the criminals are making sure that the gamblers *trust* them to retaliate if the punters do not pay. There is, however, a psychological level that Dasgupta did not write about – enjoyment.

Italian magistrates Giovanni Falcone and Paolo Borsellino were the two best organized-crime fighters the world has ever known. Better than Rudy Giuliani in New York. Far better than Scotland Yard in London. And far, far better than any other detectives in Asia. They lived – under police protection – right in the centre of Palermo for more than ten years, at the heart of the Sicilian mafia. Before their murders, they encouraged dozens of mob members to confess, to become *pentiti* and talk about the structure and business of the mob. Some of the mobsters talked of death, about the acid baths that engulfed their victims, and the trips out to the harbour to dump the bodies. They talked about the room where the head of one mafia family, Filippo Marchese, kept his victims and tortured them slowly. One mobster, who helped in the sessions by grabbing the feet of the victims as they were slowly strangled to death, testified, "Although he was head of the family, Marchese personally strangled most of the victims himself, often for the most insignificant of reasons . . . Marchese was a bloody-minded character and gave the impression of *enjoying* killing people and demanded that no one betray any emotion at the spectacle."

This is organized crime. It is not *The Sopranos*, with their moral anxieties and their psychiatric confessions. It is not Al Pacino looking sexy as *Scarface* or John Travolta in *Get Shorty*. It is desperate, horrible men who enjoy taking people away to secluded places and slowly, deliberately hurting them. Hurting them the same way little children pull the legs off ants.

"Big Sal" Miciotta was part of this world. He was a mafia hitman for the Colombo crime family in New York City. He murdered at least five people in cold blood. In the mid-1990s he was caught and became a high-profile turncoat for the FBI. He has a high price on his head. We talked about the world of illegal gambling. He, too, had become interested in the reach of the Russian mafia into the National Hockey League.

He claimed, "I know some Russians in Brooklyn that were involved with the higher NHL, the Russian mafia they call them . . . they got a bunch of Russian hockey players in the NHL, and they were doing a lot of business with them . . . the Brooklyn guys, the bookmakers, they weren't touching any hockey games . . . for a long time they shut off the hockey." In other words, the senior mob-connected Brooklyn bookmakers would not take bets on key hockey games in the mid-1990s because they were convinced that some of the Russian hockey players were throwing games for their mobster friends.

Big Sal would certainly know about Brooklyn illegal gamblers: he ran a mob-controlled casino there. He explained the structure and mechanism of illegal gambling operations in Brooklyn to me. And a lot of it sounds exactly the same as it is halfway around the world in Malaysia, down to the theatrical raids on the counting centres staged by the police.

> Me and five guys, one guy from each organized crime family, we had a place called The Club Intrepid. We had six blackjack tables, two craps tables, and ten poker tables. And we ran a casino-like business for maybe two years. We made a ton of money. We had the police on a payroll. Morals police. But when we were going to get arrested, we got, two weeks in advance, we got notice. We took all the money out of there, we left all the legitimate guys there to take a pinch, we had the lawyers waiting around to bail them out. You know, the whole deal, the whole deal.

But then he told me the real money in American sports gambling is not from running the book.

> When the guys who are betting on sports can't pay their tab at the end of the week, they automatically become a Shylock customer. That is primarily, what really, really, really spikes it up. Let's say you lose five thousand to me this week and you don't have it. I'll give you the five thousand as a Shylock loan so you can pay your gambling debt.

Hill:	And the interest is?
Miciotta:	About five points. So that is $250 a week. Just interest. A lot of money. A thousand a month.
Hill:	What happens if I don't pay you back within two months?
Miciotta:	You have to keep paying me the $250 a week until you pay me back.
Hill:	Okay, but what happens if I'm an honest, decent guy. I have a cash flow problem and I'm not lying. What happens after say two weeks?
Miciotta:	I mean, there is a lot of things that come into consideration. But mostly I would say that you're going to be bullied or hit or beaten up. They are going to smash you up. You're probably in the stages for a serious reprimand.

Mobsters must be careful how they publicize this side of the work or the real nature of a serious reprimand, for trust in illegal gambling structures is a two-way street. The gamblers must rely on the bookies to beat them up if they do not pay, but they cannot be so afraid of them that they will not bet at all. The gambler also has to trust the bookies to pay them. Steve and Don told me, "They are very good at paying. You wait two days and then they have the money for you. They will come to your door with the money. Very rare that they do not pay. And that is only when the lower bookie has spent it then they will delay. But usually never."

Even for a hard North American mobster such as Big Sal, the essential mechanism of an illegal gambling operation is the same as it is in Asia: trust and reputation. "You have to pay. Your reputation is everything . . . I never knew the Italian guys not to pay someone. Never knew that. . . ." Joe Pistone (Donnie Brasco) said the same thing: reputation is everything for the illegal bookmaker.

And once the word gets out that you welched, no one's going to bet with you any more, you know? Now, there are some . . . I'm sure this happens, but a good bookie, somebody who's been in business for a while, is not going to do that because, like I say, over the long run, the bettor's never gonna win. And, once you welch on one person, the word gets out and they're going to go to somebody else.

In the gambling business, people talk. The flow of information is a powerful, measurable force. Bettors talk about which bookmaker is honest or not, and even rival bookmakers who detest one another will share information on non-paying customers. The basic assumption in most gambling markets is that of "perfect information" or that some-one, somewhere will know everything there is to know about an event. Because of this flow of information among gamblers, after the 9/11 attacks the Pentagon floated the idea of a public futures market based on terrorist attacks and assassination attempts on President George W. Bush. Futures markets are linked to stock exchanges, so they are officially legitimate forms of investment. But they are simply another publicly approved form of gambling. Futures are usually tied in with obscure, financial commodities such as pork bellies or wheat, but basically the "investor" – read gambler – bets on the future rise or fall in the price of these commodities. The Futures Markets Applied to Prediction (FutureMAP) idea was that if any terrorist or criminal group had a serious plan to kill the U.S. president, someone, somewhere would not be able to resist betting on the plan. The futures market would then red-flag the Security Department and they would be able to increase the protec-tion for the president. The plan was abandoned as being in bad taste, but the idea of the power of information in the gambling market remains.

This emphasis on trust relationships is why the reputation of a prompt and ready payment is higher, among professional gamblers, for the illegal Asian gambling syndicates than most of their legitimate counterparts in the big British gambling companies or Las Vegas. I dis-covered this when I visited the studios of John McAllister (*), across the world, but around the corner on the Internet. He has become part of the wider revolution that in the last few years has transformed illegal betting around the world and has made fixing soccer games much, much easier.

McAllister – who, I want to be clear, does not fix matches – is one of the few who consistently makes enough money off sports gambling to live a dream lifestyle. When I visited his offices, I was hoping for something dramatic. I was hoping for a cross between Santa's workshop and a mad genius's laboratory. I imagined that the whole place would be almost dark. Through the gloom I would see rows of men wearing striped shirts, eye-shades, and smoking cigars while they muttered down the phones to sources in hundreds of different stadiums around the world.

Actually, McAllister has the pale, unshaven, math-geek look of the truly successful gambler. He worked for a few years in the financial district but then found his niche in predicting sports results. "I was always good at statistics and it came naturally to me," he told me while showing me around his offices. They look like a little boy's dream: there are TV screens showing live soccer matches, fridges stocked with pop and beer, and the walls have life-sized soccer posters on them. I met a number of other professional gamblers and odds compilers. They all have the same look: a nerd at loose in a man's world. Don't be fooled. They have nerves of steel and are willing to bet sums of money on their own intuition and intelligence that would make most people faint. McAllister not only places bets worth millions, but has also become so successful that he heads his own betting syndicate, all of whom work extraordinarily long hours to beat the bookies. He taught me some of his methods.

There are no drugs stronger than naturally produced ones. Many addictive drugs – like cocaine, heroin, or amphetamines – work not only by adding something to the bloodstream, but also in combination with the body's own endocrine system, helping secrete huge amounts of adrenalin or endorphins. Drug addicts effectively pump themselves full of natural drugs by taking artificial drugs. Others of us do the same by creating or allowing circumstances in our lives to pump us full of natural drugs: the man who drives too fast or fights with everyone, the woman who argues or dramatizes her way through life.

It is like that with most serious gamblers. The thrill with gambling is not just winning, although that is obviously better. Even losing produces great waves of natural drugs for gamblers. Even when they totally screw up their lives, lose their savings and their families, the natural wave of adrenalin is still pumping through their bodies, making them feel very, very alive. The game, be it the roll of dice, the turn of numbers, or twenty-two soccer players running up and down the pitch, is simply their way of producing a natural high in their own bodies. Big Sal Miciotta claims that the drug was so strong in some addicted gamblers that they *liked* getting beaten up: "I swear some of those guys would actually like it. They would want to get beaten."

John McAllister's recipe for successful betting is the exact opposite of the testosterone and emotional cocktail of the ordinary gambler. McAllister told me that the best traders – his word, like the Asian bookies and their agents – control their emotions and are pessimists. When he bets, he follows a strict regime:

> I do the opposite of most gamblers: when I am losing I taper down. I do not chase my loses. I think that is what may have happened to Wayne Rooney [a famous soccer player, who allegedly lost hundreds of thousands of dollars gambling], why he lost so much money. I have a set amount of money: 1.5 per cent of my betting bank a day; no more. I do not bet any more of that in one day.

McAllister was very wary about talking about his methods. At one point, he switched off a computer as I peered at some of his data. "It's the way I make my money," he said defensively. But in general there are two methods that successful gamblers use to beat the bookmakers: statistics and information. Statistics come from variations of probability theory or carefully produced computer databases with thousands of variables that churn out predictions. Information comes from inside sources: a star player has an unannounced injury, the referee is going through a divorce, the wind coming off the lake in Chicago makes baseball pitchers throw wild. The pros use both. No intuition. No feelings. No hunches. Just day after day of hard research and statistical computations.

It works. McAllister has a large house. A second home in Switzerland. And the big, legal bookmakers hate him. In fact, when they can, they refuse to take large amounts of his money. It is, according to the American gambling expert Michael Konick, the same in Las Vegas casinos or Costa Rican Internet sites. Lose money? Sure! You're welcome. Become a smart, savvy punter who wins money over the long-term? You will have a real problem getting your bets on. It is the same for Joe Saumarez-Smith. He was a successful gambler for years, yet he too faced problems getting his bets on in England:

> The U.K. gambling market has no balls. No odds-making. They won't take your business if you are a winning punter. The big companies are notorious for only catering to small punters. I go to pick up my winnings and I am told, "Oh, our shop had an off day. Sorry, but you'll have to come back tomorrow when we have had a chance to go to the bank . . ." I find it difficult enough to get £100 on a game, let alone £200,000, or the amount you need to make it worth your while. I can't place a big bet in my own name anywhere in London.

So McAllister and others in the professional gambling circuit use the illegal Asian gambling syndicates. They claim that they do so partly because their faith in the Asian bookmakers is higher than with many legal European gambling companies, even though the Asian operations are illegal. It is easier to get the bets on, the payout is quicker, and the administration fee (*the vig*, as Big Sal would say) is lower. But while the industry itself may be honest, the fixers who work inside it have devastated sports across the entire continent.

THE COLLAPSE OF THE BETTING LINE

> We lost nearly an entire generation of players, but if you are
> going to say that there is no corruption now, I wouldn't
> believe you. . . . We had circumstances where the entire team,
> including substitutes, were in on the fix.

It was supposed to be a slow night at the Singapore Pools. The multi-
million-dollar organization that is Singapore's attempt to curb some of
the interest in the country's illegal gambling market. It's a government-
run sports lottery where grandmothers can feel safe betting their money.
On April 12, 2006, Kevin Kim (*) was on duty. It is his job to watch the
bets as they come in and then adjust the betting line accordingly. Kim is
an odds compiler. The phrase *odds compiler* has a ring to it, just down
from *bookmaker*, *bookie*, or *pro gambler*, of danger, of living on the wrong
side of the law. It speaks of tough, unshaven, macho men who wear eye
shades, chew toothpicks, cigars, and unwary bettors for breakfast. From
the odds compilers that I have met, this is the wrong impression. They
are like the professional gamblers who try consistently to take their
money; gentle, nerdy types that have the paleness that suggests too much
time in front of a computer screen.

That night, Kim was a little like an all-night radar operator or a
weather watcher, checking the sweep for any bombers flying into his air-
space or storms coming to threaten the security of his kingdom. However,

that night there was a perfect storm brewing in the gambling world, and Kim and the rest of Singapore Pools had no idea it was coming.

A quarter-final FA Cup match between Singapore and the Malaysian team Sarawak was scheduled for that night. There is a great deal of tension between Singapore and Malaysia. Singapore was part of Malaysia until 1965, when a teary Prime Minister Lee Kuan Yew of Singapore came on national television to say the country was splitting up: "For me, it is a moment of anguish. All my life, my whole adult life, I believed in merger and unity of the two territories. We are connected by geography, economics, and ties of kinship . . . it broke everything we stood for . . ."

Now, there is the animosity that comes from a national divorce. Singaporeans, who tend to have to be ordered to enjoy themselves ("We have to pursue this subject of fun very seriously," a cabinet minister said once), often regard Malaysians as hopelessly lazy country cousins who simply sit around drinking and sunning themselves. Malaysians, on the other hand, tend to regard Singaporeans as their big-city cousins, impossibly ambitious, pushy, and unable to enjoy themselves without a prime ministerial decree. There is a famous cartoon that I saw hanging on a number of Malaysian soccer officials' walls. It shows two Malaysians looking at the stands of a soccer stadium before a Malaysia versus Singapore match. One section is covered in signs: "no spitting," "no talking," "no cellphones," "no loud shouting," "no chewing gum." "Ahh," says one Malaysian to the other, "it's for the Singapore fans."

In short, they hate losing to one another. So even a soccer match between a rural province such as Sarawak and Singapore should have been a tough, well-fought match.

A betting line is a reflection of all the bets on a particular game added together. It is a little like a share price. In the same way that an investor can buy a share of General Motors for $100 at nine in the morning and then see that share be worth $80 at noon when the sales result from the North American market is announced, so too can a betting line on a game shift. The star forward on one of the teams breaks his leg and the betting line moves up as more bettors place their bets against the team with the injured star. The other team announces its World Cup–winning goalkeeper is coming back from an injury and the betting line may move still higher.

However, in reality, huge shifts in the lines are very rare. When the odds compilers sit down to make up the odds on the games, they do it with a commendable nerdy energy. They have to, their very living depends not only on accurately assessing the probabilities, but also accurately predicting how the fans will think the game will end. So they pore over the injury lists. They pore over one another's odds in case a rival has some information they do not. They have long lists of statistics – which team is stronger on home ground, which team is better in the rain, which team is better early in the season – that they check with the same fervour that Southern Baptists check the Old Testament to make sure God didn't make any mistakes.

In Asia, a soccer match has several "lines" to watch. The first is the actual result of the game: who will win. It is expressed as three options: home win, away win, and draw. The most common bet in this part of the world is the Asian Handicap, which is roughly the same as the point spread of the North American sports betting market.

However, two bet types that are particularly intriguing for some match-fixers are the ones for "correct score" and the "total goals." Guess which team will win and a bettor might get odds of 2 to 1 or less. But if a gambler can predict that the total number of goals scored in a game will be over seven, they can get 30 to 1 odds or higher.

Two hours before the start of the match, Kim noticed the betting line began to move wildly. It began to move on a particular score. Not just that one team would win, but that the match would have at least nine goals. This result is very unusual (most soccer matches have total scores of two or three goals) and as such had odds of roughly 30 to 1. In the next two hours, so many people placed bets on total goals of nine or above that the betting line crashed. It went from 30 to 1 down to 1.5 to 1 – meaning that if a bettor had placed a bet two hours before the game that the two teams would score nine goals between them, for every $1 wagered, the bettor would have won $30 back. By the start of the game, the same bet would only have won $1.50.

Such a big change in the betting line is virtually unprecedented in the gambling market, where an odds shift of $4 or $5 over the course of a week is considered a significant odds movement. A change of $28 is equivalent to Black Thursday – October 24, 1929 – when the New York stock market crashed. The team management heard about the run on the gambling market, and one of the players claims that they came storming into the dressing room demanding the fix be stopped. The players, all of them, agreed and wondered who could possibly be fixing the game? They all promised to go out and play their hardest.

The result? Exactly as the fall in the line predicted: one team won 7-2. There were nine goals scored. Singapore Pools lost several hundred thousand dollars and the game was widely assumed to have been fixed by a set of gambling corruptors who lost control of their information and thus began a "run on the market." And the reputation of Asian soccer took yet another hammer blow.

It was a wet evening in Kuala Lumpur. The biggest team in Malaysia – Selangor – was playing the independent, oil-rich state of Brunei. Back in the heyday of the Malaysian league, a game against their wealthy cousins would have attracted a crowd of 30,000 to 40,000 people. The night that I sat and watched in the spring of 2005, there were barely enough people to fill in one stand out of four. The fans tried their best, but the noise they made barely came across the field. I was sitting in the VIP section, where a crowd of well-suited fat men sat around in nice chairs, discussed the game vaguely, chatted on their mobile phones, and ate a great supper at half-time. None of them stood and cheered. To be honest, there was not much to cheer about. The game was neither played at an interesting pace nor with too much skill. The best thing was that the players did not fall about and pretend to be injured, and generally, there was a gentlemanliness about them that was wholly admirable and is almost wholly missing in the European game. Even after the most atrocious tackles, they helped one another up and shook hands.

In the end, Selangor ran out easy winners by 3-0. The game mirrors the state of soccer in general on the Malay Peninsula. For the people used to watching games in the packed stadiums of the early 1990s, it is like finding a sick and dying old friend. The name is the same, but the appearance has so diminished and shrunk that it is almost too painful to see.

The national teams have also fallen in world rankings. In 1993, Malaysia was 75th in the world; it is now at 159th, just ahead of teams such as the Maldives, Grenada, and Tahiti. The situation in Singapore is almost as bad: they were at 73rd, and now they are ranked at 138th.

You don't get many thank-you notes for exposing widespread corruption. Johnson Fernandez and Lazarus Rokk certainly didn't. What Rokk got in the end was an onerous lawsuit, where his government sources refused to help him, and a bullet carved in chalk. The bullet was mailed to him with a note saying "The next time it's for real."

A few months later, their Brickfields underworld source was killed. It was, apparently, nothing to do with match-fixing. He simply got into an argument with a neighbouring Chinese gang at a pool hall. They waited for him outside and then twelve of them beat him to death with pool cues. According to Rokk, "He was a big, strong guy and fought them off, but it was just too many. And he didn't have his gang with him or any weapons to defend himself. He was left to die in the alleyway."

Fernandez and Rokk gave up. Unsupported by much of the Malaysian establishment, the story was simply too hot for them. Fernandez claims that he changed his route home every night while driving and that "I would have had to take out a big insurance [policy] for my family if I had continued. It just wasn't worth it in the end. I am passionate about soccer. I sat there watching it disappear. But there was just too much danger for us." They did their best to forget everything they once knew. They even took all their notes, including a letter that they claimed gave accurate predictions of the results of English Premier Leagues matches *before* they were played, and destroyed them.

Years later, when Fernandez and I met over coffee in downtown Kuala Lumpur, his gentle face became dark when he thinks of that time. He says that he is "totally disillusioned . . . There's no best story coming out of this. We have all been losers here; the game has been the biggest loser. The game is losing because there is no support. There are not enough passionate people there who want to see the survival of the game. We are not going to see it in our lifetime, not even our children's lifetime."

The nightmare scenario that Mohamed bin Hammam, Peter Velappan, and all the other Asian soccer officials are facing is that enthusiasm for soccer has not actually died in their countries; if anything it has become larger. A few weeks after watching Selangor play Brunei, I watched another group of fans. It was May 26, 2005, the day after the Champions League final. The night before, the soccer world had watched one of *those* games. Every few years a sporting event occurs that transcends the mediocrity of most games; it becomes a lesson in not just sport but also life. For once the overblown hyperbole of the sports journalist – where almost every game is the "match of the century" filled with "drama" and "tension" – was justified. The game was in the Atatürk Olympic Stadium in Istanbul, pitting Liverpool – from the northwest of England, and previously great but now barely surviving among the top European teams – against the superb AC Milan, owned by the prime minister of Italy, Silvio Berlusconi. The first half, for those unfortunate enough not to see the game, was a triumph of Italian professionalism. AC Milan mixed iron-clad defending with rapierlike attacks. At the end of the first forty-five minutes, they were up 3-0. Their defence was stocked with players whose names are synonymous, the way that Chubb or Pinkerton are linked to protection, with great defence: Maldini, Stam, Gattuso, and Nesta. Any reasonable person could see that there was no way back from such a score. The game was as good as over. The best thing for Liverpool and their fans to do was to slink out of the stadium in disgrace.

However, in a triumph of sheer bloody-minded courage, determination, and refusal to accept defeat, the Liverpool fans in the stadium did not accept that the game was over. There were 30,000 of them in and around the stadium and *nobody* could tell them the game was over; *nobody* could get them to stop their noise; and *nobody* could stop them from singing again and again the anthem of the great Liverpool teams of the past, "You'll Never Walk Alone." The sound echoed around the stadium; it floated down into the dressing room where their team heard it and took heart; and it was heard in an air-conditioned room 8,600 kilometres away in Singapore.

In the room were hundreds of members of the Liverpool fan club of Singapore. It was four o'clock in the morning. Any sensible person could see it was over. Their team was 3-0 down against the finest defensive club in the world. Any reasonable person would go to bed. They did not. Some of them, like their counterparts in the Istanbul stadium, sang. Most of them hunched over the television, willing their team to come back from the dead. Liverpool did. The players matched their fans in spirit and scored three goals in a six-minute spell in the second half – and then won the game on penalties. It finished at 5:45 a.m., Singapore time.

I am not a Liverpool fan. But that display of sheer bloody-minded refusal to accept defeat is what good soccer is all about. It is the finest part of the human spirit. For every cancer patient who has to walk into chemotherapy, for every rape victim who has to get up the next morning and face the world, for every person who stares at defeat and refuses to give up, it was an inspiration. This was not going gently into the good night; this was not feigning injury or giving up.

Then the party got started.

In Singapore, things are done well. The Liverpool fans hired a red double-decker bus and drove around the city. They went around dozens of times, each time with a largely different set of fans in the bus. There is a Manchester United shop on the Orchard Road shopping district, an entire shop dedicated to paraphernalia of the Red Devils. Liverpool fans are supposed to hate Manchester United. It goes along with the support. So the Liverpool fans of Singapore parked their bus in front of the Manchester United shop and cheered and sang; they did it every time that the bus went around the city.

When I went with them, there was not a single European among them. The whole group was Singaporean. Many of them had never been to England, let alone Anfield, Liverpool's stadium. Wilson Li, who has a Liverpool crest tattoo, was typical: "Liverpool is my religion, my life. My tattoo is on my chest over my heart. I am still a Liverpool man, win or lose."

His friends took off their shirts and stood, arms around one another, bellowing their lungs out. Even as a neutral, there was something oddly moving about standing in a modern car park in the middle of Singapore 11,000 kilometres from Anfield and hear a group of Chinese men sing "You'll Never Walk Alone." The hair on the back of my neck rose.

However, the scene begs a question: why?

Why does a group of people – thousands of kilometres and eight time zones away – cheer for a team that most will never see? Why are the streets and public spaces of Asia dominated with photos of such EPL stars as Frank Lampard, John Terry, and Michael Owen? Why are so many people deserting teams such as Brunei, Selangor, and Beijing Hyundai to follow Liverpool and Manchester United?

It is, in part, due to the widespread television coverage of European games in Asia. Any television viewer can see the difference in quality of play. It is in part due to the political repression of Asia. One is not allowed to speak too openly about the political situation in most Asian countries, so having a bread and circus show that is far away and politically unde-manding suits the powers-that-be in Asia. If you are a repressive govern-ment, it is better to have people shouting on the streets about Liverpool versus Manchester United than shouting on the streets about freedom of the press or democratic reforms. But the lack of support for local soccer is mostly because the credibility of most of the Asian leagues has been destroyed by the fixers. Worse still, and almost everyone admits this fact, the fixing is still going on.

Privately, there was not a single Asian soccer official who told me that they had been completely effective in cleaning up the game. One comment from one top official is typical: "We lost nearly an entire generation of players, but if you are going to say that there is no corruption now, I wouldn't believe you. . . . We had circumstances where the entire team, including substitutes, were in on the fix."

Wilson Li and his Liverpool fan friends know all about the fixing. When I asked them why they did not support Singapore or any of the local teams, they were emphatic. "We used to. Maybe ten years ago, we used to drive up to Kuala Lumpur when Singapore played. It was great; there would be 60,000 people in the stadium. But now? There is too much bribery. The fans, they pay good money for the game, suddenly their team loses 2-0, 3-0 for nothing. Waste of money!"

Contrary to legend, Ian Rush is smart. Rush was one of the great goal-scorers of the 1980s, a lithe, lean man with a toothbrush moustache. He also had the reputation of being a thickie. He went from the hugely successful Liverpool team and played for one year with the Italian club Juventus. It did not go well. On being asked what he thought of Italy, he paused and is alleged to have said, "I couldn't settle in Italy – it was like living in a foreign country." English middle-class intellectuals who fancy themselves as a "footballerati," people who cannot play but understand the game in a way that those who play it cannot, like to sneer at Rush as a typical example of a thick-headed peasant who plays it. They seriously underestimate him.

I met Rush in a Singapore bar a few months before the collapse of the betting line. We were fellow guests of ESPN journalists. ESPN broadcasts EPL, Italian, Spanish, and Champions League soccer to twenty-five countries in East Asia. Occasionally, they will bring in a big European soccer name to provide colour commentary. Rush was their guest. He was a goal-scoring coach for the Liverpool squad. He looked as he did as a player, lean and fit, although, thankfully, the moustache has gone. We talked about Liverpool's chances, how they were doing, why they played better in the Champions League than the Premier League. He was smart and insightful, with an understanding of how players work and think far beyond that of any outsider. He was good company and we shared beers. Then he asked me what I did. I told him about my research into match-fixing and asked him about Bruce Grobbelaar, the famous Liverpool goalkeeper who, allegedly, accepted money to fix soccer games. He looked at me as if I just had crawled out from a hole. "I don't answer questions at this time of night," he said and then retreated to the other end of the bar, where he was fawned over by red-faced English fans of an indeterminate age. I never intended or thought that Rush was in anyway involved in match-fixing, but not for the first time my research topic had caused me lots of social embarrassment.

I turned to the ESPN journalists. They were very, very nice guys. We chatted, but I think I may have been inadvertently patronizing. I did not mean to be, but the Rush incident had thrown me off and I said something like, "I watched your program the other night. It was quite good. What is the average audience that you have?"

One of their announcers looked at me from under his brows.

"On a good match, a final or a really big game, around 280 million people," he said, straight-faced. "On an average night, an EPL match midweek with not very much at stake, maybe only 140 million people."

One hundred and forty million people is a significant proportion of the total population of North America watching a run-of-the-mill European soccer match. For the really big matches, the TV audience in Asia climbs to more than the entire population of Western Europe. So we have a situation where there is a large population who really, really loves to gamble. They, with the rise of the Internet, have the ability to bet on games anywhere in the world. Their own leagues have largely collapsed into a state of disrepair and chaos partly due to match-fixing. The perfect storms of the collapsing lines, such as the one that hit Kevin Kim and the Singapore Pools, have diminished the credibility of the leagues. In fact, now many Asian punters prefer to bet *on* the fixes. They try to guess which particular games will be fixed and by whom, and bet on that rather than the games. And just as all this is occurring, television coverage of European matches has suddenly been introduced and the following of European clubs has grown so exponentially, that the audience for a midweek match stands at 140 million people.

So what's a hard-working Asian match-fixer to do?

Go to Europe.

EUROPE
A NORMAL WAY OF BUSINESS

PART II

PROLOGUE

(Verbatim transcript of an e-mail exchange between a European soccer player and Marc Carinci of Soccercapper.com, the researcher for this book, January 2008)

Player: I want to offer you 1 fixed soccer match that coming and its 1000% fixed.

Why i am so sure about that?

Because i will play on that match and i know that we have to lose this match.

The first match that we played at home we won and now we have to lose.

3 points for 3 points was the deal.

If you are interested just write me.

I will give you the match for 200 euro cause i sold out this information for very huge money.

date for this match is XX.03.08

Carinci: Please provide more information. thanks.

Player: This soccer match is in Macedonian league. i dont know yet what odd it will be but i am sure that it will be not under 2.00. Macedonian league is one of the most fixed league in whole europe, especially the second half of the

championship every round has a fixed match. I send
information in many websites for this events and they
paid me. i am sure that no other website for this fixed
matches does not have the right information as i do and
200 euro is nothing compare to other website for which
must pay thousands of dollars. i have soccer friends in
almost every team in macedonian league and we have
contact if some fixed match is coming. i have played in
several teams in macedinia, XXXX and XXXX [names
two other European leagues]. If your company is interested about this match just write me and i will send you
the payment link. thanks for your interested

Carinci: Thanks for your reply. If what you say is true then we
could have a very good partnership together. But how do
I know you are the real XXXXX and not just some
Internet scammer? Also will you or your friends have
any info on matches in any other league too?

Player: i will scan my passport and send you via email if you
want. i am sure that you checked my name via Internet
search. my name is XXX. born XX-XX-XXXX. i am still
active professional soccer player. former national player
. . . i have soccer friends in almost every league in europe
germany, italia, ukraine, serbia, croatia, poland, turkey
and macedonia. i have very confidential information for
example if fixed matches income. my information is
1000% accurate. i sold this fixed soccer matches very
expensive in italy and singapoure . . .

The player did send his passport, and the result of the game was exactly
as he predicted.

THE ARRIVAL OF THE LOCUSTS

It was quite dangerous . . . I was going to the plane and I got an anonymous phone call saying if I should come, they would kill me. So I was not too happy. They are really mafia boys. It's not that I am a coward, but I prefer to stay alive.

Pietro Allatta is officially known as a Belgian sports agent who has an interest in a number of footballers there, including the sometime national goalkeeper Silvio Proto. Allatta does, however, have an interesting background. He was once both an associate and then construction business rival of Carmelo Bongiorno – the former head of the Belgian Italian mob. Bongiorno was convicted in 1994 of arranging the disappearance of Stéphane Steinier, a Belgian journalist. He and his gang kidnapped Steinier, killed him, dosed his corpse in acid, and then disposed of the remains underneath one of the many buildings that Bongiorno was having constructed in southern Belgium. Steinier was not the only person who disappeared in that era: a local football goalkeeper who was a close friend of Pietro Allatta, vanished April 23, 1988. He has not been seen since and no one is entirely sure of what happened, but he is presumed to have irritated Bongiorno and received the same acid bath as Stéphane Steinier. Allatta's own brush with the law came when he and his brother were convicted of tax fraud in connection with the construction industry and sentenced to several years in prison. While Allatta's brother Salvatore went to jail, Pietro Allatta never served a day in prison.

Despite his conviction for fraud and knowledge of Italian mobsters, officially, Allatta is a soccer agent. He even has a FIFA agent's licence, although it is not from Belgium but from the Republic of Togo. He was the partner of a Ye Zheyun, a mysterious Chinese businessman who arrived in Belgium in the fall of 2004 ostensibly as the head of a textile firm – Cecilia Bilanci, of 29 Rue de Pyramides, in Paris.

In 1992, in a largely forgotten series of hearings, the U.S. Congress investigated Asian organized crime, which included dramatic testimony from actual Asian triad members about the transglobal links of the organization. The eventual report that was produced was called "Asian Organized Crime: The New International Criminal." Ye Zheyun is a sterling representative of a "new international criminal." His goal was to corrupt soccer leagues in Europe while making enormous profits thousands of kilometres away, in the gambling markets of Asia.

The Belgium that Ye Zheyun entered had a colourful history of match-fixing and organized crime. In 1984, a controversial conversation of the "referee liaison officer" Raymond De Deken at Anderlecht, the biggest club in Belgium, was caught on tape. De Deken was arranging with a criminal, Jean Elst, the attempted bribing of the English referee Keith Hackett before a vital UEFA Cup tie. They discussed the amount of money that the Anderlecht official was ready to give the referee if he accepted the bribe:

Jean: Wow! Then there won't be many referees who will say no to that amount of money.

Raymond: Yeah, but there are always some, eh, Jean? The ones in Belgium, I know all of them. But this one, I don't know. Well, I mean, I do know him, but whether he will be interested or not, I don't know.

De Deken and Elst failed with the honest Hackett, but they would go on to successfully corrupt the referee of the UEFA Cup semi-final against Nottingham Forest. The referee got Anderlecht through to the final by disallowing a Nottingham Forest goal. But after the game, De Deken and Elst had a falling-out. Elst alleges that at a meeting at the Brussels Hilton De Deken stole 200,000 Belgian francs from the payoff to the referee. The referee began to shout loudly in the hotel restaurant, so to avoid a scene Elst paid him the money and then exposed De Deken to the management of Anderlecht, who promptly paid Elst hush money to go away.

In February 2006, I felt like suggesting to the management of the Brussels Hilton that they should put up a plaque announcing that it was the scene of the corruption of one of Europe's most important games. It would not be the last time one of their hotels in Brussels was unwittingly linked to criminals and match-fixing. At the behest of Finnish television, I was examining the situation in Belgian soccer, and one of the first people I interviewed there was Senator Jean-Marie Dedecker. Senator Dedecker is fifty-five years old, but he could probably kick your ass. He could certainly kick mine. He was an Olympic judo coach for twenty years, inspiring the small Belgian team to eight medals in four Olympic competitions. He has broad shoulders and a pugnacious charm that makes him good company. When I asked him about the only other martial arts expert I know from Belgium – Jean-Claude Van Damme – he sniffed dismissively. "Van Damme is nothing. He has too much muscle. Too much push. He has done too many weights for Hollywood. Any of my team could take him."

I met him for lunch in the ornate and elaborate Belgian Senate building. In the late 1990s, Dedecker entered the world of Belgian politics and quickly stirred it up with his outspokenness. One typical incident saw Dedecker accompanying an undercover journalist into a maximum-security prison to interview a sex criminal. The prisoner had not gone to trial in six years, and Dedecker suspected that there might be a high-level cover up going on. His party was so upset with Dedecker's action that they suspended him. Dedecker professed himself completely unmoved and has turned himself into a kind of political gadfly of the cozy world of the Belgian establishment. All in all then, Dedecker is not the kind of man who lacks either physical or moral courage. But when he began to investigate the world of Belgian soccer, he had a series of warnings that made him very cautious. "It was quite dangerous," he told me, "I was going to the plane and I got an anonymous phone call saying if I should come, they would kill me. So I was not too happy . . . they are really mafia boys. It's not that I am a coward but I prefer to stay alive . . ."

Despite several death threats, in 2001 Dedecker brought out a report stating that various organized crime groups were bringing in players from the Third World to conditions that resembled modern-day slavery. It brought a flood of publicity but very little reform. He explained to me that most of Belgian soccer officials were like much of the country's establishment: relatively old, not particularly competent, and complacent of corruption so long as it did not interfere with their position.

This was the world that Ye Zheyun moved into as "a soccer investor" in the fall of 2004. Ye Zheyun and Pietro Allatta worked together. Allatta helped Ye Zheyun approach teams in the Belgian league, and then Ye Zheyun tried to get the teams to fix matches. (When I spoke to Allatta, he denied having anything to do with the fixing, claiming he was only "a soccer manager." Belgian authorities seemed to believe him. At one point they had arrested Allatta, but now they had dropped all charges against him.) One Belgian law enforcement source was amazed at Ye's success: "In total, Ye contacted fourteen Belgian professional soccer teams. They did not say anything to one another. From November 2004 to November 2005, Ye worked and not once did the teams say anything."

In what might be a prophetic warning to the English Premier League and rich foreign owners with unknown backgrounds, the law enforcement source said: "They [the soccer clubs] lose their mind when they see money. If Ye Zheyun had been smart, he would have asked to invest 1,000,000 euros. Then he could have been the managing director. He could have controlled all the teams if he had worked slowly; he could have done it all."

As it was, Ye Zheyun bought an interest in two teams in the Belgian league, but he did not work slowly. Stupidly, Ye Zheyun seemed to always be in a hurry; never more so than when he moved into the Finnish League. In the summer of 2005, after at least a dozen successfully fixed matches in the Belgian league, Ye Zheyun decided to buy the Finnish club Allianssi. Allianssi had been formed a few years before, but now its owners were looking to sell. The team was in good playing condition, high up in the league but deeply in debt. Ye Zheyun and his helpers promised to invest heavily in the club and turn its finances around. In one of his first games, he brought in five new players from Belgium and insisted they all play the match. It was to be a tough game against Allianssi's rivals Haka. But if the fans were expecting a close game, than they got a complete surprise. Their team did not just lose, but like the Singapore versus Sarawak game, they lost big: 8-0. The odds on the Finnish state gambling site, of this exact 8-0 score were 8787-1. The coach and players declared it was an accident. As in Belgium, it was not the first incident of its kind. The tabloid newspaper *Ilta-Sanomat* would reveal a few months later that a number of players had either been approached or had taken money over the years to fix games in the Finnish league.

"I have taken money for a few games. This has been going on already for years," one of the players said. "I am by no means the only one. I know by name at least two other men from other teams."

Almost unbelievably, no official authority in Finland ever said that the Allianssi versus Haka match was fixed. The Finnish police investigation seemed to start with great enthusiasm and then got bogged down; no charges or arrests were ever made. The same curious lack of action was seen when Betfair, the British Internet betting exchange, told the Belgian Football Association in the fall of 2005 that there had been "unusual" betting activity on several Belgian matches. The Belgian Football Association claims it never got the warning letters.

Soccer officials did not stop Ye Zheyun's criminal activities; but his libido finally did. Ye met an eighteen-year-old Belgian girl. He invited her out. Their first date? To see a fixed soccer match, where Ye Zheyun,

THE FIX

presumably to impress the girl, explained how he fixed the match, which players were on the fix, and the score of the game before it took place. Then he promised her a career in modelling if she agreed to some of his conditions. One of his "conditions" seemed to be that he could come and visit her late one night in her hotel room – ironically – at a Brussels Hilton Hotel. However, she had brought her mother, possibly the most sensible thing she would ever do in her life. When Ye arrived at midnight at her door, suggesting a more active, hands-on approach to managing her career, she and her mother called the police. They told them what they had seen and what Ye had told them, and that was the beginning of the end of Ye's fixing empire.

Ye Zheyun was interviewed by the police, released, and then he too fled. He has never been seen by officials again. The police investigation dragged on for a year. At first, it seemed to be going well. The officer in charge, Marc Piron, was a tough, no-nonsense character who seemed like the Jean-Marie Dedecker of the Belgian police. He did not last long. He was pulled off the case for allegedly speaking to the media. No arrests have been made since then. The charges against Pietro Allatta were all dropped; he continues his career as an agent and vehemently denies any involvement in fixing games.

Two months after Ye's disappearance, the Belgian television program *Panorama* aired a program that claimed that at least fourteen people – including players and managers – were involved in helping Ye with his activities. But the Brussels player Laurent Wuillot, who had been approached by one Ye Zheyun's people to fix a game against Lierse SK laughed when he heard that number:

Fourteen players, are you joking? They are a lot more numerous than that. You have to understand these types. They can make more money on one fixed game than in an entire season, they are so badly paid at these clubs who are desperate to survive.

Wuillot was not the only, or even the most important, player that Ye Zheyun's people approached. According to the confession of Laurent Fassotte, the captain of Lierse SK, Ye Zheyun was essentially able to control almost the entire team – management and players.

For Ye Zheyun, it was perfect. There are number of key reasons that he was able to operate so successfully in Belgium and Finland. First, the leagues were in Western Europe, so they had a reputation for honesty among Asian gamblers. Ye and his fixing syndicate could get a lot of money down on the illegal market. Two, despite this apparent honesty, the players and clubs were often so badly paid that they could be bought easily. An investment of a few thousand euros could net a potential return of millions. Finally, the Belgian league has long been complacent about corruption.

The Asian fixers scan the European leagues trying to find these conditions, and then they move in. There is one set of tournaments, however, where the paradigm of a high reputation for honesty mixed with relative corruptibility of teams is easy to find: early Champions League, UEFA Cup, and Intertoto Cup matches. Most people think of the Champions League when the big, well-known teams enter it in September. Then the national champions from the most powerful European countries – Italy, England, Spain, and Germany, plus a select group of other top teams from across Europe – compete for the trophy. However, between June and August, there are three preliminary rounds of Champions League matches, where teams from smaller and poorer European countries play one another in hopes of getting to the advanced rounds of the competition. In these rounds and in the Intertoto Cup – a trophy, ironically, designed by the European sports lotteries to give soccer gamblers something to bet on when the main leagues have closed for the summer holidays – allegations of fixing have become widespread. The games between relatively obscure teams attract more gambling than normal simply because there are no other high-level soccer games in Europe during June and July.

One European soccer official told me of a typical example in these type of games:

> We had a case recently in the Intertoto Cup. There were strange betting patterns going on. The first game had ended in a 1-1 draw. The second leg was lost by the home team 4-0. Even the referee's report said that it was a fix. He said that the home team was trying not to win. The bets on the game were that the home team would lose 5-0.

Another gambling executive gave me a list of some of the games that his organization thought were suspicious in these tournaments. The countries fitted the same paradigm – Cyprus, Belarus, Romania, Lithuania, and Greece – all countries that have long soccer traditions but all places where 10,000 euros buys a lot of influence. Many of the European sports gambling companies have already suspended betting on many games in the preliminary rounds. Indeed, it is a rare week that a game is not *pulled down* by bookmakers who are afraid of matches being fixed. A high-level European sport lotteries executive told me that the amount of suspicious games has increased so much that at one point the European Lotteries and Toto Association even considered the idea of abandoning the Intertoto tournament altogether.

In the fall of 2007, a source at the Europol, the European-wide police association, leaked the news to a German newspaper that UEFA had asked them to investigate fifteen games for match-fixing. In private, UEFA officials admit the problem is far, far bigger than simply fifteen games, but the teams will not co-operate, the cases are going nowhere, and one of the investigators has already been threatened with death.

The locusts have arrived.

If you ever have a choice of going to either the University of Oxford or Cambridge, and everything else is equal – size of scholarship, quality of supervisor, personal matters – then you should always choose

Cambridge. The reason dates back to the 1640s. At that time, England was engaged in a furious civil war, and the losing Royalist Army was besieged in Oxford, with King Charles the First using Christ Church College as his headquarters. The story goes that as the siege continued, Charles was so deeply engrossed in a book he was reading in the university library that he wanted to take it away, read it, and then return it. "Oh no, your majesty," the librarian is supposed to have replied. "The rules state no books can leave the premises; you must read it here." Now, if you ask to borrow one, the librarian usually tells you that story, finishing with some sentence such as, "And if we wouldn't lend a book to King Charles the First, we certainly cannot lend a book to you!"

This was all very charming for the first few months of my time at Oxford, but then I got to thinking about the circumstances. It was during a civil war. King Charles was about to lose the war, be captured, imprisoned, and then executed by the rebels. No wonder the librarian did not want to lend the King the book; he knew he would never get it back. On the other hand, Cambridge, Oxford's main educational rival and an equally historical institution, treat their contemporary students like adults. Cambridge students are actually allowed to take books out of the main library, read them, and then return them. To make it worse, at Oxford, academics cannot actually see the book shelves, either. Most of them are kept in vaults deep underground or at offsite storage. If you are interested in reading a book, you have to make an appointment two or three days in advance; it is then sent to a location in the library, and you go there to read the book.

I tell this story because the original material for the next two chapters was not gathered, at first, in interviews – although there were many interviews done after the archival material had been collected – but rather in a dusty, obscure corner of the Bodleian Library, the central library at Oxford. To be honest, if you have to be imprisoned in a library to read books, then the Bodleian is probably the best place in the world. Established in 1602 by an Elizabethan courtier and sometime spy, Thomas Bodley (who came up with the idea of not taking books out of the library), it is a catacomb of living history. Some of the bookshelves were designed by former prime minister William Gladstone; some of the buildings were designed by an acolyte of the great architect Christopher Wren; some of the paintings on the walls were painted by superb artists of distant eras. Amid the desks are marble statues and busts of ancient benefactors. It is so redolent in history that while I was there, parts of the library would be closed down and used as the backdrop for the Harry Potter films.

It was at a dusty wooden table that I sat and began to read the books and papers that revealed the long, long history of corruption at the heart of European soccer. I read about the foundation of the first professional leagues in the nineteenth century, in part as a defence against gambling and the fixes that were thought to inevitably attend the sport. I read about the revelation, almost seventy years too late, by the International Federation for Football History and Statistics that a 1934 World Cup qualifying match between Italy and Greece had been fixed by Mussolini's officials desperate for a triumph in the tournament. And I read, with great surprise, about the match-fixing corruption that existed at the heart of the league that enjoys the reputation as the most honest in the world – the English.

9

THE GOLDEN AGE

There were millions of people who would pay millions of pounds to do what these guys were being paid to do. There were peoples with injuries. There were invalids. There were disabled people, people who would have given everything they had to go on a pitch and do everything these guys were doing and getting paid for it. To me, they were lowlifes who were selling the club, the supporters, and themselves for a shilling. I can't accept that.

There was blood in his mouth. His head hurt. All around him was darkness and silence. He lay on his side amidst the tangled metal, still strapped to his seat. He unfastened himself, started to crawl free of the wreckage, and then saw the first dead body.

It was one of the most significant moments in British sport since the Second World War, and it happened at a German airport. Munich, February 6, 1958. The plane carrying the Manchester United team had crashed on take-off. This was no ordinary team: this was the Red Devils, the Busby Babes, the champions of England, carefully selected and crafted by their manager, Matt Busby. They were on the way back to England after a European Cup match against Red Star Belgrade. They had drawn the difficult game 3-3 in an intimidating stadium before a tough team. There is a photo of them taken before the match. They stare out at the camera. Beautiful young men in their athletic prime: muscular with the cockiness of youth, invulnerable, immortal. Now many lay in the wreck of their crashed airplane. Eight of them were dead or dying. Two others would never play the game again. But one of them became a hero that night: Harry Gregg, their tall, forceful goalkeeper from Northern Ireland.

After he got free, he staggered down the plane. The pilot appeared, a tiny fire extinguisher in one hand: "Run, you stupid bastard, it is going to explode!" Gregg could see five people scrambling away. But he turned and crawled back inside the wreckage.

It was dark. He could hear a baby crying. Frantically, he pushed and pulled at the debris until he found the infant. He checked there was nothing wrong. Then he carried the baby out and handed her to another survivor. He went back inside the plane. The fire continued to burn.

He found the mother of the baby trapped underneath the wreckage. She was unconscious. Gregg could not lift her, so pushed her out of the plane with his legs.

He still could not understand what had happened. It was too surreal, there was too much devastation: whole sections of the airplane had disappeared; the ruins of half a house tottered near the fuselage; and as the fuel caught fire, there were constant explosions.

Again, Gregg went back toward the burning plane. He found two of his teammates lying there. They were too injured to move. But Gregg managed to get hold of two others – Bobby Charlton and Dennis Viollet – and drag them by the waistbands of their trousers away from the plane.

The explosions threw flames high in the air. Finally, there was one massive blast that knocked a doctor who was tending the injured off his feet, and ended any hope of saving anyone else. Gregg was loaded into a truck and driven to the hospital.

In all, the Munich air crash killed twenty-three people. It devastated the team and its impact was felt across England.

For Manchester United, this was the very bottom for the club. Before the game, they had been in third place in the league. Now they scrambled to get enough players just to fill the team. Players were drafted in from not just the reserves, but their youth team as well. They were asked to fill in for the best players in England, the players who had died in the flames and wreckage of the Munich air crash. The roster of the players who were killed is extraordinary, including five internationals: Roger Byrne, David Pegg, Tommy Taylor, Liam Whelan, and Duncan Edwards, the man who had it all: skill, athleticism, modesty, decency, hard work, and the good looks of a movie star. The survivors who could never play again included Jackie Blanchflower, who as a player on the Northern Ireland national team had helped get them to the 1958 World Cup.

The next game at Old Trafford, Manchester United's home ground, was a sell-out crowd. Thousands more were outside the stadium, and knowing they could not enter, they stood in silence, some with tears streaming down their faces, desperately urging their team on to victory. Bill Foulkes, one of the few men to walk out of the plane, captained the team that day. Years later he wrote: "It is strange that up to the moment of the game I had been thinking so much about the boys and missing them, but when the game started all I could think about was that we simply had to win."

The shattered remnants of the team won that day. Then they won again and again and again. In the spring of 1958, against all odds, they reached the final of the FA Cup, the highest knockout competition in England. The team's emblem on their shirt was a small phoenix: from out of the ashes, they would rise again. The final was against another northern team, Bolton, and almost the whole country cheered United on as they ended up heartbreakingly losing 2-0. It was the beginning of a love affair that has continued in England and then around the world since then: through eleven league championships, nine FA Cups, and three European titles, through the rise and fall of the gifted George Best, the mercurial Eric Cantona, and the never-tiring Bryan Robson.

But it is the teams that arose in the years after the Munich air crash that most speak to the hearts of the English. They were England's sweethearts. They were champions. And a few of them were cheats.

That final verdict is given by the one man whose courage exemplified the Busby Babes, the heroic Harry Gregg. The same man who risked his life to save his friends and strangers from a fiery crash now claims in his autobiography, *Harry's Game,* and in an interview with me that on the team a few years after the crash was a small group of players that were selling matches to gamblers. Gregg claims that he was approached to fix matches by a couple of "low-life" Manchester United players, neither of whom had been in the crash. They were out to make money off illegal gambling. He went to the manager, Matt Busby, who, Gregg claims, swore, slammed the desk, and shouted, "I bloody knew."

The Manchester United team was not untypical. This is what astonished me as I read the files. This generation of soccer players were my father's heroes. In my mind, they were cloaked in a glorious light. I don't think I am alone. Ask modern English football fans about that era and many will wax nostalgic. The National Football Museum in Preston refers to this time as the Golden Age. The war was over. The world was at peace. The men wore baggy shorts, their hair swept back. The list of players is a roll-call of British soccer immortality: Denis Compton, Tommy Finney, the young Bobby Charlton, Stan Mortensen, and the greatest of them all – Stanley Matthews. They were lions. They brought light to the dark age of post-war England. And many of the players of the time, although not the ones listed, fixed games.

James Bartholomew, the English journalist and author, writes of what a wonderful place Britain was before the establishment of universal education, pensions, and medical care. How he can miss the widespread child labour, poverty, and slums that our great-grandparents had to endure is beyond comprehension. But in his book, *The Welfare State We're In,* he begins with a chapter entitled "From Stanley Matthews to Vinnie Jones." Bartholomew writes that English soccer is in a state of decline, from the halcyon sport played in the 1950s by gentlemen like Stanley Matthews, who enjoyed a nice, clean game, to the game now played by low-bred thugs.

I asked Harry Gregg about this view. He replied, "I don't know what sport he [Bartholomew] is talking about, but it certainly wasn't the one that I played."

Gregg is an intelligent, insightful, and deeply honourable man. He was also one of the best athletes of his generation. And his description of the toughness of soccer in the 1950s would curl your hair. For example, in the 1958 FA Cup Final when some of the Munich survivors of Manchester United played against Bolton, Nat Lofthouse, the powerful Bolton forward, fouled Gregg in an incident that became infamous. Gregg had the ball in his hands and Lofthouse bundled him over the goal line scoring the goal that won the game for Bolton and destroyed the dream of a nation. However, two things did not happen: one, Lofthouse was not sent off – charging the goalkeeper was simply part of the *man's game* that was soccer of the time – and two, the injured Harry Gregg did not leave the pitch – he played on.

The archival materials show clearly and consistently that some of the greatest players of the era were saying that British soccer in the 1950s and 1960s was, at times, deeply corrupt. A few examples include Brian Clough, Trevor Ford, Ken Chisholm, and Harry Gregg. Ford, Clough, and Gregg each represented one of the Home Nations: Wales, England, and Northern Ireland. Each of them played in the English first and second divisions, and each would write of the match-fixing that had occurred in that era.

Trevor Ford was a fascinating, exhilarating man. An international striker for Wales and an early campaigner for a more aggressive players' union, he was a fighter in every aspect of his life. Ford was also honest to a fault. In 1957, he wrote his autobiography, *I Lead the Attack*, based on his professional career. The first chapter, "Under the Counter," caused a sensation.

> Since I first set my sights on Soccer as a career I have met almost every known type of football fiddle. I have been involved in quite a few myself and I am not ashamed. I, like hundreds of others, have been driven to it by the miserly attitude of the authorities in their assessment of fair payment for services rendered.

Ford went on to claim that the "viper of bribery" was common among professional teams. Ford was, in all senses, an exceptional man. After the publication of the book, he was banned from the league, so he played in Holland. He was so successful there that he was able to petition the English League to overturn his ban. Ford returned to the English League and played until his retirement. He never retracted a single word of his autobiography.

It might be easy to discount Trevor Ford as an exception to a culture of fair play, except that there are many other former players who tell the truth about the state of the British game at that time. Brian Clough – then an England international, and a man who would go on to be one of the game's most successful managers – talked openly about the defenders on his team fixing games. When he publicly raised the issue of his teammates fixing, his team sold him. Years later in an interview, he was again perfectly honest about the conditions on his teams

> For five seasons in a row I scored forty goals and more, yet we never finished in the top four of our division. That's because we had a few crooks in our side that used to sell matches . . .

It was not the last time he would speak out against match-fixing. As a manager in 1973, when his team Derby County played Italian giants Juventus in a European Cup semi-final, he stood outside his dressing room and said clearly and directly to the Italian press, "I won't talk to any cheating bastards. . . ." His assistant was so angry that he had to be dragged back from hitting the Italian coach. They were furious because they thought that Juventus had paid off the referee. The incident started the great match-fixing investigation of British journalist Brian Glanville, which exposed a network of corruption among Italian fixers and European referees.

Scottish forward Ken Chisholm was also a maverick. A former fighter pilot in the Second World War, he had little time for the niceties of the soccer world. He played for a range of clubs in both Scotland and England during the late 1940s and 1950s. Years later, Chisholm's writing about the "arrangements" between teams would be included in Simon Inglis's excellent book *Soccer in the Dock*. Chisholm wrote about how he had taken part in a fixed game between Cardiff City and his own team, Leicester City. The fix had all kinds of problems, he wrote, because one of his teammates had accidentally scored a goal. The rest of the match was "a farce as both sets of players tried frantically to score in our goal." However, he defended himself by saying, like Trevor Ford, that fixes were nothing new:

> Before people get hot under the collar, this kind of "arrangement" was *commonplace* towards the end of every season in those days, and I know of many similar cases where points were given away to save clubs who commanded good support from being relegated, and also to get promotion.

The list of players who are now willing to speak the truth goes on. For example, Ernie Hunt, who was one of the sporting artists of the late 1960s (his "donkey kick" goal was shown for years on the English television program *Match of the Day*) wrote of fixing games for his team, Coventry City. But the final and most convincing primary source is Alan Hardaker. Hardaker was the secretary of the English League, one of the highest-ranking soccer executives in the country. Publicly, during his tenure he had denied the existence of any kind of problem. However, thirteen years later in his memoirs, he was to admit that corruption was rife in the league and that:

> There are many men in football today, among them respected and celebrated managers, who have good reason to remember the great bribery scandals of the early 1960s. They were deeply involved in the mess but escaped because the Law and the League could not get the evidence to nail them . . . football was ripe for corruption.

However, at the time, Ford and Clough were exceptions to a sometime culture of dishonesty covered up by a conspiracy of silence. It took an eccentric but pioneering young journalist, Michael Gabbert, to publicly uncover some of the truth about the soccer world.

Gabbert was a one-off in a profession renowned for oddballs. He became the founding editor of the *Sunday Sport*, a newspaper that featured few journalists but lots of pictures of women's breasts. Gabbert's career took off when, working for the tabloid *The People*, he along with sports reporter Peter Campling uncovered widespread match-fixing in the English league. They did it by using then-innovative techniques of investigative journalism, like secretly taping the players' and fixers' conversations. The eventual result was a series of articles published over two years, 1963 and 1964, which exposed a network of soccer players who were linked to gamblers fixing games. The middlemen were a number of former players who gave the orders for which games would be fixed. Ten players were eventually convicted, and four of them actually served jail time. One of the bookies was so upset that he committed suicide rather than give evidence.

Many English people still remember the story of the most prominent Sheffield Wednesday players – David Layne, Peter Swan, and Tony Kay – caught by Gabbert and Campling. Swan and Kay also played for the English national team. In December 1962, the three of them fixed a game against lowly Ipswich Town for £200. Gabbert and

Campling caught them on tape talking about it. In his autobiography, *Setting the Record Straight*, Swan writes of how even years later, Brian Clough, still upright, still principled, still determined to fight against match-fixing, turned his back on Swan and refused to acknowledge his presence.

However, what most people do not recognize is how widespread the match-fixing was in the league in those days. Neither Michael Gabbert nor any of the law enforcement officials thought they had even come close to tackling the real scope of the problem among the players. Roy Mason, an MP, declared in the House of Commons that "only a third of this iceberg has reared its head." Simon Inglis, who wrote of these events, claims that there was another match-fixing syndicate among Southern clubs, with a hundred players co-operating in the fixes.

For all his work and ingenuity, neither Gabbert nor his newspaper *The People* were thanked by the soccer industry for exposing the fixing. Rather, they were treated as if *they* had organized the fixing, not exposed some of it. Alan Hardaker, the secretary of the soccer league, attempted to ban *The People*'s journalists from all soccer stadiums following their stories: a difficult punishment for any newspaper, but a draconian one for a tabloid whose readers crave sports stories.

The reason why a lot of the British players of the 1950s were willing to fix a game is very simple: they were, for the most part, players from poor backgrounds who were ruthlessly exploited by their clubs. The list of what the clubs could do to them would make a modern union member blanche with horror. The clubs controlled whether they played or did not play; if a player left, the club still controlled whether he could play for another team. When and if a team paid its players, they paid a maximum salary that meant that a star player was paid the same rates as a much less valuable player, and in the off-season, they either did not pay them or paid them less. The clubs even controlled how the players dressed, drank, and ate.

In 1955, Jimmy Guthrie, the head of the powerless players' union, addressed the entire British Trade Union Congress. His description led to lots of applause but little real action:

> Mr. Chairman and delegates, I stand here as a representative of the last bonded men in Britain – the professional footballers. We seek your help to smash a system under which now, in this year of 1955, human beings are bought and sold like cattle. A system which, as in feudal times, binds a man to one master or, if he rebels, stops him getting another job. The conditions of the professional footballer's employment are akin to slavery.

The soccer books about this era are filled with more, much more, about how the players were treated. It is an intellectual antidote to the right-wing crap, like James Bartholomew's book, about the past being a kinder, gentler age. One shocking theme for a modern reader is the treatment of injured players. There was simply no widespread proper medical care of the players. If it were a less serious injury, often the players were dosed up with powerful painkillers which allowed them to keep playing, but exacerbated the injury. In his autobiography, Ian St. John, the Scottish international player turned TV personality, who also attempted to fix a game during that era, wrote, "If I could stand the pain of it I would write another kind of football book . . . about how the game treated some of its greatest performers. It would be a story filled with regret and sadness." He describes his former teammate Andy Weir as "a brilliant little winger," but Weir was injured in a match against Third Lanark, received utterly inadequate rehabilitation, then was pensioned off with a handshake and couple of pounds. He ended up in a wheelchair and died soon afterwards.

Harry Gregg spoke of the attitude to injured players in the Manchester United squad of the time. "When you got injured at Old Trafford [Manchester United], nobody would talk to you . . . you shouldn't get injured. That was just the unspoken thing. It was as if you had done something wrong." It sounds like a Monty Python sketch, but

Gregg actually practised for six weeks with a broken leg bone, before the training staff would accept that he had an injury.

I spoke to the great Sir Tom Finney, who, like Gregg, never fixed a match in his life. He played for the no-hoper team Preston North End. He was a superb forward, who also played for England, and could have played for Palermo, the Italian team. In 1952, they offered him £10,000 just to sign for them, plus a weekly salary ten times higher than his English wages. The Italians were offering to pay him, in just one fee, what it would have taken him decades to earn with Preston North End. Some believers in the Golden Age claim that Finney stayed in England out of loyalty. I asked him why he stayed, he replied, "Well, the club just said no and that was it. . . You were treated really as . . . it is very bad to say what you were treated like. I mean, I was always treated quite well at Preston, but the chairman said to me when that offer came in from Palermo, 'If tha doesn't play for us, tha doesn't play for anybody.'"

To combat against this system that gave them so few rights, some of the players did anything they could to get money. Trevor Ford wrote in his book of the prohibited practice of players selling FA Cup Final tickets to ticket touts. According to Gregg, even an icon like Sir Bobby Charlton, still rightly known around the world for his gentlemanly behaviour and decency, sold his Cup Final tickets to "heavy characters" to earn extra money.

But of more importance to fixing is the widespread presence of illegal gambling networks. In the days before gambling was legalized, the big English companies like Ladbrookes and William Hill who were offering the relatively benign "pools system" had to print their coupons in Holland or Belgium to get around English laws. Betting in person in a shop, which is now utterly normal in the U.K., was completely outlawed until 1961. One football coach remembers his childhood:

> I remember in England in the 1950s there were illegal bookies on every street. The only way you could make a bet legally, if you lived in Birmingham, was to go to the Doncaster Races. So every street had their own gambling ring.

The mental arithmetic is simple. If gambling is illegal, then the people organizing it will be criminals. In this environment moral, honest, non-fixing bookmakers (whom the law still calls criminal) are at a competitive disadvantage against the really dishonest bookmakers. There is no one to police the industry and the immoral bookmakers will survive and thrive. One of the ways that the truly immoral gamblers can thrive is by fixing lots of games, and if the players are relatively badly paid, the bookies can do a lot of fixing.

It did not help that many of the team officials of that time were also corrupt. Some of them were kind-heartedly corrupt. They organized under-the-table payments, free housing, and illegal gifts to help their badly paid players. They also organized their own fixes if their teams were in danger of being relegated, dipping into their own pockets to help their team by buying off the opposition. But many of the officials were simply venally exploitative men who were out to squeeze as much money out of their players as possible.

In 1961, the players had enough of their poor treatment at the hands of the owners. They began to talk about a strike. A meeting was called at White City, in west London. It was a historic occasion. The organizing committee was on the stage, in front of them was a room crammed with many of the league's players, from the great Stanley Matthews to the journeymen players of the lower divisions. At the beginning of the meeting, there was a general discussion about the merits of a strike, with the leaders on stage urging for a strike. Harry Gregg remembered what happened:

> One young man stood up and said, "I do not agree with you; my father works down the pit and he only gets eight or ten pounds a week and I think that my father does a better job and we should be happy with what we get." The young fella killed the room completely. It went dead. Tommy Banks, the Bolton leftback, a really broad Lancashire man, said, "Mr. Chairman, can I answer that man? Lad, tell thy dad that I'll

do his fucking shift down the pit between three o'clock and twenty to five on a Saturday afternoon, if he can mark brother Matthews here."

The players decided to vote for a strike.

The year 1961 signalled the beginning of the long and complex socio-economic battle for British soccer players that lasted from the strike vote right up to the Bosman case in the 1990s, where all players in the European Union were granted the right to play for any club. But the fixing, to a much lesser degree, went on into the 1970s. Why? Because some of the fixing players, usually the leaders or project managers, were scumbags who would have fixed games no matter what they were paid. There are always business executives on Wall Street who are paid $10 million a year and will still cheat to get another million. Or American football stars, such as Michael Vick, who will make $100 million and still design ways of torturing dogs for fun and profit. There will always be players who would sell a game no matter what their salary. Harry Gregg is absolutely sure of this. He claims that exploitation and low salary had nothing to do with the fixers who betrayed the memory of the Munich air crash in those Manchester United teams. To him, they were

> people I wouldn't want my choice to be my company in life. It was the lowest of the low. It was to betray your fellow players. It was nothing to do with suffering or the shortage of money. I cannot excuse it. There is no excuse morally or otherwise for what those players did. Maybe I would have to be fair to say, maybe a couple of them that I knew about were decent blokes who were dragged into it and regretted it for the rest of their lives. But the other bastards did it and regretted nothing. I would swear, what we were earning had nothing to do with it.

The bribery and match-fixing in English soccer in the 1950s and 1960s is an intriguing story, but why is it relevant in a book about contemporary soccer? We need to know the reasons for match-fixing in British soccer because they are repeated constantly throughout the sporting world today. Understand what was going on in that golden age and you can understand why similar things happen today in similar circumstances, even if they occur in the greatest soccer matches in the world. Some of the conditions necessary for match-fixing to flourish include:

- *There will be widespread fixing if players are exploited.*
- *There will be fixing if the players perceive their administrators and officials are making money off the players' labour.*
- *There will always be a few lowest-of-the-low players who, regardless of salary or status, will fix.*
- *Those players will be aided if there are illegal gambling syndicates around the sport. And now, with the Internet, illegal gambling syndicates are, through the computer, in everyone's home.*

We have seen *why* players fixed matches in one of the best leagues in the world at one of its most glorious times. Let us examine the decision of one of today's managers to fix games in one of the worst European leagues in one of its worst times.

TO FIX OR NOT TO FIX?

You are going to lose anyway. Why don't you lose with 30,000
francs in your pocket?

Kaliningrad is a grim, grey city stuck at the far western end of Russia. It is full of crumbling dockyards, high unemployment, and mobsters. The city is an odd outpost of the remains of the Soviet Empire. It is a Russian Baltic port, completely cut off from the rest of country and wedged between Lithuania and Poland. It also had a pretty bad soccer team, Baltika Kaliningrad.

In September 2004, Baltika Kaliningrad was in the Russian first division (meaning, in the complicated terminology of European soccer, that it was actually in the second division). The Russian soccer season runs from March to November, and by this time it was clear that Baltika was in trouble. They had had a terrible time, collecting only twenty-six points out of a possible ninety-three. If they continued in this fashion, they would be relegated to a lower division. The team president, Dmitri Chepel, decided to try to fix two games, in an effort to try to save his team. Over several weeks, his phone was tapped and his attempts to arrange the games were recorded. It is unclear just who taped Chepel's calls. The best guess is rogue, presumably soccer-loving, elements in one of Russia's myriad security agencies, such as the FSB (formerly the KGB). They leaked the tapes to a local magazine, *Novye Kolyosa*, run by a maverick and energetic editor, Igor Rudnikov. Rudnikov created a huge controversy in Kaliningrad by publishing the transcripts of the tapes in his magazine.

I was alerted to the story by a colleague who studied the Russian judicial system and its illegal alternatives. It became one of the best cases for me to understand why contemporary European club officials get involved in fixing a game. So over the next few months, in the library or at the grounds of my college, half-a-dozen different Russian students translated, retranslated, and then checked one another's work to get an accurate portrait of what went on. The transcripts themselves read like a cross between *The Sopranos* and an Abbott and Costello movie. However, Chepel is not a member of the mafia, so the whole incident is more like a Chekhov or Gogol short story: a hard-working member of the public service working in a very corrupt environment who is just trying his best to save his beloved team by whatever means possible.

Aide: So I think it is not a problem [fixing the game]. I will find him now and talk to him.

Chepel: Genya. I'm not asking you. I'm begging you. I need the result. Fuck! Life or death! Fuck!

Chepel's desperation shines throughout the transcripts and illustrates the first key question in the decision of a corrupt club match-fixer: is the game important enough to bother fixing? The answer, for most club officials, depends on the time of the game in the season. There are certain key games that are worth far more in terms of the standings than any others because of where they fall during the season.

For Chepel, in the unglamorous Russian first division, successfully arranging a fixed match at this point in the season greatly reduced Baltika's chances of being relegated. Financially, this was key. The difference for a team in England between playing in the Premier League or the Championship (effectively the first and second divisions) is estimated to be £60 million. In Russia, the figure is lower, but it still ensured that the two late-in-the-season games held enormous stakes for Baltika and Chepel.

The next question is a moral one: is it ethically right to fix a match? In his telephone conversations, Chepel and his aides seem completely unbound by any moral considerations. In fact, when one person doesn't want to fix a game for ethical reasons, Chepel's aide is unable to understand and imagines that he must be afraid.

> Aide: Hell, Dmitri, I managed to talk to [the president of the other team]; he says that he doesn't want to fucking do anything [fix a match]. Their coach is too principled ... So I said to him, "It doesn't matter: your team is already relegated." And he said, "Well I understand, but we won't fix." I don't get it! Maybe they are chicken?

Morality is a tricky thing to judge. It is easy to sit and think, Oh, I would never fix a game. But what would happen if lots of other clubs in the league fixed games? There are actually two questions that a possible fixer has to ask himself: Am I moral and is my competition moral? In this case, one of Baltika's opponents was too principled, even when the team was already relegated, to fix a game with Baltika. However, the real consideration for Dmitri Chepel is whether another team, a rival of Baltika for relegation, may fix their games.

The problem at this stage for Chepel is that he simply does not know what other rival teams might do. It is this factor that gives rise to incentive payments in the Russian league, where some teams pay their rivals' opponents to play honestly and not accept any potential fix. CSKA Moscow is one of the top teams in the Russian league, and their president, Yevgeny Giner, has spoken openly of paying incentive payments to teams so they would not take part in fixed matches that would help CSKA's rivals. Almost unbelievably, Giner was, in 2006, also the president of the Russian Premier League. So if this situation is normal in the league, Chepel's decision not to think about the morality of fixing is understandable. It is also understandable that one of the Asian fixers I met spoke of his colleague who worked out of Russia. He claimed that he had a number of regular teams that he worked with. Presumably, it saved them all the bother of fixing games themselves.

The next question a corrupt official asks himself is a practical one: Can my team win honestly? All things being equal, even fixers prefer to win games honestly: less trouble, less expenses, no headaches. However, Chepel had absolutely no confidence in his team. Nor did many other people, as this excerpt from the conversation with a team sponsor, whom Chepel approaches for fixing money, illustrates:

Chepel:	Yes, that is why I'm phoning you. I wanted you to help me with some money, fuck. Because now with the game coming up, fucking hell, it's needed! There is little hope from the players.
Team Sponsor:	(laughs)
Chepel:	What the fuck are you laughing about?
Team Sponsor:	About the players.
Chepel:	But I really wanted to make you a present – a victory.
Team Sponsor:	A victory?!
Chepel:	Yes, fuck.
Team Sponsor:	But what is needed from me, so they win?
Chepel:	I need twenty pieces (US$20,000).
Team Sponsor:	Shit! Twenty pieces? In order to beat them? Twenty pieces?
Chepel:	Yes.

The players of Baltika Kaliningrad are considered so laughably inept that they could not possibly win a game without fixing. However, strong teams will also fix games against weaker teams. In May 1993, Jean-Pierre Bernès and Bernard Tapie decided to fix a soccer match. Bernès was the general manager of Olympique de Marseille, Tapie the team president and a one-time cabinet minister of the French government of the time. Marseille was to play Valenciennes FC. On paper it was an easy match for Marseille; they were one of the strongest teams in Europe and Valenciennes were third from bottom of the French first division. But Tapie and Bernès got one of their players, Jean-Jacques Eydelie, to approach some of the Valenciennes players to throw the match.

After Eydelie contacted them, Bernès spoke to one of the Valenciennes players and dropped the line "You are going to lose anyway. Why don't you lose with 30,000 francs in your pocket?" It is a great phrase that is the key to many players and referees accepting bribes to fix games. It also sums up the question that many observers had about the affair: why did Marseille *bother* to fix the game? What on earth possessed Tapie and Bernès to risk their entire careers to fix such an easy game?

The answer is a complicated one. It is partly, as Eydelie would write later, that a culture of fixing had arisen on the Marseille team. The culture had become so embedded that the officials had all grown too confident and cocky and "cheating had become second nature." It was partly to save their players from injury; they had another big match the next week. But there is also a concept from betting that is useful in understanding what goes on in the minds of corruptors. At the heart of all wagers is the mathematical idea of probabilities: that there is predictable rate of chance that will always occur unless significantly altered in some fashion. For example, tossing a coin one hundred times, will result, roughly, in fifty heads and fifty tails. Successful professional gamblers and bookmakers use derivations of this idea to either place bets or calculate their odds. Those odds on a soccer game can be altered by buying better players or changing coaches. However, within that theory is a fundamental concept that drives match-fixing: no matter how strong one team becomes, there is *always* a chance that the weaker team could win the game. If the value of the game is low, a corrupt manager is willing to risk this chance that his stronger team will win honestly. However, as the value of the game grows – and for Olympique de

Marseille, it was a very important game; win and they could win the entire French league championship, estimated to be worth more than 30 million francs – the incentive to leave the outcome to chance diminishes on the part of the corruptor. This is why in important games, corrupt officials will fix matches, even against much weaker teams. The officials are searching for certainty in the very uncertain world of soccer games.

The next question that a fixer must answer is can he afford to fix the game? A weak team may lose to a strong team and be relegated, but the cost of fixing the game is so prohibitive that it is simply not worth doing it. For example, many people may want to fix a game against Manchester United, but aside from the players being unwilling, they just cannot afford to do so. This consideration played a large part in Dmitri Chepel's discussions. Many of the potential participants seem to be willing to discuss the possibility of fixing the game. It is whether Chepel can afford their price that is the central point of the discussions. In the following excerpt, he has negotiated a fix with the opposing team. However, he does not have enough money to complete the deal and is forced to ask for more time.

Chepel:	It's not ready. I don't have the whole amount. We have to fix. We have no other way. I have only thirty-five [$35,000]. Fuck. But I am preparing something. I could bring you the rest on Saturday. But at the moment I just don't have anything.
Rival Team Official:	Oh fuck.
Chepel:	We can give you this thirty-five now. And on Saturday, I will bring you the rest. What the fuck! You understand we only have thirty-five . . . And then I will give you the rest on Saturday. Maybe after the game, we will collect something from the tickets and I will give it to you. Fuck. I will bring it Saturday. I have to get at least three more.

I cannot make a mistake here. Maybe we will win anyway. But we may lose and I do need guarantees.

The final question that a corrupt club official asks himself is whether the league or another outside force (the police) will impose sanctions on him if he is caught. There are effectively two parts to this question: will I be caught? And then, secondly: if I am caught, will there be heavy sanctions?

Bernard Tapie got it completely wrong. He was discovered and eventually sent to jail. But, in the Baltika case, Chepel and his aides did not seem to consider any possible sanctions for their corrupt activities. Their attempts to fix the game are genuinely impressive in their thoroughness. Allegedly, they approached almost every conceivable person who could help them fix the game: rival players, coaches, administrators, and referees. Yet from what we can tell both from the transcripts and subsequent coverage, no one revealed their actions to the authorities and no soccer sanctions were ever taken against Chepel or the Baltika team.

Chepel appears to be no corruption neophyte, struggling with the decision of whether to fix for the first time. To explain this we need to know a little about the environment of the Russian league in which Chepel was operating, as the Russian soccer leagues of the past two decades have had a body count that rivals Al Capone's Chicago.

On the morning of June 15, 1997, Larisa Nechayeva, a financial director of Spartak Moscow, the most popular soccer club in Moscow, was in her dacha on the outskirts of the city with an aide and her driver. She should have been in a good mood as she had recently signed a lucrative business deal for the club, but that morning a gunman armed with a 9mm pistol broke into her dacha. He shot them all. Nechayeva and her aide probably died instantly. However, like in most mob murders, the assailant also fired a final bullet into Nechayeva's head to make sure. Then he fled.

The police took two hours to reach the crime scene and found no clues as to who had committed the murders. Nechayeva's killing has never been solved. Nor was it the only one in Russian sport in the 1990s. Stephen Warshaw, an American entrepreneur who was interviewed for the PBS *Frontline* documentary, worked in the Russian sports industry at the time, calling it the "Wild East." He said, "Well, it was frightening, in about a six-month period . . . [t]he team assistant coach, Vladimir Bouvich, was killed. And our team photographer, Felix Oliviov, was killed. Two of them gunned down mafia-style, five bullets to the head in front of their wives . . ."

His experiences and these murders are not exceptional. In Russia, two sports often share the same club, so that one club will have at least two different teams: one that plays soccer during the summer and the other playing hockey during the winter while sharing the same administration.

Both sports have seen numerous murders, pistol-whippings, kidnappings, and bombings. At one point, an elite unit of the ministry of interior anti-terror commandos faced off against fully armed Russian soldiers in a battle over control of the ice hockey team CSKA Moscow. Nor is Russia alone in these problems: in the neighbouring country of Ukraine, the entire VIP box at Shakhtar Donetsk stadium was blown up in a bomb attack that killed the Shakhtar club president, Akhat Bragin, and his five bodyguards. The most prominent club – Dinamo Kyiv – was even alleged to be connected to the mob's exporting of nuclear missile parts.

UEFA officials are aware of the situation in the former Soviet republics. After they attempted to clamp down on corruption there in the 1990s, they claimed that they had faced severe problems: "Be careful," one of them warned me. "I had the Ukrainian mafia after me for a few years in the early 1990s. We had to have police protection. I couldn't go there in the early 1990s. In fact, unless you want to get killed, I would avoid Romania, Ukraine, and Turkey. Very dangerous places – the mafia runs the place."

The UEFA official was not the only prominent Western European soccer person to be threatened by an East European who seemed "more familiar with a shadowy world more dangerous than the boardrooms and hotel suites in which transfer business is usually conducted." In his autobiography, Sir Alex Ferguson, the manager of Manchester United, reveals that both he and the chairman of the club, Martin Edwards, were threatened by a Russian agent when Ferguson refused to sell their star forward Andrei Kanchelskis. They took the threats very seriously, and sold the player.

It is difficult to blame Ferguson and Edwards. Here is a brief but incomplete list of Russian soccer officials or people close to them who have been attacked since Larisa Nechayeva's unsolved murder.

- *CSKA Moscow president Yevgeni Giner's son Vadim and driver:* shot in an attempted assassination.
- *Vladimir Valeyev, head of the Novosibirsk regional soccer federation:* murdered.
- *Viktor Skripal, the executive director of Luch-Energia Vladivostok soccer club:* murdered.
- *Yuri Tishkov, soccer agent:* murdered.
- *Vladimir Prokhorov, the 2002 president of the Kristall club in Smolensk:* murdered.
- *CSKA president, Nikolai Nino:* committed suicide, without explanation.
- *Andrei Trubitsin, CSKA official:* threatened with torture.
- *Natalya Dolmatov, wife of the coach of CSKA Moscow:* disappeared.
- *The son of Vladimir Goryunov, the honorary president of Rotor Volgograd club:* murdered.
- *Alexander Shkadov, the 1999 president of the Kristall club in Smolensk:* murdered.

The fact that the CSKA sports organization features so prominently in the list indicates just how bad the situation has become. CSKA is the Manchester United of Russia. As the former Red Army team, it was the symbol of Soviet strength and sporting prowess. Their hockey team dominated Soviet sport and their soccer team won the league championship ten times and the cup eight times. In the early 2000s, CSKA was the object of a battle between rogue elements of the FSB (the Russian state security agency) and alleged Chechen mobsters. An FSB official threatened a soccer official that he would be "torn apart molecule by molecule" if he did not follow orders. Currently, CSKA is part owned by a controversial businessman, Yevgeny Giner, the man who pays "incentive payments" to other teams so that they will not be tempted to fix games, and two other anonymous shareholders.

The question is, why have so many people been killed in Russian sport? Is it some bizarre enthusiasm for the sport? A psychopathic love of the game that produced such a bloodbath? A thuggish form of the ultimate hooliganism?

In the early 1990s, the chief reason mobsters entered the world of Russian soccer was that control of sports clubs gave them a significant commercial advantage. The story begins in 1993, when Boris Yeltsin – in a fit of imperial grandeur that would have embarrassed a Czar – made his former tennis coach, Shamil Tarpischev, Russia's sports minister. The Russian economy was in free fall, and the once-great Soviet sporting machine was crumbling. At some top-level sports clubs, the teams were so poor that the players were sharing unwashed team shirts. A few years later, on my visit to a CSKA Moscow practice, I saw the players swapping equipment as they practised. Tarpischev proposed to Yeltsin that sports clubs be allowed to import alcohol and tobacco duty-free, so the clubs could earn extra money. This was a huge concession. Jim Moody, former head of organized crime for the FBI, claimed that "almost 30 percent maybe even more" of all Russian government money came from taxes on alcohol and tobacco. The idea was that each sports club would simply import as much alcohol or tobacco as they wanted tax-free. This gave them a huge commercial advantage over other legitimate, non-sporting importers of these substances. So it took Russian mobsters all of about 3.2 seconds to figure out they should get into the sport business. As a result, various mafia groups seized control of different clubs and began to compete in the tax-free importation of goods. No single mob group was able to gain control over the sports market, although they certainly tried, as the body count shows.

Some Russian journalists I spoke to claimed most of the violence occurred in the bad old days of the post-Soviet breakup in the 1990s, when mobsters ran around the streets killing anyone who threatened the expansion of their power. Sport, runs the argument, is no exception from other industries. In 1993 for example, dozens of the presidents of the private banks in Moscow were assassinated in mob-style killings. Nor are soccer and hockey the exceptions in Russian sports; in 1999 figure skater Maria Butyrskaya's BMW was blown up by a mysterious car bomb explosion. Chevalier Nusuyev, the president of the Russian Youth Sports Federation, was killed in a mob-style murder, and eighteen-year-old European Junior Boxing Champion Sergei Latushko was ambushed and shot eight times in the head and chest as he was leaving his practice stadium. He died soon afterwards. Those are a few examples, but there are many others, from many other sports.

To some extent, however, the journalists are right: the murder rate in sports has dropped. Murders and violent incidents are still going on but not to such an extent as ten years ago. However, there are undercurrents that exist in today's Russian sport that to outsiders may seem baffling. For example, in the 1990s, the FBI revealed in court documents that Vyacheslav Ivankov was the head of the Russian mafia in America. He was convicted to ten years in jail for, among other things, running a violent extortion ring out of the Brighton Beach area of Brooklyn. Part of the court proceedings concerned a company, Slavic Inc., that was allegedly money laundering for Ivankov. However, Ivankov's name did not appear on the company registration. Rather, the president of the company was listed as Slava Fetisov, a famous hockey player, who played for top teams in the Soviet Union, North America, and for the Russian national team. In his career, he won numerous league championships, Stanley Cups, and Olympic medals. Fetisov never fully explained how his name ended up on the registration documents of a company linked by the FBI to the head of the Russian mafia. To my colleagues on the *Frontline* documentary and to Robert Friedman, the freelance journalist who broke the story, Slava Fetisov denied that Ivankov had anything to do with the company (although his lawyer Barry Slotnick actually confirmed that Ivankov was involved with the company, but it was a legitimate import-export company). Fetisov is now back in Moscow. He is, in 2008, the Russian Sports Minister.

How does someone like Dmitri Chepel go about fixing the game?

The first challenge is deciding with *whom* to organize the fix. There are three possible groups of people: the referees, the opposing players, and the opposing team administration.

Chepel and his aides spend considerable time debating which ones they should bribe, as the following excerpt illustrates. At this point in the attempted fix, Chepel has contacted the players of the opposing team. They are willing to fix the match but insist on being paid US $60,000. Chepel does not have the money, so he telephones a friend and they have the following conversation:

Friend:	$60,000?! The team wants this?
Chepel:	Yes.
Friend:	Fuck . . . Well, just give the referees the $40,000, if you don't find the rest.
Chepel:	What else can I do, fuck? Faggots! We can give them [the players] $60,000 or $20,000, fuck. The most important thing is the effect [fixing the game]. Now we will be talking with them and see and maybe we can make a deal. We will give forty, and then bring the twenty later. Fuck! So then there is a guarantee already?
Friend:	Yes, of course, the guarantee is needed.
Chepel:	Well, fuck. They also have enough. Those fuckers [the players] already have too much. This is the situation.

Friend: Maybe you fucking give the referees thirty [$30,000], fuck. And say to the players: fuck, if you don't do it for thirty, I will give the other thirty to someone else, rather than you, fuck!

The real dilemma for Chepel is how much certainty can he buy, and for how much? Which set of people – the referees or the players – can give him the best chance of a properly fixed match?

I did some statistical work on this question and the answer is actually pretty close. Bribed referees can bring about a successful fix around 79 per cent of the time; players are a little higher, they can successfully fix around 83 per cent of the time. However, lots of people in the game think that corrupt referees simply cannot guarantee a fix with enough precision to make it worth bribing them. The comments of a UEFA official, who investigated a number of fixed matches, are typical:

[Laughing] I had a case a few years ago. The referee had been bribed. So he gave a penalty. And the team missed the penalty! So you know even if you bribe people, you are not *guaranteed* to win.

But after a considerable series of negotiations, Dmitri Chepel decides not to bribe either the players or the referees. Rather, he arranges a corrupt deal with the opposing team administration. In the following excerpt of the transcripts, Chepel is speaking to Sergei (*), a team administrator of the opposition. He has already negotiated a potential deal with the players, but he is going to betray them to their own club officials:

Chepel: Okay. I'll tell it to you. Our way. I'm dealing with you. Because some of the players came and offered this [to fix the match], but I'm dealing with you.

Sergei: Who came?

Chepel: Your players.

Sergei: They contacted you themselves?

Chepel: Yes. But it is not to be talked about in a rush. I will tell
                you their names later, if you want.

Why does Chepel betray his deal with the players? It is because of the idea
of favour-banks, or "you do me a favour now, I'll do you a favour later."
In many European leagues, owners of teams do one another favours –
like ordering their team to lose a game – and then take payment in a
favour later: whether it be a "return fix" or a transfer of a particular
player. In Italy and Portugal, it is so prevalent there is a name for it: *il
sistema* or "the system."

If Chepel made a deal with the players, it would simply be a one-shot
agreement, done and then forgotten. However, if he makes a deal with
the team administration, it becomes part of the ongoing system of business that team officials conduct with one another.

But he runs into a problem soon after the conversation above. The
team administrator claims that an official from a third club had said that
Chepel had not honoured a match-fixing deal in the past. If he wants to
continue, he must clear his reputation. Chepel is furious and phones up
the third administrator:

Chepel: Grigori (*), this is Chepel. Explain to me this fact!
                Where or when do I not keep my obligations to
                your club? What are the times that I have let you
                down?
Administrator: I don't understand.
Chepel: You are telling Sergei that I won't keep my prom-
                ises! He told me that you don't trust me. And that
                I will end up tricking him. This is fucking non-
                sense! Because when I had to, I solved all the
                problems.
Administrator: I told him that you and I made a deal [fixed a
                match] but nothing else!

Chepel is not simply angry because the deal may go wrong, he also needs to re-establish his credibility quickly. Otherwise his chances of conducting future match-fixing deals will be small. This is not only important because of the present corrupt deal, but because in a league with lots of corrupt favour-banks, the ability and reputation to be able to arrange fixed matches is an important business asset for an administrator to have.

Trust is the oil of the favour-bank. The problem with most corrupt acts is that you cannot legally protect them. There is no use going into most courts and saying, "I bribed so-and-so after he promised to fix a game, and then he didn't do it." At best the judges will laugh you out of the building: at worst, you could face a whole slew of other problems. Without trust, people wanting to act corruptly would be unable to work with one another, so enormous amounts of energy are spent maintaining this favour-bank to ensure future corrupt deals can be made. Luciano Moggi, the Italian fixer for the team Juventus, was the master craftsman of a favour-bank. In 2005, in an investigation into corruption in the Italian soccer leagues, the police taped a whole series of his phone calls. The transcripts reveal that he enacted a constant series of favours with a large network of internal sports figures that allowed him to fix a number of games for his team. The following excerpt is typical. It shows Moggi's relationship with Pierluigi Pairetto, one of the officials in charge of appointing referees for UEFA, the ostensibly neutral organization in charge of running the Champions League. Moggi's Juventus team had a difficult game against the Dutch team Ajax coming up, and he requested a good referee for the match. Pairetto phones him:

Moggi:	Hello.
Pairetto:	Hey, have you forgotten me? I always remember you!
Moggi:	Oh come on!
Pairetto:	Hey, I've put in a great referee for the Amsterdam game.

Moggi:	Who's that then?
Pairetto:	It's Meier. [Urs Meier, a Swiss referee. There is no suspicion that he was corrupt; merely that he is an excellent referee.]
Moggi:	Well done!
Pairetto:	I only called you to tell you that. See I remember you, even if you these days . . .
Moggi:	Oh, don't break my balls! You'll see that when I'm back, you'll realize that I haven't forgotten you.

A few days later, Moggi helped Pairetto acquire a rare four-door Maserati. Moggi's conversations are full of these favour transactions. Here is another example: he is talking to Fabio Baldas, who was the designator of the national referees' commission, the man responsible for choosing who referees each match in the Italian League. Baldas appeared regularly on a popular TV show, *Il Processo di Biscardi*, hosted by Aldo Biscardi, also an old friend of Moggi's, to give his expert opinion on refereeing decisions from the weekend's games. Moggi essentially fixed Biscardi's show. He vetted the comments and determined which referees get the most favourable comments or criticism. Their conversation ends in the following way:

Baldas:	OK . . . if I need a favour will you do me a favour?
Moggi:	No problem.
Baldas:	You'll call me back soon?
Moggi:	Yup, soon.
Baldas:	Fine, bye.

Dmitri Chepel is not in the same class as Luciano Moggi. He simply does not have the resources that Moggi did. So midway through his fixing attempts, he runs into a problem. His credibility has already been damaged by rumours of unreliability. Now he must use another common

corrupt soccer practice: he must provide a guarantor. In this excerpt he
is complaining to a friend about his difficulties in getting the other team
administration to accept the fix.

> You understand that is how it is being talked about. Fuck! I'm saying
> [to the other team officials], that when asked [to sell a match] I solved
> the problems. Fuck! I didn't say fuck [nothing]. And I didn't try to pass
> it to other people. And I didn't tell anyone, and I didn't say, "Give it
> [the payment] immediately." You understand? And he started telling
> me stories [about Chepel's purported unreliability]. And I say, "Wait.
> If, fuck, you need the guarantees, go to the Moldovan (*) and clear up
> the situation.

In the previous section, Chepel was attempting to guarantee the match;
here he needs a third party who can do two things: re-establish his reputation and also guarantee the fix. In other words, this third party is
forceful enough to work as a quasi-legal system. This is a common practice in highly corrupt leagues – using third parties, possibly mobsters, to
"guarantee" the fix. However, it seems that as Chepel's game approached,
the opposing team administrators changed their mind and didn't
insist on a guarantor. The game took place, and Baltika Kaliningrad "won"
the match.

A month later, *Novye Kolyosa* magazine published the transcripts. One
of the other teams confirmed that Baltika had attempted to fix the
match, but they had turned down the offer. Dmitri Chepel and the
Baltika Kaliningrad administration denied the charges, claiming that the
tapes were fake and that, anyway, they had been illegally obtained.

Chepel resigned from the team management in late October, citing
his disappointment at not being able keep the club in the first division.
He did not mention the tapes, and their authenticity has never been

challenged in court. Despite repeated attempts to interview Dmitri Chepel, I was unable to contact him.

There is a theme that runs through almost all the cases of corruption in soccer, no matter where in the world they occur. The good, honourable men who try to do the decent thing and stand up against the corruption are generally punished. The villains go free. There is the case of Chinese whistleblower Gong Jianping, the referee who was sentenced to ten years in a hard labour camp after he admitted to the corruption in Chinese soccer. There is the case of Malaysian journalists Lazarus Rokk and Johnson Fernandez, who first revealed the extent of the problem in their country. They were threatened, sued, and their careers jeopardized. There is the case of Marc Piron, the aggressive Belgian police detective who was pulled off the case in the middle of the investigation. There is, of course, the case of the English tabloid *The People* that mounted a breathtakingly brilliant investigation into the extent of match-fixing in their league. Years later, the secretary of the league wrote that "he knew everything that was going on," but at the time did not thank the paper. Rather, the soccer authorities tried to ban *The People's* journalists from their soccer grounds.

But of all these cases, possibly the man who received the most harsh treatment is Igor Rudnikov, the man who published the Dmitri Chepel tapes. At the time of writing, he is in the infamous Kresty Prison in St. Petersburg. It is a nasty place: built by the Tsars, used by Stalin, and now crammed with prisoners, many of whom suffer from tuberculosis and other infectious diseases. It is known as the world's most overcrowded jail. Rudnikov's crime? He kept publishing articles about corruption in his home town of Kaliningrad. Two years after his magazine revealed the local soccer team was not only hopeless, but their management corrupt, Rudnikov made a serious mistake. He published a series of articles that alleged that some of the town police and prosecutors were running a brothel *and* also organizing a major international shipment of drugs.

The police immediately began an investigation. Not, you might be surprised, into the allegations, but into Rudnikov. Thirty-six police officers raided Rudnikov's offices. He was enraged. In fact, he was so enraged that it is alleged that he beat up eight of them. The rest of the police officers were so distressed that they *had* to arrest the powerful Rudnikov and take him to prison. While in prison, the town prosecutors felt that, in the interests of public safety, he should be removed from the city and placed in the Kresty Prison.

A disinterested person might find it difficult to imagine a magazine editor so muscular that he can beat up eight Russian police officers single-handedly. A disinterested person might also think that it was an extraordinarily unlucky coincidence that Rudnikov lost his temper so badly that he committed a violent crime just after publishing an exposé about widescale police corruption. A disinterested person might even think that the whole thing was a set up by a bunch of criminal thugs masquerading as public officials.

In many other European countries, the case of Igor Rudnikov would be a national scandal. In post-Soviet Russia, it is par for the course. The researchers at the Committee to Protect Journalists, the New York–based humanitarian group, replied wearily when I asked them about his case: "Every week in Putin's Russia, there is something like this, some journalist in a small town who is beaten up or threatened or even murdered."

A cynic may respond that this is, after all, a European country in transition. They claim that Russia will become a far less corrupt country in the future. So in the next two chapters, let us examine how the fixers work in general and then specifically how they work in the bigger, richer Western European leagues.

11

HOW TO FIX A SOCCER GAME

My personal opinion as one who has been involved in organized crime and gambling is how easy it is to do. . . . It is very easy to get a professional athlete to come "on side." We would spend a lot of time trying to get these guys to do this . . . we would deliberately target them . . . Heck, a lot of the time they would come to us!

So far, I have discussed the effects of gambling fixers. I have shown the chaos in some of the Asian leagues, how players actually perform the fixes, and the long history of corruption in the European game. But how do gambling fixers actually work? How do they go about fixing matches? In this chapter, I will show you some of their methods – but let's start with a case that demonstrates perfectly how *not* to fix a match.

Kenan Erol was a man with a plan. On April 6, 2005, he walked up to Sefer Hakan Olgun and tried to bribe him. Erol brought a bag stuffed with 500 euros to his meeting with Olgun, the goalkeeper for the Turkish Super League side Akçaabat Sebatspor. There were a couple of reasons why it might have been a good idea to bribe the Akçaabat Sebatspor keeper. Coming into that Saturday's game, Akçaabat Sebatspor was almost certain to get relegated. They were bottom of the league table, eight points behind their nearest rivals. Their opponents in the match were Kayserispor. They, too, were in a relegation battle, but they still had a good chance of staying in the Super League if they could win the game. But there was another, more compelling, motive for a fix to happen. The morning of the game, someone walked into a betting shop in the nearby town of Trabzon and bet more than 250,000 euros with a Turkish betting agency that Akçaabat Sebatspor would lose. Somebody wanted Akçaabat Sebatspor to lose the game and was willing to pay someone a lot of money to make sure that they did. Kenan Erol was their man.

Erol talked to at least three other players on the team, but he needed to make sure the goalie, the player who could save or destroy a team's chances with a couple of mistakes, was on board. Kenan Erol met Olgun. But it really was not Kenan Erol's day. Why not? Because Olgun secretly taped their conversation.

Erol:	I have spoken to all the other players about this fix. The others know about it.
Olgun:	What? The whole team knows?
Erol:	Don't worry about it!
Olgun:	I don't understand. Do you want me just to leave the goal area and "eat" a goal?
Erol:	First half you will be ahead 1-0. But Kayseri should win the game. You should let in two or three goals in the second half.
Olgun:	Can I trust these people?
Erol:	The money is in the car. Let me show you.
Olgun:	So this is both betting business and also you have an arrangement with the other team? Is that right? Does our team management know?
Erol:	If this "encouragement" went to your management, you won't get a single lira! I'm trying to do you a favour. These guys are trying to bet 500 to 600 billion lira. [He shows him the bag with the money inside]. There are

	200,000 euros in the bag and there will be more. Just get the score we want.
Olgun:	Brother! They are all 500 euro notes. I have never seen that much money in my life! Are you going to give it to me?
Erol:	When the match is finished, it will be in your pocket.
Olgun:	I have 130 to 140 billion TL [Turkish lira, approximately 84,000 euros] debt. How much will I get?
Erol:	At least 75 billion TL [approximately 45,000 euros]. The rest will go to your friends.

The identity of "these guys" who were purportedly willing to bet 500 to 600 billion Turkish lira on the game has never been revealed. But the potential payoff of the bet could have been spectacular: for getting the score line exactly right, the unknown bettors could have netted twenty-five times their initial stake. However, when Veli Sezgin, the chairman of Akçaabat Sebatspor, heard about the attempts to bribe some of his players, he fitted out his goalkeeper with a tape recorder. The fix attempt failed and the game was drawn. However, his gutsiness may have cost him. In August 2005, four months later, someone ambushed Sezgin and shot him. He was severely wounded but survived. The transcript of Erol's meeting with Olgun did give the Turkish Football Federation an accurate record of what happened. Their administrative board suspended six players for their alleged role in the fix, gave Hakan Olgun 50,000 Turkish lira as a reward for his coming forward, and invited Kenan Erol to explain his actions before their committee. Perhaps unsurprisingly, Erol declared that he was unavailable to meet with the committee, and perhaps surprisingly, the Turkish police declined to pursue the case. Possibly they believed Erol's original statement when he declared that the whole thing had been an eastern Turkish joke that had been unappreciated by the Istanbul sophisticates.

That a fix attempt or even a mob-style ambush would happen in Turkish soccer is no surprise. The league is notorious for the connections between its soccer officials and leading mafia figures. A few months before the fix attempt, in November 2004, the Turkish parliament opened an inquiry into the links between a notorious mafioso, Sedat Peker, and the soccer league. His mafia associates had been covertly taped arranging matches with referees and club officials. However, neither the attention of the politicians nor the interest of the Turkish Football Federation seemed to have stopped Peker's years of activities in the Turkish league.

If Sedat Peker were the only criminal to be involved with a Super League squad, Turkish soccer would still have a problem. But he is not. Beşiktaş is one of the big three clubs of Turkish soccer, equivalent to Liverpool or Inter Milan. However, for all their success, the Beşiktaş team management had a curious fondness for Alaattin Çakıcı. Alaattin Çakıcı was a leading member of the Grey Wolves, a paramilitary organization that tortured and killed political dissidents in the 1970s and 1980s. Çakıcı graduated into organized crime, murder, and drug dealing in the 1990s. But when the police finally came to arrest him, thirty years after he began his career of violence and intimidation, they discovered he had good friends at the Beşiktaş soccer club. In fact, the Beşiktaş manager liked Çakıcı so much that when the police came looking for him, he helped him escape the country by arranging a visa under a false name.

For all the murky circumstances around Kenan Erol, the Akçaabat Sebatspor team in particular, and the Turkish league's mafia connections in general, one thing is clear: Kenan Erol should stick to his day job. Normally, Erol is a businessman. Hopefully, he is good at "business," because he is a terrible match-fixer. His bribery attempts were inept and clumsy, his instructions were incompetent, and in conversation he displayed all the finesse of a dodgy used-car salesman. But if he wanted to, how could he improve his performance?

My intellectual mentor for this question is Michael Franzese, a character you could only find in America. He is the son of notorious mob hitman John "Sonny" Franzese. Michael became a capo for the Colombo crime family of New York while still in his twenties. His rise to prominence was partly due to his family connections, but mostly due to an extraordinary gas-tax scam scheme he organized with Michael Markowitz, a criminal connected with the Russian mafia. The scheme consisted of opening and closing hundreds of shell companies that owned gas stations in New York, New Jersey, Connecticut, Pennsylvania, and Florida. The companies collected the gas tax from their customers, declared bankruptcy, and then never paid the tax to federal, state, and county authorities. It was simple, straightforward, and it netted his "family" hundreds of millions of dollars a year. It was the perfect crime: lots of money, little risk, and low penalties if caught. On the side, Franzese fixed professional sports games, including, some people claim, New York Yankees baseball games. In the 1990s, after a series of federal busts, Franzese went straight, moved to Hollywood and became, of course, a movie producer.

I met him when he came to Canada. He had become a devout born-again Christian and was promoting an anti-drug concert tour in Toronto. I was researching the documentary about the Russian mafia and the National Hockey League for *Frontline* when we spoke briefly. Franzese was very straightforward:

> My personal opinion as one who has been involved in organized crime and gambling is how easy it is to do. . . . It is very easy to get a professional athlete to come "on side." We would spend a lot of time trying to get these guys to do this . . . we would deliberately target them . . . Heck, a lot of the time they would come to us!

Tall, dark-haired, and dressed in black leather, Franzese is an interesting man. When I met him, he was with his wife, Camille Garcia, who he credits for turning around his life. They had brought their baby with them and seemed to present the picture of a hard-working, happy family. But it is not difficult to see Franzese as the mobster he once was: he oozes intelligence, power, and danger. He knows what it takes to get a sportsman to come on side:

> Athletes like to gamble. They are confident, aggressive risk-takers. All
> the things that make them good athletes make them good gamblers ...
> Once they got in trouble with us, we got them to do things for us. They
> would shave points, you know, maybe not try so hard. Or just share
> information, let us know what was going on.

Franzese is no one's fool. He understands the psychology of people and
he used it in his fixing. I asked him whether it was difficult to get sports
people to throw games. Franzese replied that if you are a mobster, you
actually want to be friends – at first – with sports people. The idea is to
find their weakness. If it is blondes, you use blondes. If it is drugs, you
use drugs. Whatever it is, you use it to get a hold over the sports person.
Then you try to get them to throw games:

> You might approach them or set them up with a woman. She would
> get pregnant or pretend to be. That would screw their game up. Or you
> would get them partying hard the night before the game.

This amoral brilliance for discovering human weakness, which Franzese
now renounces, was at the heart of his success at match-fixing. However,
the first problem that confronts a gambling match-fixer, brilliant or not,
is how to get access to the players. If the match-fixers cannot speak to the
players, then they cannot arrange a fix. Yet access to the world of the
players is closely guarded, not only by the players but also the people
close to them. How then do match-fixers get access to the players?

For long-term match-fixers working in their own domestic league,
the process is something akin to seduction. The Prosecutor's Report of
the Berlin Staatsanwaltschaft has a description of the Sapina brothers, the
Croatian gamblers who were able to persuade Robert Hoyzer to "come on
side," and their sports bar, where many of the German referees not only
partied at but felt comfortable. Other fixers may try to establish themselves in some official capacity at the club. In international games and
tournaments, the match-fixers have to rely on other methods. Several

players and officials talked about the match-fixers manoeuvring so as to share the same hotel corridor. The fixer would then sometimes use prostitutes to establish a connection between the players and themselves.

The second method fixers use to get access to players is to hire that access. In this scenario, they employ agents, known as "runners," to ensure access between them and the players, or they may even set themselves up as "player-agents" who will represent the players in corporate and business deals. In the Asian leagues, where corruption is purportedly better established than in Europe, there exists a series of independent runners who work for corrupt players on each of the teams; these runners could then be contacted by potential match-fixers when they wanted to establish a fix. Chin Lai (*) is a former player who was approached a number of times to fix games. He also had teammates who fixed games. He claims that runners were key to the operation. They would make friends with players, figure out which players may be susceptible to bribes, and then introduce them to national-level bookies.

> ... there were runners. They were ex-players, good friends of the team. Sometimes they would be guys we would meet in a disco. The owner or someone, they would party with us for months. Then maybe say something. These guys were key. They had to be people with access to the players. They had to be people the players would trust. It was the same as the cricket fixing. You needed people who could contact the team. They were vital. They had to be people who could come to training sessions or games and matches.

The common thread between these two methods – direct contact or runner-arranged – is at this initial stage, the match-fixer is simply seeking to gain access to as wide an assortment of players as possible. How players are approached to make the corrupt deal and what is said to them is decided in the next stage.

THE SET UP

It is not enough for a match-fixer simply to be introduced to players. As Kenan Erol, the unsuccessful Turkish match-fixer showed, being in the same room does not guarantee a successfully fixed match. What is also important is *how* the match-fixer approaches a player. There are two main types of approaches, and ironically, they mirror the two principal business strategies of erotic dancers in North American strip bars.

For anyone innocent enough not to have been in a North American strip bar, this is how they work. A whole bunch of men go in with lots of money in their pockets to look at semi-naked women. They *think* the whole experience is about sex. They are wrong. The semi-naked women *know* the whole experience is about getting as much of that money out of the men's pockets as possible. In other words, it is about profit maximization. To make that money, a woman will have to do as many lap-dances as possible. A lap-dance is when the dancer will grind herself against a customer for the length of one song. She will receive a set fee for each song. Believe it or not, how the women get the men to hire them has been the subject of extensive sociological study. Some of the research has been done by traditional male academics, but lots of feminists have also studied the business and discovered that the dancers generally choose one of two business strategies: there are those who try for fast bucks – quick, direct approaches to as many different customers as possible ("Hi, honey, want to see my tits?"); and those who manufacture "counterfeit intimacy" or pseudo-relationships with specific customers ("Hi, sweetie, you look like you had a long day – want me to sit down and be your little girl?") who then spend more money on them.

The Asian match-fixers, when they are working in leagues with lots of corruption, often use the "fast bucks" approach. Tohari Paijan was a player who agreed to play in fixed matches in the Malaysian-Singaporean league. When asked about the methods of approaches, he replied, "Oh no, there was nothing subtle. They would just call us up at the hotel and propose it over the phone." This method is also common when access is limited. For example, in the 1990 World Cup in Italy, the FIFA-ranked referees were hidden away in a maximum-security compound used by the Vatican in central Rome. One source reported, "It was incredible. The phone lines were supposed to be confidential and unlisted, but the referees were receiving phone calls in their rooms from bookies offering bribes." In these examples, because there was so much corruption in the league, in the first case, and access was so restricted, in the second case, the match-fixers had to use fast, direct approaches.

In leagues where corruption is rarer, fixers face a more difficult job. It is at this point that the counterfeit intimacy method is frequently used. One example was described by a U.S. college basketball player in the early 1960s. Art Hicks was black. One day, after a white teammate made yet another racist comment, Hicks decided to fix some games with an organized crime syndicate. He was eventually caught and when he testified he revealed how the match-fixers were "experts at human nature":

> One thing you never heard about the gamblers is how good they were at what they did. They were experts at human nature and that's why so few of the kids they approached ever turned them down. They catch you at just the right time, when you're vulnerable. They can look at a kid's game and see there ain't no love there . . . Whatever the problem, they knew how to exploit it. The gambler becomes the most reliable person in your life. He replaces the coach.

This is what the former New York mafia capo Michael Franzese was talking about when he spoke of "being friends" with the players first and then using their weaknesses against them. Here a match-fixer is *not* trying the direct, fast method; it is more like a savage animal stalking its victim. The fixer is getting close to his prey (the athlete) and weakening or using weakness to propose match-fixing.

However, for all this discussion about relationship-building, how do match-fixers actually propose a corrupt deal? What language do they use?

When German referee Robert Hoyzer was persuaded by Croatian gamblers to fix matches, he struggled to explain how they were able to do so. He had always regarded himself as a very honest and a well-brought-up person, yet in a relatively short time they were able to persuade him to do something that he never would have considered before:

> It was an ongoing process that I wasn't aware of any more in the end. It affected me in a way that I stopped noticing things going on around me. I only hung out at this café, at some point it was like my second living room. I was around all the time. I was there eight days out of the week and was treated by them like a very special person.

A soccer administrator in Malaysia describes a similar pattern in proposing match-fixing where the fixers use language that would allow the players not to "feel criminal in their thinking . . . they [the match-fixers] would call it coffee money." Another popular form of corrupt invitation is for match-fixers to say, "You can get X amount of money for just ninety minutes of work. Think about it." These invitations are couched in a lovely, neutral language, as if there were nothing wrong with the proposal.

The following excerpt is a good example of *how* to set up a fixed game in a league of high corruption. It is a direct, fast-bucks approach. Chieu (*) was one of the match-fixers in the Malaysian-Singaporean league of the early 1990s. He was something of "an expert in human nature" and along with other fixers who created networks of corruption throughout the league he made himself a great deal of money. This excerpt is from one of the previously unpublished police confessions; the player is reenacting the general outline of his first conversation with the fixer. Chieu had already established a relationship with David (*) – a top Malaysian player – who then introduces him to two other players – Ali (*) and Rahil (*) – on his team to help set up a match-fixing ring.

David:	This is our friend Chieu.
Chieu:	I am Chieu. [Ali and Rahil shake hands with him]. I have come here to talk to you. I will try to help you reach the final of the Malaysian Cup. Okay, I'll make it simple! First, I help your team in five games. I will pay you 15,000 RM for winning each game. After winning those five, you will have to lose or draw the game. I will pay you 25,000 RM to draw a game, and to lose a game 40,000 RM.
David:	Don't worry! The Boss [Chieu] will help us out.
Chieu:	Okay, easy to talk. I control your coach. I brought in your two foreigners. I paid the transfer fees for them, not the state FA.
Rahil:	I will think it over fast.
Chieu:	[Gives him an envelope full of cash] This is the FA Cup money.
David:	Don't worry. Chieu will help.

This excerpt shows the difference between Chieu and the far less subtle Kenan Erol. For a start, Chieu does not show up alone to the meeting. Rather, he uses a player to introduce him to other players. This action immediately helps to establish his credibility. David, a prominent player, twice vouches for Chieu's trustworthiness.

He also shakes hands with the players. Chieu shows himself to be from a similar working-class background from the Malay vernacular he uses (this was stressed a number of times by the translator, although it is, obviously, not apparent in the English version) and is friendly and direct with the players. This is in contrast with the attitude of many club owners, who tended to patronize their players. Often players were expected to kiss the hands of the owners when they met them. Chieu, on the other hand, is courteous and, he claims, has the same owners on his payroll already. Even if this later claim turns out to be untrue, it still puts the idea in the players' heads that it might not be, making them fearful of going to the management. Again, this is in direct comparison to Kenan Erol, who, when asked if he controlled the management, showed instantly that he was an outsider with little power. So in a few sentences, Chieu has managed to both be ingratiating and to isolate the players from their management.

David C. Whelan, a former New Jersey police officer turned criminal justice professor, wrote about organized crime's involvement in point-shaving in college basketball. He claims that at the beginning of their relationship, "win bonuses" are paid by match-fixers to players to play as well as they can. Players regard the win bonuses as relatively benign: they will win and thereby keep the loyalty to their teams, but they still get the financial rewards of fixing matches. However, these payments were often what Whelan calls "gateway crimes," which brought the players into the match-fixers' net without them being aware of it.

Chieu uses Whelan's "gateway crime" approach. He claims that if the players co-operate with him, they will not only get money for winning the next five games, but that he will also help them reach the final of the Malaysian Cup. Then he gives the players money for a game they had won several weeks ago. This is an important step. For as soon as the players accept the money, they have *de facto* accepted Chieu's offer of a long-term relationship. The acceptance of the match-fixer's money by the players, no matter what the motivation, signals the closing of the deal and the end of the possible innocence of the players. A Singaporean police officer supported this view in an interview: "But you know if they take the money once, it is over. They can never turn back because the gamblers will say, "If you don't do it, we will let people know that you took the money.""

However, another match-fixer said, "As soon as [the players] take the money, they have to do what I say. I don't do this thing where I show them the money and say, 'This is yours if you do the match.' No, I give them the money. I say, 'This is coffee money. Take it. But don't cross me. Or I will get you.'"

Now the fixer is not only showing the importance of player accepting the money, but he is also showing the change in attitude, from friendliness to menace (once the players have agreed to the corrupt deal) that drives the next stage of match-fixing.

CALLING THE FIX

From all the coverage around the 2007 Cricket World Cup and the purported mysterious death of coach Bob Woolmer, someone might think fixing is new to that game. However, match-fixing in cricket has a history that is at least two hundred years old. In 1806, English cricket was rife with match-fixing. There were criminal bookmakers who set up their shops underneath the stands at Lord's cricket grounds, and like their Asian counterparts two centuries later, they were very trustworthy in paying their customers and extremely willing to fix games to cheat their rivals and their customers. William Beldham was a prominent cricketer who was approached by match-fixers to throw games. He claims that he refused, saying, "You never buy the same man but once . . . No, sir, a man was a slave when once he sold to these folk." Beldham is describing the attitude change that affects the relationship between the players and the match-fixers once the players have taken their money. It is the same transformation that Michael Franzese spoke of when he told me: "You don't treat the fixers as friends . . . you're more friendly with the guys who don't throw the games . . ."

Why would the dynamics of this relationship change so dramatically, particularly after the match-fixer has spent so much effort in getting access to the players and then setting up the fix? It is because at this stage, the match-fixer's greatest chance of loss or profit can occur. Gambling match-fixing differs from internal fixes like the ones in the Russian league. In internal fixing, the ultimate goal is to fix the result of the game. The people who fix those games, really care *which* team wins the game. In gambling fixing, the fixers don't care which team wins the game, but they do care about making as much money as possible.

There are actually two fixes going on: the fixing of the game and the fixing of the gambling market. To fix the market, the match-fixer has to look at the spread of the betting market, place the bet that will ensure the greatest profit, and then ensure that the players deliver that result. So the match-fixer has to make sure that the players will follow instructions to the absolute letter. Failure to do so ensures an enormous loss of money on the match-fixer's part. The establishment of the phony relationship with the player is over; now it is all business.

In 1919, Jewish mobster Arnold Rothstein, working with the Chicago White Sox, fixed baseball's most important competition, the World Series. The problems facing contemporary soccer match-fixers are almost identical to the ones faced by Rothstein. The chief problem is that they have to be able to get a sufficient quantity of money on to the market to make the fix worthwhile. However, if Rothstein, or any contemporary match-fixer, tried to place a heavy bet on one team, then the betting market will quickly become aware that there is something crooked going on. In general, betting companies know who the criminals are, but if Rothstein, or one of his known associates, had walked into an illegal betting shop and bet $10 on a game, no one would have noticed. If Rothstein or one of his associates had walked into an illegal betting shop and bet $60,000 on the game, then it would have been known throughout the market in hours. A fixer has to disguise the fact that he is placing the bets or his rivals will be aware of the fix. This is a problem shared by many successful gamblers who never even think of fixing a game. I spoke with a number of professional gamblers who were convinced that the bookmakers who were taking their bets were secretly stealing the bet, telling them it was not possible to get the money on and then betting themselves with other bookmakers. To overcome this problem, many successful gamblers and fixers hire their own agents to place their bets for them. These agents then hide the fact that they are placing a bet for the fixers.

A match-fixer will want the market to lean heavily against the fix – so the team he controls is expected to win. To encourage bettors to bet for the fixing team, he might spread a rumour that the other team has been weakened: an injury to a key player, dissension in the dressing room, or, ironically, that he has fixed the *other* team!

However, a match-fixer can also fix *with* the market to avoid detection, which means lower short-term profit but also less chance of detection. This is the real danger for European soccer leagues because this type of fixing can go on for years and no one suspects a thing. For example, a weak team is to play a strong team. The market expects the strong team to win. The match-fixers fix the weak team, pile on as much money as possible for the strong team and few people will suspect a fix as the result occurs as the market predicted. A Finnish fixing player testified in 2005 to this method:

> I have taken money for a few games. This has been going on for years. The most recent case is from the last season. In this case, it was just a normal league game. We had gone to the game as the underdog, and so the loss did not surprise anybody.

Because much of sport betting is done in the two hours before the game begins, the later a match-fixer can place his bet, the easier it is to place bets on the market, and the more profit he can make. Say, for example, a match-fixer has established a link with players on Team A; he sees the betting market is betting heavily in favour of Team A winning the game. Ideally, the match-fixer would want to bet heavily at attractive odds (because if he comes into the market too early, it can cause the odds to change) and then signal to his team to "open up the game" – lose – in the minute before the game is to begin. This would ensure the match-fixer of the greatest profit. However, the match-fixer faces a problem: how can he signal to his players without attracting any attention and let them give him a signal that they have understood the signal in the final minutes before a big match when all the spectators, teammates, and officials are now watching them? One solution to this problem was described by an Indonesian match-fixer, who said:

> What I do is have my runner stand beside the team box wearing a red singlet if the team is to lose. When they come out onto the pitch, they stand at the halfway line and salute the crowd. They see my runner wearing the red singlet and they know they must open up the game. If I wanted them to play hard, I would get my runner to wear a blue singlet. Now when the players see the runner, they must put their

hands on their hearts, as if they are saluting the crowd. This is their signal to let us know they have seen and understood the signal. They cannot pretend later not to have seen the signal.

The match-fixer has now called the fix, ordering the players to rig the game in a certain way. Now it is up to the players to deliver the right result.

PAYMENT

The final stage of the fix comes after the game, when the fixer pays the player or referees. These payments have to be either hidden or deniable. The players are, for the most part, public figures. Their salaries are well known. Their lifestyles are closely examined. Their honest teammates work and play with them closely. How then can they enjoy the increased money without arousing suspicion?

Johnson Fernandez, one of the heroic Malaysian reporters, wrote in his exposé that the match-fixers were giving their players winning lottery tickets. The match-fixers would buy the tickets from the winners, and then give the tickets to the players who had fixed the matches so that they could claim that the money had been won legitimately. Some of the interview subjects claimed that another way was for the players to be given their own bets on the gambling market. This had a twofold advantage: it increased their payout and it guaranteed their co-operation with the fix. However, most payments to corrupt players in gambling fixes are still relatively unsophisticated cash payments.

Generally, the gambling match-fixers have two stages in making these payments to players. The first is an advance, or "coffee and shopping money" paid before the game. This payment really settles the deal and shows that the player will take part in fixing the match. However, the main payment is reserved for after the game, when the player has successfully performed the job. The place of payment is almost always a neutral location away from the soccer world – a disco or restaurant. Here is an example from one of the Malaysian players in his confession to the police:

A few weeks after that [the fixed match] Lee (*) phoned me. He made an appointment to see me at the Shell station in Ipoh. He wanted to pay me the money for the game against Singapore. I went straight there. I met Lee and his wife there. Lee told me to follow behind. We went to an industrial area. We spoke through the car windows. Lee gave me a restaurant menu, inside the menu was 15,000 Malaysian ringgit. Then I drove away. In the afternoon, I returned the menu, without the money in it.

There is another form of payment that successful, long-term match-fixers ensure is paid to the player – the psychological one. The match-fixers try to ensure a long-term relationship with corrupt players. It may no longer be friendly, but it does need to be maintained in good account. Often players do not feel particularly good about underperforming in matches. So match-fixers will provide them with "gifts" along with the payment. Frequently, these gifts are women. Rafiq Saad took part in a number of fixed matches for the match-fixer Chieu. One in particular was against the Singapore team in Singapore in front of 50,000 fans. Because of cultural rivalries, it is very difficult for a Malaysian player to lose to Singapore and to lose in front of 50,000 fans is very difficult. In Saad's confession, he talks about the match-fixer providing the corrupt players with women:

On the XX in Singapore, we lost. I did not play all out. I went back to the hotel. The same night . . . Chieu had supplied four high-class prostitutes for four players . . .

This is not the last time we shall see that sex was used to pay people in the soccer world; here, it is the players who were "paid" with women. In the next chapter we shall see it is other people, the ones who were supposed to be the most honest and upright, who were regularly paid with women – the referees of some of the biggest soccer games in the world.

12

SEX AND THE MEN IN BLACK

Sex was used. Sometimes it would be the translator. She would come to the room and show that she was not opposed to being with the referee. Then the next morning they would come to him, the club officials, and say "If you are not sympathetic to our cause, we will let people know what you were doing last night."

So far, I have written only about the players or team officials throwing games, but what about the referees? How do European club officials who want to fix a match, but who cannot make a deal with the other team, work? How do they corrupt referees?

To find the answers, I spoke to a man who was pre-eminent in the field of soccer match-fixing: a master of his craft, an expert in human nature, and someone with an extraordinary record of helping to bribe international soccer referees.

His name is Ljubomir Barin, a Croatian described as "the human screen," "the black wallet," and "the corruptor." For years Barin helped manipulate European Cup matches for the French teams Bordeaux and Olympique de Marseille. In the 1980s and early 1990s, they were France's top two soccer teams: winning, between them, twelve domestic trophies in ten years. Barin also worked as an agent for some of the top European clubs such as Standard Liège and Anderlecht of Belgium; Bayern

Munich, the perennial German champions, and Red Star Belgrade, one of the top teams in the former Yugoslavia. He also worked with America's former favourite team, the New York Cosmos.

Brian Glanville, the English author and soccer writer, headed up an investigation in the early 1970s for the *Sunday Times* newspaper. The investigation discovered that a Hungarian agent, Dezso Solti, was working to fix matches for the Italian team Juventus. Glanville and his colleagues revealed that Solti had invited a Portuguese referee to meet him in his hotel room before a European Cup semi-final. When the referee showed up, Solti had an attractive blonde woman on his arm and offered the referee a car if he helped Juventus into the final. Barin seems to be from the same man-of-the-world mould as Solti: a sophisticated, multilingual fixer from the former Soviet empire, Barin dresses immaculately in finely cut suits. You could imagine him showing up at a referee's door with a blonde on one arm. The difference is that Barin would be providing the referee with the blonde.

For years, Barin provided referees and club owners with women, gifts, and bribes all in an attempt to help his French client clubs with European success. He established a financial network across two continents with bank payments to accounts in Zagreb, Switzerland, and Vienna. Barin knew how to fix games. He had style, a worldly knowledge, and ability to judge human nature. And on July 11, 1995, he gave the ultimate insider's tutorial in match-fixing in an office room in a Marseilles courthouse to French magistrate Pierre Philipon.

Barin claims his match-fixing began in 1981 when Claude Bez, the president of Girondins de Bordeaux, watched his beloved soccer club lose yet another UEFA Cup game on a disputed penalty from an allegedly bought referee. After the game, Barin turned to a disappointed Bez and said, "If you want us to win, you've got to make a move and do what all the others do." Bez said, "Okay."

So Barin set out to change the "luck" of the club. He would say later about his work:

When a club asks me to look after the referees, it is not because I work as a translator. But, for sure, because I can influence the referees. It was important for me to organize a favourable atmosphere for the referees before a match. To accommodate them, to make sure they were well-received, give them gifts. You have to know which of the referees have children, so when they leave, they leave with well-packed suitcases.

In other words, Barin bribed referees. He gave them fur coats, Rolex watches, perfume, expensive clothes, and stylish pens. Barin also worked for Olympique de Marseille, owned by the charismatic businessman Bernard Tapie. Barin recounted that they often met the referees before the matches on Tapie's yacht.

I remember one occasion when a referee was on the *Phocéa*, Bernard Tapie's yacht, and he remarked that it was a nice watch on Tapie's wrist. The next morning that referee got a gift of that type of watch . . . I believe that it was a British referee, but I don't remember which match he acted in.

When Barin was working for Bordeaux, they ran two sets of accounts: the first, the legitimate and public account; the second, the secret black-market accounts where they hid money from the French tax authorities. To get money for the black-market accounts, they fiddled the books on the international transfer of players. For example, they would declare publicly that a player would cost 7 million francs; however, the *real* cost would actually be much less: 3.5 million francs. Then they would take the 3.5 million off their books and put it in secret slush funds. Using these methods, Barin built a trail of secret bank accounts across Europe. It is his claim that the money in those accounts was used to bribe referees and teams in at least sixteen European games for Bordeaux and dozens of transfers for the two teams. However, in the early 1990s, the whole scheme began to unravel. He claims now that he was caught up in a series of political and economic manoeuvres. Bernard Tapie was considered a left-wing politician, so the right wing came after him.

French magistrates tell a different story. Under the French legal system, there is a role that does not exist in English common law: prosecuting magistrate. They can be remarkable investigators, launching independent inquiries with resources and power that most police forces simply cannot match. One of them began to question the hundreds of millions of taxpayers' money that went to help support the Bordeaux soccer club. Then other magistrates began to investigate the fix that Bernard Tapie and Olympique de Marseille arranged against a struggling northern club, Valenciennes. (They set up the fix without using Barin, which was a big mistake.) Barin, who at the time was one of the biggest player-agents in international soccer, was drawn into the investigation. He refused to submit voluntarily to a cross-examination by the French magistrates and a European arrest warrant was issued. Between 1992 and the winter of 1995, Barin was an international fugitive from justice. There were a series of dramatic escapes in hotels, and rumours that he was tipped off before police raids in Graz in Austria and at the Novotel Hotel in Bordeaux. Finally, on February 23, 1995, German police caught up with him at Düsseldorf airport. He was arrested and extradited to France.

The French magistrates, thinking of the trouble they had taken to get Barin, kept him in prison for five months. It shook him. He appealed to the European Court of Human Rights in Strasbourg, protesting the "inhumane conditions." It was all to no avail. Softened up by his time in prison, Barin appeared before Pierre Philipon on July 11, 1995, promising to tell all if he was released from jail. The hearing featured a dramatic meeting between Barin and Jean-Pierre Bernès, the former general manager of Olympique de Marseille. After four and half hours, a shaken Gilbert Collard, Bernès's lawyer, came out of the room and said, "Mr. Barin has pointed the finger at the entire organization of world football. It is a system of giant corruption that it is no longer possible to ignore. This dossier is going to touch upon other investigations which will go in all sorts of directions. . . . There is going to be a tidal wave that is going to submerge the world of football."

What had shaken Collard was that Barin was not only giving a tutorial in his match-fixing methods, but he was also providing the investigators with receipts, exact financial amounts, and numbers of illicit bank accounts. Between Jean-Pierre Bernès and himself, Barin revealed that Olympique de Marseille's match-fixing was more than simply a one-off event; it was a pattern of consistent and constant corruption. They had created special slush funds totalling 5 to 6 million francs a year to fix certain key, usually European, matches. At Bordeaux, Claude Bez had paid hundreds of thousands of dollars in gifts and cash payments to referees.

Among other specific examples, Barin and Bernès talked about arranging matches between AEK Athens and Olympique de Marseille in the European Cup in October and November 1989. To fix the first game, which was played in Athens, they claimed they paid the players of the opposing team to lose. The day before the match, Bernès transferred 1.76 million francs into a Swiss bank account controlled by a Panamanian company led by Greek businessman Spiros Karageorgis, who had connections to AEK Athens. For the return match in Marseilles, Barin was in charge of taking care of the referee, Helmut Kohl of Austria. Barin said, "M. Kohl was a big friend of mine. He died in 1992 of cancer. He was employed by the Austrian postal system. He was in financial difficulties. I relayed him the sum of 310,000 French francs or 698,190 Austrian schillings to his Austrian account on the 10 November 1989."

There were other revelations: receipts purportedly for bribes of 100,000 Deutschmarks to the German referee and linesmen in a European Cup tie; Italian officials being approached before a Marseille match against the Danish team Brondby (there is no evidence that they took any money); and bribes paid to the Russian team Spartak Moscow in the semi-final of the European Cup in 1991.

Years later, one of the Marseille players who also helped fix a match, Jean-Jacques Eydelie, would add to the controversy by alleging that other players had been involved in match-fixing. He claimed that there was a regular pattern, a day or so before a big match: players who had played with the upcoming team would be asked to contact their friends to see if they would "raise their foot a little." The payments were frequently money and the promise of a transfer to Marseille the next season. Eydelie even writes in his autobiography, *I Do Not Play Anymore: A Footballer Breaks the Omerta*, that after the final of the 1993 European Champions League, when Marseille beat AC Milan, two players from Milan showed up after the game looking for their payoff. It is a similar claim to the one brought out by Jean-Pierre Papin, another former Marseille player who played on the AC Milan team ("I played for Marseille, I know how these things are done…"), but other Marseille players and coaches deny these accusations, claiming that Eydelie was simply trying to sensationalize his book, two of them even threatened legal action, and Papin later retracted his claim after facing pressure from UEFA.

However, the biggest shock came from Barin's claim of the sexual accommodation of referees before big European matches. Barin said that he regularly hired a series of expensive Parisian prostitutes, £2,000-a-night women who serviced the referees.

"After word got around among the referees, they were clambering to come," said Barin in judicial testimony. "All the referees wanted to come here, it was good for the region."

"What happened when there were three officials?" asked the judge.

"There were three, four, or five hostesses," Barin replied. "When the refs were greedy, the girls stayed for two nights."

The audience in the courtroom broke into laughter.

It would be wise, however, not to underestimate Ljubomir Barin. He may seem like a kind of benevolent Santa Claus, bestowing gifts on complicit and corrupt referees. But the men he was working for, such as Bernard Tapie, had some very tough connections. There was a real "Mr. Christmas" as well – that was the nickname of Corsican businessman André-Noël Filippeddu. Bernard Tapie described him to a soccer coach he was trying to influence as "someone you can have confidence in. Him or me, it is the same thing." Mr. Christmas's list of friends and business partners extended to Francis Vanverberghe (a.k.a Francis le Belge), a notorious heroin smuggler and blackmailer. Before he was murdered in 2000, Vanverberghe was head of the French Connection, the drug rings that smuggled heroin to the United States in the 1960s and 1970s and provided the inspiration for the two films starring Gene Hackman. Tapie once intervened with a fellow cabinet minister to get Vanverberghe released early from prison. Another of Mr. Christmas's Corsican business acquaintances was Dominique Rutily, the president of the Calvi football club, a third division squad in Corsica. On March 29, 1996, four men ambushed Rutily and sprayed him with machine-gun fire; as he lay on the ground, two of them walked over to him and made sure they finished the job by shooting him in the head. This mob-style assassination was just after one of his club's matches. Mr. Christmas's brother, Jules-Philippe, was named by a Brazilian senate inquiry as being a money-laundering business partner of one Lillo Lauricella, a relative of the man called the "Treasurer of the mafia," Pippo Calò. Mr. Christmas himself was later convicted of helping run a violent extortion ring in his native Corsica.

With men like this hanging about, it was no wonder that Jean-Pierre Bernès, the former Olympique de Marseille general manager, was terrified of testifying. Once, on the stand, he told the judge he was very frightened and wanted police protection.

However, the ultimate defence of soccer insiders Bernard Tapie, Claude Bez, Jean-Pierre Bernès, and Ljubomir Barin, was "everyone was doing it." Bernès even wrote in his book about "The System of the Win" – "I discovered above all else, that if Marseille wanted to equal the great European clubs … we had to use the same methods they did… so that when the players walked on the pitch, the game was already won or lost!" Throughout their trials, Bez and Barin consistently repeated the allegation that bribing, gift-giving, and sexual favours for referees were simply the accepted way of doing business in the soccer world. Barin claimed that Real Madrid, the richest and most successful soccer club in the world, offered linesmen officiating their matches Rolex watches, costing between £1,500 and £4,000 and he added "Real win all their matches 4-0."

Their defence did them very little good. Bez died before the start of his 1999 trial. Tapie was sentenced to a year in jail and, upon his release, became the star of a TV show, restarted his business, and in 2001 became briefly the sporting director of Olympique de Marseille. Ljubomir Barin did not go to prison. He was, however, fined 76,000 euros, which, considering one covert deal that he engineered was worth 4.7 million euros, must be considered a bargain.

Let us be clear about the severity of the cases. In that era, Bordeaux and Marseille were the two elite clubs in France. They were shown to be fixing matches in the French league. They were also competing in Europe's (and arguably the world's) most competitive tournament. They were shown to be bribing referees and other teams. Finally, one of the soccer world's top agents testified that bribery, gift-giving, and sexual favours for officials were common practice among other European clubs. So what happened to the tidal wave of investigations prompted by this case that Gilbert Collard, the French lawyer, prophesized? Where were the other investigations? Did the French Football Federation investigate any other team connected with Barin's allegations? They did not. Did the Union of European Football Associations investigate? They did not. Did any other European soccer association investigate? They did not.

There were years of legal wrangling between defence lawyers and the prosecuting French magistrates, a few days of dramatic testimony, some wry news headlines about "Full bodied Bordeaux" and "Getting your kicks for free," but really very little was done. The world of international soccer was not shaken. So is it possible that Barin and Bernès were simply, as Barin now claims, caught up in a world of economic and political manipulations?

I went to Switzerland to find out.

The professional sex district of Geneva is tucked into the backstreets between the train station and Lake Geneva. Being Swiss, the red-light area is rather discreet. By day, the neighbourhood seems dominated by drab bank buildings and cheap hotels filled with United Nations officials. It is only after dark that the panoply of sex bars and massage parlours becomes obvious. Michel Zen-Ruffinen's offices were in the middle of the red-light district. They were on an upstairs floor, and to reach them I had to go through a lobby that smelt of garbage.

Zen-Ruffinen was once the second most important man in FIFA. But when I met him, he was running a small sports agency and law business. (He has since moved to Lausanne, and now has a new job with a larger legal firm, one of whose clients was the G-14, a group representing the richest European soccer clubs. At one point, they sued FIFA, demanding insurance or compensation for club players who are injured while representing their countries in international matches.) A tall, good-looking man in his mid-forties, Zen-Ruffinen has the reputation in some quarters of being an honourable whistleblower. In 2002, as general secretary of FIFA, he came out publicly to allege that his former boss, Sepp Blatter, the president of FIFA, had committed various acts of fraud. After Blatter won re-election to the head of FIFA, he got rid of Zen-Ruffinen, saying that the allegations were not true. The Swiss authorities declined to pursue the matter, saying there was "no behaviour of a prosecutable nature" and that Blatter had acted lawfully. We did not speak about those issues. I was there to ask him about other subjects, namely what it was like to be a top European referee, which he was, before he became a sports administrator. Zen-Ruffinen almost immediately supported Barin's allegations about the use of sex with referees.

> Sex was used. Sometimes it would be the translator. She would come to the room and show that she was not opposed to being with the referee. Then the next morning they would come to him – the club officials – and say, "If you are not sympathetic to our cause, we will let people know what you were doing last night."

Zen-Ruffinen was at pains to say that he never availed himself of women or in any way took a bribe. I believe him. Zen-Ruffinen has a very high reputation for personal honesty. But he does say that he heard of other people in the referees' community who did. The other thing he spoke of was the regular attempts to "accommodate him" by giving gifts or bribes.

> I remember when I was a referee, I was in Madrid for an Atlético Madrid game. We were taken to "El Corte Ingles" [a huge department store in the centre of Madrid]. It was ten o'clock and the club officials said to us, "Okay, we will be back at one. And until then anything that you buy is on the club bill." Well, being Swiss the three of us went and had a coffee. But you can imagine if we were Ukrainian or someone from the Eastern Bloc!

That Zen-Ruffinen mentions that the Spanish club Atlético Madrid as a source of bribes is not particularly shocking news. Jesús Gil, the former owner of Atlético Madrid, is known for his colourful approach to life. He began his career working in a brothel. After graduating to the sports industry, he once punched a fellow club director live on national television. He was also convicted to prison terms three times and linked to the Sicilian mafia by Spanish prosecutors. So the possibility that he may have overseen an administration that tried to accommodate referees is not surprising. But Zen-Ruffinen remembers other incidents with other clubs with better reputations, including a time when he was refereeing at one European club, sponsored by an electronics company:

> I remember I came back to my hotel room and there was a full electronic hi-fi on my bed! . . . Attached was a note saying, "We just wanted to show you what was here. But we will send it direct to your home!"

Zen-Ruffinen immediately phoned to the reception and had the electronics removed, but while conducting research in Africa and Asia, I asked other FIFA-ranked referees if the picture that he described of occasional bribe attempts and women being casually offered is true. They all confirmed the stories, and one official described his time refereeing a summer tournament in Korea as "rest and recreation":

> It was good fun in those days. We would go and they would bring in top teams. And they sent us women to our rooms. Or your translator would come to your room. But you know, that was fun. It was just friendly matches. Often, the ways to corrupt you are very subtle. Women are sent, but nothing is said directly. Some countries are simply very hospitable, it is very difficult to draw the lines.

However, another international referee in Malaysia said that the offers of sex were much more direct and much less innocent:

> It is always the same. No matter where you are in the world, money will not always get you, but sex will. If you are not gay, you will always want a woman. So they know that and they send women to your room. It happened all the time. After they have sex with a woman, the offer will be made. Sometimes it is the woman herself who does it. They say something like, "You must support me . . . You must do this and help . . ." The man feels guilty and does something.

In fact, the invitations to sexual quid pro quos was said to be so common in the 1980s and 1990s among tournaments in the Middle East that referees were given specific warnings before games involving some Arab countries.

I have, however, got ahead of myself. At the time I interviewed Zen-Ruffinen, I had not visited Asia and I was not certain how to evaluate his story. I thought he might simply be upset at the world of soccer. I thought his stories might simply be an oblique way of seeking revenge on FIFA. Even though among journalists Zen-Ruffinen has a reputation of outspoken decency, even though his story had nothing to do with

FIFA, and even though it was consistent with Barin's testimony and interview, I thought it might just have been sour grapes.

Then I went to see the officials at the Union of European Football Associations, popularly known as UEFA. UEFA is the European equivalent of the Asian Football Confederation. The UEFA headquarters is on the edge of Lake Geneva, in Nyon. It is an indication of the European dominance of the world's game and the kind of money that is available in the sport. The building has a glass front overlooking the lake, and on the afternoon I visited, light came streaming in the building, bathing it in a lovely glow. The two executives I spoke with were friendly and open. They asked that the interview be recorded as "attributable but with no names given." Under those rules, they were quite candid. One executive simply laughed, when I asked him, about Barin's and Zen-Ruffinen's stories of referees being offered women before big international matches:

> Oh yes! It was almost a tradition. "Nice ladies," money, electronics. You name it, they were offered it. It was almost standard practice that the referees were offered women. In most cases, it was difficult to figure out if it was "excessive hospitality" or bribery. It was so bad that it used to be the refs would arrive at the hotel, look at their watches, and say, "The women should be here at six."

Ljubomir Barin had been telling the truth.

In fact, the more one examines the culture of international refereeing in the 1990s, the more of these tales are revealed. Englishman David Elleray, a former top referee who is now on UEFA's referees committee, claimed that the chairman of the UEFA referees' committee had said at the time: "Only accept gifts if they are small . . . and expensive!" In his biography, Elleray also provided a stirring example of a stiff upper lip in a tight corner. It was during an evening of convivial company in a Romanian brothel before a European match. The Romanian club officials arranged the evening's entertainment, and the unwitting English referees made sure that the company did not get too convivial by all gathering together in one of their bedrooms to keep out the women. That is more than can be said for Welsh referee Howard King, who was banned from the game in 1996 when he told a British newspaper that before twelve to fifteen of the forty-four European matches that he refereed, women were made available to him. King claimed, "I never said no to the ladies." According to him, he never said no in Russia, Germany, Portugal, Spain, Holland, and Denmark. However, he also insisted that his sex life had never influenced a match, despite at one point canvassing Russian officials to provide him with a blonde before a European Championship match with Norway.

Luciano Moggi, the Italian fixer for Juventus, was in an earlier incarnation a club official with local rivals Torino. He was linked to another example of this culture: providing women for the Belgian referees in the UEFA Cup match versus AEK Athens in 1991. UEFA decided to believe that the women who spent the night with the referees were simply over-enthusiastic translators who were culturally challenged. Torino won the game. And Moggi ended up at Juventus, one of the top clubs in Italy.

Annie was delightfully sexy and in my drunken state, I pawed her tight, lithe body with great vigour. I was in Singapore, interviewing the businessman and convicted match-fixer Ong Kheng Hock. In 1995, Ong had become involved with a former international player attempting to corrupt the Singapore national goalie David Lee with an $80,000 (Singapore dollars) bribe. Ong ended up serving a couple of years in prison. So, late one afternoon, I showed up unannounced at his downtown restaurant – the unaptly named Mr. Bean's Café – and began asking him difficult questions about his past. Ong was very kind and, for the record, claimed vehemently that he never fixed any soccer games. However, he took me out for drinks and we talked about his experiences in prison and my research. I told him about the culture of sex corruption of some European referees.

I can't quite remember how many drinks we had together. Certainly at one point we had a lot of beers and not too much food at a little drinks bar, Crossroads, across from his restaurant. I seem to remember a bottle of Scotch as well. Then suddenly in the brusque way that Chinese businessmen often have, he said, "Come on, this place is boring. Let's go." I, who was deeply entrenched in a conversation with a woman who claimed to be a Singapore Airlines stewardess, disagreed, but I went along.

It was now dark and we drove out to Eastern Singapore and entered a surreal shopping mall. Surreal because it looked like a normal shopping mall: escalators, plastic roofing, sliding-glass partitions. But where there would normally be shops, there were bars. And where there would normally be shoppers, there were women. Dozens of women with short dresses and hungry eyes. Ong took me into one bar, where he seemed to be known. We had more drinks – beers and whisky – and talked more about corruption in soccer. Various women came up and offered themselves to us. Most were women from the Philippines. One said that she had met Ong when she was a thirteen-year-old schoolgirl who never wore panties. He seemed to regard her with the benevolence of a favourite uncle. I wish I could say that I was so handsome that women found me irresistibly attractive, but really it was my position as Ong's "friend" that was my strong point. Without him, I was simply one more red-faced, drunken man in a small crowd of red-faced, drunken men, encircled by a much larger crowd of Filipina women.

We went to another bar. Ong seemed to be known there as well. Annie came up, and Ong signalled for her to take care of me. At first, I was quite standoffish. This was, after all, an interview with a controversial subject. The circumstances may have been a little unusual, but it was still supposedly a professional meeting. However, Annie followed us from one bar to the other. I got drunker and drunker. At one point, I think the most gorgeous woman I had ever seen was dancing on a chair in a corner of a neon-lit imitation English pub. Her hair hung down over her face; her shirt was open to show beautiful breasts; and the red-faced men in tennis shirts ignored her. I was well gone. At this juncture, Annie moved in and started rubbing herself against me and stroking my penis through my suit trousers. Her friend Karen rubbed herself against my back. Before I knew it, I was in a corner alternating snogging and groping with Annie and her friend.

I screwed up. I made exactly the same mistake that some of the referees that I wrote about in this chapter have done. I got drunk. I got lonely. And I mixed sex with a professional situation. When I came to my senses, Ong was laughing at me. Worse he was looking at me sadly, with the loss of respect that always attends moments when you discover others' frailties, even those who show up on your doorstep and ask about your criminal record.

"So you were saying about referees and sex?" he asked.

I was an idiot.

When I interviewed him, Ljubomir Barin was facing his seventh major heart operation in six years. He portrayed himself as a victim. I asked if he meant that he was singled out because Bernard Tapie was a socialist politician. He agreed saying he was simply caught in the middle of a French political battle.

After the interviews with Zen-Ruffinen, UEFA officials, and the other top international referees, it was difficult not to have a slight sympathy for him. He was, in his pimping arrangements for referees, simply doing what seems to have been a common practice for some clubs. Were all top European clubs doing these things? No. But enough soccer clubs provided women for the referees that it came as no surprise to anyone.

A key question remains: if offering women and gifts to referees was a relatively common practice in the 1980s and 1990s, does it still happen in the world of soccer now?

If you listen to some UEFA officials, you'll believe it does not. They claim that after *another* scandal, this time featuring a heavy-gambling referee soliciting bribes, everything was changed. There were new rules and regulations to stop any corruption. For example, referees are now no longer paid directly by the clubs. In the past, at the end of the game, the club officials handed the referees an envelope with cash in it for their match fee. (You have to wonder why it took them forty years to figure out why that might not be a good idea.)

However, if you listen to Robert Hoyzer or Carolina Salgado, you'll believe that it is business as usual in the world of soccer.

In a Teutonic land of purportedly humourless public rectitude, Robert Hoyzer was an example of all that could, but shouldn't, go wrong. He is a tall, gorgeous German man who had a great career ahead of him as a referee. In his mid-twenties, he was being groomed and brought up the refereeing ranks. But he also fixed a series of matches with a group of Croatian gamblers.

In January 2005, four of his refereeing colleagues claimed that he had fixed matches. Hoyzer originally denied the charges; but then, urged on by his girlfriend, he confessed. His girlfriend quickly dumped him, and the German public turned on him with a display of hatred rarely seen.

Two weeks later, he and his lawyer appeared on television to state his side of the story. The studio audience booed him. The host was astonished, claiming that he had never seen anything like this before: his program was no Jerry Springer type show, and it was after all Germany. The lawyer talked of "the middle ages."

Hoyzer was at that time the chief prosecution witness for an investigation that would, he claimed, spread across Europe. "With the time I have spent and the contacts I made in this business I suspect it isn't only limited to Germany, and could affect the whole of Europe." He claimed in the interview: "They [the German Football Association] thought it would be limited to just one referee, but they nailed the right one with me. It was like hitting a hornet's nest. I've got a lot of information."

It seemed to be remarkably similar to Barin's allegations to the French prosecutors ten years before. The same things were said about "tidal waves" spreading across soccer. And the investigation, at first, seemed to go well. Based on Hoyzer's confessions, the German police raided nineteen homes and offices and claimed that they had at least twenty-five people under investigation – including four referees and fourteen players. Hoyzer's information led police to allegedly fixed matches in Germany, Austria, Turkey, and Greece. The betting ring had also placed wagers in a range of countries, including England.

A number of Bundesliga referees, including Torsten Koop, were removed from their duties for not telling the authorities they had been approached by Hoyzer to fix a match. Koop claimed he rejected the proposal, but the German soccer authorities, at this point, talked tough: "The name Koop won't ever surface on the referees' list again," spokesman Manfred Amerell told the German news agency DPA.

But four days after Hoyzer's infamous interview and the storm of negative publicity, the German police arrested him and he was charged with eight counts of fraud.

There followed twenty-eight months of convoluted investigations and courtroom appearances, but at the end of everything only one referee, out of all the ones accused, ended up in prison: Robert Hoyzer. There were a few suspended sentences handed out, two of the Croatian gamblers ended up in prison, but no players went to jail. The honest but overly kind Torsten Koop even went back to refereeing Bundesliga matches.

This leaves us with two situations: either Hoyzer is a corrupt referee who is lying and this was an isolated case that affected only a few matches; or Hoyzer is the Gong Jianping of European soccer: a corrupt referee who actually told the truth about how corrupt soccer was and then paid the price for everyone else's corruption.

I followed the story over those months. I visited Germany a couple of times and spoke to sources close to the investigation. Some of these sources, at one point, told me the second version was true and that the German authorities were trying to limit the story of Hoyzer because they were embarrassed about the upcoming World Cup. Later, that seemed to change their minds and assured me that all was well with the investigation.

Whatever the truth, Hoyzer made a few more allegations that, by now, will sound very familiar. He claimed that it was "standard practice" for club officials to take referees to brothels before matches. He said he had direct experience of this with other officials in the lap-dancing bars of Leipzig.

But more importantly, much more importantly, he alleges that he saw, in the car of the Croatian gambler, lists of UEFA referees and delegates for upcoming Champions League, UEFA Cup, and national team games a week before the matches. These lists are supposed to be top secret and available only two days before the matches. A group of gamblers, purportedly linked to organized crime, according to Hoyzer, had those secret lists and presumably they did not have them simply to inquire on the referee's health.

I asked some UEFA contacts about this alleged breaking of the sanctity of their organization, and they claimed rather vaguely that, "Yes, we wondered about that, but we don't understand how he could have got those lists." When I asked the German police, they said it was outside their jurisdiction to investigate.

I am not trying to excuse Hoyzer's actions in working for a Croatian match-fixing gang. His is a story of almost ancient Greek proportions: a good-looking man who almost had it all and threw it away to get a little more. But is he a pathological fantasist or is there still a deep vein of corruption running through European soccer?

I tried to interview him to find out. I visited the jail where he is currently serving time. If I had to go to prison, I would like to be there. In the front office was a note taped to the wall: "The prison closes at six o'clock. Prisoners are requested not to climb over the fence and sign in and out when they leave the building." Hoyzer was there, but he declined to see me, and the next day I got a frosty note from his lawyer asking me not to contact Hoyzer again. I respected his wishes. However, someone who was much more forthcoming was one of the men who was supposed to have seduced Hoyzer into match-fixing: Milan Sapina.

We met over coffees at his bar – the Café King – in central Berlin. Sapina was the oldest brother of the Croatians who ran the gambling fixes. He was dressed in jeans, a tight tan T-shirt, and a tighter smile. His left leg shook intensely throughout the interview, but he was remarkably cordial and polite. I had shown up at the bar late one night and asked to speak to him about match-fixing. He was with a couple of muscular friends in a booth. We shook hands and then discovered that neither of us could speak one another's language. My German is restricted to ordering coffee and polite greetings: he claimed that his English was better, but not enough to have a conversation. I said I would return the next morning with someone to translate, Sapina agreed, and I left feeling that he would not show up. However, the next morning he was there on time and spent almost an hour talking about match-fixing with me.

Ironically, he completely supports Hoyzer's view that sex is still used frequently between clubs and referees:

This is normal. Normal. It is standard that the club will pay an ex-referee to meet the referee at the airport. He welcomes them to town. Takes them to a pub. He tries to be as friendly as possible with them. Some are successful in doing so, others not. But it is part of the culture. A lot of referees go out and have some fun. It is normal to go for a beer. Women are normal. Everyone wants women. It is not necessarily that you are influencing the referee. However, referees are also men. They are human. But to influence them properly you do not say anything direct. It is all the indirect way.

He also thinks that his brother and Hoyzer were "small fish . . . and that there are much bigger fish in the aquarium." I asked who the "big fish" were. He smiled and said, "It is better that I don't say. It is better that I keep my head down at this moment. Both me and my brother know a lot of stories, but it is better to keep our mouths shut." The answer led us right to the key question: how did they get hold of the list of the UEFA referees? He looked at me quizzically and smiled a very, very ironic smile. "Look, we have a lot of good relations with people. There are a lot of people who care. We are friends with lots of people . . . [But if the authorities say it did not happen?] They are right."

On the other side of Europe is Carolina Salgado. Salgado was a prostitute who slept with a sporting official. In fact, she slept with one of the most powerful men in Portuguese and European soccer: the former boss of Jose Mourinho and owner of the team – Porto – that won two European Champions Leagues, the European Cup, one UEFA Cup, and the Portuguese league championship twenty-one times, Jorge Nuno Pinto da Costa. Ask some Portuguese people about da Costa and a resigned expression creeps across their face; they look like English people do when they speak about the dreadful English weather. He is a Portuguese phenomenon that is so dreadful, so powerful, and seemingly so natural to the environment that there is a sort of perverse, resigned pride in him.

Salgado was working in a brothel called No Calor da Noite (The Heat of the Night) when she met Da Costa. They ended up together for six years. But Salgado wrote that the world of Portuguese soccer, "compared with what I saw and experienced at No Calor da Noite, the world of brothels is almost like a daycare centre."

I am not sure what a Portuguese daycare centre looks like, but Portuguese soccer has long been beset by claims of corruption. Allegations of mafia involvement are almost routine. The use of sex bribes for referees has been detailed in several editions of the comprehensive book by Marinho Neves, *Golpe de Estadio*. João Vale e Azevedo, the former president of the top club Benfica, served four years in jail for soccer-related fraud. And for European fans, there are allegations of top fixes stretching back to the 1984 semifinal of the Cup Winners' Cup, when Porto played against Alex Ferguson's Aberdeen. The referee of the game was allegedly bribed by a man, Fernando Barata, a former president of the Farense soccer club, working on behalf of . . . Pinto da Costa.

So it was with something of an air of resignation that Portugal woke up on April 20, 2004, to find that Portuguese police had arrested sixteen people after listening to more than 16,000 covertly recorded telephone conversations. Pinto da Costa was implicated. Among other charges, he denied arranging a referee's visit to a brothel and his entertainment with several Brazilian prostitutes. He claimed that it was impossible, as the referee was gay. The referee threatened to sue him. And the investigation against da Costa seemed about to disintegrate into a farce. Then Salgado, by this time da Costa's ex-girlfriend, published her autobiography.

As successful acts of vengeance by an ex-girlfriend go, it is pretty well up there. The book became an immediate bestseller and a topic of conversation across the country. In it, she alleged that da Costa would regularly invite referees to their home to seek their favours. She also claimed that someone, somewhere in the police tipped him off about the investigation, so da Costa was able to escape to Spain to give him time to prepare his defence.

The captain of Porto defended da Costa, saying he was "a great president [who is] very ethical." But Vitor Reis, the then-head of Portugal's Association of Football Referees, welcomed the police's action. "It is time to once and for all establish who in football and refereeing has ethics and who does not," said Reis.

Reis is absolutely right. It is time for European soccer to establish once and for all who has ethics, particularly as the Asian fixers are arriving amongst them.

Unfortunately, that does not seem likely to happen.

THE GUNS ARE FACING THE WRONG WAY

We are still behind the eight ball with the Internet. We don't know what to do. It is a very scary problem. Betting companies sometimes supply us with information. But it is very difficult, as people can bet on games anywhere in the world.

I played my last ever organized game of soccer in Singapore. I wish I could say that my last game was one of those half-hours of brilliance that occurred to me so rarely. Instead, by soccer's standards, I was a fat man, woefully out of shape, melting into the sandy pitch. Worse, by some misplaced sense of confidence, I had made the mistake of talking myself up. When I arrived at the field, a guest of the star player, I saw that most players, dressed in their large shorts, had tiny little legs that peeped out like twigs surrounded by billowing sails. Better yet, at least half of my teammates had larger stomachs than me. Ha! I thought, I am clearly better than this lot. I was not. The low point was when I slid in to take the ball off an opposing player – fairly I, and the referee, thought. He, however, did not think it was a fair tackle. He tried to jump feet first on to my chest. I raised my foot and caught him as he came down. A fight started. It was, all in all, a dreadful performance.

The best part of the game, for me, was that it was on the island of Sentosa, just off the coast of Singapore. Overlooking the field was the statue of Merlion, the half lion, half fish, that symbolizes Singapore. The other icon that so symbolizes Singapore to a certain generation of Europeans was a little farther away: Fort Siloso. It is the last remaining British-built fort against the Japanese from the Second World War.

The myth is that in peacetime the troops built the guns so that they all faced out to sea rather than the land where the eventual Japanese attack would come. It is one of those enduring myths that historians love to debunk. What is undeniable is that in the 1941–42 Malaya Campaign and the Siege of Singapore, the outnumbered Japanese outflanked, out-thought, and overran the British defences. They did so partly because the Allied generals underestimated the ability of the Japanese soldiers. They did so not based on intelligence reports, but on sheer racist ignorance. One set of Australian officers declared at the beginning of the campaign that they were disappointed because they wanted a "better enemy than the Japanese." They said this because, according to the conventional European wisdom of the time, Asians had bad eyesight and therefore could not shoot straight or fly modern planes.

The awful truth is that similar attitudes still persist today. Every major investigation against Asian match-fixers in soccer by European law enforcement has, like the Belgian inquiry, been squandered in a mixture of ignorance and ineptitude. The fixers have, effectively, done what the Japanese armies did so brilliantly in 1941–42 in Malaya: they have out-flanked and out-thought the European soccer associations, the legal gambling companies, and the police. These are the three defences that are supposed to be in place to defend the European game. There are many people who argue that these three are doing a superb job in defending the credibility of the sport in Europe against any fixers from Asia.

They are wrong.

To begin with the gambling industry. They *hate* fixing. It takes money from them. They become the victims of well-orchestrated frauds. But there is a worldwide revolution going on in their industry that is provoking fundamental changes in the way they do business. It is, of course, the Internet and it is changing the gambling industry as surely as it did the music business.

Lars Jensen (*) has been swept up in the revolution. He is one of the sports odds compilers for a Scandinavian national lottery. His company, owned by the government, offers gamblers the ability to bet on sporting events around Europe. "The growth in this field has been incredible," he told me. "Five years ago, we had 90 per cent of the sports betting market in this country. Now our sports market has grown four times as large, but our share of the market has shrunk to 25 per cent."

It is the same for the FBI cops working the investigations of the Southern District of New York. It is the place to be if you are a cop in the United States. It is from there that Rudolph Giuliani began to eat into the power of the Five Families of the New York mob. It is from there that the Department of Justice investigations into Osama bin Laden were held. And it is from there that the FBI is cracking down on illegal Internet sports gambling in the United States. Special Agent David Velazquez is one of the lead investigators on the frontline against Internet gambling. "The power of this industry is mind-boggling," he told me. "We estimate that the size of the U.S. Internet sports betting industry – so that is including poker as well as sports – at $100 billion a year."

Velazquez helped put together a case against two Canadian executives who ran an Internet gambling payment company, Neteller, out of an offshore haven on the Isle of Man. The company finances listed in court documents show the power of the revolution. In 2000, Neteller Inc, was a small company that had gross revenues in the United States of $289,000; by 2006, when it had changed its corporate structure to Neteller PLC, that number had increased by over 58,000 per cent to $169 million. Perhaps more pertinently, the amount processed by the company from all gambling transactions in the entire world had gone from the low millions in 2000 to more than $10.6 billion by 2006. And Neteller was simply one of dozens of companies that helped gamblers pay their debts online.

This revolution is, for the most part, benign: a case of people innocently wagering on their favourite team. Even at UEFA headquarters in Nyon, it is possible to find soccer officials betting on games from their work computers. According to the optimists, it has made fixing of any sports fixture in the world next to impossible. But listen to the pessimists and the Internet revolution has aided the fixers working for illegal Asian gambling syndicates in a clear and significant way. They are using this phenomenon of international Internet gambling to bring sophisticated match corruption to leagues that have never even dreamed of it.

It is a daunting situation for any soccer association. One honest European soccer official told me, off the record, that:

> We are still behind the eight ball with the Internet. We don't know what to do. It is a very scary problem. Betting companies sometimes supply us with information. But it is very difficult as people can bet on games anywhere in the world.

On the record, of course, the soccer associations and some of the betting companies often say something else. Frequently, their spokespeople argue in public that the Internet has made fixing more difficult, if not impossible, because every bet is tracked and that honest bookies can see how the betting line moves. They can deduce what is going on. They can go to the soccer associations and can warn them about every possible fixed game that will occur.

This is dangerous nonsense.

Let us start with the facts. The most well-known case of Asian fixers in European soccer over the last few years was Ye Zheyun's incursion into Belgian soccer. Bookmakers and their allies point out that the alarm was first raised by the British Internet betting exchange Betfair in October 2005 because of suspicious betting patterns.

However, Ye Zheyun started fixing games in the Belgian league in early December 2004, ten and a half months *before* Betfair raised the alarm. What happened in the fall of 2005, was that Ye Zheyun had fixed so many games so blatantly that the information about the fixes had got out of the immediate circle of people involved. A key part of a good fix is control of information. Between December 2004 and October 2005, Ye Zheyun and his associates had controlled the information closely enough for him to be able to fix without detection on the European gambling market. But gradually, the information surrounding the fixes began to leak out. It was a secret that was too good to be kept. Suddenly, the bets on the fixed games skyrocketed, as many people along the chain of information either bet themselves or told more people, who then bet.

The bookmakers and their allies point out that some of the major European gambling companies, including Betfair, have now signed deals with UEFA and even FIFA to share any information about possible fixes as it comes along. FIFA even trumpets its "early warning system" as an efficient net to catch any potential fixes. It is, however, a net with very large mesh. In fact, it is largely irrelevant, because Asian fixers do not bet with Betfair or the English betting companies or European sports lotteries. They bet on the Asian gambling market. This is why it took eleven months for a European betting agency to detect that there was something wrong in Belgium. The real fixers, the people close to the fix, kept the secret by betting on the Asian market.

Many people in the gambling industry claim, publicly, that if an Asian fixer put a bet on in Shanghai, Johor Bahru, or Jakarta, the market could still trace the bet. They say that the old market discrepancies no longer exist with the Internet. They are right in some ways. There used to be massive discrepancies between the Asian and European gambling markets. Information that almost every bettor knew in Europe was largely unknown in Asia. Ten years ago in the early days of the Internet revolution, vast amounts of money could be made in this information gap. Gamblers call it "arbitrage," and there are some bettors who still specialize in playing the odds off between different bookmakers on either side of the planet. But now they have to be quick; it is rare that one bookmaker will be out of line with the worldwide betting odds for longer than ten minutes.

This is the public argument that gambling companies make: that because of the Internet there is no longer anywhere in the world where a fixer can work without being detected. Any bookmaker who takes a vast amount of money on one side from a fixer will quickly realize there is something wrong. There are even companies that specialize in scan-ning the gambling market for any shifts that may be caused by fixing.

The problem is that the fixers are not stupid.

They spend enormous energy calculating when to put their money into the market for a fixed game and the Internet has actually made it far easier for them to get money on to a fix. In the pre-Internet days, it was sometimes difficult for a fixer to get enough money into the gambling market to make the fix worthwhile. They had to hire "beards" and "runners" – people who could put their money on without seeming to be connected with the fixers. Now with a click of the mouse the fixer can place bets with a half-dozen bookmakers around the world, and with a few elementary precautions, no one is the wiser.

Two, while a bookmaker or an "early warning system" can tell that the odds may have shifted in the illegal Asian market on a particular game, they cannot tell *how* much money has gone into the fix. So if an Asian fixer has bribed the underdog team to lose – so the stronger team will win – the fix is virtually undectable. The odds will change, but all are just going the way of the team everyone expects to win anyway.

Most importantly, when a fixer fixes the gambling market, it is actu-ally *more* difficult to do it in a small league like Belgium. Even carefully hiding their bets, there is so little money placed on these games that it is difficult to get a lot of money on to the fix. But ironically, the bigger the game, the easier it is for the fixers to fix the market. When there is a lot of money being bet, the fixers can get a lot on the fixed team. If they are discreet and fix the weaker team to lose, then no bookmakers, no matter how carefully they study the market, will notice the fix.

Finally, if the gambling industry detects a fixed match, it does not change much in practical terms. Betfair, ten months after the fixes began, notified the Belgian soccer authorities that there was something strange going on in the betting market. The Belgian Football Association mis-placed the letter. However, even if they had managed to keep track of their correspondence, what could they do? In the Sarawak versus Singapore game that swamped the Singapore gambling company, the team officials marched into the dressing room and shouted at all the players, who hung their heads – but somehow the result the fixers wanted was achieved.

So if the betting industry is a willing but often ineffective partner in stopping fixes, what about the police? Have there been effective investigations by European police into the presence of Asian fixers? The answer is no.

14

NO POINT IN GOING OUT THERE

No one wants to know about this case. Everyone wants to
believe in a clean game. So the German Football Association
does not want to talk about this case.

The police investigation and subsequent trial of Bruce Grobbelaar in
the 1990s so dominates the issue of fixing that almost everyone in Asia
or the U.K. thinks of that case when they think of match corruption.
Grobbelaar was one of the best goalkeepers in the world. It was his professional misfortune to have been born a Zimbabwean. If he had played
for a country that had got to the World Cup, he would have become a
huge world star. As it was, he did none too shabbily. He played for the
same Liverpool team as Ian Rush. Together they won one European Cup,
three FA Cups, and six league championships – all with a flow of exhilarating and exuberant soccer. The team was a giant of British soccer, and
at the back of the team was the irrepressible Bruce Grobbelaar. He was a
true character. He once kept goal with an umbrella. His spaghetti legs
routine was supposed to have won Liverpool the European Cup in 1984.
He also agreed to a corrupt deal to fix soccer games.

In 1994, the *Sun*, a British tabloid newspaper, secretly videotaped him
talking about the alleged fixes with his best friend, Chris Vincent, who
betrayed him. The recordings made for racy reading. Among the many
purportedly sensational statements, Grobbelaar seems to be explicitly

discussing the Asian fixers and their organization. He claims that "The Short Man," later identified as a Malaysian living in London named Richard – Heng Suan – Lim, had linked him with a gambling syndicate in Kuala Lumpur. Here is an edited excerpt from the conversations about the purported head of the gang and his position in the country:

> Do you think I went out to Kuala Lumpur on the off chance? Absolutely not. Because the Short Man had said, "Any time you want to go to the Far East, you and your wife can go – I'll sort it out." I got an offer to go to Kuala Lumpur to play, . . . the boss man there, if it is the same person, he's fucking big in Malaysia. He'll say, that man . . . pow! That's it. Finished!

After the *Sun* published its exposé in November 1994 – "Grobbelaar Took Bribes to Fix Games" ran one headline – there were five trials in British courtrooms around the accusations. The score line going into the fifth legal proceeding was: one draw (mistrial) for criminal fraud; one win for Grobbelaar (acquittal) for criminal fraud; one win for Grobbelaar on libel against the *Sun*; one loss for Grobbelaar (on appeal). Grobbelaar's defence was that he was an innocent man entrapped by an aggressive and sleazy British press. The unsuccessful criminal fraud prosecution team argued that they had been unable to get a conviction because the juries were so starstruck (during one trial, a juror had asked Grobbelaar to sign autographs) that they would never have convicted a top soccer player of anything. Grobbelaar argued that he had not been convicted because he was innocent. So it was off on the final appeal to the highest court in Britain, the House of Lords.

Essentially, each of the trials had boiled down to the following issue: Chris Vincent – Grobbelaar's friend – was such a squalid, little fellow that it would be difficult to trust him if he said "I love you" to his mum. The only real, hard evidence against Grobbelaar was the transcript of the videotape where he purportedly discussed the tactics of fixing matches. The Law Lords looked long and hard at the Grobbelaar tapes. They wrote twenty-three pages of closely reasoned argument and by a 4 to 1 majority, they said, in essence, "Oh puuuuleeeze! Come on, of course, the tape shows that Grobbelaar had agreed to fix matches. What we cannot say is whether he actually fixed the matches."

At the end of all the trials, there are two undeniable facts. First, there was a corrupt agreement between Grobbelaar and some Asian gamblers. We know who those gamblers were, but we do not know the exact nature of their work – were they bookies or merely rich men who liked to bet? Why people don't know about those gamblers is because of an extraordinary piece of investigative incompetence. David Thomas, a British journalist, wrote a superb book, *Foul Play*, about the trial. It was mostly a psychological exploration of the relationship between Vincent and Grobbelaar. However, toward the end of the book, it contained this excerpt about the investigation:

> When the *Sun* returned from the first trip to the Far East without any solid leads, the police had known that there was no point in going out there themselves. They had no legal authority overseas, no power to detain or interrogate suspects. The only circumstances in which it would have been worth pursuing enquiries in Indonesia, Malaysia and Singapore would have been if they had known exactly whom they were going to speak to, what questions they would ask and what answers they would receive.

When I first read this, I thought it was so ridiculous that it could not possibly be true. The idea that police are supposed to follow tabloid journalists in their investigations or that they only conduct inquiries when they know the results beforehand surely must have been an error on Thomas's part. It was not. I checked with U.K. law enforcement sources close to the trial and they all confirmed that no British officer had gone out to Asia. Indeed, they used the same language that Thomas had used about "there being no point" if they didn't know who to talk to. I was so startled by this obvious ineptitude that I figured they must be trying to cover their sources. So I checked with some of the lawyers associated with the case. They, too, confirmed that no British police officer had gone out to Asia. I still thought that there must be a cover-up somewhere, so when I was in Asia I asked sources at the Royal Malaysian Police and the Singapore anti-corruption agency. None of the officers ever remembered any British police officer coming out to investigate match-fixing.

What is truly extraordinary is that while the investigation was going on in England, at exactly the same time senior members of the Royal Malaysian Police and the Singapore anti-corruption agency were cracking down on the networks of match-fixers in their country. If the European and Asian police had joined forces then, soccer might have become a great deal safer and this book might never have come to be written.

The second undeniable fact is that a member of a dangerous and violent Asian triad group was connected to "Richard" Heng Suan Lim, a.k.a. The Short Man, and that this contact would try again to fix English Premier League matches.

It took three attempts and four bullets and still "George" Wai Hen Cheung could not take down his man.

It was September 7, 1991, and the Shui Fong Triad in England was facing problems. A new group of Hong Kong "businessmen" had come into the U.K. and they were trying to take over the criminal group. So Cheung, a man who would later serve time for extortion, racketeering, drug smuggling, and carving up a man's face with a double-bladed Stanley knife, was instructed to shoot one of the interlopers – a man called Ying Kit Lam. One fall night, he followed Ying Kit Lam through the streets of London's Chinatown. He had been planning to shoot him the previous evening in a Chinese disco but had failed when Lam suddenly went to visit a brothel-cum-casino in Maida Vale in West London. This time as Cheung moved in to shoot Lam, two teenaged girls got in the way and he had to turn around quickly and pretend to stare at a window.

Finally, Cheung had his opportunity. He came up behind Lam, stuck his gun in his back, and fired twice. But even this did not go according to plan. The wounded Lam grabbed him and the two of them fought in a deadly struggle in the middle of the street. Cheung fired twice more, but his gun jammed and he fled, dropping the weapon.

The eventual trial at the Old Bailey was one of the most intriguing in triad history. For the first time, a made member of a Chinese gang – "George" Wai Hen Cheung – publicly described his initiation rites. He talked about going at two o'clock in the morning to the basement of the Princess Gardens restaurant in Fulham. There a gang member, Ng Lo, a.k.a. No. 5, told him and the other initiates to take off their clothes and any jewellery. They were to kneel on the floor in front of a table covered with red paper, a pot with burning joss sticks, a bottle of wine, and paper cut into the shape of a man. Cheung then had to hold the burning joss stick with four fingers of his left hand and five fingers of his right and repeat a series of traditional oaths. The most important of these oaths, he testified, were: "never to betray a brother, never to steal from a brother, and never to commit adultery with a brother's wife. If we broke these oaths, we would be punished severely. I was told I would be crippled or killed."

Despite the warning, Cheung testified at the trial that he had been ordered to do the shooting by six members of the Shui Fong Triad. One of them was "Danny" Wai Yuen Liu, thirty-one, who at the time had a conviction for helping to run a stolen and forged credit card ring. In the trial four of the defendants were acquitted of planning the attack, although two were convicted of visiting Cheung in prison and threatening him if he testified. Then Liu disappeared from public life until six years later when he surfaced in the most serious attempts to manipulate a soccer match England has seen.

On February 10, 1999, Liu was driving a BMW containing two Malaysian criminals. As they left, Charlton FC's stadium in southeast London, armed members of the Scotland Yard's Organised Crime Squad arrested them. It was a dramatic ending to a series of fixed matches, called the "floodlights swindles." Essentially, the scam had involved a number of English soccer games that were being televised in Asia. The games were all between teams of varying strengths. But if the underdog was either tied with the favourite or losing by only one goal and it was the second half of the game (so the bets could not be called off), the Asian fixers would switch the lights off. Since most of the Asian betting public were gambling on the favourites winning, the fixers were estimated to make up to £30 million per match.

The gang was caught when their English assistant had unsuccessfully tried to recruit another man to help them. There were three members of the group. They were all arrested, and two of them, and possibly the third, have interesting connections to the other match-fixing trials. The first of these men was "Danny" Wai Yuen Liu, the driver who had been involved, although acquitted, in the triad shooting trial. The second was "Mark" Chee Kew Ong, who had been arrested for illegal gambling in Malaysia. In 1987, Ong had written to "Richard" Heng Suan "The Short Man" Lim, the alleged go-between in the Grobbelaar match-fixing plot, saying, "You must try your best to tackle Wimbledon and some other club [*sic*]. Make use of your time, for you can do it." Lim had just arrived in London and was trying to cultivate connections in the soccer world. Ong told Lim that they could both make a lot of money on the Kuala Lumpur gambling markets with the right kind of information.

The third member of the gang was also called Lim – Eng Hwa. He was from a small northern state in Malaysia called Penang. All three Asians in the floodlights gang were convicted to time in jail. It was the one unequivocal success that European law enforcement has had against Asian fixers, but the information does not seem to have permeated to other European police forces.

The most recent trial took place in Sitzungssaal 1 – or Trial Room Number 1 – in the State Regional Court of Frankfurt. It was, like many things connected to the justice system, slightly underwhelming. It was a modern courtroom with subdued neon lights and a large seal on the wall. Five judges sat behind a long desk at the top of the room.

On the left side of the courtroom sat the seven defendants and their fourteen lawyers. Most of them – at least, the defendants – slouched down behind the low-slung table like a bored UN delegation. On the right side of the court, facing them – alone – for the prosecution sat a young, attractive, blonde woman.

It was the most important case of Asian match-fixing in Europe since the floodlights case and there was practically no one watching it. The case was so obscure that I had spent forty-five minutes in the court-house trying to find the right room. Few of the officials had known where the trial was, or what it was about.

In the actual courtroom, there were exactly three people watching the proceedings: an elderly lawyer in an ill-fitting suit who turned out to be the German Football Association's representative, a fat, Lebanese-looking fellow wearing a bright lime green T-shirt who continually spoke into a cellphone, and me.

The case had been jogging along since March 2006, when the German police announced they had caught a gang of unsuccessful fixers who had tried to rig ten games in the Austrian and German leagues. At the centre of the trial was yet another Malaysian Chinese by the name of Bee Wah Lim, or William. He, like the Lim at the centre of the floodlights trial, had been born in Penang, a northern state of Malaysia, in 1962. He was, according to the press reports, a poor hapless cook who had lost at least 700,000 euros in attempting to fix ten games in the German and Austrian leagues. I had wondered about the case. It seemed strange to me that a purportedly unemployed chef could afford to lose hundreds of thousands in euros fixing games.

Then even the small press interest died and I heard no more about the case until I phoned a contact in June 2007. He was connected to the

Asian fixers and told me that one of them was in Frankfurt. What was he doing in Frankfurt? I thought. It was the off-season. There was no soccer. He is not the type to get on planes for the fun of it. What business would be so important that he would want to go to Frankfurt? Then I remembered the trial.

I knew nothing and phoned the court lawyers. They told me that Lim had been in jail for more than a year, but that week he had agreed to confess. So on a dreary Friday afternoon in June, he revealed to the court how he had arranged the fixes. His defence lawyer claimed that his wealthy wife had died, leaving him with a lot of money. Lim had used some of the money to get a Serbian former professional soccer player, Dragan Anić, and a Lebanese petty criminal, to approach the players to throw games. The lawyers read into the court record the text messages between the accused. Then the judges put a 30,000 euros bail on Lim and asked him to come back next week to the court.

He disappeared, just like Michael Vana, the Czech star player in Singapore. He disappeared the same day my Asian fixer source was in Frankfurt. And no one – not the police, not the prosecutors, not his own lawyer – knew where he had gone. I asked the German law enforcement officials what happened to him. They replied:

> We think he left the country. We were told that he left the country, but we really don't know. There was a court date the next week and he did not show up for it. He has a number of passports: British, Malaysian, Singaporean, Chinese. He travels under them all, so he could be anywhere.

What they also do not know was where exactly Lim was betting his money. They don't know with whom or which Asian organization. They didn't even know what language he might have been talking to his contacts in Asia (Hokkien or Hakka would be the answer). His methods, manner, and finances all suggest that Lim may have been connected to a far larger organization. Yet the German authorities let him go. It is yet another example of how the Asian fixers completely outwit the European authorities. Here was a prime catch, a man who used precisely the same methods and manner of fixing matches that Ye Zheyun was using in Belgium at precisely the same time. But again the Asian fixer was allowed to disappear: and again the German police, like the English police before them, had not been to Asia and had no idea of the scale of organization that may have been behind Lim.

There is no suspicion that the police were corrupt. Rather, they were purely and simply ignorant. To paraphrase the former U.S. secretary of defense Donald Rumsfeld, they did not know what they did not know. But how good was the German Football Association? One of the police officers said something interesting to me, when we spoke about why there was so little discussion of the trial:

> No one wants to know about this case. Everyone wants to believe in a clean game. So the German Football Association does not want to talk about this case.

This is not to suggest that there was an explicit cover-up, the German FA did form a match-fixing committee to look into the Hoyzer allegations, but it does echo the comments from the English detectives and lawyers who were connected to the Grobbelaar investigation. One of them said, "At first, they wanted to help. But as the trial started, the soccer world banded together and would not help us at all. They wanted the bad publicity to go away."

The final chapter of the Siege of Singapore in 1942 was, if possible, the most shameful of all. The outnumbered Japanese army had come so far, so quickly that their supply lines were shattered: they were to the north of Singapore but were at the end of their equipment. The Allies had 120,000 men in Singapore; the guns, contrary to legend, could swing around and face north – and yet they surrendered. There is all kinds of debate around the surrender but the psychological side of what happened to the Allied army is clear: they panicked. The streets of the city were full of chaos and disorder. Few people knew what to do. There was no effective central command and from stupid overconfidence based on racial prejudice, they turned quickly to stupid unnecessary panic.

The same is true of the European sports world.

Three years ago when I first started speaking out about the Asian match-fixers, I was greeted, for the most part, with skepticism and disbelief. It was a little like being an Old Testament prophet. I would come wandering out of the desert of research with tales of destruction and doom about the sport being in peril. People would listen politely but essentially not believe me. After a couple of years, I noticed that people had reached the rationalization stage: now they believed there was a problem but they would say things like, "Sure there is fixing, but it is only in the lower divisions, not the big games. The top teams would never fix a match." Now they have reached the stage of resignation. "There is nothing that anyone can do," they say shrugging the problem off as if match-fixing was as inevitable as cold in the winter.

They were wrong to deny there was a problem, they were wrong to think that top teams cannot fix games, and they are wrong to believe that there is nothing that can be done. I have shown that there is, in some clubs, a culture of supplying women to referees before big matches. There is a very easy, simple way of stopping that culture dead in its tracks – have more female match officials. "Hey, did you like the girl I sent to your room last night?" becomes, in most cases, redundant if you are talking to a woman. So if soccer associations *really* want to stop that culture, they should simply fast-track women officials. Of the top referees in Europe at the moment, the ones who handle the big Champions League matches and European Championship, none are women.

Want to stop the players from taking any bribes? Tell them about the change in their status – from coveted friend to slave – when the match-fixers start "calling the fix." The U.S. National Collegiate Athletic Association does that: they have the former Mafia capo Michael Franzese lecture their players about how the mob really works. At the moment, not a single European soccer association has any education or training for their players on how to avoid criminals or the dangers of dealing with them.

I am not trying to be unfair to the European soccer associations or the police. There are inept and incompetent officials among them; there are also very good people trying to the best of their abilities to defend the sport and the law. But they do lack some very basic tools. For example, very few European soccer associations have a security department, which is standard in North American sports, like the NFL and NHL. Not even UEFA, a sports body that runs the Champions League and European Football Championship (tournaments that produce billions of dollars in spinoff revenue), has a unit specifically interested in protecting and policing the game. There is no one who can tell interested but uninformed law enforcement officials in other countries, possibly unrelated facts – for example, that there was a Richard Lim and a William Lim at the heart of two major match-fixing trials. Or that Richard Lim had been connected with a triad member who was involved in later match-fixing attempts, and that all of the cases had links back to illegal organized crime syndicates in Malaysia, Singapore, Hong Kong, and Vietnam. Until such organizations are put into place, then the fixing will continue.

Outside the Frankfurt courtroom, after the day's proceedings had ended, I introduced myself to the lawyer from the German Football Association. He told me he was monitoring the case and that he had been on the Association's investigation committee of match-fixing. I took him to one side and explained what I did, who I was connected to, and that if he needed any corroborating information to vouch for my honesty I would be happy to make sure someone provided it to him. I gave him my e-mail addresses, phone numbers, and all my contact details. Finally, I told him that I suspected that the same Asian fixers who had escaped this particular trial may have successfully targeted the Bundesliga, the top German league. The lawyer's response? He ran away. He disappeared out of the court, past the security scanner, and out the door waving his battered briefcase at me as if to ward off any more knowledge. To this day, I have not heard from him. His response is typical of the reaction I have met from European police. As a researcher, it is not my job to work for the police, but on several occasions, the fixes that I was hearing about were occurring at such an enormously high level that I felt it was my public duty to go to the police. I did not walk into an ordinary police station and ask to speak to the duty officer. Rather, I went to units that had been organizing criminal investigations into match-fixing. I offered to brief them on what I knew. None of them took me up on the offer. It's too bad, because the Asian fixers came back, and I believe they fixed some of the very highest games in the world.

Robert Hoyzer (left) refereeing a fixed game. A player tries to protest one of the calls.

Café King in central Berlin, where many of the Hoyzer fixes were organized.

The author and Milan Sapina, one of the fixers who helped Robert Hoyzer.

The author and Rajendran "Pal" Kurusamy, the former match-fixer in the Malaysian-Singapore League. Kurusamy served several years in prison and has now retired from any fixing.

The ticket scam in action with German police about to stop any photographs.

Celebrations after Brazil's first goal against Ghana at the Dortmund Stadium.

The reach of soccer: a bar in Accra, Ghana, advertising a match played in Toronto, Canada, between an African and an Asian team, and another Latin American match.

Richard Kingson (holding the ball) during a practice on the beach.

The hard stare of one of the best midfielders in the world: Sulley Muntari of Portsmouth and Ghana.

The intense Michael Oti Adjei interviewing Asamoah Gyan, the star forward of the Ghana national team.

Luciano Moggi (kicking the ball), the Juventus general manager, in 2005. At the end of the season, Italian police released his incriminating telephone conversations.

Alaattin Çakici, the Turkish gangster who had connections with the Beşiktaş soccer club.

After being interviewed by the Belgian police for match-fixing, Ye Zheyun fled and has never been seen by officials again.

Dmitri Chepel, in his days as president of the Russian team Baltika Kaliningrad.

The girls of the Mathare United Under-14 team handling press interviews in Norway after winning the tournament. Rosemary Njiru is speaking into the microphone.

Boys playing on the pitch where a young Stephen Appiah played in his hometown of Chorkor, Ghana.

THE
WORLD
CUP

PART III

PROLOGUE

My time in Oxford growed me up. Two incidents in particular changed me. The first was coincidental to the university. I was working as a freelance journalist during the spring vacation of 2004. I was back in Iraq, a year after the invasion. It was a normal morning at the Kirkuk Business Centre, in the oil-rich north of the country. The business centre had no customers in it. The halls had metaphorical tumbleweeds floating through the corridors. All the Iraqis working there told me that they were about to leave for places like West Virginia, Florida, or Los Angeles, or that they would do so as soon as their visa came through. Every American I spoke to spun a line about how the city was going to be "the Houston of the Middle East." Then they told me that they were leaving in nine days or two weeks or next month and their eyes told me a story of the fear in which they lived.

I got it then. I got it as if someone had tattooed it on my forehead. The United States had lost in Iraq. It had lost as surely and certainly as if it had been defeated in battle. It was over. Then I watched while, in the next three and half years, hundreds of thousands of people died to sustain something doomed to die anyway. They died needlessly. They died from a lack of imagination. They died because of bullshit. They died because thousands of other people in Washington, London, and obscure little caves in Pakistan kept pumping out clouds of bullshit to hide unpalatable facts – like it was an unwinnable war for any side and all that will be left after the years of misery and bullshit is chaos and death.

I had a similar experience one day while walking through one of the sub-branches of the Bodleian Library at Oxford. This part of the library was where the social science books are kept and, for the most part, students can actually see and touch these books. I walked past stacks and stacks of books and found a few, a painful few, books that I actually wanted to read. Actually, I found painfully few books that I could read. In recent years, the language used in the social sciences has become so increasingly obtuse and convoluted as to be unreadable.

It was not always so. My great-grandfather taught the now-forgotten art of rhetoric at a university. I have some of his writings. He was essentially trying to teach the trick of conveying complex ideas in a simple way. Most academic papers are now completely the opposite: they convey extraordinarily simple ideas in the most complex manner possible. In the 1930s, when my great-grandfather retired from his university, it was still possible for an intellectually curious person of almost any educational level, to pick up a university journal article and read it. That person may not have been able to understand every nuance, but they could get the general direction of the debate. It is no longer so. I defy most readers to pick up an article from sociology or psychology or linguistics and, as the author goes on about postmodernism or Foucault or structuralism, even understand the introduction.

Those experiences in Iraq and Oxford changed me. I began to look around and see factories of bullshit everywhere. I do not mean the usual corporate hucksterism that we see all the time on television. I mean places like government ministries, international development agencies, think tanks, Royal Commissions, corporate public relations departments that all pump out documents, studies, and reports that will never be read in a thick, turgid, seemingly unending stream.

Sport is different. At its best, sport gives us the truth. It is one of the rare places in this modern age where anything might happen. There may be a freak weather pattern. The underdog team, playing their hearts out, may achieve a miracle and upset the odds. The strong team, full of people who dedicated themselves to making the difficult – winning –

look easy, may inspire us. But whatever happens, sports, played honestly, is unscripted and truthful.

We all have our favourite moments in sport. One of mine came when I watched a cross-country ski race in the 1998 Olympics. If you know anything about ski racing, you know Bjorn Daehlie. He dominated his sport, winning twelve Olympic medals, fourteen World Championships, and setting a host of individual records. The race that I watched was typical Daehlie: he won easily. In fact, he finished so far ahead of the rest of the competition that he could have gone home, made a cup of tea, drank it, and returned before many of the other competitors had finished. But he did not leave. He waited by the finishing gate and shook hands with as many of the other competitors as he could. They left. He stayed. Daehlie remained behind because there was one final competitor who was taking part in almost his first ski race. He was at least twenty minutes behind everyone else. It was bitterly cold. Most of the spectators had left. Most of the media people had packed their gear and left. Most other athletes would have contented themselves with a handshake in the warmth of the Olympic Village. But not Daehlie. Not a man who demonstrated the true nature of what it is to be a champion. He waited. He waited in the freezing temperatures. He waited until he saw that last racer come around the final turn and he cheered him on, clapping and waving as the other man finished the race.

This is the beauty of sport. It produces events that inspire us to become bigger than who we really are, be it Liverpool and their extraordinary comeback in the Champions League Final; be it the courage of the survivors of the Munich air crash trying to win the FA Cup for their dead teammates; be it a ski champion at the end of a race cheering on another competitor.

Match-fixing destroys all of that. Match-fixing ruins our dreams and ideals. Match-fixing turns sport into one more area of predictable bullshit. I am going to introduce you to some people who claim they fixed a number of international soccer games. It may shock and disturb you, but from what I can tell, it is the truth.

THE STORY OF PAL

Lawyer:	In your evidence in the trial-within-a-trial, you told the judge you made millions [from match-fixing]?
Kurusamy:	Yes.
Lawyer:	How much?
Kurusamy:	Actually, I earned over $20 million.
Lawyer:	How much goes to yourself?
Kurusamy:	I also have to pay the players. After all those, I had $16 to $17 million for myself.
Lawyer:	This is one year's work in 1994?
Kurusamy:	Not one year, five months.

Rajendran Kurusamy is a genius. In a few years, he was able to take over much of the fixing in the Malaysian-Singapore league from the traditional Chinese-Malaysian horse racing gangs and essentially run the games. Kurusamy is not like Ljubomir Barin or other urbane, sophisticated fixers such as Luciano Moggi. He is not a player-agent, so he does not care too much about judging players' abilities. He does not dress in immaculate suits. He claims to be almost illiterate. He has a number of nicknames: Raj, Ah Sing, but the most popular is Pal. "Pal" in Tamil means "milk," and Kurusamy got the name after his first job delivering milk. His parents were Sri Lankan peasants. But Pal reckons he could teach most professors of psychology a thing or two about human nature.

"Any game, anywhere in the world, I could fix it," he told me confidently. "I could tell within the first twenty or thirty minutes of talking to him if a player would take a bribe. That's all it took."

I tracked him down after weeks of searching, including a night of touring around the Sembawang area of northern Singapore. The anti-corruption investigator that I spoke to would not give me Pal's address. "He is a very dangerous character, and I do not want to be responsible if anything bad happened to you." His organization had a lot to do with Pal. They had used him as a prosecution witness, then arrested and finally convicted him for his match-fixing. They were, seemingly, still frightened of him. One of the senior officers told me about one of their investigators being threatened by the match-fixing gangs with a snake in his car. He assured me solemnly, "Anything is possible with those people."

After I spoke to the police, I spent some time going through the court archives that detailed Pal's testimony of match-fixing. I found a number of addresses for him in the files and on a hot night in June set out to try to find him. Sembawang is a working-class area of Singapore, full of identical-looking apartment blocks between ill-used patches of grass. I walked up the long concrete stairs and banged on doors, only to be received by bewildered, non-gangster residents. After the third fruitless visit to an apartment, the taxi driver asked me what I was doing.

"I am trying to track down a bookie called Pal. Do you know him?" I replied.

The driver paled. "Yes, I know him. You don't want to be a clown. No monkey business with those people." He spent the next forty-five minutes telling me stories of Pal's gangster reach into the world of Singapore sports. Then every time he parked the car, he was careful to park it so we could get out of the lot quickly if necessary. He seemed very frightened.

He was not the only one. The legends of Pal's work spread all over Singapore sports. I met an official from the Football Association of

Singapore. He was petrified of talking to me publicly, so we met in an anonymous little coffee shop just off Bencoolen Street and he looked carefully around to make sure no one saw us together. It was not just the gangsters he feared, but the Singapore authorities. Like many soccer people in Singapore, he was still traumatized by the disappearance of the Czech midfielder Michael Vana. He felt that there had been some kind of covert deal between officials and Vana to get him out of the country: "I believe they let Vana go," he whispered across the table at me, "I think there may be some truth to the accusation that there were a lot of players in Singapore involved, and if they had put Vana in the dock he would have opened up a whole can of worms."

He was also concerned that one of his colleagues would find out that he had told me that he thought there was still match-fixing going on in the Singapore league. He need not have bothered; a year later there was yet another major trial publicly showing his suspicions were correct. However, when he spoke about Pal, his voice dropped even lower and I had to hunch over the table to hear him properly. He told me he had seen Pal once inside a soccer stadium just before a match actually talking to one of the goalkeepers. He had ordered his security people to creep quietly up to Pal and try to get a good photo of him. Pal had discovered them doing it. He went straight up to the official and said, "You want a photo of me? I'll fax you a photo of me anytime. Just let me know." The official declined his offer.

However, a macho Chinese "businessman" that I met laughed sardonically when I asked him about Pal's reach into the criminal world. "Pal? He is a chicken gangster," he said "The real tough gangsters were above him. They were businessmen, insurance sales people – whatever. Most of them connected with horse racing. Now Pal is broke. He runs around the north side of Singapore doing little labour deals but there is nothing to be afraid of. He is broke and penniless – yesterday's man."

The businessman's description was not particularly reassuring, as "chicken gangsters" can still kill you. In fact, to prove that they are not "chicken," they may be more likely to do something violent than a non-chicken gangster. Also, the businessman had made the description over beers, in a bar, at least sixteen kilometres away from Pal with absolutely no intention of going up to Sembawang to help me track Pal down. In life, nothing is impossible for the man who does not have to do it himself. And most men's bravado mounts proportionally to the declining probability of their actually doing anything.

I kept remembering the descriptions of the trial of Lutz Pfannenstiel, the German goalkeeper who was convicted of match-fixing in the Singapore league in 2000. It was revealed that Wilson Raj Perumal, a muscular Indian fixer had arranged an attack on one of Pfannenstiel's teammates, the Croatian defender Ivica Raguz. Raj and an accomplice had ambushed him while he was walking on a Singapore street, using a field hockey stick to smash in his left knee. During the trial, some of the other players testified that they had received calls from people threatening to break their legs. What was even less reassuring is that the Singaporean soccer official thought that Wilson Raj and Pal sometimes worked together, but that "Wilson Raj is more gentle than Pal."

I went up to northern Singapore. This was his home territory: vast apartment blocks where Indian workers lived. In the courtroom, this area was described as Pal's "power base." Pal acknowledged the truth of the claim, but said, "It was because, people were grateful to me. If you do good, there will be a 'power base' . . . As far as I was concerned, I have done good only."

In the end, I simply sent Pal a fax asking him if we could do an interview. Then I followed up a few days later with a phone call. His secretary and he were both polite and open. When we actually did talk, Pal was forthcoming and seemingly direct and honest about his match-fixing. He is also supremely confident. He claims that in his prime he could have fixed almost any soccer game anywhere in the world, including top international matches:

First thing I did was fake a card. I said that I was from the Singapore press, something like that. Then I met the player and had an interview with them. I took them to a restaurant, treated them well. I talked about the game for a little bit. Then I would start to talk about their family. I showed them that I cared. I could figure out very quickly if they were supporting their family, how they cared about them. Then I could tell if they were ready to take my offer or not.

We spoke in his company's offices. Pal was dressed in a casual shirt and jeans. He drives a black German salon car. He seemed like a normal, hard-working businessman. The only unusual thing was that when we went upstairs into his private office, there was a six-foot-tall statue of the Goddess Kali, with multiple arms, and the figure of a hapless and bloodied man being trampled under her feet.

The tactic he mentioned, the fake journalist card, sounds exactly like the method the English Premier League goalkeeper Ian Bennett of Birmingham City said was used on him when he was offered £20,000 by two men who claimed to be Singapore journalists. So Pal certainly talks a good game, but can he deliver fixed matches? History suggests he could.

It was Pal that built a network of corrupted players, coaches, and officials across the Malaysian-Singaporean League. He was not the first, last, or only match-fixer, but in his day he was by far the most successful.

A referee told me what it was like to officiate one of the many fixed games between one team and Selangor, the most popular club in the league.

I am not stupid. I knew the game was fixed. Sometimes you could see the signs, but I didn't care; it makes my life easier. I go to the game mentally and physically prepared for a tough game. Then nothing happens! It makes my life easier. It is not my business if the teams want to do stupid things.

In the summer of 1994, the Malaysian and Singaporean police decided that it was their business and they moved in. It was difficult for the investigators. The more people they arrested, the more the police realized how big the fixing network actually was. By the end of their investigation, more than 150 people had been arrested, and police estimated that 80 per cent of the games played in the league had been fixed.

Rajendran Kurusamy was the master conductor of a superb orchestra of match-fixing. Again, he was not the only fixer, but he had established match-fixing syndicates on not just one, but at least nine of the league's teams. On the witness stand, he testified to netting more than US$16 million in five months by fixing matches.

The players fixing the games were not junior players. They were some of the top talent that their country and continent could produce, and they talked about how they were recruited into the fixer's networks. One player, Junaid (*), who worked for Pal, said:

> Pal contacted me. He was speaking Tamil on the phone. He wanted me to sell the match. I was scared. Pal said, "Don't worry. I already control your entire team." He then asked me to inform Zahid (*) that if he [Zahid] does not co-operate, Pal will break his legs. I told Zahid. He agreed to fix the match. Pal then asked me to inform the rest of the group. All of them agreed. They promised us 20,000 RM [approximately US$7,500] each to fix the game. We had to lose or draw, make sure we did not win.

In this excerpt, Pal reveals himself to be a brilliant strategist. First, he spoke in Tamil, a language that is used by only a small, ethnic, working-class community in Malaysia. By speaking in this language, Pal establishes a kind of "us against them" bond with the player. Then he follows up with a threat, but not, of course, directed at the player. "Could you tell Zahid that I will break his legs?" There is nothing to stop Pal from telling the player directly that he will break his legs but that would destroy the friendliness and confidence he is trying to establish. After the player tells Zahid of the threat, he not unsurprisingly joins Pal's network.

I asked him about some fixers' habit of giving women to players and referees. "Of course," he said, sounding amazed that anyone would make a big thing out of it, like a dentist wanting to know why you would not have magazines in the waiting room. But he used an interesting phrase, one that revealed the inner menace of his charm: "Then we could buy their heart from them."

Officially, the Singapore anti-corruption police are known as the Corrupt Practices Investigation Bureau (CPIB). In Chinese their title is the Foul Greed Investigation Bureau. They are a feared lot in Singapore, famous for dawn raids and strong-arm tactics. Many Singaporeans both inside and outside the bureau believe that their success is key to the country's economic strength. Over forty years ago, just after independence and the split with Malaysia, Singapore was simply another Asian city-state dependent on trade and corrupt to the core. Upon assuming power, the authoritarian president Lee Kuan Yew declared that corruption was a competitive disadvantage to the country and that henceforth the government would use the carrot-and-stick tactic of both paying civil servants well and founding the CPIB. The strategy seems to have worked, and Singapore now has the reputation of a purportedly rare corruption-free zone in Southeast Asia.

At the CPIB headquarters is a museum where visitors can go on a tour of the artifacts of decades of investigations and successful convictions of a range of con men, crooks, and corruptors. There is a display announcing the success of Operation False Start, when the CPIB investigators smashed a horse-doping ring at Singapore's prestigious Turf Club. Another display boasts of Operation Ah Gu or the conviction of six corrupt house inspectors who were extorting cash from developers. There is even a display showing that the CPIB mounted Operation Drugnet against their own Singapore police Central Narcotics Bureau. In one corner in this hall of busted infamy is a StarTAC mobile phone. It is broken and bruised. The CPIB officers had to go into a sewer to recover it, after the phone was flushed down a toilet. But it is a mute testimony to the extraordinary powers of both the CPIB and Rajendran "Pal" Kurusamy.

Pal's moment of glory came in 1998. He had been arrested for match-fixing in the Singapore league. He was in jail. Singaporean prisons are not places for the weak-kneed. The authorities do not subscribe to the idea of prisons as houses of reform or gentle correction. They are nasty, brutish, and savage places. The German goalkeeper, Lutz Pfannenstiel, who was jailed there for match-fixing, described conditions inside: "At night there were people being raped. Someone died and I remember them carrying him out . . . I could hear the screams of people being caned. It was horrific." But somehow, maybe by his ability to judge human nature, Pal thrived in the place. He managed to get a prison guard to smuggle in a mobile phone. From then on, he was set.

"I did everything," he said happily. "I worked from inside the prison. European matches, World Cup matches, international games."

"Hold on," I said. "Did you say that you were gambling on games inside a prison or you were fixing from inside the prison?"

"Both. I did both. I fixed games as well. Or I did until they caught me."

"I'm sorry. I can't believe you. You say you fixed a World Cup game from inside a Singaporean prison?"

"Oh yes; once you have the network it is easy. I tell you, I could tell any games that are fixed. Doesn't matter what they are. And I could fix almost any match."

Then he told me the story of how he achieved the ultimate soccer fixer's goal, arranging a match in the World Cup Finals.

Ironically, Pal began match-fixing in prison. In 1990, he was in prison for a mob murder: he and a group of Tamil criminals had surrounded a labour contractor and stabbed him to death. No one confessed to the actual killing, so they were all convicted with a reduced sentence. Inside the prison, Pal had "a life-changing experience"; he discovered volleyball and his talent for successful sports corruption:

> While I was in prison, I was a champion volleyball player. The best. There was a lot of betting going on in the prison on these games. The prisoners would bet $1,000 or $2,000, to be paid by their families, family to family outside. I would find out when there was a lot of money on the game. And I would play badly to lose and make money that way. I came out of the prison with a lot of money.

He may have come out of prison with a lot of money, but he had almost no skills, apart from knowing how to throw volleyball games. So he took the natural step and began to get interested in the business of gambling. The vast networks of illegal gambling intrigued him. The whole peninsula was obsessed with soccer, and Pal started to bet like almost everyone else. But he noticed that when he bet, he routinely lost. It was only when friends told him that many of the games in the league were fixed that he began to understand why he was losing money. He decided to try to beat the fixers at their own game.

At first, Pal went to work for a group of Chinese-Indonesian gang-sters, run by a fixer who called himself Uncle Jimmie (*) or Uncle Frankie or Chong – depending on what day it was or who he was speaking to. Uncle Jimmie had been fixing matches in the Malay Peninsula for a long time. In one confession, a player speaks of Uncle Jimmie paying his team off in matches dating back to 1987:

> One week before the game, Uncle Jimmie would contact me. Uncle Jimmie will tell me whether he wants us to win or lose. Then one day before the match, Uncle Jimmie will confirm whether he wants us to lose and by how many goals. Normally one day after the match, I would collect the money from Uncle Jimmie in different places around the town.

The player had a long, relatively complicated relationship with Uncle Jimmie. When the player lost a contract with his team and was unemployed on the streets of Kuala Lumpur, Uncle Jimmie did what few soccer officials would presumably do – he met him and lent him money:

> I was walking around in Kuala Lumpur. I phoned Uncle Jimmie. We met, I can't remember where. Uncle Jimmie gave me $2,000 just for "pocket money."

If you want a good diagram of the fixing networks in the league, than just draw a picture of a shark frenzy. Anyone who could fix, did fix. Alongside Pal and Uncle Frankie, was a Chinese bookie – Ong, a.k.a. The Blind Man – from Malaysia – whose territory was concentrated in Kuala Lumpur and Malacca. There were reports that he too had made vast amounts of money from fixing – up to $10 million. There was another group of fixers based out of the racecourses who had a reputation of absolute brutality based on the murder and maiming of a number of jockeys and trainers. There was a gang of loosely connected Indonesians, one of whom would strut around Marine Drive in Singapore loaded down with gold jewellery. Their reputations for corruption and violence were equal to anything in the Pal storybook. Even ten years later, when I spoke with a Kuala Lumpur crime reporter about these gangs, his hands shook when he spoke of them. It was the rivalry between these fixers that led to the violence. Teams were divided into cliques, some of whom followed one set of fixers, while another clique followed another group. There was actually a fight inside the dressing room of Selangor, one of the top teams in the league, between players representing different fixers. Another Singapore fixer told me much the same thing. We had talked about the North American mafia. He said:

> Here a runner can also be a bookie. In North America, maybe you have a hierarchy but here, money talks. They will do everything. Take

money, gamble, fix games . . . see that their bookie is taking odds heavily one way, so go to the other side and take other odds that way or fix the game. There is no control over them.

However, when Pal entered this world, he found he had a great competitive advantage over the other fixers. Many of the players in the league were either Indian or working-class Malays. The Chinese were at a disadvantage. For all kinds of cultural and economic reasons, few of the players were Chinese. When the Chinese fixers tried to talk to the players, they couldn't do so in their own language. Pal, on the other hand, had grown up in the same area as many of the players. He understood them in ways the Chinese fixers simply could not. Uncle Jimmie and Pal worked closely together through the 1993 season. In one of the Royal Malaysian Police confessions, Uncle Jimmie tells a player looking for direction that "his partner" Pal will help him. It was, seemingly, a friendly relationship. However, for all the cordiality, Pal began to undercut the other fixers. Ironically, his chief weapon was the same one used by the Singaporean government to combat corruption – he paid the players more money:

> The other fixers only paid the players 2,000 to 3,000 ringgit. But I paid each player 30,000 ringgit. So because of the money a lot of players knew me, a lot of players came back to me.

Finally, according to Pal, in the spring of 1994, Uncle Jimmie shared with him the secrets of fixing international tournaments. At first, Pal was not really interested. He was making all the money he could by fixing in the local leagues – why bother with international competitions? But Uncle Jimmie came to him before the 1994 World Cup and allegedly said:

> We have a team. It is the Cameroon team . . . The guy he came to see me. He is my runner.

I said, "Are you sure? The Cameroon team? Who have you got?" [Names a player on the team, claims he is "their runner" for a network of corrupt Cameroon players . . .]

So I said, "Are you sure? Okay what's the deal?"

He proposed me. He talked to me about the price. About the function of what he is doing and then he asked me for $100,000. Then I met them. I see them. I talked to them. They said, "We are willing to do the business in our game against Brazil." Then he recommended the Russian team. So many teams.

Because of the time that has elapsed, it was impossible for me to confirm if these stories of fixing at the 1994 World Cup were true. Certainly it is not the first time that elements on a Cameroon team were alleged to have thrown a game at the biggest tournament in the world. In 1984, Italian journalists Oliviero Beha and Roberto Chiodi claimed to have spoken to a mysterious source from Cameroon who told them that the game between Cameroon and Italy in the 1982 World Cup Finals had been sold.

Back at home in Malaysia and Singapore, the end was in sight: Johnson Fernandez, Lazarus Rokk, and other journalists were publishing stories on the fixing. The police investigations were beginning and the tension was ramped up. Runners began to betray fixers, and Pal claims he was betrayed by one of his Chinese runners.

The Chinese guy informed to CPIB. . . . He was my runner. We were betting on a game. We had $8 million one way. He took $5 million and put it in his own pocket, only gave me $3 million. That was stupid. The betting market very small [sic], you always find out what is going on. So I got on the phone and worked the market in Indonesia, Thailand, and I switched the odds. I got $22 million on. I turned the game 2-1. It was a counter-fix. The Chinese guy lost the money, so he was angry with me so he informed on me to the CPIB.

It was all like something out of a sinking ship. As the investigators moved in, the fixers scrambled to protect themselves. One player claimed he was frightened of the investigation, so he phoned one of his fixers to ask what to do:

> 10 December 1994, I contacted my fixer and I was afraid of being arrested so I phoned him. He warned me, "Don't mention my name. Mention the other guys. If you mention my name, I will do something to you . . ."

The problem for Pal was that here, he was at a serious competitive disadvantage to the other fixers. As a former labourer, his strength was his contacts with working-class players and their families from disadvantaged Indian and Malay backgrounds. When the police moved in, he did not have the political protection that the Chinese fixers could claim. Push a police investigation with a Chinese triad–connected fixing gang and somewhere, somehow there would be repercussions for the police investigator. Push a case against Pal and his Indian cronies and a police officer was safe, at least from political repercussions. It also, of course, did not help Pal's cause that he was guilty, very guilty.

So Pal did what countless other major criminals have done before and since then. He cut a deal with the police and agreed to testify on their behalf. In 1994 to 1995, there was a series of dramatic cases in Singapore courts, all featuring one Rajendran Kurusamy as a prosecution witness. Thiru Rajamanickam, a FIFA-ranked referee, was convicted of aiding and abetting in a fixed match. The Michael Vana trial, the great Czech disappearing act, if it had gone ahead, was to feature Pal as a witness. The hugely popular midfielder Abbas Saad, the "Maradona of Singapore," was convicted of accepting bribes to win games, thanks in part to Pal's testimony. And Ong Kheng Hock, the match-fixer who helped get me drunk and distracted in a bar, was sent away for a number of years based again in part on Pal's performance in the witness box.

It was all hugely irritating for the Singapore Chinese establishment.

Here was an Indian labourer with no political connections running the most successful match-fixing network in their national soccer league, defrauding hundreds of thousands of gamblers, helping to ruin the league, and even causing a scandal between neighbouring Malaysia and themselves. And any establishment members who were connected to the Chinese triads must have been even more furious, because Pal had largely cut them out of the fixing business for a year and a half. And at the end of the day the same Indian labourer was not serving a single day in jail but was going about his business, after cheerfully testifying in court that he had made between $16 and $17 million in five months.

Pal should have laid low, very low. His lawyer warned him, the CPIB special investigator warned him, even the CPIB director warned him, not to fix matches any more. But Pal did not listen. Like the addict who discovers that crack is not a benign party drug but cannot help himself, Pal started fixing matches again.

After the glamour of the alleged World Cup fix, the games that the police eventually got Pal on were very low level. They took place, practically in his backyard in the summer of 1996: Woodlands Wellington versus Sembawang Rangers and Woodlands Wellington versus Balestier Central United. It would have been difficult to find anyone, outside of northern Singapore, and even then not too many, who cared about the matches. But the trial featured Pal and his two accomplices, Maran A. Jagannathan and Devaraj Doraisamy, the captain of his team and national team player. Pal was supposed to have paged the two of them the figure – $80,000 – just before kick off. At which point Devaraj took out a pair of *blue* socks from his bag and put them on. It was a secret signal to the rest of the fixing players on his team that the fix was on and they should try to lose. If he had pulled out a pair of *white* socks, it would have meant that they should ignore the offer of the fix and simply try their best. In vain did Pal argue that the money was for a business debt that Jagannathan had incurred opening a flower shop. He wasn't helped by the fact that Jagannathan had broken down in a CPIB interrogation room and confessed the whole crime. Then in the middle of the trial when Jagannathan realized that his mates had not betrayed *him*, he very dramatically began to testify *against* the prosecution. Neither the trial judge nor the appeal judge was persuaded by his last-minute change of side, and they convicted all the defendants to jail. The appeal judge added in his statement the heartfelt sentiments of most of the Singapore ruling class:

> Soccer is a sport with a wide following. Offences of this nature have attracted much public attention lately. If left unchecked, they are capable of tarnishing the image of Singapore.

In the spring of 1998, Pal was finally back in prison, and the various appeals of the case were quashed. There was a certain biblical cycle to his life. His fixing games had begun in prison and they would end in prison. What is known both from Pal himself and the CPIB is that he paid a prison guard tens of thousands of dollars for a cellphone and replacement batteries. Even that, given Singapore's stance on corruption, is pretty remarkable. But seemingly completely unfazed by his surroundings, Pal claims to have set out to fix games in the World Cup in France in 1998. The CPIB official I spoke to said:

> Pal continued to match-fix, even in prison! He had a hand phone smuggled into his jail cell by a corrupt prison guard who we also caught.

What the CPIB did not say was the story that Pal told me. He claimed that a few weeks before he entered prison, he had gone to Cameroon:

> The game I fixed from the prison cell. I made $3 million. I had gone to the Cameroon before the prison. I had met X [a player that had allegedly been his runner at the 1994 World Cup]. I arranged for water pipes to his village. That is how I fixed the games.

Pal claimed that in return for cash and the water pipes, the runner arranged with some of his Cameroon teammates to sell one game in the 1998 World Cup Finals. I was not able to confirm or deny this story. I put it here simply for the public record, but I will add a few further pieces of circumstantial evidence that may be of importance to readers in deciding for themselves the truth of Pal's claims.

One, the CPIB official did say that Pal was match-fixing on the phone in the jail when they arrested him. He did not specify which match or matches, but he did claim that had been the nature of Pal's business inside the prison.

Two, in June 1998, a furious Mike Saunders, the managing director of Victor Chandler, a large British bookmaker, announced to the press that he was convinced that there had been a fixed match in the World Cup. He said that there had been massive amounts of bets coming from Malaysia-Singapore, all on one outcome of one particular game. The rumours in the market was that one team had been bribed. The game Saunders claimed that had been a "bribery target" – one featuring Cameroon. He would tell me later, "We had agents working the Asian market, they were swamped. Their phones were going crazy. There is no doubt in my mind there was a fixed match in that World Cup."

Finally, I had heard the story of the water pipes, Cameroon, and the World Cup fix from three different sources in Singapore *before* I had met Pal. If the story is a fantasy, which it may be, it is at the very least a consistent fantasy. It is a story that Pal has not changed in its essential details.

Whatever the specific truth of his fixing claims, Pal's generous nature in prison got him into trouble. He claims he told the entire wing of his prison that they all should take France in the final:

> Even in prison. Who will take the Cup? You know? But I know. I tell them – take France. Happens. Happens to beat them. Most people I tell them.

This final piece of flamboyance ensured that the prison authorities got to know about his activities, and one day they staged a sudden raid on his cell. Pal was on the phone and he frantically flushed the phone down the toilet. The CPIB, who by now were really angry with Pal, went down the sewer to get it.

The prison authorities were even more furious with him. Singapore prisons are not designed to be nice, but there is a further section which is for the *really* hard cases. Alone for twenty-four hours a day, no windows, no contact with other prisoners, Pal was placed in it for more than two years.

> You see I am alone in prison. In prison a lot of people but I am in the
> Shell. I am alone. I cannot go down. I cannot see the sun or the night.
> I am alone for twenty-eight months.

When he emerged from prison in 2001, Pal fit at least one of the descriptions of the Chinese businessman. He was broke. Labour duties on his imported workers had bankrupted his company. He had a young family and lots of responsibilities. When I met him four years later, he was like any hard-working businessman, trying to get deals. We even spoke about the possibility of writing a book. He claimed he had given up on match-fixing, although he did seem nostalgic for the days when he caused such havoc on the highest stage of international soccer. But, he assured me, he had completely retired from match-fixing; his son was too important to him. This was in contrast to the fixer I would meet next, who was definitely in the thick of top international soccer matches and, in fact, allegedly proceeded to fix them as I watched.

BEHIND THE DOOR

All the leagues in the world – EPL, Champions League, World Cup – they can be fixed. I had players on Crystal Palace, Wimbledon, and Liverpool. You say these are great teams. They are bullshit. We can bribe them. You think because the clubs make big money in the transfer that it means that the players won't take a bribe. That is not true. They will take the money.

Saturday, November 26, 2005, 8:00 p.m., Bangkok, Thailand. For months I had been tracking down one particular match-fixer. His name is famous among the Asian gambling community. He has a track record of fixing games for more than fifteen years. His name was associated with some of the major match-fixing trials in the last decade, but always as the "shadowy figure" about whom not much is known. But he supplies the bets or the money or the guarantee of violence. I will call him Lee Chin (*).

It had taken months of faxes, calls, and abruptly cancelled meetings. A few weeks before, I had received a phone call inviting me to a meeting. It may have been because I had recently learned how to look at a business card in the proper Chinese fashion: holding it in both hands, studying it, and then asking a question that showed you understood the rank of the person who had given you the card. I had, unknowingly, done so to one of Chin's associates when I had met him in the VIP section at a soccer match, showing him proper "face." I heard through the grapevine that the gesture had been appreciated and that an interview might be possible.

Then Chin and I spoke on the phone. He invited me to meet him. So I dropped everything and flew out. Then followed ten days of cancelled meetings and unreturned phone calls. Finally, we had agreed to meet on Saturday afternoon. It had been confirmed, but at 6:37 p.m., one of his assistants had abruptly cancelled the meeting: "Mr. Chin is very busy. You must understand that. If you state the nature of your business he might be able to see you in the next few weeks." The thought of having flown all the way out to Asia to cancel yet again, made me furious. But I kept my temper as best I could and pleaded that we already had made plans for an interview. I had already made it clear what the interview was to be about. The assistant hung up, and I did not rate my chances too highly of getting the interview, at least not for that day. Then at 8:07 p.m. I received another call.

"Hello, is that you?" a voice said.

"Yes," I replied. "Is that Mr. Chin?"

"Yes. Where are you?"

"I'm downtown near the central shopping centre."

"You know the – Country Club?" He named an expensive golf club on the outskirts of the city.

"I can find it."

"Good. Take a taxi. I'll see you there in one hour. Very sorry to have been late. My room is at 1104 on the ground floor, just come straight there."

"Thank you. Thank you very much. I look forward to seeing you."

Actually, I was not completely looking forward to seeing him. I was very nervous. However, I was not too surprised. It is almost standard operating procedure when meeting criminals that the location changes at the last minute. I once met a couple of enforcers for the Hells Angels, in Barrie, Ontario. The Hells Angels biker gang at that time were in the midst of a bloody war with another biker outfit called the Rock Machine. We were supposed to meet at a local restaurant; I sat there for half an hour until one of their former girlfriends arrived. She apologized and told me that I was to go with her, and she would take me to meet them at an undisclosed location. We ended up at a half-empty suburban shopping mall where the enforcers were waiting. That time had been nerve-racking. As I had got into her car, I had wondered about whether I would ever come back. The Hells Angels were expanding into the English-speaking part of Canada and they did not have a reputation for gentleness. However, I was a representative of a national television network, and a colleague was sitting in another car nearby. We were in mobile phone contact. If I did disappear, it would not be long before someone came to inquire about me.

Having gone through that experience did not make me feel any better going to meet Mr. Chin. Courage is like a bucket filled with a mysterious liquid. You use up your supply of the liquid in the bucket and there is none left. This time I was alone. Through my own life choices, I had ceased to be a representative of a powerful media organization and was now a relatively poor graduate student. The Thai police are not really into rescuing impoverished people from the clutches of million-aires at their country clubs. A friend had promised to call me at mid-night, and we had worked out an elaborate code for him to ask me if I was all right. But really what could they do if I did not answer or said the code word for "I'm in trouble"? I remembered the British graduate student who was murdered while researching drug gangs in Bristol in 1970s. I thought of Jim Thompson, the art collector, silk merchant, and sometime CIA operative who had disappeared in Malaysia in the 1960s. His body still has not been found.

As instructed, I got in a taxi. Time speeded up and I viewed every-thing as if in a dream. The very oxygen I breathed seem valuable. The taxi driver chatted amiably and I tried to do my best to make sure he remembered me and where he had dropped me off, in case someone had to follow my last known movements. We drove up to the club. Beside the driveway executives practised their golf drives by floodlight. Then the taxi pulled up and I got out.

It was 9:55 p.m. and the restaurant and lobby were empty. It was an old, classic building surrounded by a long veranda that looked out over grass lawns. It was like a set for a 1930s film noir. And, like a cliché from every movie about the tropics, I could hear crickets sounding loudly in the darkness. I went over to the staff behind the front desk and made sure that I questioned them enough that they, too, would remember me, if asked. I couldn't hear the sounds of any other guests. Apart from the people in the lobby, the place seemed deserted.

I walked quickly down the empty corridor toward room 1104. I didn't want to slow down. I didn't want to give myself time to think or consider. I had now been conducting my research in Asia for months, asking embarrassing questions, probing where local journalists had long since given up. Was this entire meeting Chin's way of luring me to his territory and then beating the crap out of me or worse?

I stood in front of the door.

I had stood, in fear, in front of other doors, not knowing what lay behind them, one part of me not wanting to know, another part not wanting to turn back. There was the time with the Central American crime lord, who had taken me and an entire television crew on a tour of his house. We had gone through his recreation room, complete with a bar, full-sized polar bear skin rug and medieval sex sculptures. Then he stood us in front of a door. He smiled and said, "I bet you won't guess what is in here. It's my favourite." Then he pushed open the swing doors. Inside, and this was right beside the love-pad bar, was a fully functional, state-of-the-art, scrubbed-down gynecological operating room, with a full set of extra-large forceps, drills, and a saddle-shaped table. I still have nightmares about what takes place in that room.

But what was behind this particular door at night in a Bangkok golf club? Would it be as surreally sick as the gynecology lab? Would there be an explosion of violence? A smashing of field hockey sticks, like Wilson Raj's attack on the Croatian player? If an attack was to come on me, I hoped it would be with a field hockey stick. I was vaguely comforted by the thought, somehow it seemed less frightening than a baseball bat. A baseball bat was what Al Capone had used. A field hockey stick was what upper-class girls at Cheltenham Ladies' College used: if the mobsters hit me with a field hockey stick it would be bad, but I would be alive. With those irrelevant and probably erroneous thoughts running through my head, I knocked on the door.

There was a voice behind the door. I stood away from it so if the attack came, I would have a few feet of room. My hand was in my pocket, holding a small can of pepper spray. But I tried to make my face look as reassuring as possible. The door opened. An Asian man opened it; he did not look particularly threatening, and he asked me to come in.

I walked in the room. The door closed behind me.

There were three people: two men, Chin and one of his assistants; on the bed, a beautiful woman watched a movie. The curtains were open and I could see around the room. There was no one on the balcony. As I had walked past the bathroom, I pretended to be a little lost and pushed the door; there was no one there.

I was not attacked. I was not threatened or menaced in anyway. There were no scenes of torture or brutality featuring gynecological forceps, field hockey sticks, or any other kind of weapon. What followed for the next two hours and fifteen minutes was one of the most bizarre conversations I have ever had.

To this day, I am still not entirely sure how much was bullshit and how much was the truth. In some ways that is irrelevant in journalism: there is bullshit, facts, and legally provable facts. I have omitted the specific names of many of the players and coaches that Chin named. I include some of the games that he alleged were fixed because it is in the public interest to know that a major Asian fixer claimed that those particular games were fixed. But I do not make any claims to knowing whether the games were actually fixed or who were the specific individuals who might have been fixing those games.

Here then are the major points.

Stephen Fleming, the great New Zealand cricket captain, claims he was approached by a gambler in 1999 who had told him that there was a syndicate of Asian bookies arranging top international games of cricket and soccer. "Look, these things are not coincidences," the gambler was alleged to have said about a recent soccer match. "If you want to know where the real money is, it's in the syndicate that's going on around the world right now, speculating on the likelihood of certain results or occurrences." The gambler, according to Fleming, said prominent sportsmen were involved, including some in English soccer and tennis.

In essence, this is what Chin told me. The only difference was that he claimed to be one of the men at the centre of a network. He claimed to have sixteen runners around the world working exclusively for him.

There were two phones on the table. One rang almost as soon as I sat down. Chin answered and started talking in what I think was Bahasa Indonesian mixed with English. He talked amiably, saying a few players' and coaches' names that I recognized, then he put down the phone. He turned to me.

"You see, Mr. Hill, I am getting call. It is from the Philippines. You know the SEA Games that are going on now. I am arranging all the matches. Laos only lost 1-0 to Singapore. Everyone thought that Singapore would win 3- or 4-0. I control the Laos team I told them to go all out. I knew they could keep the score level."

The SEA Games are the Southeast Asian Games, equivalent to the Pan-American games or the All-Africa Games: a continent-specific version of the Olympics with athletics, soccer, and other events such as sailing. They had started a few days before in the Philippines. It was not a complete surprise that a fixer would be alleging that the games were fixed. A top Asian sporting official, the same one that had the fixer's number in his speed-dial, had told me that the events were plagued with "caring and sharing" or "through every pipe a little water must flow." In other words, the various sports officials divided up the games to make sure that each nation would get at least some medals to make sure their home governments were not bothered by any lack of sporting success. If it were just him, I would not bother to mention it, but a few days after my meeting with Chin, I had read that the weary Thai prime minister repeated the same allegation, saying very publicly that many of the competitions in the SEA games were fixed; the chef de mission of the Vietnamese delegation had even given a press conference at which he announced how many medals would be won by each country *before* the SEA Games had begun. That Chin would tell me that the games were fixed was no surprise, but he went on to tell me that he and his associates travelled the world fixing international soccer matches.

I asked him what the biggest event he ever fixed was.

Chin shrugged. "The Olympics? The World Cup? I don't know. Which is bigger?"

This seemed absolutely bizarre.

"I went to the Olympics in Atlanta in 1996," Chin said. "I fixed a game in the 1996 Olympics: Tunisia versus Portugal. I bribed some of the Tunisian guys to lose outside of the spread. They did it."

We spoke about the fix. He claimed that it was one of the rare ones where the players he approached would not even consider doing it for money: they were too religious.

"Finally I get this beautiful Mexican girl. I paid her $50,000 for the whole tournament. That is a lot of money for them. She would hang out in the lobby . . . met him [one of the players from Tunisia], they went up to his room, did it, and then she proposed to him. Then I went in . . . 'Will you do the game for me?' He said 'Yes, opening game.' They lost to Portugal 2-0 . . . I make a lot of money and everyone was happy."

One of his phones rang at 10:27 p.m. There was a conversation that lasted two minutes in a language that I could not understand. Like many Asians, Chin speaks at least four languages. I could not follow what was being said. He put the phone down.

"You see this I just got a call. Hannover is going to win by at least two goal. It is arranged. I have only put $20,000 down. Not much."

"Not much! Maybe to you," I said, "but $20,000 is a lot of money to me."

The woman on the bed laughed. It was the first and last time in the whole conversation that she showed even the slightest interest in what was said. I turned to look at her. She shrugged and flicked the converter of the television and continued to watch the movie.

"The game starts right now. Hannover will win the game by at least two goals. You watch."

A translation might be in order. The top German league is known as the Bundesliga, literally "best division." On November 26, 2005, Hannover was a middle-ranking team; they were playing another Bundesliga team, Kaiserslautern, in Germany. Chin was claiming just *before* the match began that Hannover would win by a score line of at least a two-goal difference. He did not say or reveal in any way how this result might be achieved whether it was a network of players or referees. He did say, in the course of the conversation, "Some German referees are bad . . . I have referees that work for me in many places, U.S., Greece. Many places."

I in no way want to imply that those specific referees were on the take to throw the Hannover versus Kaiserslautern match. That was never stated directly at any point in the discussion. However, it was by this time well known that Robert Hoyzer had taken money to throw games in the lower German leagues. So possibly Chin was simply repeating that fact. But what I can say is that throughout the next two hours, the phone rang five or six times, and I presumed one of his colleagues would tell him if a goal had been scored in the Hannover match.

I told Chin that I did not believe his claims about fixing top leagues. The games were worth too much. The players are paid too much money. He smiled.

That is a common mistake. People see the amount of money that is paid in transfer fees but that does not go to the players. You approach their agents; that is the way to get to the players. Say they get £50,000 a week. Then we offer them £150,000 for an hour and half's work. Think they will turn that down? Very easy to get them to say yes. But all the leagues in the world, EPL, Champions League, World Cup, they can be fixed. I had players on Crystal Palace, Wimbledon, and Liverpool. You say these are great teams? They are bullshit. We can bribe them. You think because the clubs make big money in the transfer, that it means that the players won't take a bribe. That is not true. They will take the money.

It was my time to smile. I expressed disbelief. He shrugged again and told me some years ago one of his associates told him of a business opportunity.

I remember one of my runners told me, "You can be a director of X [names a relatively prominent team in the U.K.]. You just have to pay £20,000 to £50,000." I said, "Forget it. Let's just make money."

We spoke about the network of Asian fixers. I said it was too difficult for Asians to get access to European players. He nodded:

Yes, I have heard that the English gangs are now trying to fix EPL games. In the last four to five years, the Englishman comes to Asia . . . The Asians taught them how to fix games. One time they wanted to meet me but I refused. They are doing the same thing in boxing and rugby.

When I had asked Pal whether he had sometimes used prostitutes to pay or to encourage corrupt players and officials, he was amazed that anyone would ask such a simple question. When I asked Chin whether he had links with top Asian team officials to fix matches, he too looked amazed that I would even have to ask.

Last year for X [names a top Asian team] . . . the head of the team, phoned me. He paid me $300,000 so they could win a tournament . . . I fixed it so they would win.

At this point, you might be wondering, as I was, why Chin would want to talk to me. Unlike Pal, who had been convicted and served jail time for all his fixes, Chin was claiming to tell me about current fixes and situations that were not public knowledge, let alone ones that had been prosecuted. As we talked, it became clear that he was interested in the possibility of my writing a book *on him*. I mention this because it gives Chin an important motivation to embellish or even fabricate entire incidents. He undoubtedly had fixed matches, even international tournaments before. He was rumoured, by English law enforcement sources, to have been approaching Premier League players. But how many of his stories were true at that point, I could not say.

At quarter after midnight, I left the room. Unhurt. But my mind was stirred to the core. Chin and I shook hands. I left. For the record, a few minutes before I departed another call came through from his correspondent: Hannover had beaten Kaiserslautern five goals to one. It fitted Chin's prediction – a victory by more than two goals.

A few days later, I sat on the beach of Sentosa Island, Singapore. I had flown in, played my last game of soccer, and now I sat in the fashion parade beside the beach bar having a drink. Normally, Sentosa Beach is a "place to be," full of gorgeous bikini-clad beauties and muscular men. Music plays and it seems a little like an Asian version of a California beach movie, minus the surf boards, circa 1962. But today, I missed all of that. My head was in a whirl. I was trying to figure out the answer to questions that ran through my mind.

Was there, as Lee Chin claimed, really a network of international gamblers fixing matches? Or was it all nonsense designed to get a book deal for him? Even if Chin wanted a book deal, if he were making such large amounts of money, it would not be worth it. Nor would it do him any good. Maybe it was all a question of personality. I knew he had a long track record of fixing games, but maybe he was the Baron Münchhausen of match-fixers? Maybe he was a fantasist that spouted off great-sounding stories to fool impressionable researchers? On the other hand, he had never granted an interview before, so why start now with a line of nonsense?

But I knew from trials and police investigations that this was a man taken very seriously by soccer and law enforcement officials. I also knew from interviews with sporting officials that there was a set of gamblers, linked to Chin who attended the big international tournaments trying to fix games.

There was the example from 1995, when a series of fixers had been arrested at the World Under-20 Championship in Doha. Two young Portuguese players had been invited up to a room to discuss an interesting proposition by an attractive young Thai woman. When they got there, they discovered a pile of money on the table, two "well-known fixers," and a group of players from the Cameroon team.

Somehow those "well-known fixers" were not prosecuted. Even an honest soccer official of the AFC had told me, "The bookies are well known. We know who they are. . . . We see them regularly." Which of course, begs the question: if you knew who they are, why don't you have them arrested or banned from future international tournaments?

There was also the case of the German game. The game had taken place, in front of me, with the result Chin predicted, but was that simply a coincidence?

Four months later, I visited the offices of the professional gambler John McAllister. He has a database the size of a small space agency. It contains almost every detail of every match played in Western Europe, as well as the movement of the betting line before the games. Pledging him to secrecy, I asked about the Hannover versus Kaiserslautern match.

Funny you should mention that game, because it was very odd. There were a number of "dodgy" Bundesliga games at around that time. I was working with a colleague on that game. And we tried to get in [place a bet] with these agents who were Chinese but working out of Vietnam. Often when they hear our bets they turn around and just bet it themselves. And then say to us, "Oh we're so sorry, but we couldn't get it on in time . . ." That happens all the time. So we were very suspicious of these guys. But we decided to give them one last chance coincidently for that game. And we wanted to put on a punt and they said afterwards, "We couldn't get it on, because the market moved so quickly. It was not us, but someone else." So we were trying to take Hannover and then the line got absolutely snorked. Assuming it was someone else, they had moved in very heavily.

McAllister showed me a chart of the betting line of the Hannover versus Kaiserslautern game: sure enough, about one hour before kickoff, there was a line like a seismographic chart announcing an earthquake.

Again, maybe it was coincidence. But a few days after I'd been thinking on the beach, it was announced that some of the soccer matches of the 2005 Southeast Asian (SEA) Games had been fixed by a series of gambling match-fixers. The results of the entire soccer section of the tournament were in doubt.

If those two events indicated that there may have been some truth in what Chin had told me, they still did not answer another fundamental question I had. Chin may have wanted me to write a book about him, but I still did not understand *why*. I had told him that the money he could make from any possible book deal was peanuts compared to what he made fixing, and any publicity would kill off his chances of long-term fixing.

Almost two years after our first meeting, I think I partly understand why Chin was, at least, at the beginning willing to consider the idea of a book. Chin comes from a minority background. Although he is powerful, he is not a big shot politically connected wheeler-dealer. He often travels, but most people would pass him by in the airport without looking twice at him. He is also extraordinarily good at what he does. Leaving morality aside, I believe him to be a psychological genius. He is a man who, using his wits and intelligence, is capable of corrupting players and referees from different cultures and countries around the world and then manipulating the Asian gambling market in such a way that he can make enormous amounts of money.

There is also a form of cognitive dissonance for most match-fixers. They think in very particular terms. When I approached them, it was always in a very businesslike manner. I think that after years of operating in the shadows, it was hugely flattering that an outsider, particularly from a world so utterly alien, an English university, would be studying *them*.

However, at that time in December 2005, I was still very skeptical of Chin's claims. I told him this frankly and directly, so he invited me to watch while he fixed matches in the 2006 World Cup Finals.

17

THE SET-UP

At KFC, you took a photo, yes? I could see you. I know that
you were trying to get photo. I know that. I know everything.

They fixed the World Cup at an anonymous Kentucky Fried Chicken
restaurant in northern Bangkok. There were four men. They sat at a little
table hunched over so they could hear one another while they spoke.
One was black, tall, and athletic, wearing a tight blue shirt and jeans. The
other three were Asians: one was Chin; beside him sat two younger Chinese
men. They met at 12:00 p.m. on May 25, 2006, and continued their discussion for almost an hour and twenty minutes. After ten minutes, a tall
white man dressed in an unironed shirt came to a nearby table. He
looked harassed and had problems with his mobile phones. He went
outside a number of times to try to get them to work.

The four men were discussing how to fix a World Cup match in the
2006 finals. It was a little bizarre. In an anonymous, suburban shopping
mall in northern Bangkok, the four men were planning to make lots of
money and at the same time destroy the dreams of millions of people
around the world. I was the tall white man. I was also trying to covertly
tape their meeting. I had two secret audio recording devices. Unfortunately, my hidden camera was not working properly, so I was reduced to
taking photos of the meeting with my mobile phone.

There was pop music playing over the speakers, and until I got the

KFC manager to turn it down, it ruined my recording. The "problem" with the mobile phone was me trying desperately to get my phone to take enough video and photos to link the four of them together without being seen by them or any of their henchmen, who I had to presume were somewhere close by. It was harrowing work. I pretended to read newspapers while I eavesdropped on their conversation. I glanced at my watch frequently, to try to look like an overstressed businessman waiting for a call. Then from time to time, I would pick up my phone, make a fake call, and pretend to have a conversation, all the while trying to take a picture.

Their meeting was about *how* they were planning to rig the gambling market. From what I heard then, and from what Chin told me later, their conversation was along the following lines. The black man was the runner or match-broker from one particular team. He claimed to have a number of players and officials from his country willing to consider throwing a game. But Chin and his associates had a problem. They did not have enough money to cover the initial payment it takes to ensure trust with the team.

The match-broker for the team wanted to work with them. He had worked with them before. There were good levels of mutual trust on either side. But he needed "shopping money" to convince the allegedly corrupt members of the team to agree to the deal. The amount of money needed in these situations depends on the level of the game. For a local Asian league match or a youth international tournament $1,000 a player will do. But to arrange a game at the World Cup Finals is serious stuff. The match-broker was asking for at least $100,000 to cover the network.

Chin wanted to introduce him to another syndicate – or investors – who could front the money. Chin would surrender control of the fix, but still receive some money for the deal. The match-broker did not like this. He didn't know who the new people were. It was going to be a difficult task to ensure that there was trust on both sides.

On the other side, the broker allegedly had two team officials who wanted to take part in the fix. Chin and his associates didn't like this development. They had, they claimed, worked with the team before.

They knew the players in the network. They didn't like the idea of bring-ing in officials at this point.

The four men talked back and forth about the various issues.

All the time, I was trying to listen as closely as possible, without looking as if I was listening, while trying to maintain my appearance as an overstressed businessman. A KFC restaurant is not the kind of place that one sits in for a long time. I finished my meal. I read every page of the two tabloid newspapers I brought with me, twice. At one point, a young couple came in and sat between me and the group. I almost hit them. I got up and walked past the men. As I did so, I heard a discussion about goalkeepers. I stood just outside the door and frantically took photos and video of the group.

At 1:20 p.m. the group of men stood and walked out. Chin walked with one of the Asians, the black man with the younger-looking Asian. Chin did not look at me. I tried to avoid eye contact with him. I stared at the black guy, trying to soak as much information as possible into my memory.

At 1:59, I got a phone call. It was Chin. He sounded exultant. The problems were being solved. The fix was on.

Throughout the winter and spring of 2006, Chin and I kept in contact. He had talked about organizing the fix for the World Cup and one country had been mentioned repeatedly: Ghana.

According to Chin, back in 2004 at the Olympics in Athens, some of his group were able to get close to some of the Ghana team and get them to throw their last game against Japan. I had no idea how good Ghana could or would be as a soccer team. Chin laughed at my ignorance.

Do you think Japan could ever beat Ghana? You have to be kidding Ghana has a good team. There is a player. I paid him $15,000 [pre-payment]. I know very quickly if someone will take a bribe from me or not. If they say they are willing to see me, it means that they will take a bribe. The whole game cost $550,000 to fix.

It is always the same. No trust, no deal. Fortunately for Chin, he claims the Ghana team had a bad experience with another fixer in the past. Chin claimed he was able to convince them that he is a good fixer to work with, and since then he had a good relationship with various corrupt Ghanaian players. I was doubtful, but Chin seemed very confident in his ability to deliver this fix. He told me:

> You want to come with me to Ghana? I will go to Ghana a month before this World Cup. I will fix the World Cup there and then. . . . I will show you what I do. But you must be in the background, not say anything. You will just see me work.

Then in late April we talked on the phone. He claimed he could not talk on the phone. I had to come to see him in Bangkok.

We met again, this time in an anonymous office on the outskirts of Bangkok, just as the sprawl of the capital city begins to mould into the countryside. I am, unlike most tourists, not a huge fan of Thailand. I have visited the country a number of times. It seems like a society where almost anything is possible so long as you have money. Want a girl? Pay money and you can have one. Want a little boy? Pay a little more money and you can get one. Want to chop down a rain forest and plant drugs? Pay a lot more money and you can get it done. Anything, except insulting the Royal Family, seems to be okay there if you have the money. There is corruption in other Asian countries, but not on the same scale as Thailand. It is also, ironically, the smiling that disturbs me. Singaporeans and definitely Malaysians and Indonesians can be very grumpy. Thais smile all the time. I feel as though a knife could slide into my stomach and the person holding the knife would never stop looking at me with a pleasant, polite smile.

Nor do I like Bangkok. It is steeped in traffic and to get anywhere takes hours of sitting in a cab. The office Chin is in this time is a far cry from the country club. This is bland walls and laminated office furniture. Again, I am carrying two covert audio recording devices. It makes me nervous, as Chin has another man with him. He looks much more threatening than the fellow at the country club. This man stares at me as if trying to figure out if I am recording anything. I try to cover up my nervousness by talking a lot. Chin, too, is nervous so it makes for a strange meeting.

He tells me that the fix is on. The allegedly corrupt contingent of the Ghana team will play along and, so he claims, will two of the officials. Here is the soaker. He wants money from *me*. Not money as a book advance, not money as deposit, but money as an investment. I am to give him $100,000 and he will invest it for the two of us in "coffee money" for the corrupt members of the Ghanaian team. I tell him absolutely not. We talk briefly. I leave.

Again my head is in a whirl. What happened to the network of sixteen associates around the world? What happened to the Mr. Big at the country club? He is asking *me* for money? I am so broke by this point of years of travelling and research that I stay in the absolute cheapest hotel I can find anywhere in Bangkok that still has a lock on the door. I share the bathroom with fifteen other people, including an entire family from eastern Thailand. Have I come all this way to be fed a ridiculous line about match-fixing, the World Cup, and a team that is probably as honest as a collection of Mennonite preachers?

Late that night, I hunker down with a cup of tea and examine my options. It seems that there are three possible scenarios:

1) It is all a big con job. Chin has heard about my research and thinks it will be a way to make some money and have a good laugh. If I had money to give, which I don't, he would take it and then disappear with it.

2) He was a big fixer but now has fallen on hard times. He is sincere. He still has contacts. He genuinely can fix a World Cup game. But he is desperate and wants to finance it somehow.

3) He is still a big fixer. He is telling the truth. His money is in Switzerland, as he claimed, but is tied up in a transfer from Credit Suisse. He is genuinely trying to do the deal.

The only real option, I realize, is to stay in the region and keep working. I will not give him any money, and so I rule out the first option. But I will stay in contact with Chin and see what will happen.

What happened next was the meeting in the KFC. Between the meeting where Chin had asked me for money and the KFC incident were two weeks where I hung out in Bangkok and Kuala Lumpur. I did more interviews with players and agents. When anyone got curious about my research, I would talk about Singapore and Indonesia. I never mentioned Bangkok. And almost every day, I would call Chin and ask him what was happening. Our relationship had grown rather strange. He seemed to take it as a personal affront that I was skeptical of his claims. He told me he was determined to prove to me that the fix was on.

We met two days after the KFC meeting. Chin was in a great mood. This time we were alone. No associates, either muscular or not. We talked in the same bland office on the outskirts of Bangkok. I asked him what the meeting was like. He told me about the disagreements of bringing in new people on either side of the deal: the new Asian investors on his side, and the new players and officials on the team side. Then I asked how he knew that the runner was not fooling *him* – did he really have the clout in the Ghanaian hierarchy?

Hill:	He is powerful enough in the Ghanaian Football Association?
Chin:	Yes! He is an Under-17 coach for the Ghanaian team.

Hill:	So he knows everyone?
Chin:	Yeah. He knows everyone.
Hill:	Because I was thinking of you. Because I saw in the newspaper that they are going to pay everyone on the team US$20,000 for every game they win.
Chin:	Win is not 100 per cent. You think win is 100 per cent? . . . But I'm paying each player. Each player gets US$30,000. Right? So I know about the Ghana team . . . He told me, "Okay, boss, now we got eight players."

We spoke a little more, and then near the end of the conversation, I almost peed myself when Chin leaned forward. "At KFC, you took a photo, yes? I could see you. I know that you were trying to get photo. I know that. I know everything." I stammered and tried to look as calm as I could. The problem was that I was recording this meeting too and now my hidden camera was working. The only problem was that it threw out a little red light. As he said, "I know everything," Chin seemed to be staring right at the lens. I leant forward across the table and tried to distract his gaze. It seemed to work. It was a good reminder that I was engaged in a very odd dance with some people who could be extremely dangerous. Chin may have asked me for money. He may be playing some bizarre game, but he had the capacity and capability to really hurt me if he wanted. I had to be very careful.

A few days later, I flew back to Europe. The latest developments played over and over in my mind. Either there was one of the biggest scams in sports history going on or some very weird game was being played at my expense.

A SMALL TOWN IN GERMANY

FIFA dismisses the possibility that players or officials could
be open to temptation, saying no player would want to do
anything but their very best at a World Cup.

I fell in love with the World Cup in the Allianz Arena, Munich. It was a
few minutes before the opening match between the host Germany and
Costa Rica on June 9, 2006. The thousands of balloons, doves, and bits
of coloured paper had fluttered up into the sky. The opera notes had
faded away. I watched a laughing Michael Ballack, the captain of the
German team leading a group of his team in a ballet warm-up. I watched
the red-shirted Costa Rican fans dancing in their section of the stands. I
waved my waffleboard in time with everyone else.

I was over in Munich to deliver a lecture on match-fixing to a group
of European gambling executives. They paid me enough that I could
continue my research for another few weeks, but the real treat was a
ticket to the opening game. It is a heady feeling, being present at an event
that the entire world is watching. The air itself seems coloured and distinct. There are invisible lines going out from the event to streets and
houses around the world.

The game itself? There is a famous, much-repeated quote from
Uruguayan writer Eduardo Galeano: "Years have gone by and I've finally
learned to accept myself for who I am: a beggar for good soccer. I go

about the world, hand outstretched, and in the stadiums I plead: 'A pretty move, for the love of God.'" Galeano would have been delighted. The game was perfection. Lots of goals. Skill. And spirit. It started early: in the sixth minute, Philipp Lahm, a German defender who looked so young that it seemed as though the ballboy had wandered onto the pitch by accident, suddenly cut past a defender and blasted a shot in the corner of the Costa Rican goal. I rose with the rest of the stands and we roared.

It was over. All over. How could Costa Rica, tiny Costa Rica, playing in the opening match in Germany, against the powerful Germans, now down 1-0, outplayed in the first few minutes, ever hope to come back from that goal? Someone must have forgotten to tell Paulo Wanchope, the tall, athletic Costa Rican striker, because a few minutes later, he ran through the worryingly weak German defence to equalize 1-1.

The game went back and forth, all the time played at a frantic pace. All the time the crowd, German and Costa Rican, cheered and roared at every piece of skill and magic. All the time we were caught, 66,000 of us, in the spirit that not one of us, not a single one of us, wanted to be anywhere else for that moment.

What a game. What a time to be alive.

For men like me, whose fathers and older male relatives had served so long and hard against the Nazis, it had been a worrying thought to go into a stadium with so many Germans shouting in unison and waving flags. I know that is not a politically correct thing to say, but it was true. As I approached the stadium with the flags everywhere, hackles that I didn't even know I had rose on the back of my neck. To see tens of thousands of Germans, many dressed in identical soccer uniforms, all chanting and singing; it had too many resonances from too long ago. But after ten minutes, I realized I was wrong. Not at this wonderful tournament, staged in a glorious June where the sun shone bright and it seemed like the whole world was watching. Not when all of Germany came out, charming and hospitable. Not when some of the dreadful ghosts of the past were laid to rest.

After the game came the street party along the boulevards of central Munich. In the cobbled courtyards, steeped in history, Iranian and American fans waved to one another. They were not the only ones: fans from almost every part of the world sang and partied together. The marvellous, wonderful Germans offered around bottles of beer. The Costa Ricans staged an impromptu salsa party. The Mexicans jumped up and down, arms around one another, arms around anyone else, and we danced and sang until our throats ached. When it was over, I staggered through the train station and saw that the floor was covered with hundreds of sleeping fans. I saw three young German teenagers dressed in lederhosen and green felt hats, asleep leaning against the wall. I saw no violence, no fights, no racist shouts, no thefts, no pickpockets, no stealing. I may have been lucky, but it was a wonderful, international party. I came back to my hotel at 7.30 in the morning, exhilarated by life, by singing, by soccer.

The idea that two weeks before, and 8,700 kilometres away, I had been huddled in the back of a Thai fast-food outlet listening to plans to fix a game at this wonderful gathering now seemed ridiculous. After five days in southern Germany I flew back to Oxford full of the life of the tournament. Chin had claimed that a friendly match against South Korea in Scotland on June 4 might be fixed. It was not. I read the news that the Ghanaians had ripped the Koreans to shreds in a 3-1 victory with a sense of diminished curiosity.

Then on June 12, came Italy versus Ghana. It was one of the matches that Chin claimed might be fixed. He had said that the corrupt members of the squad would give up two games in the tournament. For the Italy game, the aim was to beat the spread. Italy was to win by at least two goals. I raced home from the university to watch it in my apartment in north Oxford. By this time, seduced by the heady brew of the opening match in Munich, I was watching mostly for the sheer pleasure of the match. I longed to see the Italian team, possibly all good men, but now the representatives of a league that had produced the infamous Moggi match-fixed games, humiliated by a team of underdogs from Africa. I watched the BBC feed flat on my couch.

Midway through the first half, I felt like I had chewed on glass. I felt sick.

The camera had panned across the team benches, and there just behind the Ghanaian coach, Ratomir Dujković, was a group of officials. I could almost swear that the man from the KFC was there. I waited, hoping that the television director would choose to swing the camera back. He did not and I spent some of the rest of the match with my head cocked at an odd angle trying to peer around the sides of the screen.

The Ghanaians were playing oddly. Sometimes beautifully, the mid-field controlling it, touching the ball one to the another. But in the final thirty-five yards, the forwards always seemed to miss the goal or put the ball into touch.

Their spirit seemed odd as well. They did not signal or slap hands when they were together on the field. Their faces were always dead. The Ghanaian team had 53 per cent of the possession. But they never seemed to do anything when they had the ball. A couple of times a Ghana player almost seemed to stroke the ball into touch at the thirty-five yards. I thought of Chin's comments about how to lose a match. How a corrupted team has to keep the ball, do small things, then give the ball way.

As for their defence, both Italian goals came not from attacking prowess but from dreadfully simple mistakes by the opposing defenders. The commentary of the BBC studio experts after the match was scathing about Ghana. Martin O'Neill, the former player and now the manager of Aston Villa of the English Premier League, who looks like a studious priest, was particularly harsh: "There is absolutely no excuse for that," he said about the first goal. "They have been warned all the way through the first half . . . They were punished."

It is all subjective. Possibly the players were simply too nervous to be world-beaters. I had never watched Ghana play before; maybe this subdued energy was simply their natural way of playing. Yet the result was exactly what Chin had claimed that it would be: Italy had won by two clear goals, enough to record a loss on the Asian gambling market. To this day, I have no definite idea if there was something wrong with the game, but on a scrap of paper that I had grabbed during the match I wrote in big, block letters my opinion:

THIS WAS A FIXED GAME.

It was time to go back to Germany. It was time to put aside the heady enthusiasm of the opening game and visit the Ghanaian team hotel and headquarters. It was time to figure out if the man sitting near the Ghanaian coach was the KFC man. It was time, finally, to understand if what I had seen in Bangkok was a wisp of fantasy or something more solid: a genuine attempt to fix the games at the biggest tournament in the world.

The first Ghanaian I saw in Germany was taking out the garbage. In the 1960s and 1970s, thousands of Ghanaians had escaped the grinding poverty of their homeland and moved to Germany. They still work mostly in menial jobs as janitors, gardeners, or garbage collectors. He was there among the crowds at the Würzburg station. A middle-aged man, probably in his fifties. He was silent and dignified, collecting pieces of garbage. There was no outward racism. No one that I saw called out or threatened or treated him badly. But what most white Germans seemed to do was ignore him. It was as if the space that he occupied did not have any cells in it. It was simply blank. I saw about a dozen Africans in Germany that June, and it was usually the same. No overt racism. No American-style fear. Simply utterly blank spaces where people were but were not supposed to be.

When you leave the train station in Würzburg, you can see a hill stretching up past the railway line covered with vineyards. Würzburg is a lovely town. The Main River flows past a wonderful collection of historic buildings that make up its centre. The local joke is that the town has more churches than houses, and certainly down near its gorgeous seventeenth-century law school, the joke seems true. Nothing much has happened in Würzburg since 1631, but suddenly for a few days in June 2006, it felt like the whole world was looking at the town. The Ghana camp was at a hotel in the centre of Würzburg. After the Italy game, the Ghanaians had beaten the favoured Czech team 2-0. Then the night that I arrived, Ghana had just beaten the United States 2-1, and half the town was down at the Maritim Hotel to welcome the team home.

I went down to the hotel. I had no idea what I was doing. When I left the U.K. to go to Germany, I had expected that the World Cup camp for the Ghanaian team would be in some castle high on top of a German mountain. Access would be restricted and tightly guarded. Security would be tight to stop would-be suicide bombers, scandal-seeking journalists, and match-fixing gamblers.

It was blessedly, wonderfully, and worryingly not like that. When I reached the hotel, a huge party was going on. Half of the inhabitants of Würzburg seemed to be at the doors of the hotel to welcome the team back. I watched the crowd. They were straining to get into the hotel. There were flag-draped, middle-aged Ghanaians dancing in the streets while bemused small-town Germans cheered them on.

This was the flip side of the subtle racism that I saw at the station and throughout Germany. Over the next few days around the hotel I saw that Africans were not ignored; now they were *happy* people who danced in the streets. I had a drink across from the hotel with a Ghanaian. Enthusiastic Germans there exclaimed about the *happy* Africans and gave us lots of thumbs-up about their spirit. Here is the problem: the Ghanaian I drank with was a founder of his own welding supply company in the West Ghana gold mines. He had been a gold miner himself for five years. He was a tough businessman in one of the toughest environments in the world. But to the people in the bar, he was a *happy African*. It is the inability to see a person as a person, rather than as a blank space or a cliché, that defines racism.

I drank a glass of wine with the ex-miner. Two Ghanaian players in white T-shirts wandered past the window. They were holding hands. I was touched. Amid the hurly-burly of flags waving, fans dancing, and cars honking, they looked like two villagers, who happened to be World Cup players, wandering almost innocent through the joyful chaos that they had helped to cause.

"The world says thank you for beating the United States," gushed the middle-aged German woman in the hotel lobby to the Ghanaian player. She was dressed in black leather trousers and had dyed-blonde hair. She held the young player's hands for too long and smiled. "You know every-one hates the United States. They are doing all these bad things in Iraq. They have such a terrible reputation around the world and you beat them!" She beamed at the player. He said nothing and had the decency to look embarrassed.

It wasn't supposed to be like this. Everything that I read spoke of stern-faced officials pushing back the hordes of people to keep teams separate from potential dangers. There was an article from the 2002 World Cup by the London *Evening Standard* sternly stating that "FIFA had not established any specific rules to limit the contact between players and officials at the World Cup and bookmakers." FIFA's reply in the article had been:

> FIFA dismisses the possibility that players or officials could be open to temptation, saying no player would want to do anything but their very best at a World Cup . . . FIFA says the security will be so tight that players, managers and officials will not be contactable.

Well, that may have been true in Japan and Korea, but it certainly was not true in Germany. I had got so close to one of the players within ten minutes of arriving that I could see how red his ears turned when he was embarrassed.

In fact, over the next six days, I contacted pretty much all of the players, managers, and officials that I wanted to. I did it by taking a strategic decision within about twenty seconds of arriving at the hotel. First, I took a deep breath. Then I mentally counted my remaining euros from the gambling executive lecture. Then I took another deep breath and walked up to the reception desk and booked a room. It is an expensive hotel and a long way, both figuratively and literally, from my place in the backstreets of Bangkok. However, I got a room on the second floor, just past the dining hall where the players, officials, and soon I would eat. Now I could and would wander around talking to anyone I wanted to. I thought to myself repeatedly over the time I spent there that if it were this simple for a penny-pinching academic researcher, it must be very easy for a rich gambler.

Even booking into the hotel was probably unnecessary. Everyone and anyone seemed to wander around almost at will. I watched the televised matches of other games, sitting two along from the most famous African players of their generation: Abédi Pelé and Tony Yeboah. There was something disconcerting in both how young and how normal the atmosphere was around the Ghanaian team. If you have ever been in a sports tournament, then you know the atmosphere: half family, half athletes preparing for the bout. Injuries are discussed. A round of small commitments dominates the time. Two of the younger players came down from the elevator, late for the reception at the town square.

"What time is it?" snapped Anthony Baffoe, one of the stars of the great Ghana team of the early 1990s who was helping out the current squad.

The two of them smile, embarrassed.

"You were supposed to be down here at six thirty. Let's go."

One morning I saw Michael Essien, the Ghanaian star of Chelsea, having breakfast a few tables over from me. On the television screen during games, he looks like a snarling pit bull of a player. In person, he seemed far younger and less muscular. All the players looked like that. So young and *normal*. It seemed a contradiction that at the centre of the marketing hype, the nationalistic fervour, the countless TV programs and newspaper articles, the World Cup is just another tournament of young players playing soccer.

The first thing to do was track down anyone who was an Under-17 coach. Chin had claimed that his runner was an Under-17 coach. They were two youth coaches with the delegation: Sam Arady and Cecil Jones Attuquayefio. I asked to meet them on the restaurant patio. Before they arrived, I paced nervously up and down, wondering what I would say if it either of them turned out to be the same man I had seen a few weeks before in Bangkok. I need not have worried. As soon as I saw them, I realized that neither of these men was the person I had seen in Thailand. They were much older and they were extraordinarily talented men. Between the two of them, they had coached teams to successes in, among other things, an Under-17 Africa Cup, an Under-17 World Cup, and an Olympic medal. I asked Arday what his best moment had been in a long, storied career:

> The best moment I have had with Ghanaian football was in Barcelona. It was the first time an African team had won a medal in the Olympics, and for me, it was like something had happened to my life. And when we went to the [Olympic] village and we saw our team, I was very happy . . . It is something I will cherish and cherish forever.

Until I spoke to Chin, I had never really taken much notice of Ghanaian soccer. It was a huge oversight. In terms of youth soccer, Ghana is an international powerhouse. In the last twenty years, the number of Under-17 World Cups either won or placed second by the Ghanaians is just behind Brazil. The morning that I spoke to them, the Serbian team had failed in the World Cup. They had failed ignominiously badly. The Ghanaian coach was Serbian. I told Arday and Jones that they should fax in their resumes to the Serbian FA. They laughed. But there was a painful side to their laughter. It is considered a joke that an African coach should submit his resume to a European team, even when an African coach has won youth continental championships, youth World Cups, and Olympic medals. It is racism that still afflicts the sport in Africa. I asked them about this issue.

This is the problem in the whole of Africa, and I think that we African coaches have not been given the opportunity to offer ideas that would be very crucial to the development of football in our country or Africa in general. When it comes to the coaching of the national team, they want to go for an expatriate. They don't seem to have confidence in us. In this whole of Africa, Ghana included, they have never had confidence in us, and therefore it is difficult for us even to have access to the national team.

This attitude may have something to do with the mysterious paradox that has plagued Ghanaian soccer for the last twenty years. They dominate youth soccer to such a degree that their only consistent rivals are Nigeria and Brazil. At the senior level, over one hundred Ghanaian players are playing or have played in the top European leagues. Yet they have never, until 2006, shown what they are capable of on the world stage at the senior level. The team that typifies this paradox is the one of the early 1990s. That team should have dominated African and international soccer. Its stars – Abédi Pelé, Tony Yeboah, and Anthony Baffoe – were high-ranking European players. Abédi Pelé was voted African player of the year three times; he had won a European Champions League medal with Olympique de Marseille. On paper there was no way that they should not have challenged for the World Cup. Yet they did not. In 1993, there occurred a heartbreaking game that every Ghanaian fan remembers only too well. The team was to play the winners of the 1990 World Cup, the Germans, in Germany. In the first half, the Ghanaians played like *they* were the World Cup winners and were leading 1-0. The second half was so bad that it would have been funny, if it had not been so painful: the Germans came storming back, utterly outplaying the Ghanaians. They even scored three goals in one minute, and won the match 6-1. In Ghana it is known as the "Bochum Disaster," and one popular theory that explains the odd match is that at half-time the Ghanaian officials came into the dressing room and explained that there would be two different levels of pay for the game: the foreign-based stars on the team would receive one level of payment, and the Ghana-based players would receive another, much lower, pay. The players who played in the Ghana league were not happy with the proposal and made their discontent clear in the most obvious way possible.

The man who first told me that story was the best of the Ghanaian journalists, the cerebral and insightful Michael Oti Adjei. He runs a TV talk show on sports in Ghana and loves his country and team with a passion. We struck up a friendship and one day over coffee, he tried to explain to me how much this team meant to his country:

> You know, for a country like Ghana, football victories mean so much. It is very, very symbolic. It's one of the few occasions when this country really feels like it belongs to the world. Because constantly you can't compete; you can't hold on to your best doctors; you can't hold on to your best teachers. People are completing first-degree programs and running away to the United Kingdom and the rest to do menial jobs scrubbing dirt, you know, do all sorts of jobs, wait on people and the rest. So you know, football is when we see them on TV, when they are the centre of attention of the world, [and it] provides a really good source of patriotism that nobody can channel.

I spent six days there, and each day the tension at the hotel increased a little more. Once the euphoria of beating the Czechs and the United States had faded, everyone's attention, including my own, began to focus on the Brazil game coming up on Tuesday, June 27. Conversations focused on tactics, strategy, and preparation. One evening, I interviewed Stephen Appiah, the captain and talismanic player of the Ghana team, in the lobby of the hotel. He is a former Juventus player, now with Fenerbahçe, the Turkish league champions. He told me that their main focus for the Brazil match was to defend well:

We have to defend very well, because they have players, you can see their matches, they always come like three, no, four, five. They come to attack. We have to take our time to get a counterattack and if we can make use of it then I think we can put them into trouble. Because, they always go, they have players that they can't even defend, only to attack. So we have to use our head to beat them.

He was charismatic, charming, and seemingly completely focused on winning the game. Surely this man, with so much money and talent, could not be tempted to take money from an Asian gambler?

Everything seemed fine on the surface. There was no sign of any fixers anywhere. There was no sign of any dodgy Under-17 coaches. I searched the squad again and again. I sat in the restaurant watching them all eat. I sat in the corner of the lobby and I took photos, sweeping the room and taking shots of everyone. Then, late at night, I would examine the shots to see if there was anyone I could recognize. But there was no one either in person or in the photos who reminded me of the people in the Bangkok KFC. I went up to every Asian man or woman I found in or near the hotel. I struck up conversations. Nothing. Not a stir of memory. Not a trace of recognition.

The truth was, there was absolutely no sign of any of the people around the table at the KFC. No sign of the runner who was supposed to have eight players and two officials ready to throw the match. No sign of any Asian fixers with briefcases full of cash. No sign of anyone who raised the slightest amount of suspicion.

As for the thought of players fixing a game, it dissolved almost completely from my mind when I walked down the corridor toward my room. In a meeting room at nine at night, the team would gather to sing Christian hymns, their voices echoing down the hall after me as I went to my room.

The idea of a fix being perpetrated now seemed like a dream. The Ghanaian team seemed like a group of good guys who held hands in public, were polite to idiotic fans, and sang hymns every night before they went to bed. The whole thing was crazy. An absurd trick had been played on me. My view of the Italy game must have been wrong. So what if some of the players had seemed dazed during the Italy game? It was a natural reaction to one of the biggest games of their lives. If Chin had got the score right of the game, it was simply by accident.

Another thought occurred to me: maybe Chin had switched countries on me for security reasons? Maybe he was actually fixing another African team at the World Cup? Togo, for example, was having huge problems. I had read in the newspapers that their German manager had ordered his team to not speak with Asian journalists. Togo had a game against South Korea coming up. The coach did not want any of the players to be bribed. His thoughts were that the journalists or fixers pretending to be journalists would approach his Togo players to throw the game. Then suddenly, the German manager announced his resignation. Then he was reinstated. Then the players went on strike, demanding that their appearance money be paid directly into their bank accounts and not to the Togolese Football Federation. The players feared that the Togo soccer officials would steal their money. In the end, the Togo team only played when they were guaranteed by FIFA that FIFA would pay the players directly. So if Ghana was such a peaceful team, maybe Chin's real connection was with the Togo team?

While these thoughts floated through my head, I began to realize that there was something else going on at the hotel and among the Ghana team. Something that was odd and something that I couldn't quite figure out. It was symbolized by an event that means nothing except in its image. I went out of the hotel on the Sunday morning. The sun was shining and for once the square in front of the building was empty. It was lovely, quiet, and deserted. I looked back at the hotel and there sitting at an open window was a gorgeous young German prostitute. She stood there, large breasts packed into a red boustière, blonde hair floating across her shoulders, silently announcing to the world who she was and what she did. She was absolutely certain of her effect on the world. She looked down at the square from her perch with wonderful self-assurance. And she looked down at the square from the floor where many of the rooms belonging to the Ghanaian delegation were located.

This is not an anti-sex observation. It is that there was some thing, some strain that was underneath the surface that I was not catching. Something that was at odds with the hymn-singing enthusiasm.

After a few days of eating and living in the same hotel, I noticed that there was a distinct class difference between the players and the officials. The players were the working-class. The officials were the Big Men of Africa. The officials strutted around the lobby and dining hall, showing off their control and power. The players actually looked like small-town guys. They did not seem to have the ego or swagger of North American athletes, but rather one got the feeling of a local team on tour. They were mostly surrounded by their friends, young guys from the same neighbourhood who acted as their gofers and aides.

It was like the story of the success at the Under-17 World Cups. On the first day after talking to Sam Arday and Cecil Jones Attuquayefio, I had become a gushing fan of the development of Ghana soccer. But I got a different perspective talking to the president of the Ghana Football Association, Kwesi Nyantakyi. It was late one morning. I was sitting, by mistake, in the team section of the restaurant. He was waiting for his coffee and seemed slightly officious. However, when I started to ask him questions, he was remarkably forthcoming. I asked him about the paradox of why Ghana had such strong teams at the youth level but, until this World Cup, not at senior level. He trotted out what I suspect were a roster of usual excuses: the players change all the time (they are supposed to, they are young), Ghana had no resources, no facilities. But most interestingly, and with great honesty, he told me that if Ghana had done well in the past at youth level it was because a lot of the players had not actually been under seventeen. They had really been nineteen-, twenty-, or twenty-one-year-olds pretending to be younger. His predecessor had announced that this practice must end, and Nyantakyi was doing his best to make sure that players were actually the right ages. However, since this policy of honesty, Ghana's youth teams had not been as successful as in the past.

Later, some of the Ghanaian journalists at the hotel explained to me that the use of overage players was so common among their squads that many players had two ages: the official one, which was improbably young, and their real ages, which were at least two or three years older.

There were other more worrying stories of alleged corruption. Michael Oti Adjei told me the story of the Ghana national team losing to Nigeria in the last qualifying match before the 2002 World Cup. It meant Nigeria went through to the finals while Liberia did not. Ghana was already out of the running, and they lost 3-0 to Nigeria. At the farewell banquet after the match, the former president of the Ghana Football Association accepted $25,000 from the Nigerians, which he promptly shared among the players and officials. The Nigerians claimed that this was simply a traditional gift in their culture.

Then I watched the Ghanaian delegation selling their ticket allocation. When Ghana got into the second round, FIFA issued a round of tickets to the team. Over the weekend, the tickets arrived for the Ghana Football Association. Outside the hotel, an orderly lineup of Germans formed immediately. The Ghanaians promptly ignored the line and went around to the side of the table and ordered dozens of tickets each. Not surprisingly, within twenty minutes the supply of tickets ran out. Then some of the Ghanaians went into the hotel lobby and sold the tickets for at least twice what they had paid for them. I bought a couple of tickets from Michael, who did not charge me anything extra, but the German fans were not happy. They started to protest. Some journalists began to take pictures of the corruption in action. Then the local police stepped in. They lost their heads. So in love with all things Ghanaian were the people of Würzburg, that the police did not stop the ticket scam from going on. Rather, on the "orders" of the Ghanaian officials, they told the journalists that we could not take photos of the corrupt ticket sales. They even threatened to arrest a Brazilian journalist who was demanding to do so. Why German police felt able to tell citizens in what was purported to be a democracy when they could or could not take photos is beyond me. It left a sour taste. It made me realize that although I had wonderful access to the team, I was not getting a complete picture of what was going on.

And then there were the phone calls.

While I sat in my room away from the carnival atmosphere of the hotel lobby, I would speak to Chin. He was back in Bangkok with his business associates, but we would talk every few days. On June 25, two days before the Brazil game, we spoke. We were watching the Ecuador versus England game, and Chin was telling me that one of his friends had helped to fix that game. The problem was England was so bad that they were having difficulty even beating a partially compliant team. But he had news of the Brazil versus Ghana game.

Chin:	Yeah, yeah, my friend told me. But they called me and they are interested doing. Ghana and Brazil.
Hill:	Brazil is going to win?
Chin:	No, Ghana will lose. They will do the business with Brazil. [Really?] Yes it is confirmed.
Hill:	Confirmed, confirmed?
Chin:	Absolutely. 100 per cent confirmed. They say against Brazil, they really want to do the business.
Hill:	I don't understand why they would want to do that? They get paid by the football association.
Chin:	Yeah. [laughs] But you gotta know, sometimes in football, there are players . . . they will do the business . . . But today the same guy told me that they arranged the game with Ecuador to England to win. 2-0.
Hill:	Yeah, I don't know, I am watching the game here, and England look as if they are much worse than Ecuador. Ecuador looks very good.
Chin:	Yes, England is very very bad. . . . They are playing 4-5-1. It is a fucked-up arrangement, you know.

Hill:	But I think the Ghana-Brazil one we have more informa-
	tion on. We have people inside the camp. We are more
	certain about that . . .
Chin:	Yes, absolutely. Absolutely. Absolutely. It's true.

Chin was saying two things. One, some of his associates had contacts with a few players on the Ecuadorian team who had arranged for them to lose to England. Yet the English team was so bad that they could not let them score a convincing goal. It struck me at the time as typical of the kind of Asian gambling talk that is common. England did eventually win 1-0, which is not the score that fixers would have wanted, but Chin was quite complacent saying that when he arranged fixes he would often get the team to play well in the first half and then have a bad second half. He thought that is what had probably happened with the game. I remain uncertain, knowing absolutely no other details of the purported fix. Again, I include this conversation because of the public right to know. However, Chin was guaranteeing that Ghana would "lose" the game against Brazil, which meant in gambling terms that for that particular game, Ghana would lose by at least a two-goal margin. The conversation was two days before the game. He predicted "with 100 per cent certainty" that Ghana would lose by at least two goals.

JUNE 27, 2006: DORTMUND STADIUM, GERMANY

I cried. I stood in the stands and I cried.

I'm sorry to write that I was so emotional. It may seem silly. It may seem undignified or not masculine. But I want to be honest. I am not sure why I cried. I think I cried for the lonely, dignified Ghanaian man who picked up the garbage at the train station. I think I cried for the millions of people around the world willing their team on against the greatest favourites in the sport. I think I cried because of the couple beside me in the stands: a forty-year-old father and his twenty-year-old son. They had never met until a few weeks before the game. And now they were so in love with one another, it made you smile. I think I cried because of the Brazilian man with a twisted face dressed in a chicken outfit outside the stadium. A man so intent on seeing his heroes in action that he had spent an enormous sum of his money in travelling to Germany and now he desperately begged for a ticket outside the game. I think I cried because of all the emotions and symbolism that gets placed in the great and beautiful game. I think I cried because at an emotional level, I am sure that game was fixed.

I watched the match in the Dortmund stadium surrounded by tens of thousands of chanting, flag-waving supporters. The Brazilian fans had all the accoutrements the world has come to expect of them: the samba drum, the gorgeous women in bikinis, the casual arrogance that comes from being the world champions. The Ghanaians had hope. I stood among the supporters of the underdog team. To many of the supporters, their soccer team represented their dreams, aspirations, and dignity. They cheered on their team with desperate enthusiasm: every successful pass, every successful tackle, every successful run seemed to mean so much more to them than a mere soccer game.

I don't know how. I don't know the mechanics. I watched the game skeptically. I had heard Chin's story before the match. But I still watched the game with disbelief that anything corrupt would happen. It was simply impossible. The teams came out. They seemed to play with all their hearts. They seemed to be trying as hard as they could. They seemed to be doing everything they could to win the match. But there were a string of stupid mistakes: shots were missed, offsides were not played well, defenders' attention wandered, and three stupid, silly goals were scored. They were goals that a youth team would have been ashamed to give away.

There was something not right about the game, something that stunk.

The final score was the exact one Chin had told me it would be. I was – and still am – convinced that *something* went on in that game. I had watched a fixed match take place.

The supporters left and I stood alone. It was then that I cried. I did not cry for long – a minute or so – but there were tears. Then I pulled myself together and phoned Chin.

I congratulated him on his victory and told him that I had never quite believed him, but now I did. He was remarkably calm. "If I'm such a genius," he complained, "how come I can only make a couple of hundred thousand?" Then he said, "But I have another one for you. Another fixed match."

The match was Ukraine versus Italy. According to Chin, another of his associates had a few corrupt players on the Ukraine team. They were willing to throw the game against Italy. The score would be above the Asian goal spread, so more than two goals. He told me this before and during the game. Frankly, I didn't have the same emotional attachment to the Ukraine team. I had not seen a KFC-style meeting. I had not met with the players before the game. I watched the game on television. All the Ukraine team seemed to be trying their best; they seemed to be charging about trying to beat a technically superior Italian team. They still lost, though. And they lost by the result that Chin had told me that they would lose.

The situation was now incredible. In four games in the World Cup Finals I had been told before the matches started or during the matches what the results of the game would be. In three of those matches, the results had been absolutely accurate. In the fourth, the result had been off by only one goal. Was it all coincidence? Was it all just sheer luck and a good story by Chin? I desperately wanted to investigate. I desperately wanted to find out what was going on.

And then I was stopped from investigating.

19

THE GOLD COAST

Yeah, yeah, yeah, I remember in Malaysia in '97 in the Under-20 World Cup. There is one guy, I see him everywhere, even during the World Cup, he was there. I think this guy is from . . . Japan or China. So he came to us and he said, "Hey, you people have to score first goal and we are going to bet, because they are gambling, and I am going to give you this amount of money."

For the last few months, it had been difficult to juggle the roles of a doctoral graduate student and an investigative journalist. At this point, for a variety of university-related reasons, I had to promise the Sociology Department not to conduct any more research or investigations outside of my academic, now mostly statistical work. I could not phone Chin or any other of the Asian fixers. If I broke the agreement, I would have faced very serious academic consequences.

I kept my word. For a year, I did no work on investigating the possible match-fixing at the World Cup. It was the year of the Big Wait. It was a year of cooling my heels. It was a year of statistics, dark walls, and bits of paper thrown off a pier. It was a year of glorious Oxford, of long runs with friends over the beautifully green Port Meadow, of swims in the Thames and sunsets making the whole town glow. But all the time at the back of my mind were the questions of what I had seen and what it all meant.

Then, finally, the next June I was free. I handed in my thesis to my supervisor. The investigative wolf that lives inside me was let off the chain. I was off to track down what happened that last year.

At this point, it is probably worth considering what I knew and did not know.

First, there was some evidence that was purely circumstantial. Ghanaian journalists had told me that their national team may have thrown a World Cup qualifying match to Nigeria a few years before. So the *idea* of selling games was not as unknown as it might have been.

Second, I had seen some matches that made me very suspicious: one where I was so convinced that I had seen a fix that I had cried. Big deal. In the cold light of afterthought, it still seemed unbelievable that a fixed game would be played at that level.

The major piece of evidence that games had been fixed in the world's biggest soccer tournament was, of course, that a well-known Asian fixer had told me the essential results of four matches before they were played. It could, of course, have been luck. The games all followed a particular pattern. If Chin was to be believed, all four matches were between relatively poor underdog teams and heavily favoured teams. The predictions of the alleged fixes followed what most gamblers would have said would be the result: Italy would beat Ghana and Ukraine, Brazil would beat Ghana, and England would beat Ecuador. Possibly then, Chin was having me on, telling me with great secrecy the results of games that any outsider could have predicted. But he had, of course, done slightly more than that; he had told me the gambling spread of each game.

At one point in the year of the Big Wait, I asked one of the rising stars of the Sociology Department, Steve Fisher, for advice. Fisher is a statistician who, along with his work on tactical voting, does things such as help run the BBC's election night specials as a number cruncher in the studio.

We spoke a little about the situation. He said, "It is very simple. Just add up the odds for each of the games with the predicted results, because the odds depend on the result of each game. You should be able to figure out how lucky that prediction was. . . ."

I did so. The number was not particularly high (for I had been given only the exact result – win by more than the spread rather than the exact score), roughly 5.5 to 1. However, it is worth remembering that most bank managers – or drug dealers – would be very happy with a return on investment of 5 to 1.

I had also seen things aside from the actual matches. I had not only spoken to the fixer, Chin, who was purportedly helping to arrange the fixes, but he had also shown me a meeting with a man he alleged to be a runner, in which they had discussed the possibility of fixing games.

So along with the accuracy of the predictions, I knew that there was *something* going on. I knew that it was not whole teams; rather, the fixers were supposed to be small groups of corrupt players. However, I had absolutely no idea of the truth of the allegations about unnamed players on the Ecuador or Ukraine team. I did not have a single player talking about being approached to fix a game. Most importantly, I had no idea of who the runner was at the KFC. I had never seen the runner near the Ghana camp, nor had I knowingly seen any of the gamblers.

I believed the possibility of *something* having occurred. If Chin had been telling the truth, the runner would have the following characteristics:

- *He would have had some connection with the Ghana team, enough to be able to get easy access to the players.*
- *He would have been an Under-17 coach.*
- *He would have been involved with the Olympic team in Athens against Japan.*
- *He would have been in Würzburg, but there would have been some reason that I had not seen him. Either he was at another hotel or in deep hiding, which seemed unlikely.*

I decided to go to Ghana.

To find that man, if he existed, I had a grainy photograph and my memory. On the surface it was a ridiculous task: to find one man who may or may not be in Ghana, out of all the millions of Ghanaians. I had spent hours in the hotel in Würzburg trying to find him. I had taken photo after photo of groups of Ghanaians and then had gone through them. I had found no one who looked like the man I had seen in the Bangkok KFC. However, if I did not go to Ghana I would always wonder about the truth of what I had seen in Germany at the World Cup.

Ghana was one of the first of the former British colonies in sub-Saharan Africa to gain its independence. In 1957, the charismatic Kwame Nkrumah, Ghana's first prime minister, was interested in uniting the rest of Africa into one country. One of the ways he tried to do so was through soccer. In Ghana, massive amounts of money were spent on developing soccer in a vain attempt to convince the rest of the continent that they should unite under African, read Ghanaian, rule. So it was ironic that the day I arrived in Accra, it was the opening of the African Union Summit: a huge shindig for African leaders to get together and talk about building a united Africa. From what I could gather, the meeting left most people in Accra completely unmoved, both literally and figuratively, so there were lots of complaints about the traffic jams that the meetings caused and the millions of dollars that were spent on refurbishing a downtown conference centre, but little enthusiasm and interest in the summit. Moammar El-Gadhafi, the Libyan leader, had driven with his entourage through the Sahara Desert to be at the meeting. It was an imaginative stunt, but the real problem facing most people in Ghana is not African unity – it is poverty. One of the older Ghanaian coaches would tell me that in the middle of a famine in the early 1980s, he motivated the national team during a tournament by providing them all with bags of rice and beans. Then he gave the players the weekend off so that they could take the food back to their families. This way, the players were not preparing for a major competition while worrying if their families would starve. The country has developed tremendously in the last twenty-five years and its literacy rate is among the highest in the continent, but over 75 per cent of the population still make less than $2 a day.

What really interested most people in Ghana, aside from their family's survival, was soccer. The exploits of the Black Stars were still dominating Ghanaian social life. The heady brew of world attention is rarely tasted in the country and Ghana was still a little drunk from the events of the World Cup the year before. The politicians had ensured that the city was covered with flags and photos of the various African summit leaders. The people covered themselves, their cars, and their buildings with photos of the Black Stars players and the team logo.

The obsession with the Black Stars was partly because of the positive attention the team had brought Ghana on the world stage, but partly it was that the players had won the lottery of life. And for the most part, they had won it fairly. They were not corrupt African politicians driving around in limos tying up traffic and giving windbag speeches in multi-million-dollar conference halls. Rather, the young men who played soccer in Europe and for the national team had achieved the Horatio Alger success story in a poor African country. They were mostly very poor, very young men who with nothing but their talent, hard work, and enterprise had succeeded in making relatively large sums of money. The sports newspapers reflected this phenomenon; they were dominated with news from Europe. The well-read magazine *African Sports* is twelve pages long. The issue of late June had seven and three-quarters of its pages devoted to the doings of the European Champions Leagues, and only four and a quarter pages on sport in Ghana.

There was, however, one item of home-grown soccer news that was of great interest in the spring of 2007. Abédi Pelé had been the dominant African player of his generation. He was one of the players I had watched games with in the hotel in Würzburg. He was part of the golden generation of Ghanaian players from the early 1990s. He was an African Player of the Year, the lead scorer of the Ghanaian national team, a European Champions League medal winner, and in the spring of 2007, many Ghanaians thought that he had been involved in a fixed match.

In March 2007, the team that Abédi Pelé owned, FC Nania, had been challenging for promotion to the Ghana Premier League. They had come to the final round of the season tied on points with rivals Great Mariners. If the situation stayed that way, the championship would essentially depend on which team had scored the most goals over the season. Their games began at exactly the same time and at least in the first half seemed to be played normally: both FC Nania and Great Mariners were beating their opponents 1-0 and 2-0 respectively. Then things got strange, *very* strange. Goals started to be scored in each game, *lots* of goals, so many goals that one of the referees began to get dizzy. You cannot really blame the poor fellow; just writing down the numbers of goals scored must have put a severe strain on his wrist, let alone having to count them all. By the end of the game, FC Nania had, of course completely coincidently according to Abédi Pelé, won their last match of the season 31-0, while their rivals, Great Mariners, had managed to win *their* last game of the season 28-0.

It was not the first time that such ridiculous scores had been recorded in last matches of a Ghanaian soccer season. But it was still hugely embarrassing. The equivalent would be Roberto Baggio or Wayne Gretzky or Sir Bobby Charlton owning a team that won by such an improbable score. Worse, Abédi Pelé is a luminary of FIFA, a member of their Football Committee. He is even one of FIFA's ambassadors for the upcoming World Cup in South Africa in 2010. It was not just a problem for soccer in Ghana, but also for African and world soccer.

To its credit, the Ghana Football Association (GFA) moved relatively quickly on this issue. Their disciplinary committee banned Abédi Pelé, the two teams, and most of the players involved in the matches for a year from the sport. FIFA had still to decide on Abédi Pelé's fate when his wife started a lawsuit against the GFA. Abédi Pelé himself released a statement that said in part:

I will go wherever I can to get justice as we have been banned on con-
jecture . . . The only possible accusation is that my team scored more
goals. And if that is the case, my contention is that while the score line
may raise eyebrows, it does not point to an irrefutable conclusion that
the match was fixed.

The excuses began to flow fast and furious. One of the coaches from a
losing team declared that the reason his team played so badly was that
they were all recuperating from food poisoning. One of the referees
said that he "couldn't understand what happened at the games." Abédi
Pelé himself, at one point, claimed that he had actually left the stadium
before the end of the game. He was then contradicted by his own
brother, who said that Abédi Pelé not only stayed to the end of the game
but was carried shoulder-high around the field by the victorious players.

It was not the first major case of alleged match-fixing to be seen in
Ghana. One Internet blogger wrote, "I'm surprised that people are lambasting those 4 teams involved. Can somebody who is football fanatic
[sic] tell me that no team in Ghana has not been involved in match-
fixing[?]" The year before, two top teams in the Premier League had,
allegedly, been taped arranging fixes. And I also spoke to a Ghanaian
Premier League team owner, who assured me that match-fixing occurred
regularly and that he had bought matches. "I got the other team's goalkeeper to let in goals at 50,000 cedi each goal. Every time he gave up a
goal he would raise his right arm as if swearing, but it was really a signal
to me . . . The final score was 4-1 to us, so I paid him 200,000 cedi in all
[200,000 cedi is about $20]."

However, when I arrived in Accra, the GFA Appeals Committee had
just overturned the ban on Abédi Pelé and his teams. The whole case was
making its way through the court system, to the interest of soccer fans
across the country. (A few months after I left the country, the official
legal charges against Abédi Pelé were dismissed in court, but the bans
against the teams and players all remained.) The situation may have
been bad for Ghanaian soccer, but at that time it actually made my job

easier. I was not looking forward to researching a possible case of corruption in the one institution in Ghana that people respected and admired as being utterly corruption-free. Now, with the Abédi Pelé case, no one would be particularly suspicious if I wandered around interviewing people about match-fixing.

I hired Michael Oti Adjei, the intellectual turned journalist who had so impressed me the year before. He was to get phone numbers and help arrange interviews, but when I spoke to him I kept the actual story that I was working on deliberately vague. I did that for two reasons. First, because I wanted him to have deniability if anyone asked him what I was doing. It is relatively easy being an international journalist. At the end of the story, we get to fly out. What is often far more difficult is to be the local person who helps the international journalist. Those people have to stay around and carry the can with the people who have been upset by the story. It is often better not to fill them in completely so they can honestly say to people, "I had no idea what they were doing."

Second, for all my respect for his intellectualism, I noticed that frequently many Ghanaian journalists seemed to think that they were working for the soccer association or their favourite team. I was not sure if this would happen with Oti Adjei, but I did not want to take a chance. We met the night of my first day in Ghana. We sat in the front garden of the Avenue Club, an outdoor restaurant at the centre of Accra. There was a canopy of palm trees and stars. As Oti Adjei briefed me, I began to understand that there had been more, much more, going on at the camp at Würzburg than I had realized.

The most important thing he told me in the darkness of the garden was that there had been a big fight in the camp between the players and the officials about how much they were to be paid. This story was confirmed later in the trip by both some players and the president of the Ghana Football Association (GFA). The meetings had included almost everyone in the team, all the players and the senior officials of the GFA. One of the players had stood up in the middle of the meeting and shouted at the executives, "You are not the people who deserve the money. You cannot play football. You are useless. We are the people who play the game, we deserve the money." The argument had been over the allocation of the sponsorship and FIFA money. The players had thought that they should get paid well for their efforts. The officials claimed that they wanted the bulk of the money for the future development of the game in Ghana. For the officials, unfortunately there was a high level of distrust of the soccer authorities by players. Some of the players thought that the officials simply wanted to skim the money for themselves. The feelings between the players and officials were, evidently, so bad that a senior Ghanaian politician had to intervene personally to make sure there was peace. I asked Oti Adjei why few people had heard about these meetings. The fights between the Togo players and their officials were in the newspapers. He replied:

> I heard about it, but I managed to suppress it, along with the other Ghanaian journalists. We journalists tend to be motivated by patriot- ism. I think that other [foreign] journalists would have run big head- lines on it. You know: "Key Meetings Over How to Share the Money."

His response made me glad that I had not shared too much infor- mation with him about the investigation. If this was the way Oti Adjei, one of the best journalists in the country, treated a story of salary discus- sions, what would he do if he thought I was investigating the possibility of some corrupt players on his national team fixing games? Would he work to uncover the truth, whatever it was, or suppress it? Possibly, he would want to uncover the truth, but possibly not. I have the highest respect for Oti Adjei, but I could not take that chance.

However, the really important thing about the news of these salary negotiations was the *timing* of those meetings. The first meeting, which was very acrimonious, was in the first week of June. In other words, it was *after* the meeting at the Bangkok KFC on May 25. If there were dis- satisfied players who resented the pay settlement, they would have a strong motivation if approached by the runner to say that they were willing to fix the game. They may have changed their minds after the meeting to discuss the salary, but certainly the mood of some of the players would have been very resentful at exactly the time the runner was going out to Bangkok.

The timing of the second meeting was also interesting. It occurred *after* the match against the United States. The team had got through to the second round, and the players wanted to make sure their pay reflected that difference. It occurred at the same time that Chin was assuring me that some of the players had "100 per cent confirmed" that the fix would occur in the Brazil game. Again, this does not prove that there was a fix, but it certainly changed my perception that the camp was full of well-behaved, well-paid hymn singers. Rather, the players may have been singing hymns, but some of them did not consider themselves well paid.

The second thing was another phenomenon that Oti Adjei noticed about his country's sporting culture. At the Avenue Club, we spoke long into the night about the Brazil match and the ridiculous goals that the team had given up. Finally, he gave a long sigh and said:

> The thing is, who cares? Even after we lost to Brazil, we still celebrated. Getting to the second round is considered an achievement. Whatever happened after Czech and the U.S.A. games, the players knew they were going to be treated like heroes. The attitude was "We are not big boys, we have come in the world as far as we can." The players were given the highest honour in Ghana. This is setting the bar too low.

If this perspective were true, it again may have made the decision to fix a game easier for a corrupt player. They had got all the glory they were going to get at the World Cup. They knew that they would not have to face an irate press like the English do when they go out of tournaments at the quarter-finals. To paraphrase Jean-Pierre Bernès, if they were going to lose to Brazil anyway, why not lose with $30,000 in their pockets?

As I mentioned, the ideal fix should have a goalkeeper. So I went to speak to Richard Kingson, the man who played in goal for Ghana for all of the games in the tournament, to see if he had been approached.

I went out to his house in an eastern suburb of Accra. It was an hour-and-a-half drive along the coast road. The neighbourhood surprised me. For a star player, and Kingson had just signed for Birmingham in the English Premier League, the house from the outside was surprisingly modest. The road was unpaved and had potholes three feet deep. I know because we saw a taxi stuck in one. The wheels were completely immersed and the back door would not open because the car had sunk so deeply into the hole. Kingson was not there and Oti Adjei and I sat for two hours waiting for him to return. We went into his compound and discovered that outside appearances can be deceiving. Beyond the gates, there was a large paved courtyard and a life-sized statue of a goal-keeper saving a ball. There were also four men sitting playing cards and whiling away the time. It is something of the nature of professional soccer players in Ghana; there are always three or four young men hanging around them. They are usually buddies from the former neighbourhood, and they control access to the players. It is also some-thing of the nature of Ghana's society and economics. It is a poor country and does not have the money to establish the great factories of bullshit, universities, government departments, and the like, that create so much employment in the developed world. So the streets in Ghana are full of young men just hanging around waiting for some-thing, *anything* to happen. We chatted to them for a while. Finally, Kingson phoned me and apologized, saying we would not be able to meet that night.

I caught up with him in a five-star beach resort the next morning. Kingson was not in a mood to be interviewed. He was a professional athlete, he had a three-hour training session ahead of him, and he wanted to train. However, he sat down with me for a few minutes in a little bar. I had arranged the situation so that there would be no other journalists or hangers-on around. But a few minutes is not a lot of time to do a thorough interview, so I was as blunt as possible. The first few minutes of our conversation went like this:

Hill: Do you know about Asian gamblers who were trying to buy World Cup games?

Kingson: No.

Hill: Did anyone approach you to fix a game?

Kingson: No.

Hill: Did you fix a game?

Kingson: No.

Hill: Heard anything about games being sold?

Kingson: No, nothing.

Well, that was just about as clear as it could be. Our interview continued, with Kingson becoming more comfortable. He urged me to speak to Stephen Appiah, the team captain. He was uneasy at the thought of that game. But he said that if any fraud had happened he would have been the last person to be approached. All the other players knew him as a deeply religious person, he was almost the pastor of the team. He told me he, too, had cried at the end of the game.

I feel like crying, feel like crying because of what you are saying. I didn't know anything about this. I mean, before that game I was crying, because I was full of inspiration, 'cause I had the confidence and the faith that we are going to win the game, no matter what they do. Yeah ... now, now I'm thinking back, and was previewing the game ... [pause] maybe that is how they won it. It's very bad, if that is going on, then it's very bad. How can you sacrifice this? ... After the game I was crying. I was crying. I was asking myself why? Because I saw the glory of God, we would become champions.

Kingson was absolutely positive that no one would have approached him to fix the game and if they had done so he would never have taken any money. After the interview, I went along to his training. It was an extraordinary scene. On a white sandy beach beside the rolling waves of the Atlantic Ocean, some of the top goalkeepers in Ghana were having a private fitness session. Something that most amateur players do not have is the intensity of professional athletes when they practise. Generally, the lower the level of player, the greater the ego on the practice field: to most professional athletes, practice is work and most practices are conducted with complete focus. The training session that I saw was like that: a range of goalkeepers, either the ones who had contracts to play in Europe or the ones who wanted contracts in Europe, diving, jumping, catching, leaping, time after time for hours.

As I was watching, I got into conversation with Yussif Chibsah. He is a midfielder and he had just finished practice. We stepped away to do an interview in a little hut along the beach. Chibsah is one of Ghana's top players; he had just missed making the World Cup squad. He had come to Germany and had been cut from the team a week before the tournament. But he had been the captain of the Ghana team in the Olympics, the one that Chin had claimed took money to lose to Japan. He very quickly confirmed that Asian gamblers had contacted the team during the Olympic tournament. Chibsah said:

> They approached us, I think it was the game against Paraguay and then the game against Japan. Against Paraguay they said, they have a bet. They are gambling. They went for Paraguay, so they would like us to lose that game. Yeah. We told them for lose, we cannot lose this game. Already our first game, it was a drawn game. So we cannot afford to lose the second game. They tried and tried. But we did not give in. Stephen was telling us something about Malaysia in 1997, when they went there. Those kind of things were common over there during the Malaysian tournament. Those kinds of gamblers were around. It was common over there.

I was equally blunt with Chibsah. I asked him directly if he had ever taken money from gamblers either to win or lose a game. He said, "No, no, never. But I have heard there are a lot of gamblers at all the big tournaments. They approach a lot of the teams." I asked him if he knew if any gamblers had approached the Ghana team at the World Cup, and he said he would not know because he had been cut at the last moment.

In the first week of my stay in Ghana, I interviewed two more stars of the Ghana World Cup team: Asamoah Gyan and Sulley Muntari. I did not suspect either of being involved in any type of fix: they had both scored goals in the World Cup. Both denied right away that there had been any fixing going on. Muntari is surprisingly nice. I say surprisingly because he has the reputation of being the Ghanaian Roy Keane, the former enforcer for Manchester United. Muntari, who had just signed for the English Premier League team Portsmouth, is an absolutely ruthless midfielder who has walked out on international camps because of disagreements with the management. He is just about the last person you could imagine taking money to throw a match. But he did say something interesting: that the team was very unsettled by the money situation during the Italy match. That part of the problem with the players, that I had thought might have been corruption, was actually that the top stars could not concentrate because of the financial argument that was going through the camp. But he, like almost everyone else in Ghanaian soccer, urged me to talk to Stephen Appiah: "We are leaders, we are all leaders, but Stephen is our main leader."

Sulley Muntari is not alone in his respect for Stephen Appiah. Appiah's name towers over Ghanaian and African soccer like a colossus. He represents the dream for millions of young men across the continent. He came from a small house in the middle of the Accra slums and by sheer talent, focus, and drive has now earned millions for himself and his family. I went to Appiah's home neighbourhood, Chorkor, a fishing village-cum-suburb on the outskirts of Accra. Say the name of the area to most people from Accra and they look worried. It is a tough area. The roads are paved, there is some electricity, and most houses are cement or brick. But definitely a very, very poor neighbourhood. Appiah would tell me later that Chorkor has the reputation of a hard, dangerous place: "I see my old friends. And I see myself. I feel that God has blessed me. I know what I have come through and all of these guys they dead, they have been killed for armed robbery. And some of them are spoiled with drugs. So I see myself like this . . . the type of level that I am on now. I really feel that I have come from a long way."

Appiah's brother Ernest took me on a tour. He wore cheap flip-flops, a black T-shirt, ill-fitting white pants, and a diamond earring. In his clothes and manner he was utterly indistinguishable from anyone else in Chorkor, except for the earring. He and another brother were repairing the family house where Stephen Appiah was born. It is a low-slung building where half a dozen people still live. Nothing shows the lottery of life that the players have won better than this house and the comparison with his brother. I saw one of the pitches that a young Stephen Appiah played on when he was a boy. It was beside the ocean, covered with garbage and without a scrap of grass.

Appiah has not forgotten where he comes from. I caught up with him after he appeared at an event promoting a national health insurance program. Appiah had posed for a photo shot to publicize the scheme and then had personally paid the fee for a hundred elderly people from Chorkor to be insured. When Michael Oti Adjei and I got there, Appiah had just left, pulling away in a gleaming, black Infiniti 4 x 4. However, in the midst of poverty and altruism came near-Hollywood glamour to save our day. Oti Adjei introduced me to Appiah's press attaché-cum-general factotum, Akosua Puni. She is a former beauty queen and was utterly glamorous in completely unlikely circumstances. Thankfully, she felt sorry for me, smiled when I asked about the possibility of an interview, and said she would make it happen.

The interview with Appiah was like something out of a movie. Akosua Puni did make it happen. We, Oti Adjei and me, raced in the taxi to a little industrial sideroad in another area of Accra. On one side of the street was a Volvo backlot; on the other was an empty lot with steel girders piled on top of each other. Pulled up on the sidewalk was Appiah's black Infiniti. The licence plate read "demostix." There were, as in any good film, two tough-guy aides, Vladimir and Moral. One of them, with his red-ringed eyes, looked very much the worse for wear. The two glamorous aides, Akosua and her sister Coco, had their wraparound sunglasses on.

Appiah sat inside the Infiniti. He looked smaller than he does on television, and he was wearing a tight white shirt with three buttons in the collar, and two jewelled earrings in the left ear: one silver, the other diamond. We leaned back in the front seats; they were white leather. He was very friendly, and his English was shaky but good.

We talked about his career, how far he had come. I asked for a piece of advice to the millions of people who wanted to be him. Appiah told me that it was very hard, starting in Chorkor; often they did not have enough to eat. But he urged people "to do everything possible to make the dream come true. You cannot give up."

Then I asked if anything had happened in the Brazil game.

"Nothing happened. I think we made some mistakes with underestimating the quality of the players that they have. Every mistake you do, they will get their goal, so, that's what happened."

Then I asked him about the fixers. He was staggeringly direct about them.

Hill:	Have you ever been approached by gamblers to fix games?
Appiah:	Yeah, yeah, yeah, I remember in Malaysia in 1997 at the Under-20 World Cup. There is one guy, I see him everywhere, even during the World Cup he was there. I think this guy is from Japan or China, little round face, very friendly. So he came to us and he said, "Hey, you people have to score first goal and we are going to bet, because they are gambling, and I am going to give you this amount of money."
	"Okay," I said. "Okay, let me talk to the players."
	"No," he said. He wanted to give the money to me.
	I said, "No, I'm not going to take any money." If I take the money, maybe something will happen, it will be a

shame for me, so I said, "Let me talk to the players. There is this guy who wanted to . . . how do you say? To promise the team, if we [score] our first goal he will give us this amount of money." So yeah, I approached the players, and they said, "Okay. Fine, fine, fine."

But I called the guys and said, "Okay, we are not interested in our distance." So when we played against Uruguay, semi-finals, the guy came to me and said, "Hey Stephen, we are gambling a lot of money. You know what? Talk to your goalkeeper. So they will score the first goal."

I said, "What are you talking about? I can't do that. I can't do that. We don't need your money, I'm not going to do it."

Then Appiah talked about the Olympics in Athens.

Appiah: When we went to the Olympics, Athens 2004, this guy came to us and he said, "Okay, here is $200,000. You have to let in first goal."

And I said, "No, because we wanted to go far . . ." So you know what he said, you know you have to try, and win the game.

Hill: Go all out?

Appiah: Yeah, yeah, go all out. So this guy gave me $20,000. And I share with the players. Yeah after that game, we won 2-1 and I shared the money with the players.

Hill: What did they do this last World Cup? Did they approach you?

Appiah: Yeah, yeah, they came to me and they said, "You have to win the game against the Czech Republic." Because we lost the first game, I didn't give them a chance to talk to

me. I said, "Hey, man, don't talk to me, I am concentrat-
ing on the game." I don't want to talk about anything.

Hill: Okay. But do you know if that guy goes to other teams?

Appiah: Yeah, I think they go, go, go around. They go around.

Stephen Appiah, the captain of the Ghana national team and a top international player, had confirmed that there had been an approach made to
him by fixers during the World Cup tournament. The fixer, and others
like him, go to many of the international tournaments that Appiah had
played at. He had known the fixer who had approached him for several
years. In the 2004 Olympics, he had taken $20,000 from the fixer for
winning a game and then had distributed the money around the team. I
phoned Appiah a few months later to check these details. He again confirmed everything that he said, adding only that when they received the
money at the Olympics, he had waited until after the game to make sure
that there was no ambiguity from the fixers. They win, they get paid, no
other stuff going on. I asked him about other fixes and he laughed. "If
you go writing this in your book, these people will come and kill me." I
asked again and he assured me that he was only joking.

If what he said were true, Appiah and his teammates were breaking
a number of FIFA regulations about accepting money from outside
interests. However, it in no way proved that there had been a fix at the
World Cup. Quite the opposite, all the players told me that they had
nothing to do with any corruption.

Then I saw the runner.

20

I SWEAR, I'M INNOCENT

> He came to my room, knelt, and said that he was sorry, he's
> not a bad person, but he was tempted by the devil, and all
> that. Well, I thought he should go tell that story to a priest,
> I'm no priest, I'm a football administrator.

The inside of a live television studio is the same the world over. It does not matter if you are in the CNN studios in London when they are interviewing their Jerusalem correspondent or putting out an overnight program for the Canadian Broadcasting Corporation or the TV3 early morning sports show in Accra, Ghana. There is a kind of organized chaos in the director's studio during a live television broadcast. The editors and producers sit in a row of chairs staring at a bank of television monitors. In pretty much any of those studios there will be at least one producer who complains constantly: "Who do we get to film these pieces? Did you see the shot of the watch in the middle of the interview? What are we now, an advertising program?" They are generally ignored by their colleagues, who have heard them complain about everything countless times. The director is the conductor of the technical orchestra, dealing with five different issues at once, calling which shot should go to air, talking in the host's ear about which segment is coming up next, or telling one of the cameras to close in.

No, it is a nice watch, which is why they focused on it. Camera two, go in tighter. Thirty more seconds for this section. I like it when the cameraman show little details like the watches the players wear, it makes it easier to cut. Camera two, have you got the shakes this morning? Have a coffee and focus in. Okay, let's come out of this item in five, four, three, two, one – go!

TV3 in Accra had all of those things. I was sitting at the back of the studio at 8:15 one July morning watching Michael Oti Adjei in action. As a performer, he was very good. The same cerebral intellect he shows in daily life was useful in the bustle of a live show. Asamoah Gyan, the star forward for the Ghanaian team, had cancelled his appearance at 7:10 a.m. The show began at 7:30. They had no studio guest and an hour and a half of blank air to fill. They had twenty minutes to fill it. Many TV performers would have thrown a hissy fit, stomped on the floor, and shouted at the least powerful person they could find in the room. Oti Adjei did none of those things and kept a program going almost by pure improvisation. To fill the time, they decided to take a lot of viewers' calls.

The callers were from across Ghana, some who spoke in different languages that Oti Adjei would translate off the cuff, and they were the same as they are everywhere, from the deeply insightful to the utterly inane.

Caller:	Hello, hello. [Screech of feedback]
Oti Adjei:	Hello, caller. Please turn off your television.
Caller:	[Presumably staring at the TV screen in a vain effort to seem themselves live . . .] Hello, hello. I want to talk to you about football.
Oti Adjei :	Yes, you can talk to me, but please switch off your set!
[More feedback]	
Caller:	Hello. Hello. Hello
Oti Adjei :	Yes, hello. Please turn off your set.

Caller: Hello, yes I can hear you.

(More feedback)

(Oti Adjei finally ends the call.)

The producers had scheduled the items in the following way. First, there was a discussion about where Stephen Appiah was going to play in the next season. Would he go to Glasgow Celtic or the Ukrainian club Shaktar Donetsk or stay in the Turkish league with Fenerbahçe? Then there was an item on the visit of a couple of the Black Stars to an unbuilt stadium. Asamoah Gyan, the star who had cancelled at the last moment, had earlier that week decided to record a CD of music. Then there was a filmed item on him playing music, followed by a general discussion about whether that would distract from his soccer career in the Italian league. Finally, just dropped in as a news item, they mentioned that a Ghanaian coach had been fired for allegedly trying to fix an international match the week before between Ghana and Iran.

What?!

I jumped out of my chair in the back of the studio. The producers and even the director looked at me oddly. The program was almost over. The complaining producer told me that yes, one of the coaches of the Ghana Under-23 team had got some of the players to visit "friends" of his from Malaysia or Hong Kong. They were to pay the players for losing the game.

I frantically searched and then found a newspaper; fortunately they seemed to have more news sense than the television journalists. There on the front page of the sports section, directly under the headline "I swear, I'm innocent" was a large photo of the man I had last seen in the Bangkok KFC. I knew him instantly, and I knew, whatever he might say, he was not innocent.

The coach's name was Abukari Damba. He had played for the great Ghanaian national team of the early 1990s, the one that featured Abédi

Pelé. Now he was in trouble. I immediately phoned him, and we agreed to meet that afternoon for an interview.

Before the interview, I went over to the Ghana Football Association. Their headquarters are in downtown Accra, near the overpriced conference centre for the Africa Summit. It is, like much of the developing world, a mixture of the highly modern, a newly built office building, and the shambolic. The day I was there, the building had a twenty-foot puddle, like an impromptu moat, in front of it. Journalists and soccer administrators stood around waiting for passing taxis so they could get through the water.

The president of the GFA was the same man, Kwesi Nyantakyi, that I had met the year before while he was waiting for his coffee in the Würzburg restaurant. Again, he had the slightly officious air, but he was still relatively forthright. When he spoke, I had the impression that the GFA actually understood how important the issue of match-fixing was to their sport. It seemed like the exact reverse of European countries, where the journalists would be salivating after a story of match-fixing while the officials would try to play it down. Here the officials were forthright about there being a problem while the sports journalists, with the one exception of the newspaper that put it on the front page of their sports section, did not rank it higher than a discussion about the musical taste of a star forward.

He spoke about the presence of fixers – he called them gamblers – at international tournaments.

> In every competition you find gamblers around. Yes, every competition, every competition, they are there. It is done all the time in major competitions. In all the major tournaments, World Cup, Cup of Nations. The gamblers are not Africans, they are Europeans and Asians. So they have a lot of money to do bet on these things.

I asked him whether he thought the same thing may have occurred in the World Cup in Germany.

I would not rule out the possibility of gamblers approaching our players. We put in place in Germany precautions to stop unauthorized persons from entering the room of our players. But it is impossible to stop it.

I thought back to my experience in Germany when it had been relatively easy to contact the players. Even if you could not meet them in the hotel, which I did all the time, the players were still wandering out to bars where any fixer could meet them. Nyantakyi seemed to realize the same thing and said:

> They may not necessarily have to come to the hotels. Some have agents who establish links and then they do their business. Even at the World Cup in 1991 when we won the Under-17 World Cup, there were gamblers around, offering a lot of money to the team to throw away the match.

He laughed. We spoke about the meetings with the players to discuss salary in the 2006 World Cup – he said they were "hectic" with "free and frank" negotiations – and the current allegations of bribery before the Iran game:

> Even last week when we played Iran in a friendly match, gamblers were at the team, they bribed our players. They did it to one of our assistant coaches ... The coach let an official of a gambling company to see the players one by one; and the players were paid $1,000, and the coach took $500 as his commission from each of the players. So he got about $3,000 worth, each player got about $500 each.

After the interview, Nyantakyi passed me on to Randy Abbey, who was the GFA official in charge of the trip to Iran. Abbey looks like a tough, no-nonsense character, but he claimed that "this was the first time he had encountered such a thing [match-fixing]" and he was in still in shock from the events.

One of our coaches got involved with some people. I hear two of them
were Chinese-looking, and one was supposed to be an Iranian. And he
had these people in his room, and he would go speak with the players
... and ask them to come meet these people.

Abbey claimed that in the hotel room the players were supposedly
instructed on how to throw the game, and then they received $1,000. It
was this money that the coach was taking his cut from. Whether the
players were angry about that, or genuinely remorseful, one of them
went to the captain of the team, who went to the coach. Abbey immediately fired the assistant coach. But that night he had a visitor.

The coach came to my room and knelt, and said that he was sorry, he's
not a bad person, but he was tempted by the devil, and all that. Well, I
thought he should go tell that story to a priest, I'm no priest, I'm a
football administrator.

Not everyone in the Ghanaian delegation at the Würzburg hotel in
Germany was an innocent fan. I discovered soon after arriving in Ghana
the story of Kofi Boakye. Boakye was the police officer appointed to
head up security for the Africa Cup of Nations to be held in Accra in
2008. He went to Germany with the team to gain experience of a major
sporting event. Two months later, it was revealed that part of his time
in Würzburg was spent phoning back to Ghana to find out who had
covertly taped him meeting with a group of Ghanaian drug traffickers.
During the meeting he was heard saying that he would "sort out" some
Colombian business partners of the drug barons if they gave them any
trouble. There was also a question of seventy-six bags of cocaine that
had been discovered by police in a raid and then had gone missing. After
a year-long trial, the two drug traffickers who had met and taped Boakye
were convicted to fifteen years of hard labour, while the trial judge stated

that he was displeased with the attorney-general for not also prosecuting Boakye. One of Boakye's favourite bars, and one where he allegedly would sit and discuss his business, was called the Bus Stop, located on the side of the busy ring road that circled the centre of Accra. Strangely it was the same bar where the coach had chosen to meet me. As I took the taxi down to bar, I thought about the Hilton Hotels in Brussels and how, by coincidence, that particular hotel chain has attracted a lot of the match-fixing history of Belgian soccer. Now it seemed that one bar in central Accra was an unwitting magnet for tales of corruption.

When I got to the Bus Stop, I realized I was not particularly nervous. I was tired and curiously unexcited. This was not like the first time I met Chin. Well, to be honest, *every time* I met Chin, I was terrified of what would happen to me. It had now been thirteen months since the meeting in the Bangkok KFC. It had been a long chase. I had gone across three continents. I had gone through countless disappointments. I was prepared for it not to be the same man.

Then I met Damba.

It was him. I know memory can prove fallible, but it was the same person that I had seen thirteen months before in Bangkok. One of the things that had struck me as true about Chin's story in Thailand was how clearly athletic the man was who had met them in the fast-food outlet. His body and physique had the hardness that only comes from the absolute focus of the professional athlete. One of the first things I recognized about Damba was that he had that same hard, professional athlete's body.

We shook hands amiably. He did not seem to recognize me. We sat down. Unlike the last time we had been in the same room in public, I tried to make sure no one was around to listen to our conversation. Almost immediately, and almost without any prompting, he told me the story of his life.

As I listened, a series of clicks went off in my head confirming that he was the man I had seen.

He had been one of the regulars in the great Ghana team of the early

1990s, along with Abédi Pelé. *Click.* (The reputation of the squad was such that any member of it would have instant access to the Ghanaian team, even to its dressing room.)

He had been an Under-17 coach for the Ghana Football Association. *Click.* (Exactly as Chin had claimed him to be.)

He had been in Athens during the Olympic Games. *Click.* (He could have helped put the purported fixes and payments together that Appiah and Chin had spoken of.)

He had not been in Athens officially; rather, he claimed that he had financed himself privately to go there. *Click.* (I wondered about the nature of the private financial arrangements that had allowed him to go.)

He had played in Malaysia, just after the great collapse of the league through match-fixing. *Click.* (Surely, he would have met some of the fixers then.)

In Malaysia, someone who he thought was a friend had stolen more than $100,000 from him. *Click.* (A good reason for wanting to get into match-fixing?)

He had been in Würzburg, again ostensibly to improve himself as a coach. Again ostensibly, he had been privately financed. He had left just before I had arrived. *Click.* (That is why I had not seen him there.)

I asked him what had happened in the game against Iran the week before.

He claimed that he had made a mistake. He had thought his friends were simply agents who wanted to recruit some of the players. The whole thing had been a terrible misunderstanding. Then he claimed that he was trying to lure the gamblers into giving up the money, but not make the players play badly. Then he claimed that if people could come inside him, they would know how innocent he was. In truth, he was a mess. His eyes darted around the room and he looked completely devastated.

I listened to Damba's entire life story. He said he was a chief's son from the poorer Muslim area in the north of Ghana. It is an area that, generally, Ghanaians from the richer, more urban south of the country speak of with some disdain. Damba's father, at first, would not let him become a soccer player, insisting that he finish his education, but after completing his teacher's training Damba began to play as a professional goalkeeper. He worked hard, becoming at his time one of the best goalkeepers in Africa. At the end of his career he moved to Malaysia and played there.

I felt sorry for him. It was all rather sad to see a former great player reduced to such a state. I also did not like what I was going to do: betray him. I was going to pretend to be friendly and in the meantime, collect information on him. Some journalists thrive at this kind of thing, pandering to interview sources or sucking up to famous people before putting the knife in. I don't like it, but it was the only way that I could get more information on Chin's gang of fixers.

So at a pause in our meeting I leaned forward and told him that I had friends who were friends of his.

I told him that he had been in Bangkok in May 2006.

He shuffled, blinked twice and said, "No, I don't think so."

I smiled and said, "I think you were."

"I am not sure. I must remember. Maybe."

We fenced around each other like swordsmen on a sheet of ice. The real question he was asking me was, "Who are you?" It was a question that I was not sure I wanted to answer, but I tried to be as honest as I could. I told him that I had done research on match-fixers in Asia. His colleagues had helped me out.

We shook hands and agreed to meet the next day.

The next day I met his wife. She was not a glamorous Ghanaian beauty queen, but she was a tough-minded, politically well-connected woman who wore hijab and stared intently at me. They were also clearly very much in love. They held hands at one point and when they laughed they looked into one another's eyes. However, that was about the only light point in the first hour and a half of the meeting. If the atmosphere around Damba and I had been tense the night before at the bar, it was now *really* tense. We were meeting on the patio of the Beverly Hills Hotel, a tiny, white-painted establishment in the centre of Accra. It looked like the kind of place where married couples, who are not necessarily married to one another, go to stay. It was near my hotel. So we agreed to meet there. Mrs. Damba eyed me up and down as if I were a blackmailer.

I don't really blame her. I must have been a living embodiment of the expression that no matter how bad something is, it can always get worst. Here was her husband's reputation destroyed and his job gone, and now a man who could be anything from a spy for the Football Association to a match-fixer's assistant to a blackmailer was sitting in front of them telling them back their secrets that neither thought anybody should have known.

I managed to reassure them. I told Mrs. Damba that her husband had "friends who were my friends. They had been very good to me." Now I was nervous. I was speaking the literal truth, but I was also using the deliberate code of organized crime. I was implying that I was one of the gang. We had a cup of coffee. Then they asked me to come to a radio station, Joy FM, to see Damba being interviewed. I helped him prepare for the interview, which made me feel extremely uncomfortable.

In the afternoon, I went back to the notes of my conversations with Chin that I had made thirteen months before. I realized I had missed a key detail. In a number of different places, he had actually used Damba's first name – Abu – to describe the runner. As in:

Hill: Why do you think you're going to have to meet the players? To coach them on how to fix?

Chin: No, No. Myself, No problem. I trust Abu, I know. He tell me to play, I play. I trust him, He do this only a few years, a couple of years. I trust him, OK?

Abu is a pretty standard title in some Asian cultures, a bit like a younger person calling someone "Uncle." I had put it down to Chin not wanting me to guess his runner's name. Now I was realizing it actually was the runner's first name.

I also began to do some more research into the Iran versus Ghana fix. There were a number of interesting things that struck me. One, it was exactly like the purported World Cup fixes. The favourites, the Iranians, had won the game. Even though it had been advertised as a full friendly international, the Ghana team was actually not their full-strength team. Rather it was a considerably weakened Under-23 team. The Iranians, however, fielded their top national squad. Therefore, no one would have suspected a potential fix if the Ghana team lost.

Two, the loss was one of the easiest to arrange for the fixers. The weaker team, the Ghanaians, simply had to lose above the spread, by two clear goals. Presumably, it is generally easier for fixers to convince players who expected to lose anyway to lose.

Three, after all the hysteria, after all the investigations, after all the team meetings about potential fixes, the final score of the game was 4-2. A result that the fixers had wanted was still reached.

I managed to get the summarized transcripts of the July 3 GFA hearings into the affair. They had not been publicly released and they were very damning. The hearings had actually occurred before the press stories about the attempted match-fixing. The meeting opened with prayers and the announcement that testimony could be given in any of the indigenous Ghanaian languages, not just English. Four of the players had testified. Their stories were remarkably consistent. They said that Damba had approached them. A couple of them said that he either asked them directly or was in the room when they were asked to fix the game. There were two Chinese men and an "Iranian-looking" man who he introduced them to.

Sampson Cudjoe was one of the players who testified. Part of his summarized testimony reads:

On the day of the match Coach Damba came to his room and took him to a room where he met three people. After shaking hands with the people, they gave him $1,000 for shopping and that Mr. Damba will tell him what to do next. As he was about to leave, they told him to throw the match by a two-goal margin.

Emmanuel Allan was another one of the players; he gave his testimony in Ga, a southern Ghanaian language.

He said before they emplaned for Iran, Coach Damba told him that his friends from Hong Kong would come and give him money. In Iran Coach Damba introduced those people to me after we [the players] had finished our meeting with Mr. Abbey. He said he was informed but was not given any money. When I went to the room with Coach Damba, I met the three people who promised me money for shopping. They told me that we must allow them to score two goals in the first half, then one in the second half before we will pull a consolation goal in the dying minutes of the game. The people were very particular about the score line.

Coach Damba confirmed that Allan's story was true.

I don't know what the expression for "Gotcha" is in Ga, but that pretty well expresses Damba's status in any language. He was fired after the hearings.

The players' testimonies also present a larger problem and possibly the reason why the GFA did not want the tribunal made public. If the players' testimony is to be believed, it sounds as if someone from Iran was also involved. There was an "Iranian-looking man" who was with the two Asian fixers to ensure the fix went to plan. But the corroborating support for this theory is Emmanuel Allan's testimony. He claims that there was the offer of the Ghanaians being allowed to score a goal in the final minute, which implies that the fixers were also working with some of the Iranians, so they could guarantee the Ghanaians a goal.

Damba and I met again on Monday afternoon. Again we met at the Beverly Hills Hotel. Again Damba tried to waffle around. I had asked him to bring his passport. He was still maintaining that he had not gone to Bangkok in May 2006. He brought a new passport and claimed not to be able to find the old one. He started on another line of nonsense. I stopped him. I told him:

Here is the deal I would like to propose to you. I will tell you exactly where you were and then I would like to have a no-bullshit conversation with you. You were in Bangkok last year. On May 25, you met people at a Kentucky Fried Chicken. At twelve noon. You sat with three other guys. They were Chinese. They wore white shirts. One of them had a round face and wore glasses.

He interrupted me.

Yes, that one was Alan! That was the guy I was telling you about. He lived in America for some time.

The dam burst.

For the next hour, we talked about his activities. It started with his description of meeting "Alan," the Malaysian fixer. The same Alan had helped him try to fix the Iran game. They had met when Damba was playing in Malaysia. He had lost more than $100,000 in a deal to invest in a marble business. His business partner had taken his money and walked off with it. Damba was distraught. He had no way of getting his money back. He told his troubles to another goalkeeper in the Malaysian league. The goalkeeper introduced him to Alan. Alan's reaction to Abu's story? Kidnap the businessman's children until he "found" the money to pay back Damba. Alan would then split the money 40/60 with Damba. Damba claims that he agreed to the offer, then decided against it. Alan was angry. "*What?*" He had already got his people in place to do the kidnapping. Eventually, they agreed not to kidnap the children and had a table talk with the businessman. Alan was able to get some of the money recovered by these means.

They had first worked together during the 1997 World Under-17 Cup in Malaysia. Damba had introduced Alan to members of the Ghana team. It was, claimed Damba, their modus operandi. Damba would get access to the teams. He was, after all, one of the great stars of the past team. People looked up to him. However, he claimed that he never proposed fixing matches to the players, he just got Alan into the room with them. Then he would leave.

"How could I ask the players to throw a match?" he asked me plaintively. "How could I ask them to do such a thing?"

His most serious claim was that both he and Alan had been in Würzburg together. They had been at a hotel across the square from the Maritim Hotel but had contacted and got access to the players. It had been relatively easy, because by this time Alan knew one of the players himself:

> We were together in Würzburg, myself and Alan. He had established friendship with Stephen Appiah. They have a relationship. Not a friendship, but an understanding. Alan approached him to fix something up. I don't know what happened.

For the record, this is not what Chin claimed was Damba's relationship to the team. Chin had claimed that Damba knew and represented a corrupt group of players on the team. He claimed Damba had flown out at his expense to broker a deal with the Asian fixers. But Damba denied this, saying his job was simply to get access for Alan. Any fixing that took place was Alan's job.

Stephen Appiah had told me that he had met someone who matched the description of Alan in previous tournaments. He had even taken money from him for winning games. But he absolutely denied fixing any game during the World Cup or any other tournament with him. I asked Damba about the Brazil game and whether that had been fixed. Damba claimed not to know, but felt there was a defender on the Ghana team that was very suspicious. He drew a long diagram on the napkin showing how ridiculous a number of the goals had been.

On my last day in Ghana, Damba and I met again. We tried to talk in the restaurant of the Beverly Hills Hotel. But a man sat right behind Damba and was obviously interested in what he had to say. So we got nervous and shifted down the road to the Avenue Club. Damba told me about receiving a number of anonymous phone calls in the middle of the night. The caller would say, "Are you there?" Damba would reply, "Yes." The caller said, "Just checking." Then the line would go dead.

"I tell you, I was very frightened the first time it happened at 2:00 a.m. Do you know anything about it?"

I told him no, and despite the calls, Damba was more confident and more comfortable. We leaned back in the chairs at the club, and he told me that he was shocked to find out that Alan bet in the millions of dollars.

"I would like to propose that you and I work together. You are almost my agent, so to speak. Because I swear to you, what you're telling me about the gambling market I had no idea about these sums of money. You and I should work as a team."

The last time I saw Damba, he was helping a little boy. I had seen the boy lying on the sidewalk. He looked unconscious. People walked over him or around him and ignored him. So we walked over, picked him up, and took him to a nearby food stall. The boy, who was mentally challenged and desperately hungry, did not seem to be able to take in what was happening. He claimed to be from another section of town. As I left them to pack before going to the airport, Damba was picking him up and putting him in his car. He told me he was going to make sure he got home.

As I sat on the plane, I thought about what I now knew. I knew that fixers approached the Ghana team during the Olympics. The captain of the Olympic team claims that they were rebuffed. The fixers claim that some of the Ghanaians took money to lose a match. Stephen Appiah, one of the star players, says that he took money to *win* a game, after it was over, and he distributed the cash around the team.

As for the World Cup, Chin, the Asian fixer, told me the essential score of four games before they were played. He then showed me a meeting with a man he claimed was the runner for the Ghanaian team. I found the runner in Ghana. He had all the attributes described by Chin. He was an Under-17 coach. He knew the players on the team. He had been in Greece during the Olympics. He confirmed that he had gone to Würzburg and that another fixer, an associate of Chin known as "Alan," had contacted the Ghana team. Stephen Appiah also confirms that the fixer approached him, but he claims that the fixer wanted to give him money to beat the Czech team. Appiah claims that he turned down the fixer because he was so intent on winning the game. I want to stress that no one claimed *all* the players on the team were in on the possible fixes. Rather, it was made clear that some of the players would be playing as hard as they could, while others would not.

So it comes down to what do you believe? There are two alternatives. One, it could be that the gamblers were lying: no one on the Ghana team took any money and they just got lucky with a series of predictions and strange coincidences. Two, it could be that the gambling fixers actually told the truth and that someone on these teams did take money and a fix occured.

The very least is that all parties, soccer officials, players, and the fixers themselves, agree that organized crime gamblers do regularly approach teams to fix games at international tournaments. They are able to do so easily, and sometimes they succeed. The question is, who is trying to stop them?

21

WHO GUARDS THE GUARDIANS?

I think it is not true. I think it is not true. I think it is not true. Or if something happened it did not influence the final result ... [but if it were true] then I would say that then all the work that we have done in FIFA over the last thirty years, to develop the game, and to make the game accessible to everybody. To say that the game is an education, it is a school of life. It is part of a social cultural program. It is entertainment. It is emotion. It is passion. Then we have failed. We failed.

On August 27, 1869, one of the largest crowds in England in a generation watched a sporting event. It was not a soccer match, not a horse race, not a track and field event. It was a unique race that caught the imagination of much of the Western hemisphere, in one of its most popular sports, rowing. Earlier that spring, the Harvard University rowing team had written a formal letter to both Cambridge and Oxford universities challenging their teams to a four-and-a-quarter mile race down their home river, the Thames. Cambridge, to their shame, declined. Oxford did not.

The Harvard team arrived a few weeks before the race in a storm of publicity. It was four years after the bloody American Civil War. The Northern states had won, but official British government sympathies had largely been with the Southern, slave-owning states. The two countries seemed to long for a symbolic resolution of all the tensions that the conflict had created. A contemporary British journalist wrote that the race, "is in the eyes of the public a race between England and America." Charles Dickens, the greatest English writer and celebrity of the time, called the Oxford crew, in a speech dedicated to them at Crystal Palace, "the pride and flower of England." In the United States, interest was even, if possible, more intense. The City Hall in New York was prepared with flags and a 100-gun salute in case of victory. The *Aquatic Monthly* wrote:

> In the city of Milwaukee preparations were instituted for a grand pow-wow in case the American crew should be victorious. A public meeting was called at the City Hall, a salute of fifty guns was to be fired, and the ringing of bells and blazing of bonfires, were to add their effects to the general rejoicing.

The day of the race, *The Times* reported that a million people lined the Thames to watch; *Harper's Magazine* claimed there were more spectators than any other event in that generation, except "when the Prince of Wales first brought his wife home" and that the crowd during the competition was a "dense mass on shore [that] has been swaying and struggling, and now, like a mighty river, is sweeping on over fields and fences, ditches and hedges, wild, mad with fierce excitement, yelling at every breath, and with all its might."

Those spectators watched a tight race. For the first two miles, the American crew led. Then slowly, inexorably, the Oxford crew pulled them in. The Harvard cox made a fatal error that reduced the lead and Oxford charged ahead. But the Harvard team had not given up, not by a long shot. Coming into the final stretch, the home team was still two lengths ahead. The crowd, delirious for most of the race, now went crazy: shouts, screams, cheers. In the final five hundred yards, the Harvard team tore into the English lead. They reduced it to one length, then a half-length. Then, as the winning line came close, the Oxford team dug deeply into whatever resources they possessed and just held off Harvard on the finishing line. The painting of the two teams, with Oxford winning, is still, 140 years later, in print.

The next day, the front page of the New York Times was dominated by news of the contest, a map of the course, and biographies of the Harvard rowers. This was not an accident of a slow news day. In the late nineteenth century, rowing was one of the biggest sports in North America and Western Europe. A large group of American newspaper correspondents had accompanied the Harvard team. In North America, sporting fans were obsessed with the fates of various rowing teams such as Biglins or Wards. The races between the top single scullers of each country were even bigger events. When the great Canadian Ned Hanlan (a.k.a. The Boy in Blue) raced an American champion on the Hudson, 200,000 people watched the contest.

Now the popularity of professional rowing seems like a distant dream. Rowing, compared to soccer, baseball, or tennis, is a relatively minor sport. Even in England, apart, ironically, from the annual Cambridge versus Oxford boat race, it is largely ignored. The reason for rowing's demise is partly societal – it is difficult to overstate the snobbery of some nineteenth-century rowing officials ("the ignorant prejudices of illiterate professionals" is how one official described working-class rowing coaches) – and partly technological; with the invention of the marine engine, far fewer people rowed at the turn of the twentieth century than one hundred years before. But one of the strongest reasons for the demise of rowing was fixing led by gamblers. Put simply, the hundreds of thousands of people who came out regularly to watch those races began to have less and less faith in the credibility of the sport. Even the Harvard team in the weeks before the great race down the Thames against Oxford had two sets of meals brought to them. The first were public meals that they pretended to eat. The second, a secret supply of food prepared only by "Harvard men," were the meals they actually ate. The reason for all this dietary subterfuge? The same one that the German tennis star Tommy Haas claimed in the summer of 2007 when playing a Davis Cup match in Russia: they were afraid of being poisoned by match-fixing gamblers. This was not an isolated incident. As in modern-day tennis, the fixes in rowing were rumoured to be so prevalent that some would happen *during* the race. It was this constant gamesmanship, cheating, and fixing that meant eventually professional rowing became discredited and it faded into that graveyard of sports the public has largely abandoned, such as cockfighting, bear-baiting, and archery.

The comparison with the demise of professional rowing is not to say that soccer will disappear overnight, but it is to say sports rise and fall. Remember the fuss over possible match-fixing in professional pedestrianism? You would if you had lived in the nineteenth century when it was one of the most popular sports of the era. Lets look at the situation of soccer, the most popular sport in the world today. We have seen that in Asia, the credibility of entire leagues have effectively collapsed due to corruption. We have seen that some leagues in Europe are plagued with consistent and chronic corruption. We have seen that matches in European-wide tournaments are being fixed. We have seen that match-fixers are approaching players at the biggest international soccer tournaments in the world.

If soccer is under threat, who is guarding it? Who is protecting it from the outsiders who will try to kill it? Who is safeguarding the sport? What is the organization that is mandated to stop soccer going the way of rowing, professional pedestrianism, and cockfighting?

I have mentioned FIFA throughout the book. They are the organization that runs all soccer games everywhere. Well, almost all soccer games: the Saturday-morning matches with heaps of jackets for goals and teams that are thrown together are not run by FIFA. But just about every other organized game of soccer, from youth leagues in Arkansas and Zambia to the final match of the World Cup, falls under their jurisdiction. Or, to be precise, the jurisdiction of a national soccer federation that makes up FIFA. Every country in the world has a national soccer federation. In fact, there are some places that are not even countries that have soccer

federations. It is often repeated that there are more countries represented in FIFA than there are in the United Nations. Each of these soccer
federations officially make up both their continent organization such as
UEFA or CONCACAF in Europe and North America, and also the world
organization based in Switzerland, FIFA.

Thirty-five years ago the president of FIFA was a suit-and-tie
Englishman, Sir Stanley Rous. There is a certain nostalgia that creeps into
many English journalists when they write about the days of Sir Stanley;
presumably, it reminds them of the days of an empire purportedly run
by decent chaps who could be trusted to do the right thing. Whether
that is actually how FIFA or the British Empire was run is open to
debate, but what happened for certain was that in 1974 a couple of new
boys rode into town and changed everything in international soccer.

The new boys were two men who understood better than anyone
else the influence of sport for power and profit. They were the head of
the Brazilian Football Confederation (CBF), João Havelange, and
Horst Dassler, the head of the giant German sporting company Adidas.
Together, they revolutionized soccer. First, Havelange beat Sir Stanley
Rous in a FIFA presidential election. Almost immediately, the English
way of doing things went out the window and international marketing
came in. Multimillion-dollar sponsorship deals were signed with Adidas
and whole host of other multinational companies. There were deals for
international television rights. The World Cup was expanded from
sixteen to eventually thirty-two teams, becoming the most popular
sporting event on the planet. FIFA, from an organization that lived hand-
to-mouth in the early 1970s, became one of the most powerful sporting
organizations in the world.

The organization was deeply hierarchical and allegiance to the
President João Havelange was absolute. I saw Havelange once: on the
train from Dortmund after the Ghana versus Brazil match. He was
in the first-class compartment – tall and athletic even in his nineties.
He was dressed in a beautiful suit and his presence shone through the

carriage like a grey, diffused light. He had been an Olympic athlete for Brazil. A businessman who had made his fortune in the bus industry in Brazil. A soccer executive who oversaw the growth of the game in the poorer countries of the world. A man who genuinely transformed soccer from a place of first among equals to the preeminent sport on the planet.

However, there was another side to Havelange. The British investigative journalist and author David Yallop claims in his book *How They Stole the Game* (marketed as "the book that the FIFA president tried to ban" when FIFA took out an injunction against the work) that Havelange was connected to the Brazilian intelligence agency responsible for many of the human rights abuses in the military dictatorship of the 1960s. An article in the Brazilian version of *Playboy* claimed that he had helped ship arms to the military regime in Bolivia, renowned for its human rights abuses. But worse, much worse, was the revelation in 1994 by a Rio de Janeiro attorney general of the connections between him and the head of a multimillion-dollar illegal gambling syndicate Castor de Andrade. De Andrade's criminal gambling empire was infamous in Brazil. He employed tens of thousands of people to sell his *Jogo do Bicho* lotteries. He, allegedly, helped launder the profits of the Colombian and Brazilian drug gangs. And after a raid on de Andrade's house, the Brazilian police realized they had a problem. Illegal gambling, as Joe Pistone the U.S. undercover cop pointed out, breeds corruption. The corruption in Brazil linked to de Andrade's illegal gambling reached very high indeed. Top judges, politicians, and policemen were all found to have been paid off by de Andrade. At the same time, a personal letter of reference for Castor de Andrade written by none other than João Havelange surfaced.

> . . . Castor de Andrade is a sportsman. I am President of the International Federation of Football Associations (FIFA) and Castor is an outstanding patron of this sport in Rio de Janeiro where he is patron of the Bangu Atlético Clube. For his distinguished contributions, Castor has received decorations from Football Federations of the

States of Rio de Janeiro and Minas Gerais. . . . Castor de Andrade, a controversial man with a strong personality, is an amiable and pleasant creature, who can make friends due to a predominant feature in his character: loyalty . . . Castor de Andrade is a good family man, a devoted friend and is admired as a sports administrator . . . Those who attack him perhaps ignore these positive traits of his personality. I authorize Castor de Andrade to use this statement as he deems appropriate . . .

If de Andrade's crimes had been almost anything else – murder, drug-dealing, blackmail – it would have been better. To have the top executive of the world's biggest sport linked to the head of an illegal gambling operation presented all the wrong images. Then Havelange and his son-in-law, the head of the Brazilian Football Confederation, argued with Pelé, the greatest of all former soccer players, who was trying to reform Brazilian soccer. It all began to be too much and at the 1998 World Cup, João Havelange, citing age – he was by now eighty-two – resigned. A set of administrators led by his Swiss general-secretary Sepp Blatter won the elections and took over FIFA.

Blatter's jump into the chief executive role was supposed to be the arrival of a new broom. FIFA would become a Swiss-run organization that would be administered efficiently by professionals, all of whom had ethics, codes of conduct, and morals. Unfortunately, ten years after the election it is not entirely clear that this has happened.

There have been a whole series of allegations about voting fraud at FIFA elections, of money in envelopes for delegates' votes, and ticket scandals at the last World Cup. In the fall of 2007, the Swiss police declared that they were charging a number of executives of the agency that managed FIFA's marketing and television rights for more than twenty years. The charges the Swiss police brought against the executives included embezzlement, fraud, fraudulent bankruptcy, harming creditors, and the falsification of documents in a US$100 million case.

It may sound incredible to an outsider that some of the top people connected to the administration of the world's biggest sport are under investigation for a range of serious financial crimes. Actually to a FIFA executive it may sound all rather familiar. For the year before, in a multi-million-dollar court case in New York over competing sponsorship deals between MasterCard and Visa, four FIFA marketing executives, including Jérôme Valcke, their director of marketing and TV rights, were cited by the judge for deliberately lying and document forgery. Her judgment did not make for comfortable reading for FIFA executives:

> While the FIFA witnesses at trial boldly characterized their breaches as "white lies," "commercial lies," "bluffs," and, ironically, "the game," their internal emails discuss the "different excuses to give to MasterCard as to why the deal wasn't done with them," "how we (as FIFA) can still be seen as having at least some business ethics" and how to "make the whole f***-up look better for FIFA."

The judge even rejected some of the testimony of Chuck Blazer, the general secretary of CONCACAF and a current member of FIFA's Executive Committee, writing it was clear that he had *fabricated* part of his testimony. A few months later, there was an appeal that referred the case back to the courts asking the judge to clarify which contract was in force at the time, but FIFA decided to settle with a $90 million payment to MasterCard. Jérôme Valcke, one of the men whom the judge had accused of lying to the court, was then promoted to the post of the secretary general of FIFA, second only to Sepp Blatter. With a corporate culture that was so distinctly odd how could this organization protect soccer?

From England, I spoke to Jerome Champagne. Champagne, a former French diplomat, is FIFA's director of international relations. He has a difficult job. He has to deal with almost every controversy, problem, or scandal that touches international soccer. A contact had told me that he was an honourable man, so I phoned him up, told him about the book, how I had spent three years researching it, and that I, unfortunately, had bad news for him.

Champagne at first, without waiting to hear what the "bad news" was professed himself completely unmoved and said, "Life is made up of bad news." He told me that if there was corruption in soccer, it was the fault of society in general. If there was racism in the stadiums, it was because there are racist people everywhere. He went on:

> Our societies are trying to evade taxation, or to violate regulations, that is why we have all these kind of things. Our societies are greedy that is why we have some people trying to use football in order to make money. So it is not bad news, it is a fact of life. And that is why we are fighting on the regulation aspects in order to try and correct these misdeeds. But unfortunately, we live in an unperfect world [sic]. We are very aware of these problems and we are fighting them.

Champagne added that the international media, with their concentration on scandals and sensationalism, was unfair to FIFA. He claimed that he and his FIFA colleagues did not care, that they maintained "a cool distance from these things" because the media only focused on scandals and they never talked about all the good things that FIFA had done. Champagne spoke of building fifty-two artificial fields in Africa. "No one talks about that." Champagne spoke of the construction of stands by FIFA in a stadium in Palestine: "No one talks about that," he repeated. He spoke about FIFA's efforts to stop government interference and corruption in soccer in Kenya, Peru, and Iran: "No one talks about that," he ended. By this time he sounded far from cool or distanced, saying, "That is the reality. But, basically, we don't care. Because we realize that people [who] are writing on football on the scandals or these things [are trying] to make money out of football."

I said, "Jerome, can I clarify something for you?"

"Yes."

"I risked my life to get this information. I've put my physical safety on the line for football . . . [and] I am talking about matches organized by FIFA at the very, very highest level."

"Which ones? The finals?"

"Yes, the finals."

"Yeah. Well I am ready to listen."

A few weeks later, after intense negotiations by phone and e-mail, I went to Zurich to FIFA headquarters to meet Sepp Blatter. I was prepared to dislike him. Instead I found Blatter to be a mixture of the deeply charming, the utterly dictatorial, and the oddly moving. It started well: in the morning I was gazing around the science-fiction-like reception hall of the FIFA headquarters. (It is a completely modern, emissions-free building and the staff's fingerprints are coded into a central computer that opens doors for them.) Blatter was in the hall with a group of executives. He stopped talking to them for a few moments, came over, introduced himself, and said he was looking forward to our interview in the afternoon. It was a small, but beautiful example of professional diplomatic manners that was very engaging.

The beginning of the interview was enjoyable as well. Blatter roared with laughter talking about his own, modest, soccer playing ability, "I was a striker. I was number nine [and] my coach said [to his teammates], 'When you give the ball to Sepp and he is thirty metres from goal, then all of you should go back to the middle line, because either he scores or he will lose the ball!'"

However, once I began to get into the more controversial questions the mood changed. I asked him about the 2004 game in China, the match-fixing scandal, and when he was booed at the stadium. He drew back, folded his arms across his chest and looked at me as if I had farted in an elevator, "My recollection [of the game] was a wonderful atmosphere. I would not believe in a Chinese stadium that someone would take the risk of booing an official speaker. It is not up to my recollection."

It was a strange Emperor's New Clothes moment. All his aides agreed and nodded sagely at what Blatter had said, but his recollection is at odds with a number of other witnesses that I interviewed, several newspaper articles written by journalists who were in the stadium, and, presumably, tens of thousands of Chinese fans. But it was clear that he had spoken and that his mind would not change. So we talked about the match-fixing attempts by Asian gamblers and he told me that he had known of this phenomenon since the late 1970s. I asked for his reaction to the fact that I had been told the essential scores of games by an Asian gambler in the World Cup Finals *before* they had taken place. He paused for eight seconds, his manner now utterly stone-cold, then:

> I think it is not true. I think it is not true. I think it is not true. Or if something happened it did not influence the final result . . . [but if it were true] then I would say that then all the work that we have done in FIFA over the last thirty years, to develop the game, and to make the game accessible to everybody. To say that the game is an education, it is a school of life. It is part of a social cultural program. It is entertainment. It is emotion. It is passion. Then we have failed. We failed.

It might be important to consider exactly what FIFA or any soccer association could do to prevent widespread match-fixing. Blatter is very proud of the "Early Warning System" or a method of using the information from betting companies to monitor the gambling markets for fixes. The idea is that if a warning comes in, FIFA executives will swing into action and stop any problems from occurring. I explained to him why I, and many gambling executives, consider the warning system a good, useful tool but not particularly effective at detecting all potential fixes at a World Cup Final. (The amount of money bet on a World Cup match is so great that you cannot see many of the betting anomalies caused by fixing, particularly if the fixers are helping the favourite team win.) He replied that the system was so good that the International Olympic Committee (IOC) was considering implementing it at the Beijing Olympics to monitor any potential rigging of their games.

Blatter is also very proud of his work over the last ten years on increasing the standards of referees. "The most sensitive person is the referee and I have been advocating [for] professional referees. It took a long time to realize they are not only in their hobby, they are in their job. And if you are in your job, you take it more seriously."

I suggested the implementation, as in North American sports organizations, of security departments made up of former police officers who can specialize in action against match-fixing. (In the morning, I had suggested the idea of promoting women referees to counteract the boys-only culture of top referees to one FIFA executive, who dismissed it as "nonsense.") Blatter replied that they did have one person who was very experienced and that besides security is something that everyone at FIFA should take seriously and they did not need a particular department.

We did not have time to discuss the dozen other methods that I believe can reduce the chances of match-fixing in international tournaments, but the conversation ended amicably. Blatter seemed both shocked and disbelieving about the possibility of a fixed match at a World Cup tournament. But he did speak about a game in the last World Cup that he watched and wondered if it were fixed. (He was not suggesting, in any way, that he had information that the game had been fixed.) Then he said, "I have spent over thirty years working at FIFA. Football is my baby. I want to protect it. Thank you for your investigation, but if you are right, it hurts." Then with a significant, backward look at me, he walked out of the room.

If those are the *words* of the chief executive of FIFA, how have the organization's *actions* been towards potential match-fixing, particularly since the foundation of the "early warning system"?

This book began in China; it ends in China.

It was the Women's World Cup in 2007. The tournament was held in China, the same country that had suffered a collapse of the credibility of its own soccer league three years before due to gambling match-fixing. It is the same country where the Beijing Olympics, including a soccer tournament, will be held in the summer of 2008. It is the same country, that is now bidding to host the 2018 Men's World Cup.

The tournament in China was, for the women's game, a big event. If you consider that almost every player there had faced some form of discrimination in playing a "man's game." If you consider that only fifteen years before the women's sport had trouble attracting more than a few thousand players outside of North American and Scandinavia. If you consider that three years before, Sepp Blatter had said that women playing soccer should consider wearing tighter, smaller shorts to attract more attention to the game. If you consider all those factors, the Women's World Cup was, publicly, an immense success. Hundreds of millions of people around the world watched the matches. There were high-profile sponsorship deals. There was widespread television coverage. There were matches in five different cities, with the final between the exhilarating Brazilians and the efficient Germans (how little national styles change between the genders) attracting more than 30,000 people.

There were also two cases that brought the very credibility of the sport into question. They were discovered and then went utterly unpunished.

The first case attracted widespread attention in Scandinavia and was largely ignored everywhere else. It happened to the Danish team. They were drawn in their first group match to play the hosts, China. The day before their match, the Danish coach was to hold a strategy meeting with his team. It was to be in a meeting room in their hotel. At the back of the room was a large mirror. Just before the meeting started, one of the coaches noticed that there was something very odd happening behind the mirror. He went up to the mirror, peered in and realized that it was not simply a mirror, but behind the mirror was a small room and in the room were two Chinese men with a video camera who were about to film the team talk.

The Danes were furious. They blocked the entrance to the room and called for the hotel security. When the security people arrived there was an embarrassing stand-off. The hotel security staff would not open the door and when they finally did, they took away the two men, but did not give the Danish team the tape or their names. It left the whole incident surrounded in mystery.

Was the Danish team being filmed for some sexual perversion? Would the resulting tape have been peddled on the web with an exotic title like *Hot Scandinavian Babes in their Hotel?* Were the two men members of the Chinese government who wanted to give their own team an advantage and simply could not understand that the rest of the world does not appreciate the corrupt tactics of a repressive government practiced against their sporting guests? Or were Chinese organized crime fixers filming the Danish team, intent on doing to the Women's World Cup what they had done to their own league?

We do not know. We do not know because when the Danes went to FIFA, the organization who is supposed to protect international soccer, a FIFA representative claimed that they and the hotel security people had investigated the entire incident and determined that it was not related to soccer. When Danish journalists asked how they knew it was not related to soccer or who they had investigated, a FIFA official told them: "We don't have to give details on how we conduct an investigation . . . Everything that we have had to say on the issue has already been said."

The Danish Football Association wrote a letter requesting FIFA tell *them* how they knew that the men behind the mirror were unrelated to soccer. They really wanted to know as this was the *second* case of mysterious Chinese men videotaping their team. The previous day during one of their purported closed-door practices they had caught someone else filming their team and again nothing had been done about it.

At FIFA headquarters, I found the same executive who in China had refused to reveal how they knew the two men filming the Danish team had nothing to do with sport. I asked him directly for a copy of the report on the incident or if he could simply explain to me how the investigation had proceeded and how it was possible they could rule out any connection with sport. Yet again, he refused to provide any details on the investigation.

However, when I spoke to Sepp Blatter, he told me that it was a case of "tactical spying by a Chinese television station," so all the questions over the incident still remain open, as does the mystery of why FIFA had allowed a television station to act in this appalling manner, or whether anyone was punished or sanctioned for "tactical spying."

There was a second series of incidents in the same tournament, featuring FIFA and match-fixing, that is even more worrying for the sport. It has not been reported outside of Ghana until now, but even there most of the following details are unknown. Blatter told me that he had been at this particular game, but that he knew nothing of the case. The executive who would not talk about the investigation into the filming of the Danish team claimed that this particular series of events did not happen, until I told him, in front of Blatter, that I had the FIFA documents concerning the case and gave him the reference number of the file.

It concerned, again, the Ghanaian team. They were staying at the Radisson Plaza Hotel in Hangzhou. The team had not had a good tournament. They had lost their first two matches, and had only one more to play – against the heavily favoured Norwegian team. Two days before the game, a couple of the players reported that fixers had approached them to throw their last match against Norway by five clear goals. In other words, the team had to lose by a score like 5-0 or 6-1. The fixers were not trying to make a deal with the whole team, just selected players: the goalkeeper, defenders, and a midfielder. The fixers phoned them a number of times, and one of them was reported walking around the hotel lobby trying to find the room numbers for the players.

I spoke to several Ghanaian officials. They confirmed everything the players had said. In fact, they went further. One of them said, "The fixer phoned the players in their hotel room. Some of the officials listened in on the conversation using the telephone in the player's room. [The fixer said that] he was going to give each and every player [US]$22,000 and a laptop. This is what he promised them. He [the fixer] said on the phone that they would be 'very sorry' if they told anyone about the deal."

Even with the implied threat, the Ghana officials really seem to have done a good job. They collected the names of the fixers, the numbers of the hotel rooms, and they were even ready to testify about what the fixers had offered their players. They wrote up a report for FIFA, but again the reaction of the local FIFA representative was, according to the Ghanaian officials and players, very odd. FIFA did say they would monitor the match carefully, but then they implied that the fault was with the Ghanaian players and told the team officials to remind them of the penalties for match-fixing. Then the FIFA representative refused to investigate the case and instead passed it on to the local Chinese organizing committee: the same type of people who had such a problem investigating match-fixing in their own league, the same type of people who could not figure out what happened with the two men filming the Danish team. Those same type of people listened to the complaints of the Ghanaian team officials and then said there was no point in arresting the match-fixers as, "There was no evidence they had done anything wrong." At this point a reader may be wondering what a match-fixer has to do to get arrested in China, certainly the Ghanaians were left scratching their heads, for the fixers were allowed to leave the city.

The score in that match? Norway 7, Ghana 2 – a gap of five goals, probably a coincidence, but exactly the score the fixers wanted to achieve.

THE SALVATION OF SOCCER

On January 27, 2007, at around 11:00 p.m., Geoffrey Chege was on his knees in a street in Nairobi. Robbers had stopped his car and pulled him and his wife out. Chege was a regional director of the international aid agency Care in Nairobi. He was unarmed, and there were four men with guns around him. It was a simple robbery, no other motive: so he gave them his wallet. He offered them the keys to his car. His wife cried and begged the thieves to let them go. Her pleas seemed to have worked. The men started to walk away. And then one of them turned, put his gun to Chege's head, and shot him. Chege died instantly.

That same day, when I was in Nairobi, two American women were killed in a similar way. Both attacks made a few headlines, and then in the general levels of Kenyan crime, they were forgotten.

The murderers of both Chege and the American women were purported to have come from the slums that loom over the centre of Nairobi like dark clouds. They are not pleasant places. Nairobi has a total population of three million; over half of these people are crammed into the Kibera and Mathare slums. Inside these areas, the rates of easily preventable diseases are shockingly high: tuberculosis, malaria, and AIDS affect more than 30 per cent of the population.

This last story is about what life is like inside one of those slums. It is about a fight involving mafias, political interference, and salvation through soccer. It is about hope appearing out of darkness. I write it because I have shown you some of the murders, the bombings, the attacks that have happened over the control of international soccer. I write it because I have shown you some of the ways of bribing and corrupting the sport. I write it because I have shown you that the world's biggest soccer tournament may have been corrupted. You might feel cynical. After all, if that is the way of the world, why fight to change it? Why bother? Corruption occurs in all things: why not in soccer? Why not simply sit down, enjoy the game, and not think about the litany of forgotten, good people who have to tried to stand up and change the game? But I write this last story because I love soccer. I write it to show the power of the beautiful game to change people both inside and outside. I write it because from one of the most unlikely places in the world, a Nairobi slum, comes a solution that offers hope for us all.

I met Rosemary Njiru after her soccer game. Rosemary lives in the middle of the Mathare slum. She is a thirteen-year-old girl, who has a perpetual half-eaten toothpick stuck in the side of her mouth, a glint of humour in her eyes, and an old soul. Some of her former schoolmates are prostitutes; one, she claimed, began at nine years old, and with the wisdom of someone far older, she explained child prostitution to me: "Anywhere in the world that you have some people with lots of money and lots of people with no money, you will get situations like this."

The field where Rosemary plays soccer is right in the centre of Mathare. It is a scrap of bare earth. There are sheets of garbage, plastic bags, used toilet paper that litter one corner of the field. Rosemary plays with other girls and as they do so, drunken men stagger across the pitch. Three of the players do not have boots. It doesn't seem to bother them as they chase the ball barefoot into the garbage. Some girls have soccer boots; two girls share a pair. One girl wears a boot on her left foot, the other wears the right one.

Joyce Motio is another player on Rosemary's team. She is also thirteen, and she lives in a two-room hut with her mother, who runs a tiny vegetable stall, and her three sisters. Her worst problem about Mathare?

"The flying toilets. You know there are few toilets. So some people in the night, they do their thing on a piece of paper, then they throw it in the air and it lands in front of your house. It is very common."

I meet the two of them because they are both about to embark on an extraordinary journey. The league they play in has more than 16,000 players across Mathare, but every year a very few of them are selected to go, all expenses paid, on a trip to Norway to play in a youth soccer tournament. It is an incredible opportunity for girls who struggle to get the bus fare to get to the other side of the city. When asked, neither of them has any idea what Norway will be like: they tell me, "Just like Kenya, only colder." In January, the trip to Norway is a long way off, and both girls have not made the team yet. The competition is stiff: more than 125 of the best girl players in Mathare struggling for sixteen places. Make the team, a child's life can change forever. Miss it by one spot and they are back where they started.

The two girls take me on a tour of their community, the Mathare Valley. There are thousands of tiny huts made of corrugated iron and mud. The roads are dirt tracks. There are pubs full of desperately drunken men and just desperate prostitutes. There is a long series of one-room Protestant churches: the Cathedral of Praise, the African Independent Gospel, the All Nations Gospel Church, the Redeemed Gospel Church, each of them promising heavenly salvation. However, seemingly oblivious to their lure, drunk men who have sought solace in other spirits lie all over the dirt tracks. Two things, however, are immediately clear to an outsider. The first is that every common area in the community seems to have a layer of garbage over it. The smell of fetid excrement hangs in the air like a thick, heavy, sickly jam. The second is once your nose gets used to the smell, and your eyes used to the poverty, you realize that the great majority of Mathare Valley people are just trying to make a living with as much decency and dignity as they can.

One morning, I went to the local school where the girls go. There are tiny little crammed rooms about two by three metres, with twenty-five or thirty kids to a class. All or most of them walk there with their knapsacks and pressed uniforms. Their parents, the lucky ones, work long hours on the other side of the city to make sure their children can get the educational opportunity. Others are like Joyce's mum, who has a little stall beside the soccer field where she sits all day selling a few meagre vegetables and fruit. When we passed by on the way to her house, we shook hands, talked a little about the girls' prowess at soccer, then walked on. A few minutes later she came panting up to the house, hair dishevelled and sweating. She said something in Gikuyu. I didn't understand, so Joyce translated.

"My mother invites you to our home and wants to know if you would like a soft drink or a biscuit." Her house was a two-room walled shack. A soft drink would have put a substantial dent into her entire day's salary. I declined as politely as I could and invited the girls to lunch.

The girls were now joined by their two friends: Patricia, who they call Pablo, and Mary, who they call the Bishop. We all went for lunch in a little restaurant. We ate beans and drank cokes and then after lunch they explained, with all the wisdom of thirteen year olds, the ways of the world. In some ways, little Pablo was the most moving. She was about half the size of Joyce, and she stared earnestly back at me as she struggled to say what soccer meant to her:

> When I play soccer, I forget about my companies at home, which are bad people. They go to a place called Koinange Street. A girl like me, a thirteen-year-old girl, is being married by an old man, because she does not have a helper.

I asked Rosemary about the girls that don't play soccer. She replied with all the fervour of a religious convert, follow the path – soccer – and you will be all right. Don't follow the path and you will end up in hell.

> Some girls just go for prostitution. They get married very early. Some have to drop out of school. And maybe some are helpless. No school fees. But if they could be playing football, they could avoid all those

things. I can advise them to just come and play with us, and they'd see the changes in their lives.

All the girls talk this way, about how soccer is a road to salvation. It is more than just a potential trip to Norway. It is hope in the middle of darkness.

Clare O'Brien is a doctoral researcher at Oxford who spent time looking at girls' soccer in the slums of Nairobi. She claims that in some places, soccer has become so well organized it is replacing church in the girls' lives. I was deeply skeptical when I first heard her. But after listening to the children, I began to understand what she meant. She told me about part of her research where she gave some girls who were soccer players cameras and told them to bring back photographs showing what soccer meant to them.

I got back pictures that were so shocking, that I wouldn't have thought that this is what football would mean to someone. One of the pictures was of two girls, scaling a little mud wall, and there is a sewer going between the two walls, and there's a boy sitting down, sniffing glue, and I was looking at this thinking, "Hmm, okay, what could this possibly mean?"

The girl who took the photo said, "This is a sewer, and there's no way to get out of here except to walk through the sewer. This boy here, sniffing glue, he's given up. There's no reason for him ever to leave this part of the slum. And maybe he never will. He might spend the rest of his life there, because there's nothing that's motivating him to get out of there and to do something more. But these two girls are going to a football game. What they're doing is they're scaling the wall and they're taking the chance because they know that there's nine other girls waiting for them to play football. And they're willing to take the risk of falling in the sewer because they think that there might be something better for them out there. This is what football means for us. It's a chance. It gets us out of our current situation because we believe that there's something else better than what we have right now, and we know that there's other people that are doing the same thing, that are waiting for us."

This story of salvation through soccer has an unlikely starting point: the small town of St. Catharines, Ontario. In 1987, Bob Munro, a Canadian development consultant who grew up in that town playing hockey in leagues organized by veterans of the Second World War, went into Mathare to pick up his daughter, who was teaching an English class. She was late. So Munro wandered around the compound. He saw children playing soccer with string and paper balls. He remembered his own childhood and he thought, Why shouldn't the kids in Mathare have the same chance that I and my friends had when I was a kid?

Munro contacted the chairman of a local church group with the idea of starting a small soccer league. "So I made this deal with them. I said, 'Look, if you and your friends get together a little committee. I'll work with you. The deal is this: if you do something, I'll do something, and if you do nothing, I will do nothing.'" At the time he thought it was a pretty clever deal, which would prevent him from being too caught up in an organization. It hasn't turned out that way.

On the first day of the new sports league, Munro showed up with a clipboard and whistle expecting a small group of kids, maybe enough for six or eight teams. He was surprised. The children had lined up before dawn and there were enough boys there for twenty-five different teams. It was the beginning of the Mathare Youth Sports Association (MYSA), an organization that has had an influence far beyond this community. Its genius was to link the enthusiasm for sport with development.

The kids loved playing soccer, and each season more and more teams joined the league. So the MYSA organizers added an original twist to the league standings: each team got the normal three points for a win and one point for a draw, but they would also get six points if they helped with some community development project. At first, Munro and the other leaders were not sure what it would be:

We looked at a variety of things, and then the obvious thing jumped out: all this garbage, it was killing kids, and adults, in the slum. . . . because when it rains twice a year for several weeks, it flows down the hill and through their homes. So they are surrounded by contaminated water all the time. When you're walking through contaminated water, if you have the slightest cut, it'll kill you. You get infected, the medical care is not good in the slum, you get diarrhea or cholera, or meningitis and typhoid, you know, diseases that we think belong to the Middle Ages.

For the garbage clean-up, each team had to show up and a "referee" would be there to make sure that all the players were there. If not all of them showed up, the team wouldn't get the points. So the captains really put pressure on all the team members to show up or their chance of winning the league would be gone. The idea proved immensely popular both with the boys, but also with their parents, who could see an immediate and significant benefit to their children playing soccer. But then in the early 1990s, MYSA did something really revolutionary: they decided to organize soccer for girls.

We had three problems. One problem was that the boys, and it was a boys' organization then, they knew that girls couldn't play football. The girls didn't think they could. And the mothers didn't want them to, because by the time they're seven, eight, nine, the girls, while the mother is working, are looking after the younger brothers and sisters. So we would put tents up beside our field so that the girls could come with their little brothers and sisters and we ran a little daycare centre, which became very popular. And then the girls could play and the little ones would be looked after, and that's how we got girls' football started.

Since those early days, MYSA has expanded to other programs: scholarships, loans, anti-HIV education campaigns. They have now directly helped more than 17,000 children in Mathare with scholarships and tens of thousands of others with library facilities, drama groups, and video production courses. But at the heart of all MYSA's work is a key value: do something for us, we'll do something for you; do nothing, you'll get nothing. At first it may seem hard, tough love, but it stops the charity handout complex and is extraordinarily empowering.

Bob Munro may have kicked off MYSA, but much of the organization has long outgrown him. It now has hundreds of leaders, most of whom came up the ranks of MYSA, first as players on youth teams, then on scholarships for helping to organize tournaments. It has just opened a brand new training centre for its teams on the edge of Mathare. It has offices, meeting halls, a video production studio, a weight room, and fitness centre.

But amid all this good news and hopes of salvation through self-help and soccer, there is a problem. Its called the mafia. The precise name for it in the Mathare Valley is the Mungiki. They run things in the slum. They are the effective government. In Mathare, they've hijacked the water pipes that bring free water to the area and then sell water to the residents. The area is also a no-go area for any electricity meter reader. Mathare does receive electricity. But the inhabitants have to pay the mafia, not the electrical company.

There are other mafia groups in the slums of Nairobi. Some have names taken from current events, so there is a gang called the Baghdad Boys and another ironically named the Taliban. The Taliban, who have absolutely no relation to Afghanistan, Osama bin Laden, or Islam, are the Mungiki's big rivals in Mathare. They established a *chana*, or African whisky distillery. I went down to see it. The distillery is three smoked, lined plastic barrels. The water that is the principal ingredient is taken straight from the garbage-choked Mathare River, just downstream from a dozen open sewers. The actual whisky is not bad, considering it was brewed for forty-five minutes and then poured straight into plastic jerry cans, and it is a very lucrative business.

In the fall of 2006, the Mungiki and Taliban fought a murderous war up and down the streets of Mathare for control of the distillery, which

left several hundred people homeless. Both Patricia and Rosemary witnessed the fighting. They were afraid. They told me about fleeing from
their homes and seeing a young man caught by the Mungiki: "They outnumbered him. They just stopped the car. Seeing it was a Taliban, they
took him out, they burned his car, then they beat him, then they cut off
his head."

I had a small sampling of what violence could be like in Mathare. I
was working with a young Norwegian woman, Gunhild Forselv, who had
been a colleague in Iraq and Turkey. We were staying at the home of one
of the local MYSA leaders in the middle of Mathare. It was a small, mud-
walled hut, next to the garbage dump. There were two rooms; we were in
the kitchen-bedroom for his family. It was 10:20 p.m. There was a small
pot of fish on the stove, the children were still awake, and we were joking
about learning Norwegian. It was all very domestic, all very comfortable.

There was a sudden bang on the door and screams in the alleyway.

A young man dressed in a blue shirt staggered in with an inch and a
half cut on the back of his head. It looked as if it had been sliced open
with a machete. There was blood trickling down the back of his neck and
soaking his short hair. Everyone rushed to close the wooden door. Over
the top of the door, I could see another young man screaming and trying
to push his way in. It felt like there were others outside. Our guys pushed
him away. There was a smash on the window. A stick with a knife actually came through the mud wall. Everyone was screaming.

I figured it was over. The Mungiki or the Taliban had come to get us.
They must have heard the rich foreigners were there. There was nowhere
to run. Nowhere to hide. We were trapped. There was no help we could
call on.

The guys ran outside and there was a fight in the alleyway. I gripped
the pepper spray in my hand and stood by door. Only later did I wonder:
if I were a real man would I have run outside and fought beside the
others? But frankly, I didn't think too much about it. I was ready to fight.
I expected at any moment a horde of gangsters to set upon me and do
worse to Gunhild.

The guys come back in. One of them, still smiling, nodded at me. "Time for us to go?" I asked.

"Time for you to go," he replied.

On the side of the main Juja Road, one of the other guys, Julius, invited us back to his place. I refused, saying, "I'm a coward. I feel scared. I want to go home . . ." There was relief in Julius's and the other guys' eyes, but shame in our former host. He hunched over as he walked along beside me. "I was happy. Now I am sad. My heart does not feel good . . . I will find those boys and I will break their necks." He did not meet my eyes for the rest of my stay in Mathare. As we left, they were planning to roam the streets to find the men who attacked the house and kill them.

In May 2007, just as the final practices for the Norwegian tournament began, the area exploded again. This time it wasn't the Mungiki versus the Taliban. It was another group of criminal extortionists, the Kenyan police. The Mungiki killed a police officer. That was a really bad move for the entire Mathare slum. The police moved into the area and declared open war on pretty much everyone. They beat up hundreds of men, women, and children. They killed at least thirty people and every corpse, they declared, was a Mungiki killer. It is hard to believe when one of the people they shot was a ten-year-old boy. Throughout all this violence, Rosemary, Joyce, Mary, and Pablo all kept practising and kept dreaming about their possible trip to Norway.

It would be relatively easy to stop the violence in Mathare. But each of the mafia groups is connected with top politicians. They provide the politician with votes at election times: the politicians provide them with protection when their violence provokes too many headlines. And some of those politicians *really* didn't like Bob Munro.

Munro's problem was that after he helped establish MYSA, he had been asked by MYSA to turn his attention to the problem of corruption in Kenyan soccer as a whole. MYSA had launched an adult professional team made up from its best youth players. It was a success, quickly gaining promotion to the Kenyan Premier League. As it climbed, Munro began to be aware of the corruption in the league: the unpaid referees, the theft of gate receipts, the mismanagement of schedules, the pocketing of fees from illegal transfer deals.

Kenyan Football Federation (KFF) politics can be *very* dirty. Two recent soccer executives of the KFF were beaten up by thugs, purportedly hired by their rivals. Two other executives are facing court trials for embezzling tens of millions of Kenyan shillings. Part of the problem is that a post in the Kenyan Football Federation is regarded as an excellent step toward political prominence: of the last seven Kenyan Football Federation presidents, six have gone on to become national politicians. So after one powerful team refused to be relegated, Munro helped found another rival Premier League backed by a number of corporate sponsors. It was an immediate success and it was stepping on all the wrong toes. When I visited Kenya in January 2007, things looked really bad for Munro, MYSA, and Kenyan soccer. The Kenyan minister of sport had threatened to deport Munro claiming that he was bad for the game. The Commissioner for Sport, Gordon Oluch, had been attacked after he brought riot police to close down a match of Munro's Premier League. And FIFA, tired of the whole mess, had stopped Kenya from competing in international soccer.

In the midst of it all, Munro was unrepentant. He said:

People would come to me and say, "Bob, the problem with you is that you need to learn how to compromise." And I say, "Look, I've spent thirty years in the UN, and compromises I know a lot about. But let's look at this issue. What do you mean by compromise? Do you mean by compromise is that the previous regimes stole $55 million and they're in court being charged with stealing $55 million, so should we compromise by saying this existing regime, they can steal $25 [million]? Or, you know, the previous regime, they broke over half the articles in the KFF constitution, so do you mean that we should compromise by saying, "Okay, you're only allowed to break a quarter of them? Is that what you mean by compromise?"

There are certain things in which compromise is not possible. You steal or you don't steal. You respect the constitution or you don't respect the constitution. You have the rule of law or you don't have the rule of law. So there's certain things that are absolutes and areas that are not negotiable.

There is a happy ending to this story.

Over the course of 2007, the international soccer authorities like FIFA and the Confederation of African Football stepped in and did what they are supposed to do: help clean up the game. They got people to the table, administratively banged a few heads together, and now finally Munro is safe, Mathare United is back in the league, and the corruption is beginning to leave the game in Kenya.

In July 2007, the Mathare United Under-14 girls team went to Norway. Rosemary, Joyce, and Pablo all made the team. It was their first trip out of Kenya and after six hard-fought matches they won the whole damn tournament. I saw a photo of Rosemary Njiru after the final. She is standing in front of her jubilant teammates, being interviewed by the Norwegian press. She doesn't have her toothpick, but she has grown so much since I first spoke to her. She looks like a professional: poised, happy, and confident. She looks like a young girl who has come a very long way.

The moral of this story is that if a bunch of little girls from a slum and an unarmed Canadian can take on the mafia, violence, and corruption in soccer and survive and thrive, then so can we all. We can take the game back. We can clean up this sport. We can establish leagues that help their own communities instead of being nesting grounds for hooligans, mobsters, and corruption. We can stop referees from being bribed. We can make sure that the biggest tournaments and leagues in the world are not infested with match-fixers. We can win this fight and the sport deserves us to fight it. I will finish the book with one of my favourite quotes. It was from the great English anti-slavery advocate, William Wilberforce. In 1789, Wilberforce took on the entire English slave-owning class and gave a three-and-a-half hour parliamentary speech that outlined the horrors and atrocities of the slaving ships. He ended his speech with the words, "Having heard all of this, you may choose to look the other way, but you can *never* again say that you did not know." The sport, our young people and all who come after, need us not to look the other way.

ACKNOWLEDGEMENTS

Blanche DuBois famously said that she depended on the "kindness of strangers." In writing this book I have relied on the kindness of just about everybody: colleagues, friends, relatives, acquaintances, and strangers. In particular, I would like to thank all the people who consented to be interviewed, many of whom have asked not to be identified. Because of this reluctance, I will not mention anyone who gave me an interview, to stop guessing games as to identities, but I do want to thank everyone who spoke to me for their time and patience in explaining the sometimes unseemly side of a sport that we all love so much.

The book would never have been written without Marc Carinci, a tireless researcher, who worked on fact checking and research reports. His enthusiasm never waned despite long hours and he was absolutely dedicated to getting facts right: any mistakes in the text are mine. Chris Bucci, the senior editor at McClelland & Stewart, guided me with wonderful calmness throughout the editorial process. And Emma Parry, my agent, is ever ready with a good word, a great smile, and a superb meal!

In the management and processing of information I owe much to Ben Spurr, Noah Bush, and Nolan Little for their work in transcribing the hundreds of hours of tape; Alyn Still and Emma Link for their help with statistical calculations; and Dominic Bown for keeping my computers and various hidden cameras and recording devices working.

At Oxford, there were two great English gentlemen who made my stay there largely a pleasure: Dr. Andrew Markus, my colleague advisor, who gave mostly gentle advice, kept my spirits up, and taught me how to tie a bow-tie; and, of course, Professor Anthony Heath, a supervisor who with wit, grace, and intelligence saw me through to the completion of my thesis. Other colleagues who gave plenty of intellectual contributions to the work and deserve my thanks are Professors Diego Gambetta, Tom Dawson, Uwe Ackerman, Sean David, Keith Frayn, Raman Saggu, Derek Jewell, Steve Fisher, Michael Biggs, Peter Hill, Matthew Bond, Jay Gershuny, and Edmund Chattoe, for their encouragement and ideas.

There were dozens of other people who helped read manuscript drafts, make cups of tea, and generally keep me sane, they include Michael Drolet, Anders Krarup, Lucie Cluver, Jamie Salo, Paddy Coulter, Anne Millard, Allison Gilmore, Jackie Davis, and Nigel, Glen, Darren, Mick, and the rest of the porters at Green College. Thank you as well to the members of the British Council, who were kind enough to give me a Chevening Scholarship that financed some of my studies at the university.

In Malaysia, I was fortunate to be adopted by two mentors: Ian "Mr. Malaysia" Stratton and Gerry Bodeker. Also Sharon Saw, Ngooi Chiu Ing, and the gang at the Oxbridge Society of Malaysia who on occasion would make me forget my research and take me dancing. Thank you as well to my friends and contacts at the Royal Malaysian Police who helped me with great patience and graciousness. Other people who were helpful were Tunku Adnan, Effendi Jagan, Ann Lee, Hilary Chiew, Jahabar Sadiq, Patrick Chalmers, Richard Ryan, and Roshan Jason.

In Singapore, Andrew Leci and the ESPN gang were extremely hospitable. Steve "the wisest man in Asia" Darby, Rafiq Jumabhoy, Jose Raymond, and Jeffrey Lau were all very insightful into the ways of Singapore society.

In Thailand, a couple of people watched my back and have requested not to be named. I know who you are and what you did – thank you.

I have never made a sports bet in my life, so the gambling world was largely unknown territory. A group of people taught me an enormous amount and then patiently helped when I returned to them with all kinds of what must have seemed very silly questions. Those people are, in the English gambling world, Andrew "Bert" Black and Robin Marks (Betfair),

Graham Sharpe (William Hill), Alistair Flutter, and Matthew Benham. In the European Lotteries world, Göran Wessberg, Tjeerd Veenstra, Stefan Allmer, and Wolfgang Feldner of the FIFA "early warning system."

I have a number of contacts at FIFA and UEFA; in particular I would like to thank Andreas Herren of FIFA for helping arrange interviews and getting me access to information.

Around the world (and all flights were offset by donations to carbon reduction programs), there was a band of brothers: fellow journalists and football lovers who shared their information, stories, or translated with wonderful generosity. In Belgium, Kees t'Hooft, Stefan De Wachter, Frank Van Laeken, Douglas De Coninck, Jan Hauspie, and Peter Verlinden. In Finland, Risto Rumpunen, Tiina Ristikari, and Ari Virtanen. In Croatia, Mislav Ivanišević. In Northern Ireland, Malcolm Brodie. In Italy, Stefania Battistelli, Graziano "Primo" Lolli, and Andrea Patacconi. In Germany, Professor Johann Lambsdorff, Mathias Nell, and my colleagues at ACTC who deserve special thanks for their patience while I was working on the book, also – Julika Erfurt, Thomas Gerken, Franziska Telschow, Anna Zimdars, and Söhnke Vosgerau. In Russia, Pär Gustafsson, Natasha Gorina, Ekaterina Korobtseva, Ekaterina Kravchenko, Svetlana Guzeeva, Eugene Demchenko, Alisa Voznaya, and Maria Semenova.

In Brazil, Colombia, and Argentina, Rafael Maranhao, Mike Ceaser, and Ezequiel Fernandez Moores. In China, Stewart Park. In Turkey, Chris Wade and Emre Ozcan. In the United States, David C. Whelan. In Kenya, the long-suffering Odindo Ayieko and joel kinuthia; Anthony Husher for cold beers and good counsel; and James Njugush, Cosmos, and the guys for fighting so well in a dark alley. In Ghana, Dr. David Abulai, "Paca," and the numerous informants, particularly in Tamale.

In Canada, Anthony "the great Tony" Blundell, Rachel Vincent, Bruce Livesey, Sharon Klein, Clive Doucet, Tad Homer-Dixon, James Orbinski, Richard McLaren, Alan Guettel, David Nayman, Dick Miller, and, of course, to my long-suffering teammates on the Pangaea Soccer Club who through the seasons had to put up with my constant exhortations, petulant temper tantrums, and over-intensity when playing the beautiful game.

NOTES

In the course of the research for this book, I conducted more than two hundred interviews. Because so many people requested anonymity, in fear either of the police, criminals, or sports officials, I have the following code in the notes to help the reader understand the role of the person giving the interview.

Gambler (G): any bettors, odd compliers, or gambling industry worker from executives
    to runners
Corruptor (C): any match-fixer or criminal who was involved in the sport
Player (P): former or current soccer player
Referee (R): former or current referee
Sports Official (SO): any league or team administrators, including coaches or managers
Law Enforcement (LE): police officers, anti-corruption agents, or state prosecutors
Journalists (J): journalist who had direct knowledge of fixing
Others (O): miscellaneous roles – diplomats, businessmen, members of the Malaysian
    Royal Family, academics, politicians, and political dissidents

INTRODUCTION: BIRDS OF PREY
Weather conditions, TV ratings, on day of final:
Notes on the weather that day available at:
www.ngdc.noaa.gov/nmmr/public/viewRecord.do?xmlstyle=FGDC&edit=&recuid=19
16&recordset=NCDC.
    "U.S. Helps World Cup Make Global TV History." *Atlanta Journal-Constitution*
(Atlanta, GA). July 19, 1994. D1.
    Vader, J.E. "All Was Ready, Then the Teams Failed to Deliver." *Oregonian* (Portland,
OR). July 18, 1994. D1.

Description of VIP section:
Interviews with Chuck Blazer, Alan Rothenberg, Sunil Gulati, Cathy Scanlan, Karen Bybee (all either FIFA, U.S. Soccer, or protocol officials who were present that day), January 2008.

Kikalishvili in the VIP section:
Interview with Anzor Kikalishvili, February 1999.
    Also, Fyodorov, Gennady, "Godfather of Sports Denies Mafia Link." Agence France Presse. November 19, 1996.

Kikalishvili's reputation:
Hearing before the Permanent Subcommittee on Investigations of the Committee on Governmental Affairs, United States Senate: One hundred and fourth Congress, Second Session. May 15, 1996. 86, 88.

Background on 21st Century Association:
Friedman, Robert. *Red Mafiya: How the Russian Mob has invaded America.* London: Little, Brown and Company, 2000. 115, 125, 130, 154, 194–195.
    See also Baranovsky, Igor. "Mafia: Young Wolves vs. 'Authorities,'" *Moscow News* (Moscow). October 1, 1993. No. 40
    Trifonov, Vladislav. "Kvantrishvili Killed by Soldier." *Kommersant* (Moscow). June 14, 2006. Available at www.kommersant.com/page.asp?id=681819.

For general background on the Russian mob:
Handelman, Stephen. *Comrade Criminal: The Theft of the Second Russian Revolution.* London: Michael Joseph, 1994.

Kikalishvili's activities in Florida:
Interview with LE 12, 20, May–June 1999.
    Friedman, 154.

For Havelange's connections with Castor de Andrade:
Renato, Claudio. "Havelange e Avalista Moral de Castor." *O Globo* (São Paulo). April 9, 1994. 12.
    Rodrigue, Ernesto. *Jogo Duro, a História de João Havelange.* Rio de Janeiro: Editora Record, 2007. 284–285.
    Yallop, David. *How They Stole the Game.* London: Poetic Publishing, 1999. 73, 210.
    Rocha, Jan. "Lottery Bribes Scandal Snares Rio's Elite: Fifa's President and the Police Figure on an Alleged Mafia Payroll," *Guardian* (London). April 9, 1994. 16.

"most notorious capo . . ."
Vincent, Isabel. "Not Told of Probe, Suspect Complains." *Globe and Mail* (Toronto). April 13, 1994.

For situation in Russian soccer:
Hansam, James. "Murder, Mystery and Suspensions in Moscow." *Evening Standard* (London). February 6, 2001. 78.
 Brennan, Dan. "Soccer Russian style." *Scotland on Sunday* (Edinburgh). July 6, 2003.

For situation in Colombian soccer:
Interview with O7, January 2008.
 Macalister Hall, Malcolm. "Hero, Scapegoat, Martyr." *Mail on Sunday* (London). April 19, 1999. 11–13.
 Price, S.L. "Shadow of Shame: The Specter of Violent Drug Cartels Haunts the Formidable Colombian National Soccer Team." *Sports Illustrated* (New York). May 23, 1994. Available at http://vault.sportsillustrated.cnn.com/vault/article/magazine/MAG1005218/index.htm.

Information on TV program:
The documentary "Mafia Power Play" was broadcast on *The Fifth Estate*, CBC Television, October 6, 1999, and *Frontline*, PBS, October 10, 1999.

Explosion at 21st Century Headquarters:
Solovyova, Yulia. "Hotel Open for Business as Bombing Investigated." *Moscow Times* (Moscow). April 28, 1999. Available at www.themoscowtimes.com/indexes/1999/04/28/01.html.

Background on Friedman and his work on the Russian mafia:
Friedman was called "The Best Investigative Reporter You've Never Heard Of" by Sherry Ricchiardi in the *American Journalism Review,* January/February 2000. Sadly, in 2002, Friedman died of an illness contracted while researching a story in India.

Pavel Bure:
Friedman, 173–201.
 "Mafia Power Play." *Frontline.* PBS TV, October 1999.

For background on other Russian hockey players:
Interviews with LE 20 and J 23, April 1999.

Joseph Kennedy's bootlegging history is explored in:

Hersh, Seymour. *The Dark Side of Camelot*. London: Harper Collins, 1997. 44–60.

Russo, Gus. *The Outfit: The Role of Chicago's Underworld in the Shaping of Modern America*. London: Bloomsbury, 2001. 359–362.

Hersh cites various eyewitnesses and also FBI documents linking Kennedy to the illegal booze supply to the mob. Russo cites an RCMP document from 1929 showing Kennedy as one of the suppliers to Al Capone.

Corruption in other sports:

Basketball: Both in U.S. college basketball (NCAA) and the National Basketball Association (NBA), there have been cases of professional gamblers attempting to fix games. The most recent and high-profile is the former NBA referee Tim Donaghy: see Bender, William, "Donaghy's associates indicted in betting case." *Philadelphia Daily News* (Philadelphia, PA). February 9, 2008. 42.

Cricket: A number of top cricket stars have been involved in fixing games in international matches with criminal bookies. For more information, see Judge El King, "Commission of Inquiry into Cricket Match Fixing and Related Matters, 2nd Interim Report," Republic of South Africa, 2000; or Ganapathy, M.A., "Report on Cricket Match-Fixing and Related Malpractices," New Delhi: CBI Special Crimes Branch – Central Bureau of Investigation, October 2000.

Tennis: A number of top tennis players from Russia's Dmitry Tursunov to the U.K.'s Andy Murray to former U.S. great John McEnroe have discussed the presence of criminal fixers in the sport.

See Associated Press, "Tursunov Multiple Match Fixing, Bribe Offers," September 28, 2007. Harman, Neil. "ATP Summons Andy Murray after Claims over Match-fixing." *The Times,* (London). October 10, 2007. (On John McEnroe) Hodgkinson, Mark. "The Russian Mafia Could Be Involved. That's Scary." *Daily Telegraph* (London). December 7, 2007. 15.

CHAPTER 1: THE CONQUEST OF THE LOCUSTS

For Yang Zuwu's walk-out:

Watts, Jonathan. "China Struggles to Quell Football Revolt: Country's Most Popular Spectator Sport Rebels against Bribe-taking and Match-fixing." *Guardian* (London). November 4, 2004. 19.

Shao Da. "Chinese Soccer on Defense." *China.org.cn*. October 31, 2004

For general conditions in China Super League:

Interviews with Peter Velappan, former general secretary of AFC, June 2005 and May 2006.

See also "Velappan Warns Corruption Could Kill Football in China." Agence France Presse. June 10, 2005.

Davis, James. " 'Black Whistle' casts a shadow." *Observer* (London). Sport, 9.

For accusations of China's team in the World Cup, throwing games:
"China accused of match fixing." Reuters. June 26, 2002.

For information on the "Black Whistle Scandal":
"Black Whistle Fighter Remains Indomitable in Isolation." *Shanghai Star* (Shanghai). July 3, 2002. Available at http://app1.chinadaily.com.cn/star/2002/0703/pr231.html.

Gittings, John. "Chinese Fans Riot at Ref's Foul Decision." *Guardian* (London). March 28, 2002. 20.

Soccer development in China, radioactive comment
Gidney, Charlie. "Football Development in China: It's a Funny Old Game." Available at www.chinalyst.net/node/14262. Retrieved May 21, 2007.

See www.chinasuperleague.com:
- "More Black Whistles Blown." January 19, 2002.
- "CFA Response Imminent." January 23, 2002.
- "Newspaper Makes 'Black Whistle' Revelations." February 1, 2002.
- "'Black Whistle' Arrested." April 18, 2002.
- "Chinese Referee Jailed for Ten Years." January 29, 2003.

For Sepp Blatter's idea on young players being sent to Asia:
Kynge, James. "Send Football's Young Stars to Play in Asia, Says FIFA Chief." *Financial Times* (London). July 17–18, 2004. 10.

For the booing in the stadium:
Interview with Peter Velappan, June 2005 and May 2006.

See also Xianfeng Chen and Fei Li. "AFC Official Apologizes for Tirade of Misunderstanding." *China Daily* (Beijing). July 20, 2004.
Available at www.chinadaily.com.cn/english/doc/2004/07/20/content_34975/1.htm.

"Beijing Olympics Questioned as Asian Cup Opens Amid Uproar." Agence France Presse. July 18, 2004.

In an interview with Sepp Blatter, February 2008, he denied that any riot, booing, or confrontation occurred at the stadium.

For information on Hong Kong players fixing:
Stewart, Anne. "Footballers' Confessions Admissible." *South China Morning Post* (Hong Kong). February 12, 1999. 6.

Staff writer. "Football Match-fixer Tells of Sorrow for Former Teammates." *Hong Kong Standard* (Hong Kong). February 11, 1999.

Speech by Deputy Commissioner Tony Kwok. "Sharing 25 Years' Experience in Law Enforcement Fighting Corruption & Organized Crime." ICAC, Hong Kong, 22nd International Asian Organized Crime Conference.

Indonesian Referee's Mafia:
Staff writer. "PSSI Believes report on Collusion Practices." *Jakarta Post* (Jakarta). February 21, 1998. News.

"Betting." Agence France Presse. May 18, 1999.

Match-fixing in Vietnam and the Nam Cam case:
Nam Cam engaged in a wide range of corrupt activities, and one of the charges on which he was convicted was of fixing football matches. There are many articles on other match-fixing scandals in Vietnam; one case even sparked a World Bank investigation. Two other typical ones are:

Staff writer. "Vietnam Football Needs to Be Clean to Grow." Agence France Presse. October 12, 2002.

Staff writer. "Match-fixing Scam in Vietnam." Agence France Presse. October 30, 2002.

Bruce Grobbelaar quote in:
Grobbelaar vs. News Group Newspapers Ltd and another, Court of Appeal (Civil Division), 18 January 2001, paragraph 178.

For an excellent overview of the entire Grobbelaar case, see Thomas, David, *Foul Play: The Inside Story of the Biggest Corruption Trial in British Sporting History.* London: Bantam, 2003.

For violence by the fixers, see:
Mcdonnell, David. "One Player Died in a Mysterious Accident and Another Found a Cobra in His Car." *Daily Mail* (London). March 30, 1999. 77.

Also interviews with P 2–13, J 4–9, LE 1–5, SO 1–10, April to May, November to December 2005; May 2006.

The Rambo-knife incident is from a confession made to the police by the player, shared with me by the Malaysian police in May 2005.

"We know where your granny shops . . ."
Interview with SO 9, June 2005.

For foundation of league and its subsequent collapse:
Seneviratne, Percy. "History of Football in Malaysia." Kuala Lumpur: PNS Publishing, 2000. Published with assistance of the Football Association of Malaysia.
　　Interviews with SO 1, 3, 4, and 8, in both Singapore and Kuala Lumpur, April to June, 2005.
　　Williams, Russ. *Football Babylon 2*. London: Virgin Books, 1998. 109–126.

"I worked a couple of times for the bookies . . ."
Interviews with J 3, 8, and 9, May 2005, December 2005, May 2006.

For background on Johnson Fernandez and Lazarus Rokk:
Interviews with J 2, 3, and Fernandez and Rokk, May 2005 and May 2006.

"For years, we had been trying . . ."
"He was a great guy . . ."
"They use former players . . ."
Interviews with Fernandez and Rokk, May 2005.

"There were rumours all the time . . ."
"What happened with our mob . . ."
Interviews with Scott Ollerenshaw, December 2005, May 2006, November 2007.

Hansie Cronje
See Hansie Cronje's statement before the Judge Edwin King Commission, June 15, 2000.

1919 Chicago White Sox fix
Asinof, Eliot. *Eight Men Out: The Black Sox and the 1919 World Series*. New York: Henry Holt, 1987. See also the 1988 film by the same name, directed by John Sayles.

Liverpool vs. Manchester United 1915 fix
Inglis, Simon. *Soccer in the Dock: A History of British Football Scandals, 1900–1965*. London: Willow Books, 1985.
　　Sharpe, Graham. *Free the Manchester United One: The Inside Story of Football's Greatest Scam*. London: Robson Books, 2003.

General information about networks and fixers strategies:
Interviews with P 7, 8, 9, 32; Cor 1–4; B 3; November, December 2005 and February 2008.

See also Fernandez, Johnson. "A Worldwide Plague." *Malay Mail* (Kuala Lumpur). July 28, 1993. 74–75.

CHAPTER 2: "WHAT THE HELL DO YOU THINK YOU'RE DOING?"
British repression of civil liberties in Malaysia:
For a critical view of Britain's role in the Malaya war of the 1950, see Purcell, Victor, *Malaya: Communist or Free"* London: Victor Gollancz, 1954. Purcell was a former British Army officer turned colonial civil servant who revisited Malaysia in 1952, describing it as, "a vast armed camp in which no one could call his soul his own . . ."

The other side of the argument can be seen in Parkinson, C. Northcote, *Templer in Malaya.* Singapore: Donald Moore, 1954; also the entertaining but dated Brigadier Richard Miers, *Shoot to Kill.* London: Faber and Faber, 1959.

See also Short, Anthony. *The Communist Insurrection in Malaya: 1948–1960.* London: Frederick Muller Limited, 1975. 295–96 and 380–87.

Malaysian repression of civil liberties:
Amnesty International Report. *Another Guantanamo in Malaysia?* May 26, 2006.

The Anwar Ibrahim Case:
The intelligence officer testified: "Basically we do a quick assessment on our target [a prisoner], then we see how the possibilities are to turn over their stand. If it is a certain political stand, we may neutralize the stand if it is a security threat. It is known in the Special Branch as a turning-over operation. The procedure is to turn them over so that they will change their stand . . . My Lord, [to the judge] this is a Special Branch secret. It is a great secret." ("Malaysia's Intelligence Chief tells Anwar Trial He would lie," CNN Kuala Lumpur, November 5, 1998. Available at www.cnn.com/WORLD/asiapcf/9811/05/anwar.02/.)
See also Pereira, Brendan. "Ex-Special Branch director asked about 'trade secrets.'" *The Straits Times* (Singapore). November 5, 1998. 26.

For details of Operation Bola:
Williams, 1998. 112–130.

"'Drastic' Action Vowed if Soccer Corruption Not Curbed." Associated Press. July 5, 1995.
"Three More Picked up for Alleged Match-fixing." *New Straits Times* (Singapore). March 12, 1995. 8.
"Six Malaysian Footballers Banned for Life for Match fixing." Agence France Presse. November 16, 1995.
Veera, R.V., Navaratnam, C., Nambiar, Ravi. "Almost an Entire State Team to Be Banished." *New Straits Times* (Singapore). February 16, 1995. 1.

"World Soccer Body Seeks Assurance Tournament Won't Be Fixed." Associated Press. April 21, 1995.

Rafiq Saad's confession:
From the Royal Malaysian Police files.

Genoa versus Venice Fixed Match:
Preziosi, Enrico. "Una Chiamata Durante la Partita." Associated Press. 24 June 2005.
Dellacasa, Erika. "Ecco la Telefonata Che Mette Nei Guai Il Genoa." *Corriere Della Sera* (Milan). June 24, 2005. Available at www. corriere.it/Primo_Piano/Sport/2005/06_Giugno/24/genoa.shtml.
Hawkey, Ian. "Genoa's Top Flight Dreams Rest on a Pile of Cash." *Sunday Times* (London). July 3, 2005. 57.

Bologna versus Juventus Fixed Match:
Petrini, Carlo. *Nel fango del dio Pallone.* Milan: Kaos Edizione, 2000. 110–112.

Canada versus North Korea Fixed Match:
See McKeown, Bob. *The Fifth Estate.* CBC Television. October 10, 1989.
Interview with Paul James, December 2005. Note: Paul James was in no way involved in fixing the game. Rather, his courageous stand brought the matter to light.

Finnish Goalkeeper Fixing Tactics:
Staff writers. "Kaksi Maalivahtia Kertoo IS Urheilulle, Että Lahjuksia on Tarjottu" and "Maalivahti Sami Sinkkonen: Kieltäydyin Kolmest Lahjukssta." *Ilta-Sanomat* (Helsinki). December 12, (2005): 2–3.

"There was one game . . ."
Interview with P 7, December 2005.

The Suicide Pass:
Borristow, Michael, Bernard Jordan, Harold Pendlebury, and Robert Greaves. "This Is the Way Soccer Matches Are Fixed." *Daily Mail* (London). October 10, 1960. 1, 11.

"It was ridiculous mistakes":
Interview with P 7, December 2005.

Fred Pagnam and "what he damn well meant . . . ?"
Staff writer. "Players Suspension: Claims for Damages and an Injunction." *Daily Dispatch* (London). July 6–7, 1917.

Players "buy time":
Interview with C 3, December 2005.

CHAPTER 3: EXPERTS IN VERBAL BULLSHIT
Disappearance of Michael Vana:
Staff writer. "Singapore May Legalize Soccer Bets." United Press International. April 1, 1996.

  Miller, David. "Ex-national Striker, Club Manager Nabbed." *New Straits Times* (Singapore). October 25, 1994. 1.

"The best player I have ever coached."
Interview with SO 15, March 2006.

  Despite being banned for life by FIFA, Michael Vana denied taking ever taking any bribes; see Staff writer. "Czech Soccer Player Rejects Bribery Charges." CTK National News Wire (Prague). May 18, 1995.

There are all kinds of tales:
Interviews with J 8, 9; C 1, 2; SO 8, 10; B 3.

"I think the one that capped . . ."
Interview with SO 15, March 2006.

The Jackie Pallo story:
Pallo, Jackie "Mr. TV." *You Grunt, I'll Groan: The Inside Story of Wrestling.* London: Macdonald Queen Anne Press, 1985. 8–32.

"Also it is important for fighters to respond to one another's moves . . ."
Pallo, 20.

"It is all the verbal bullshit . . ."
Interview with P 7, December 2005.

"Football is very subjective . . ."
Interview with LE 5, May 2005.

On Academic Economics:
For similar views expressed far more cogently, see the writings of the great Professor Terence Hutchison of the London School of Economics, particularly *The Significance and Basic Postulates of Economic Theory* (1938), still cited today, and *Knowledge and Ignorance in Economics* (1977).

Examples of investigative economics in sport:
Taylor, Beck A., and Justin G. Trogdon. "Losing to Win: Tournament Incentives in the National Basketball Association." *Journal of Labor Economics.* 2002, vol. 20, issue 1. 23–41

Moul, Charles C., and John V. Nye. "Did the Soviets Collude? A Statistical Analysis of Championship Chess 1940–64." Available at http://ssrn.com/abstract=905612. Retrieved May 2006.

Duggan, Mark, and Steven D. Levitt. "Winning Isn't Everything: Corruption in Sumo Wrestling." *American Economic Review.* 92.5 (2002): 594–605.

Compilation of database:
The two colleagues who were most helpful were Dr. Johann Lambsdorff and Marc Carinci. Lambsdorff is the creator of a fascinating survey: for the group Transparency International, he ranks most of the countries in the world on how corrupt they are perceived to be. It is an immensely complicated and controversial, piece of research that is used in almost every country in the world. Lambsdorff and I also work together as anti-corruption consultants of the ACTC group. Carinci is a successful professional gambler who also helped in the research of this book. Ironically, one of the most difficult parts of the database was to compile an accurate control group of matches that could be assumed to be both honestly played and culturally equivalent to the fixed mtaches. I spent a considerable amount of time researching this control group.

Sins of Omission versus Sins of Commission:
Aquinas, Thomas. "Prima Secundae Partis Summa Theologica." (1920).71–89. Available at http://www.newadvent.org/summa/

Measuring Sins of Omission:
I also thought about measuring things like offsides. The offside trap is not only useful for corrupt defenders but also forwards. Tohari Paijan was a Singaporean international player. He took money from bookies to win a game, but he also played with a lot of players who took bribes to lose games. He told me, "One of their favourite things is to go offside all the time. I would play with one striker; he like to do Kelung. He would score

one goal. But go offside ten times. He would say, 'No one can accuse me of Kelung, because I scored a goal.' But it would totally jeopardize the team." Unfortunately, I simply could not get enough consistent data to be able to measure this effect.

"There is a specific referee . . ."
Interview with SO 29, May 2007.

Penalty kick results:
There is a further note that may be of interest to football fans. The second control group was composed of the penalty statistics for five European leagues – the English, Dutch, French, Scottish, and German – during the 2005–06 season. However, I had deliberately excluded the Italian Serie A. I had the same statistics for that league, but in 2005–06 there were simply too many fixed matches (at least nineteen) for it to be an accurate indicator of honest play. I noticed something at the end of my statistical analysis. In the presumed honest European league, the rates of penalties per game was some where between .19 to .24 (or roughly one penalty every four to five games). In matches where fixing was going on by corrupt referees, the rate of penalties rose to .42 (or just under a penalty every two games). In Italy, where it is known that fixing by corrupt referees went on, there was a rate of penalties significantly higher than the other leagues, at .32.

Story of Vlado Kasalo
There was a lot of coverage on this case in 1991, but for a good recent summation of it see Kistner, Thomas. "Druck von der Kroatischen Wettmafia." *Süddeutsche Zeitung* (Munich). January 27, 2005, and Harding, Luke. "Football: Germans mount matchfix inquiry: Dubious goals and heavy bets raise suspicion about obscure league game." *Guardian* (London). December 16, 2004. 33.

"They don't know what they are doing . . ."
Interview with C 4, December 2005.

Discussion of the fixing players:
McGinniss, Joe. *The Miracle of Castel di Sangro*. London: Little, Brown and Company, 1999

"shoddy accommodation"
Glanville, Brian. *The Story of the World Cup*. London: Faber and Faber, 1993. 256.
The arrangement was so blatant that a group of fans from Algeria, the team that had been cheated out of a place in the next round, stormed onto the pitch led by a member of their Royal Family.

CHAPTER 4: MISSING THE BIG BOYS

"Even several of the senior . . ."
Interviews with SO 1, 6, 13; R 2; J4, 5, and 8; P 2; C 1, 2; May to June 2005.

"There was nothing obvious . . ."
Interview with SO 6, May 2005.

"Was the [team] management ever involved in the fixing?"
Interview with P 9, November 2005.

"They arrested a lot of the players . . ."
Interview with P 7, December 2005.

"Johnson Fernandez discovered similar stories . . ."
Fernandez, Johnson. "End of Innocence." *Malay Mail* (Kuala Lumpur). July 30, 1993. 59.

"They [the football officials] are sweeping it under the carpet . . ."
Fernandez, Johnson. "End of Innocence." *Malay Mail* (Kuala Lumpur). July 30, 1993. 59.
See also Dorai, Joe. "A multinatural corporation." *Straits Times* (Singapore). November 20, 1993.

"In West Asia [the Middle East for Europeans] I once picked up a newspaper . . ."
Interview with Peter Velappan, June 2005 and May 2006.
AFC statistics are from a mural painted on the front entrance lobby of AFC Headquarters, May 2005.

Saddam Hussein's henchmen had beaten up one of those referees . . .
Interview with R 2, May 2005.

"It was in an international tournament in West Asia . . . :
Interview with R 3, June 2005.

"In 1882, a British colonial official . . ."
Blythe, C.M.G. Wilfred. *The Impact of Chinese Secret Societies in Malaya: a Historical Study.* Oxford: Oxford University Press, 1969. 219–220.

"Kuala Lumpur, Malaysia's capital, for example, was founded by two rival triad operations . . ."
Blythe, 119, 173–174 and 193.

"At the heads of these groups are . . ."
Interviews with O 5, 6; J 4, 5; B 1, 2.

"You won't understand Malaysia if you look at the government . . ."
Interviews with B 2, O 6, May 2005.

"Success in politics and business in Asia . . ."
Lintner, Bertil. *Blood Brothers: Crime, Business and Politics in Asia.* Crows Nest, NSW: Allen & Unwin, 2002. 16–54.

Linter also writes (pages 8–9) of the links between the Chinese Communist government and the criminal triads, and how Deng Xiaoping, the former Chairman of the Chinese Communist Party, declared that many triads were "good" and "patriotic." The head of China's Public Security Bureau stated that the people who had demonstrated for democracy in Tiananmen Square would not be released from prison; however, the government would "unite" with the triads in Hong Kong.

"They are illegal . . ."
Interview with Joe Saumarez-Smith, February 2006.

CHAPTER 5: KEEPING THE SYSTEM TURNING
In 2006, Macau "officially" surpassed Las Vegas . . ."
Watts, Jonathan. "Macau Beats Vegas at Its Own Game." *Guardian* (London). July 20, 2007. 27.

Comparison between American porn industry and Asian gambling industry:
Much of the difficulty in understanding the size of the American porn industry lies in the fact that many very large corporations make a lot of money out of the industry but most do not want to admit that they do so. For example, some international hotel chains make a large proportion of their "in-room" profits on guests renting sex videos.

For a good discussion of this issue, see the sex industry magazine *Adult Video News;* also Lane III, Frederick S. *Obscene Profits: The Entrepreneurs of Pornography in the Cyber Age.* London, Routledge, 2000; and Rich, Frank. "Naked Capitalists." *New York Times Magazine.* May 20, 2001. For a skeptical view, see Ackman, Dan. "How Big Is Porn?" *Forbes.* May 25, 2001.

Foreign Policy estimate of Asian gambling industry:
Holliday, Simon. "Risky Business." *Foreign Policy.* March/April 2006. Available at http://fparchive.ceip.org/story/cms.php?story_id=3406. Note this estimate also includes casinos, bingo halls, and national lotteries, as well as sports betting.

See also Booth, Martin. *The Dragon Syndicates: The Global Phenomenon of the Triads*. London: Bantam Books, 2000. 378–379.

Booth writes that Asian gambling profits are in the billions of dollars. In Hong Kong alone, "[c]omplete universities, schools, hospitals and even Ocean Park, Asia's biggest seaquarium, have all been funded entirely from racing profits." 378–379.

Estimate of Asian pharmaceutical industry:
Liew Kou Yew. "Asian Pharmaceutical Outlook," Pharma Focus Asia, 2006. Available at www.pharmafocusasia.com/Knowledge_bank/articles/asia_pharmaceutical_sector.htm.

Soccer betting in Hong Kong and Singapore
Husock, H. *Soccer Betting in Hong Kong: A Challenge for Home Affairs*. Boston: Harvard University, 2002.

Staff writer. "Soccer Bookie Gets $1m Fine, Jail." *New Straits Times* (Singapore). August 21, 2003.

"A passion for gambling pervades . . ."
Blythe, 219–220.

There are about two dozen international-level bookies . . .
Interviews with B 1–4, B 6, 7; C 2, May to June 2005, November to December 2005.

Figure 5.1 – the structure of illegal gambling market
Interviews with J 4, LE 1, B 1, 2, May, 2005.

When we talked we would say ten sen, which would mean a hundred RM (Malaysian ringgit, or $30) or one RM, which means a thousand RM ($300).
It is a similar kind of code that was used in the gambling networks around the American baseball player Pete Rose. See: Dowd, John M. "Report to the Commissioner In the Matter of Peter Edward Rose, Manager, Cincinnati Reds Baseball Club." Office of the Commissioner of Baseball. May 9, 1989. 53–59.

"We were paying off police officers, sure . . ."
Interview with Joe Pistone, June 2007.

"Right, and they make a bust . . ."
Interview with Pistone, June 2007.

"the biggest and most thorough inquiry . . ."
Williams, 1998. 115.

"I do remember that one . . ."
Interview with LE 4, May 2005.

Government-appointed commission:
The Royal Commission to Enhance the Operation and Management of the Royal
Malaysia Police, established by the King on February 4, 2004, reported to the prime minister April 29, 2005, and then publicly released their findings on June 12, 2005. See, for
example: Kent, Jonathan. "Malaysian Police, 'Brutal, Corrupt.'" *BBC News.* August 10, 2004.

CHAPTER 6: THE MOB, TRUST, AND SERIOUS REPRIMANDS
Visits to Petaling Street Market: April to June 2005, November to December 2005; burnt-
out stalls appeared in the market in May 2006.

Interview with LE 20, who investigated the pirate DVD industry in Kuala Lumpur,
June 2006.

"Better selection, cheaper too, la . . ."
Quote from Malay friends, May 2005.

"You can go to them . . ."
Interview with B 1, 2, May 2005.

Description of Falcone and Filippo Marchese:
The testimony of Vincenzo Sinagra cited in Stile, Alexander. *Excellent Cadavers: The
Mafia and the Death of the First Italian Republic.* London: Jonathan Cape, 1995. 162–166.

Partha Dasgupta once described the need for people to trust . . .
Dasgupta, Partha. "Trust as a Commodity." *Trust: Making and Breaking Co-operative
Relations.* Oxford: Department of Sociology, University of Oxford, 2000. 49–72.

"I know some Russians in Brooklyn . . ."
Interview with Big Sal Miciotta, June 2007.

"Me and five guys . . ."
"When the guys who are betting . . ."
Interview with Big Sal Miciotta, June 2007.

"They are very good at paying..."
Interview with B 1, 2, May 2005.

"You have to pay..."
Interview with Big Sal Miciotta, June 2007.

"And once the word gets out that you welched..."
Interview with Joe Pistone, June 2007.

For more information on the Futures Markets Applied to Prediction (FutureMAP), see Report to Congress regarding the Terrorism Information Awareness Program – in response to Consolidated Appropriations Resolution, 2003, Pub. L. No. 107–8, Division M, 111(b).

Also Hulse, Carl. "Threats and Responses: Plans and Criticisms; Pentagon Prepares a Futures Market on Terror Attacks." *New York Times* (New York). July 29, 2003. Available at http://query.nytimes.com/gst/fullpage.html?res=9d0defd71f3ff93aa15754c0a9659c8b63.

"I was always good at statistics..."
Interview with B 6, February and April 2006.

There are no drugs stronger than naturally produced ones...
For a good anecdotal description of this phenomenon see Huxley, Aldous. *The Devils of Loudon*. London: Chatto & Windus, 1952.

Two recent scientific journal articles exploring similar topics are Shinohara, K., et al., who write of the "fever" of naturally produced drugs produced by playing pachinko in long-term gamblers in their article "Physiological Changes in Pachinko Players." *Applied Human Science – Journal of Physiological Anthropology*. Vol. 18 (1999) No. 2. 37–42, and Meyer, Gerhard, et al., "Neuroendocrine Response to Casino Gambling in Problem Gamblers." *Psychoneuroendocrinology*. (2004) 29. 1272–1280.

"I swear some of those guys..."
Interview with Big Sal Miciotta, June 2007.

"I do the opposite of most gamblers..."
Interview with B 6, April 2006.

Las Vegas casinos or Costa Rican Internet sites...
Konick, Michael. *Smart Money: How the World's Best Sports Bettors Beat the Bookies Out of Millions*. New York: Simon & Schuster, 2006.

"The U.K. gambling market has no balls ..."
Interview with Joe Saumarez-Smith, December 2007.

CHAPTER 7: THE COLLAPSE OF THE BETTING LINE
Description of the events of the evening of April 12, 2006
Interviews with B 11, P 10, SO 9, C 3, May to June 2006.

"For me, it is a moment of anguish ..."
Staff writer. "A Pledge by Lee: We Want to Co-operate with Central Govt." *New Straits Times* (Kuala Lumpur). August 9, 1965. Accessible at http://ourstory.asia1.com.sg/merger/headline/mpledge.html.

"We have to pursue this subject of fun very seriously,"
de Ledesma, Charles, Mark Lewis, and Pauline Savage. *The Rough Guide to Malaysia, Singapore and Brunei.* 4th edition, London: Rough Guides, 2003. 612.

Malaysia and Singapore football rankings
Rankings as of December 2007, current rankings accessible at www.fifa.com/worldfootball/ranking/lastranking/gender=m.

"You don't get many thank-you notes ..." to "We are not going to see it in our lifetime, not even our children's lifetime."
Interviews with Johnson Fernandez and Lazarus Rokk, May 2005 and May 2006.

Description of European Champions League Final, May 2005, and bus tour around city ...
Personal observation and interviews with Wilson Li and other Liverpool fans, May 2005.

Reasons for rise of EPL in Asia ...
Interviews with O 1, 2, 4; J 3, 8; SO 1, 10, April to June, November to December 2005.

"We lost nearly an entire generation of players ..."
Interview with SO 1, May 2005.

"I couldn't settle in Italy – it was like living in a foreign country."
Rush now claims that the quote was made up. See Honeyball, Lee. "Been There, Done That: Ian Rush Rebuts His Italian Myth." *Observer Sports Magazine.* February 6, 2005. 33.

Footballerati
The term is used with great scorn by Richard Giulianotti in *Football: A Sociology of the Global Game.* Cambridge: Polity Press, 1999.

"On a good match, a final or a really big game, around 300 million people . . ."
Confirmed in later interviews with ESPN communications.

Asian punters betting on the fixes.
See, for example, www.superbesttips.com, which purports to give its subscribers inside information about which games are fixed.

CHAPTER 8: THE ARRIVAL OF THE LOCUSTS

Background of Pietro Allatta:
Interview with LE 15, J 16, 17:
See also Staff writer. "Bruxelles Procès de Négriers du Centre. Des Fraudes Réglées Comme du Papier à Musique." *La Nouvelle Gazette* (Brussels). January 7, 1999.
Mathieu, Elisabeth. "Négriers de la Construction." *La Nouvelle Gazette* (Brussels). February 18, 2000. 1.
Xavier, Lombert. "Chapelle Interpelle pour Faux et Escroquerie." *La Nouvelle Gazette* (Brussels). April 1, 2000.
Empein, Michel. "Cour D'Appel de Bruxelles." *La Nouvelle Gazette* (Brussels). June 30, 2001.
Poncau, Ludivine, and Jean-Paul Cailleaux. "Demirkaya Est Sorti de Prison," and "Il N'A Jamais Rien Avoue." *Sudpresse* (Belgium). January 5, 2006. 10.
Dupont, Gilbert. "Le Fantôme de Gattesco." *La Dernière Heure* (Brussels). February 6, 2006. Available at www.dhnet.be/infos/faits-divers/article/143727/le-fantome-de-gattesco .html.

The Hearings on Asian Organized Crime:
The New International Criminal and Asian Organized Crime: Permanent sub-committee on investigations of the Committee on Governmental Affairs, United States Senate, Washington D.C., 1992.

Transcripts of Elst and De Deken:
Van Laeken, Frank. *Blunderboek: van het Belgisch voetball.* Brussels: Icarus, 1997. 179–279.

"Van Damme is nothing . . ."
Interview with Senator Jean-Marie Dedecker, February 2006.

Background on Senator Jean-Marie Dedecker:
"Belgian Senator Suspended from Party for Enabling TV Interview with Pedophile."
BBC Monitoring International Reports (London). January 30, 2002.
    See also "Fallout of Dutroux interview continues to haunt party of Prime Minister
Verhofstadt." Text of report by *Belgian RTBF* radio. January 30, 2002.

"It was quite dangerous,"
Interview with Senator Jean-Marie Dedecker, February 2006.

Allianssi versus Haka match
Interview with J 16, 22; LE 15; SO 41, February 2006, 2008.

Figure of 8787 to 1
While this figure of 8787 to 1 is accurate, it should not be taken as an indication that the
fixers would fix on the Finnish National Lottery. Rather, they did their work on the Asian
illegal gambling market.

"I have taken money for a few games ..."
Staff writers. "Kaksi Maalivahtia Kertoo IS Urheilulle, että Lahjuksia on Tarjottu" and
"Maalivahti Sami Sinkkonen: Kieltäydyin Kolmest Lahjukssta." *Ilta-Sanomat* (Helsinki).
December 12–13, 2005. 1–5.

No official authority in Finland ever said that this match was fixed.
The closest Finnish football authorities ever got was to say that the team was "insuffi-
ciently prepared" and to fine them 10,000 euros (Reuters, August 4, 2005).

Interview with SO 41, February, 2008.

The same curious lack of action was seen when Betfair . . .
Van den Abeele, Chris, Eric Dupain, Wim Straemans, Tom van de Weghe, and Kris
Dechamps. "Tackling the Mafia." *Panorama*. VRT Belgium. February 5, 2006.
    Taildeman, Yves. "L'UB a Déjà Contacte Betfair." *La Dernière Heure* (Brussels).
February 10, 2006.

Ye Zheyun's libido
Suspension of the investigation
Interview J 16, LE 15, February 2008.

Fourteen players, are you joking?
Delepierre, Frederic. "'On M'A Proposé 200,000 Euros.'" *Le Soir* (Brussels). February 7, 2006. 36.

The confession of Laurent Fassotte
Laurent Fassotte appearing before the Union Royale Belge des Sociétés de Football Association Commission d'Enquête. March 8, 2006.

Problems in Intertoto and early Champions League matches:
Interviews with SO 29, B 9, 12, 18, 19, March 2004 to February 2008.

He had a case recently in the Intertoto Cup . . ."
Interview with SO 28, March 2004.

UEFA estimating that fifteen to twenty-seven games were fixed:
Interview with SO 29, 30, May and December 2007.
See also: Hawkey, Ian. "UEFA launches inquiry after claims of 15 fixed matches." *Sunday Times* (London). December 2, 2007.

Foundation of the first professional leagues
Vamplew, Wray. *Pay Up and Play the Game: Professional Sport in Britain, 1875–1914.* Cambridge: Cambridge University Press, 1988.
Inglis, Simon. *Soccer in the Dock: A History of British Football Scandals, 1900–1965.* London: Willow Books, 1985.

1934 World Cup qualifying match between Italy versus Greece had been fixed
Hersh, Philip. "Allegations of Corruption Marring Sport." *Chicago Tribune* (Chicago). June 7, 1998. Sports 13.
"Weltmeisterschaft 1934 – World Cup 1934, Fussball Weltzeitschrift." *Journal of the International Federation of Football History and Statistics.* Kassel. No. 28–31, 1995/96.

CHAPTER 9: THE GOLDEN AGE
Sources for description of the crash:
Gregg, Harry, and Roger Anderson. *Harry's Game: The Autobiography.* London: Mainstream, 2002.
Arthur, Max. *The Manchester United Aircrash: 25th Anniversary Tribute to the Busby Babes.* London: Aquarius, 1983.
Charlton, Bobby. "I Survived – and Still Feel Guilty." Excerpt from *Manchester United Limited Edition Opus,* 2006, printed in *The Times* (London). December 11, 2006 5–7.

Connor, Jeff. *The Lost Babes: Manchester United and the Forgotten Victims of Munich.* London: HarperSport, 2006.

Crick, Michael, and David Smith. *Manchester United: The Betrayal of a Legend.* London: Pan Books, 1990.

"It is strange that up to the moment . . ."
Arthur, 21.

They were cheats . . ."I bloody knew"
Gregg, 92–96.
Interview with Harry Gregg, August 2005.

"Golden Age"
The National Football Museum at Preston can be accessed at www.nationalfootballmuseum.com/pages/news/04/finney.htm.

Nice, clean game . . .
Bartholomew, James. *The Welfare State We're In.* London: Politico, 2005. 9–14.
Stanley Matthews was considered the greatest English player of his generation, roughly equivalent to the contemporary Ronaldinho. His name was also a by-word for gentlemanly conduct. Vinnie Jones is a footballer turned actor, famous for his toughness. The picture of him squeezing the testicles of another player was a bestseller in England in the 1990s.

"I don't know what sport he . . ."
Interview with Harry Gregg, August 2005.

"Since I first set my sights on Soccer as a career . . .
Ford, Trevor. *I Lead the Attack.* London: Stanley Paul and Co, 1957. 13.

"Viper of bribery . . ."
Ford, 21.

Background on Ford
Ford, Trevor. "Trevor Ford in Conversation with Ron Jones." Rec. *Wales Video Archives* in conjunction with the National Library of Wales, Cardiff. November 3, 2000.
"Football great Ford dies." *BBC Sport.* May 29, 2003. Available at http://news.bbc.co.uk/sport1/hi/football/internationals/wales/2948388.stm.

Richards, Huw. "Ford, Trevor (1923–2003)." *Oxford Dictionary of National Biography.* Online ed. Oxford: Oxford University Press, 2007. Available at www.oxforddnb.com/vew/article/89974.

See also "New soccer bribes sensation – nine named: Trevor Ford Confesses." *The People* (London). April 1963. 1, 11.

"For five seasons in a row I scored forty goals . . ."
Pearson, Harry. "North-East of Eden." *When Saturday Comes.* November 2004, 24–25.

"It was not the last time he would speak out against match-fixing . . .
Clough, Brian, with John Sadler. *Walking on Water: My Life.* London: Headline Publishing, 2004. 88–94 and 201–203.

Glanville, Brian. *Champions of Europe: The History, Romance and Intrigue of the European Cup.* Enfield: Guinness, 1991. 82–112.

Ken Chisholm and "Before people get hot under the collar this kind of 'arrangement' was commonplace . . ."
Inglis, 76.

In going through the newspaper archives, I found another twenty-four players who spoke of the fixing that was going on in that era.

Ernie Hunt was one of the footballing artists . . .
Westcott, Chris. *Joker in the Pack: The Ernie Hunt Story.* Stroud, Gloucestershire: Tempus Publishing, 2004.

There are many men in football today,
Hardaker, Alan, with Byron Butler. *Hardaker of the League.* London: Pelham Books, 1977. 90–95.

Some of Gabbert and Campling's stories are:
Gabbert, Michael and Peter Campling. "How Two 'Bookies Cashed in on Fixed' Matches." *The People* (London). May 3, 1964. 1.

Gabbert, Michael, and Peter Campling. "The Day the Fixers Were Fixed – by Blackmail!" *The People* (London). April 1963. 1.

Many English people still remember the story . . .
Gabbert, Michael, and Peter Campling. "The Biggest Sports Scandal of the Century" and "Soccer Bribes: Today We Accuse Three Famous Players." *The People.* April 12, 1964. 1–6.

Swan, Peter, with Nick Johnson. *Peter Swan: Setting the Record Straight*. Stroud, Gloucestershire: Stadia,2006. 15–26, 125–146, and 159–160.
What most people do not recognize . . .
Inglis, 202.

Hardaker's attempts to ban The People *. . .*
Ibid, 200.

Conditions for players in the league
Ford, 14–16.
Interview with Harry Gregg, August 2005, and Sir Tom Finney, June 2007.

Speech at Trade Union Congress
Imlach, Gary. *My Father and Other Working-class Heroes*. London: Yellow Jersey, 2005. 67.

"If I could stand the pain of it I would write another kind of football book . . .
St. John, Ian, and James Lawton. *The Saint: My Autobiography*. London: Hodder and Stoughton. 63.

"a brilliant little winger"
Ibid, 57–66.

When you got injured at Old Trafford . . .
Interview with Harry Gregg, August 2005.

Background on Sir Tom Finney
Imlach, 148–149.

"Well, the club just said no and that was it . . .
Interview with Sir Tom Finney, June 2007. Note: Sir Tom Finney also disagreed with James Bartholomew. He claimed the level of player violence in the sport is about the same level as it was then.

Tickets touts and the players
The example of Sir Bobby Charlton and Harry Gregg selling their FA Cup tickets is in *Harry's Game*. The practice was very common, and many players knew the infamous Stan Flashman – The King of the Touts. For example, Frank McLintock, the Arsenal captain of a later era, writes of players and football officials partying with the King of the

Touts, Stan Flashman in *True Grit: the Frank McLintock Autobiography*. London: Headline Publishing, 2005.

Illegal gambling on every street
Interview with SO 15, March 2006.

Mental arithmetic
See, for example, Preston, Ian, and Stefan Szymanski. *Cheating in Contests*. Oxford: Oxford University Press, 2003. 612–24.

Many of the team officials were also corrupt . . .
See Ford, Inglis, St. John, and Imlach's books for numerous examples of the owners' corruption exploitation of the players.

"And one young man stood up . . .
Interview with Harry Gregg, August 2005.

Interview with Tommy Banks, February, 2008. Banks confirmed this incident and made two points: one, he *had* worked as a coal miner and so could have done the father's job; and two, when news of his speech and its impact on the other players was printed in the newspapers, he was fired from his team and never played professional football again. Banks also confirms the match-fixing that was going on and says that he was even approached once to sell a game for £1000, which he immediately turned down.

"People I wouldn't want my choice to be my company in life . . .
Interview with Harry Gregg, August 2005.

But the fixing, to a much lesser degree, went on into the 1970s
See, for example, McLintock, 186–87, where McLintock writes of the Leeds manager Don Revie offering him a free holiday if "takes it easy."

Harry Gregg says after he left Manchester United there were, he heard, other fixes.

CHAPTER 10: TO FIX OR NOT TO FIX?
Social conditions of Kaliningrad
Campi, Giovanni. "Is Kaliningrad Taking Its First Steps Toward the EU?" Cafebabel.com. July 26, 2006.

Tapes of football match being fixed
These transcripts were published in October 2004 by Kaliningrad's *Noviye Kolesa* newspaper, and their validity was confirmed by a number of independent sources. My thanks

to Paer Gustafsson, Natalia Gorina, Eugene Demchenko, Ekaterina Korobtseva, Ekaterina Kravchenko, Svetlana Guzeeva, Alisa Voznaya, and Maria Semenova for their translation and insight on this case.

See also O'Flynn, Kevin. "Tapes Expose Russian Football Bribery Scandal." *The Times* (Moscow). October 14, 2004. 41

Cost of relegation to lower division
Hughes, Rob. "Relegation Battle Could Play in Court." *International Herald Tribune.* U.K. ed. May 7, 2007 . Sport, 17.

Yevgeny Giner, has spoken openly of paying incentive payments to teams
"CSKA president admits paying incentives to clubs." Reuters. November 20, 2006.

In May 1993, Jean-Pierre Bernès and Bernard Tapie decided to fix a football match . . .
Broute, Remi. "La Match de VA-OM Se Joue Maintenant Devant la Justice." *Les Archives Integrales de L'Humanite* (Paris). March 13, 1995.

Staff writer. "Tapie Projects Secret." *Le Point* (Paris). October 21, 1995.

"Go-Between Describes Corruption Throughout European Soccer." Associated Press. August 12, 1995.

Value of Manchester United
In 2004, the club was valued at close to £740 million. Available at www.forbes.com/lists/2007/34/biz_07soccer_Soccer-Team-Valuations_Value.html.

No legal action was ever taken against Chepel or the Baltika club
Staff writer. "Head of Russian Football Club Baltika Quits After Match-fixing Claims." *Moscow News* (Moscow). October 28, 2004.

O'Flynn, Kevin. "Soccer Awash in Match-fixing Scandals." *The Times* (London). November 10, 2006. 41.

Details of Larisa Nechayeva's murder
"Woman Boss of Moscow Soccer Club Shot Dead." *Daily Telegraph* (London). June 17, 1997. Available at www.telegraph.co.uk/htmlContent.jhtml=/archive/1997/06/17/wmos17.html.

"Well, it was frightening, in about a six-month period . . ."
Stephen Warshaw, interviewed for PBS *Frontline*, October 1999.

Transcript can be accessed at www.pbs.org/wgbh/pages/frontline/shows/hockey/interviews/warshaw.html.

Stand-off between the commandos and Russian soldiers
Wallace, Scott. "Treading on Red Ice: Hockey and the Russian Mob." *Penthouse* (New York).July 1997. 28.
The entire VIP box at Shakhtar Donetsk was blown up
Boggan, Steve. "How Bribes and Secret Bank Accounts Led to a Bomb in the Directors' Box." *Independent* (London). August 7, 1999. 3.

Alleged to be connected to the mob's exporting of nuclear missile parts . . .
Kuper, Simon. *Football Against the Enemy.* London: Orion, 1994. 55–63.

"Be careful, I had the Ukrainian mafia after me . . ."
Interview with SO 28, March 2004.

Story of Alex Ferguson and Manchester United being threatened . . .
Ferguson, Alex, with Hugh McIlvanney. *Managing My Life: My Autobiography.* 2nd ed. London: Coronet, 2000. 307, 364–65.
    The agent, who ended up as an official of Spartak Moscow, denies the incident took place.

List of murdered Russian soccer personalities
From the following articles:
- Brennan, Dan. "Soccer Russian style." *Scotland on Sunday* (Edinburgh). July 6, 2003.
- Smirnov, Mikhail. "Soccer Becomes Increasingly Dangerous in Russia." *RIA Novosti.* February 10, 2005.
- Hughes, Rob. "One Law for Big, One Law for Small." *International Herald Tribune.* February 18, 2005. 20.

"Molecule by molecule," and the battle for CSKA Moscow
Badkhen, Anna. "Soccer Tale of Guns, Ransom, Fear." *Moscow Times* (Moscow). December 6, 2000. Available at www.moscowtimes.ru/article/881/49/256878.htm.

CSKA ownership structure
Wilson, Jonathan. "Why It Is Boom Time for Russian Football." *Guardian* (London). October 31, 2006. Available at http://blogs.guardian.co.uk/Sport/2006/10/31/why_its_boom_time_for_russian.html.

Unwashed shirts
Warshaw, PBS *Frontline*, October 1999.

"Almost 30 per cent ..."
Interview with author, January 1999.

Dozens of the presidents of the private banks in Moscow were assassinated in mob-style killings.
For a good overview of life in Russia at that time, see Stephen Handelman's book.

Skater's car and killing of Nusuyev
"'Pure Human Jealousy:' Car Bomb Derailed Russian Skater's Preparations." Reuters. December 29, 1999.

"Former Russian Sports Official Linked to Olympic Scandal Killed." *Pravada* (Moscow). August 30, 2005. 1.

See also: Jackson, Jon, with James Pereira. *On Edge: Backroom Dealing, Cocktail Scheming, Triple Axels, and How Top Skaters Get Screwed.* New York: Thunder's Mouth Press, 2005. 209, 291.

Boxing Champion
"European Junior Boxing Champion Sergie Latushko Was Gunned Down." Reuters. March 3, 2000.

Story of Slava Fetisov
Friedman, 179–186.

Also PBS *Frontline;* see Fetisov's interview at www.pbs.org/wgbh/pages/frontline/shows/hockey/interviews/fetisov.html.

"I had a case a few years ago ..."
Interview with SO 20, September 2004.

Trust is the oil of the favour bank
There are a number of academic journal articles and books that examine how covert, corrupt deals are put together. See, for example, Lambsdorff, Johann Graf. "Making Corrupt Deals." *Journal of Economic Behaviour and Organization.* 2002: 48, 221–41. Also della Porta, Donatella, and Alberto Vannucci. *Corrupt Exchanges: Actors, Resources, and Mechanisms of Political Corruption.* New York: Walter Gruyter, 1999.

The Moggi Tapes
In July 2006, the Italian Football Association held a hearing into the case, and confirmed that Moggi and Juventus had been fixing games. Moggi was banned from the game for five years; Juventus was demoted into a lower division.

Most of the tapes were released by the Italian media in the first week of May 2006; see, for example, Toti, Giuseppe. "Suscitano Scalpore le Conversazioni fra Personaggi Eccellenti Arbitri & Telefonate." *Corriere della Sera* (Milan). May 4, 2006.

The transcripts are also in English on the web at http://calcioitaliascandal.blogspot.com/ 2006/05/wiretaps.html.

Moggi has, in general, kept a low-profile, refusing most media interviews. One of his exceptions was when a journalist reportedly asked him if he would ever return to soccer. "Of course . . . but this time I'm going to be the guy who breaks everybody's balls. I'll finger them all, by their first names and their surnames. I'll break the balls of all the false moralists of this world who think that everything is clean now because they got rid of . . . Luciano Moggi."
See, Burke, Jason. "Paradiso to inferno," *The Observer Sport Monthly* (London), July 30, 2006. Available at www.guardian.co.uk/sport/2006/jul/30/footbal.com/features.
See also "Moggi contro tutti: Ritornerò!," Calcio, Blog.It. July 27, 2006. Available at www.calciobloc.it/post/1196/moggi-contro-tutti-ritornero.

The tapes were fake and that, anyway, they had been illegally obtained.
O'Flynn, Kevin. "Tapes expose Russian football bribery scandal." *The Times* (London). October 14, 2004. 41.

Staff writer. "Head of Russian Football Club Baltika Quits After Match-fixing Claims." *Moscow News* (Moscow). October 28, 2004.

Rudnikov story
Poleskov, Konstantin. "For what 'Kolesa' is overrun. The Kaliningrad Court closed the opposition newspaper. The Publisher and Journalists do not give up." *Novaya Gazeta* (Kaliningrad). August 2007.

Interview with Igor Rudnikov, January 2008.

Rudnikov was finally released in the fall of 2007, after spending months in the Russian prison system.

International PEN Writers in Prison Committee. "Half-yearly Case List." June 30, 2007. 54.

"Every week in Putin's Russia . . ."
Interview with Human Rights Watch, June 2007.

CHAPTER 11: HOW TO FIX A FOOTBALL GAME
Kenan Erol, Sebatspor attempted fix
According to news reports, Kenan Erol claimed that there had been an attempt at match-fixing, but that both Olgun and Szegin had actually been part of it.

See Staff writer. "Prosecutor Probing Soccer Rigging Case." *Turkish Daily News* (Istanbul). October 15, 2005.

Available at www.turkishdailynews.com.tr/ article.php?enewsid=25941.

See also Staff writer. "Fix: What Is Going on in Super League?" *Turkish Daily News* (Istanbul). April 13, 2005. Available at

www.turkishdailynews.com.tr/article.php?enewsid=10663&contact=1.

"Bahis mafyası." *Star Gazete* (Istanbul). April 10, 2005. Available at

www.stargazete.com/ gazetearsiv/index.asp?haberID=69496&gun=10&ay=4&yil=2005.

Tuncer, Yasin. "Sali Hakan Şikeyi 90'dan çıkardı!" *Zaman, Spor,* (Istanbul). April 12, 2005. This is the article that contains the transcript of the conversation between Kenan Erol and Hakan Olgun; my thanks to Chris Wade for his translation and insight into Turkish Football.

Arslan, Mehmet. "Paralarýn sahibi telefon kaydýnda." CNN-Turkey (Hürriyetim). Anasayfa. August 27, 2005.

Staff writer. "Sebat Inquiry Rumbles On." *Turkish Daily News* (Istanbul). September 3, 2005. Available at www.turkishdailynews.com.tr/article.php?enewsid=22498.

Sedat Peker Inquiry

"Turkish Football Federation Probes Sport-Mafia Links." Agence France Presse. October 26, 2004.

"Turkish Parliament to Probe Match-fixing, Fan Violence in Soccer." Associated Press. November 23, 2004.

Kilinç, Erdal. "Mafya yesil sahada, Polisin dinlemesine 'sike diyaloglari' da takildi." *Milliyet* (Istanbul). July 28, 2006. This article contains a series of dialogues, allegedly between mafia aides discussing various fixed matches. My thanks to Emre Ozcan for translation.

Staff writers. "Beşiktaş Accused This Time." *Turkish Daily News* (Istanbul). July 28, 2006. Available at http://ankarafootball.blogspot.com/2006/07/besiktas-accused-time.html.

Beşiktaş and Alaattin Çakıcı

Komisar, Lucy. "Turkey's Terrorists: A CIA Legacy Lives On." *Progressive*. April 1997. Available at http://findarticles.com/p/articles/mi_m1295/is_n4_v61/ai_19254727.

Kinzer, Stephen. "Top Fugitive's Arrest Revives Turkish Corruption Inquiry." *New York Times* (New York). October 15, 1998. Avaliable at http://query.nytimes.com/gst/fullpage.html?res=9B02EFDB123AF936A25753C1A96E958260.

"Intelligence Officer, Football Manager Charged in Turkish Mafia Scandal." Agence France Presse. November 2, 2004.

Michael Franzese
Hearing before the Permanent Subcommittee on Investigations of the Committee on Governmental Affairs, United States Senate: One hundred and fourth Congress, Second Session – May 15, 1996. 36–43.

    Mortensen, Chris. *Playing for Keeps: How One Man Kept the Mob from Sinking Its Hooks into Pro Football.* New York: Simon and Schuster, 1991.

    Schoenfeld, Bruce. "Personality: The Fixer." *Cigar Aficionado.* Online ed. Mar/April 2003.

"My personal opinion as one who has been involved in organized crime . . ."
"Athletes like to gamble. They are confident, aggressive risk takers . . ."
"You might approach them or set them up with a woman . . ."
Interview with Michael Franzese, January 1999.

Berlin prosecutor's report on Hoyzer
Staatsanwaltschaft Berlin, June 2005.

"There were runners. They were ex-players . . ."
Interview with P 9, November 2005.

Business strategies of erotic dancers
Boles, J., and A.P. Garbin. "The Strip Club and Customer-Stripper Patterns of Interaction." *Sociology and Social Research.* 1984: 58, 136–44.

    Enck, G.E., and J.D. Preston. "Counterfeit Intimacy: A Dramaturgical Analysis of an Erotic Performance." *Deviant Behavior.* 1988. 9:4, 369–81.

"Oh no, there was nothing subtle . . ."
Interview with P 3, November 2005.

"It was incredible . . ."
Interview with anonymous sources, August 2005.

"One thing you never heard about the gamblers . . ."
Cited in Whelan, David C. "Organized Crime, Sports Gambling, and Role Conflict: Victimization and Point-Shaving in College Basketball." Unpublished Ph.D thesis. City University of New York, 1992. 137.

"It was an ongoing process that I wasn't aware of any more in the end . . ."
Johannes B. Kerner Show. "Interview with Robert Hoyzer." ZDF Television. February 9, 2005.

NOTES

"Not to feel criminal in their thinking ..."
Interview with SO 1, May 2005.
"You can get x amount of money for just ninety minutes of work ..."
Interview with C 4, December 2005.

Chieu's Fixing of a Match
From a Royal Malaysian Police confession, 1994–1995.

Kissing of hands
This is the customary way of greeting Malaysian royalty, of whom there are a great number as the country is a conglomeration of several indigenous kingdoms. Many of these people own or run football teams.

"Gateway Crimes"
Whelan, 142–52.

"But you know if they take the money once, it is over ..."
Interview with LE 4, May 2005.

"As soon as [the players] take the money ..."
Interview with C 2, December 2005.

Cricket match-fixing
Pycroft, James. *The Cricket Field.*(1851). London: St. James's Press, 1922. 133–40.
 The sport was actually codified specifically because there was so much gambling around it in the 1730s. For more background, see Rae, Simon. *It's Not Cricket: A History of Skulduggery, Sharp Practice, and Downright Cheating in the Noble Game.* London: Faber and Faber, 2002.

"You never buy the same man but once ..."
Pycroft, 134.

"You are more friendly ..."
Interview with Michael Franzese, February 1999.

Problems of Fixing a Gambling Market
Interviews with C1, 2; B 1, 2, 6, 7, 8, 15.

"I have taken money for a few games . . ."
Staff writers. "Kaksi Maalivahtia Kertoo IS Urheilulle, että Lahjuksia on Tarjottu" and "Maalivahti Sami Sinkkonen: Kieltäydyin Kolmest Lahjukssta." *Ilta-Sanomat* (Helsinki). December 12, 2005. 2–3.

"What I do is have my runner stand beside the team box . . ."
Interview with C 3, November 2005.

Lottery tickets used for payment of bribe
Fernandez, Johnson. "A Worldwide Plague." *Malay Mail* (Kuala Lumpur). July 28, 1993. 74–75.

Payment strategies
Interviews with C 1, 2
   Malaysian Police Confessions 1994–1995.

"On the xx^th of xxxx in Singapore . . ."
Royal Malaysian Police Confession, 1994–1995.

CHAPTER 12: SEX AND THE MEN IN BLACK
Biography of Ljubomir Barin
Interview with Ljubomir Barin, August 2005.
   Much of the research in this chapter is from the books written by the various participants and players of Olympique de Marseille at this time. See, for example:
   Eydelie, Jean-Jacques, and Michel Biet. *Je Ne Joue Plus! Un Footballeur Brise L'Omerta.* Paris: L'Archipel, 2006. After the book was published, Bernard Tapie tried to sue Eydelie for libel, but the case was dismissed.
   When I contacted Jean-Pierre Bernès about the possibility of doing an interview, he replied that he was not interested and that his book was his "last word" on the subject. The book is:
   Bernès, Jean-Pierre, with Bernard Pascuito. *Je Dis Tout: Les Secrets de l'OM sous Tapie.* Paris: Albin Michel, 1995.
   See also:
   Boli, Basile, with Claude Askalovitch. *Black Boli.* Paris: Bernard Brasset, 1994.
   Dessaix, Marcel, with Philippe Broussard. *Capitaine.* Paris: Stock, 2002.
   Other general books include:
   Lecasble, Valérie, and Airy Routier. *Le Flambeur: La Vraie vie de Bernard Tapie.* Paris: Bernard Grasset, 1994.
   Peraldi, Michel, and Michel Samson. *Gouverner Marseille: Enquête sur les mondes politiques Marseillais.* Paris: La Découverte, 2005.

See also:

Dubourg, Bernadette. "Ljubomir Barin Rejugé Seul." *Sud Ouest* (Bordeaux). May 3, 2001.

Gattegno, Herve. "M. Barin Dévoile L'Ampleur de la Corruption dans le Football Européen." *Le Monde* (Paris). August 12, 1995.

Story of Solti and bribe attempt
Glanville, Brian. *Champions of Europe: The History, Romance and Intrigue of the European Cup.*" London: Enfield, 1991. 86.

Barin provided referees and club owners
Gattegno, Herve. "M. Barin Dévoile L'Ampleur de la Corruption dans le Football Européen." *Le Monde* (Paris). August 12, 1995.

Ultimate insider's tutorial
Staff writer. "VA-OM; La Coupe Jusqu'à la Lie." *Le Point* (Paris). July 15, 1995.

Claude Bez and the beginning of the fixing
Webster, Paul. "Referees 'Bribed with Prostitutes' in European Games." *Guardian* (London). March 4, 1999. 12.

When a club asks me to look after the referees . . .
Dubourg, Bernadette. "Des 'Faveurs' aux Arbitres." *Sud Ouest* (Bordeaux). March 3, 1999.
"L'OM Aurait Acheté L'Arbitre d'une Rencontre Contre Athènes en 1989." *Le Monde* (Paris). August 2, 1995.

"I remember one occasion when a referee . . ."
Staff writer. "Tapie Projets Secrets." *Le Point* (Paris). October 21, 1995.

Transfer Dealings
Dubourg, Bernadette. "Les Millions des Transferts." *Sud Ouest* (Bordeaux). March 2, 1999.

Using these methods
Sage, Adam. "Referees 'Bribed with Rolexes and Call Girls.'" *The Times* (London). March 4, 1999. 21.

I was caught up in a series
Interview with Ljubomir Barin, August 2005.

Barin as a fugitive
Gattegno, Herve. "L'Homme-cle des Affaires du Football a Été Arrêté en Allemagne." *Le Monde* (Paris). February 27, 1995.

    Gattegno, Herve. "L'Ancien Vice-président de l'OM Jean-Louis Levreau a été Placé en Garde à Vue." *Le Monde* (Paris). April 27, 1995.

Imprisonment and confession of Barin
Dubourg, Bernadette. "Ljubomir Barin Rejugé Seul." *Sud Ouest* (Bordeaux). May 3, 2001.

    Staff writer. "VA-OM; La Coupe Jusqu'à la Lie." *Le Point* (Paris). July 15, 1995.

Mr. Barin has pointed the finger at the entire organization of football . . .
Staff writer. "A la sortie d'une confrontation de quatre heures entre Bernès et Barin, hier matin, dans le bureau du juge Philipon, l'avocat de l'ancien directeur de l'OM a annoncé que l'intermédiaire croate avait 'pointé du doigt l'organisation générale du foot mondial.'" *Sud Ouest* (Bordeaux). July 12, 1995.

Creation of slush funds
Broussard, Philippe. "Bernard Tapie Tiendra a Nouveau la Vedette dans le Proces des Comptes de l'OM." *Le Monde* (Paris). May 12 1997.

    'L'Histoire d'un Pillage." *Sud Ouest* (Bordeaux). March 4, 1999.

Specific games that were fixed
Staff writer. "VA-OM: La Coupe Jusqu'à la Lie," *Le Point* (Paris). July 15, 1995.

    Staff writer. "Tapie Projets Secrets." *Le Point* (Paris). October 21, 1995.

    Webster, Paul. "Referees 'Bribed with Prostitutes' in European Games." *Guardian* (London). March 4, 1999. 12.

    Gattegno, Herve. "L'Enquête sur l'OM de Bernard Tapie Dévoile des Faits de Corruption." *Le Monde* (Paris). January 3, 1997. 6.

The culture of fixing that had arisen on the Marseille team . . .
Eydelie discusses this culture throughout the book, particularly in Chapter 1.

"I played for Marseilles, I know how these things are done . . ."
Gattegno, Herve. "Deux Enquêtes Judiciaires Dévoilent la Corruption du Football Européen." *Le Monde* (Paris). August 12, 1995. 1.

Bribing referees with women
Webster, Paul. "Referees 'Bribed with Prostitutes' in European Games." *Guardian* (London). March 4, 1999.

Dubourg, Bernadette. "Des 'Faveurs' aux Arbitres." *Sud Ouest* (Bordeaux). March 3, 1999.

Two prominent French referees, Michel Vautrot and Joel Quiniou, testifying at the trial, claimed that although small, appropriate gifts were given to referees, they were only received in front of the UEFA match official.

Links to Gangsters
"Tapie, Courbis, Filippeddu, le Belge, mafia(s), foot, argent sale et coups tordus." Université Panthéon-Assas (Paris II), Institut de Criminologie de Paris Département de Recherche sur les Menaces Criminelles Contemporaines.

Follorou, Jacques, and Vincent Nouzille. *Les Parrains Corses: Leur Histoire, Leurs Réseaux, Leurs Protections.* Document J'AI LU. Paris, 2004.

Henley, Jon. "Gangsters Kill to Control Paris Fruit Machine Racket." *Guardian* (London). July 30, 2001. 13.

"'Brise de Mer:' Grand Banditisme, Milieu du Football Politique et la Mort de Dominique Rutily." *L'investigateur* (Paris). 2001. www.investigateur.info/affaires/corse/articles/rutily.html

Bernès testimony.
Staff writer. "Bernès: 'Chaque année, quatre à cinq matches étaient achetés.'" *l'Humanité.* July 10, 1995. Available at www.humanite.fr/1995-07-10_Articles_-Bernes-Chaque-annee-quatre-a-cinq-matches-etaient-achetes.

Williams, 119–120.

Everyone is doing it . . .
Bernès, 43–44.

Sage, Adam. "Referees Bribed with Rolexes and Callgirls." *The Times* (London). March 4, 1999. 21.

After prison career of Tapie
Jeffries, Stuart. "France Sells its Soul for a Fistful of Francs." *Observer* (London). July 1, 2001. 4.

Sentencing of Barin
Dubourg, Bernadette. "Ljubomir Barin Rejugé Seul." *Sud Ouest* (Bordeaux). May 3, 2001.

Wry Headlines
Staff writer. "A Really Full Bodied Bordeaux." *United Press International.* October 31, 1990.

Sage, Adam. "Getting Their Kicks for Free." *Ottawa Citizen* (Ottawa). March 4, 1999. B1.

Michel Zen and G14
Staff writer. "G14 Starts Legal Fight with FIFA." *BBC Sport.* September 6, 2005.
Staff writer. "Swiss prosecutor throws out charges against Blatter." Reuters, December 4, 2002.

"Sex was used. Sometimes it would be the translator . . ."
"I remember when I was a referee . . ."
Interview with Michel Zen-Ruffinen, March 2004, November 2005.

David Elleray, the British referee claims the same thing was done when he was refereeing a Real Madrid game. Elleray, David. *The Man in the Middle.* London: Little, Brown and Company, 2006. 132.

Jesus Gil
The Internet links showing Jesus Gil in a shoving match with other club owner is at www.youtube.com/watch?v=YycOiakbsus.

Staff writer. "Espagne – Jesus Gil: Président de l'Atletico et Politicien Controversé." Agence France Presse. May 15, 2004.

Staff writer. "Spain's Atletico Boss Gil Linked to Sicilian Mafia." Agence France Presse. June 24, 1999.

"Only accept gifts if they are small . . . and expensive!"
Elleray, 132.

Night at Romanian brothel before a World Cup qualifying match
Elleray, 129–130.

Howard King
"Top Ref Banned for 10 Years." Agence France Presse. February 15, 1996
    Williams, 1996, 196–198.

Moggi at Torino
Vulliamy, Ed. "Turin Judges Turn to Sex and Soccer." *Guardian* (London). December 8, 1993. 10.

Ong Kheng Hock
Staff writer. "Ong, Kannan Plead Guilty to Other Charge of Match-fixing." *New Straits Times* (Singapore). November 23, 1995. 47.

Caught in the middle of a French political battle.
Interview with Ljubomir Barin, August 2005.

NOTES

Robert Hoyzer

Nicola, Stefan. "Organized Crime Threatens German Pastime." United Press International. October 18, 2005.

Kirschbaum, Erik. "Ban May Not Be Worst of It for Hoyzer." *National Post* (Toronto). April 30, 2005.

Hoyzer on television

Kerner, Johannes B. "The Robert Hoyzer Interview." ZTF Television. February 9, 2005.

An investigation that would spread across Europe

Kammerer, Roy. "Referee Given Prison Sentence in Match-fixing Trial." Associated Press. November 17, 2005.

"With the time I have spent . . ."

Langdown, Mark. "Football: Hoyzer says Fixes Commonplace." *Racing Post* (London). June 22, 2005. 89.

"They thought it would be limited to just one referee . . ."

Kirschbaum, Erik. "Ban May Not Be Worst of It for Hoyzer." *National Post* (Toronto). April 30, 2005. 13.

The investigation, at first, seemed to go well.

O'Driscoll, Brian A. "German Referee Searched In Dawn Raid." *Goal.com*. February 2, 2005.

Starcevic, Nesha. "Referee to Stay in Custody; Federation Suspends Another." Associated Press. February 14, 2005.

Staff writer. "Ringleader in German Match-fixing Linked to Galastaray Match." Associated Press. June 8, 2005.

"The name Koop won't ever surface on the referees' list again . . ."

Kammerer, Roy. "Hoyzer Arrested in Germany's Match Fixing Scandal as Investigators Say More People and Games Could Be Involved." Associated Press. February 12, 2005.

Four days after Hoyzer's infamous interview . . .

Staff writer. "Referee in Germany Soccer Scandal Arrested." Associated Press. February 12, 2005.

Goodbody, John. "Match-fixing Fears Grow." *The Times* (London). February 14, 2005. [*The Game*, p. 21.]

Standard practice to visit brothels
Staff writer. "Vorspiel für die Schiedsrichter." *Der Spiegel* (Hamburg). February 21, 2005. 17.

UEFA list in car of gamblers
Staff writer. "Schiedsrichter-Skandal Erreicht Uefa." *Der Spiegel* (Hamburg). March 24, 2005. Available at www.77-77.com/news.php?id=31301.

"Yes, we wondered about that . . ."
Interview with UEFA officials and German police.

This is normal. Normal . . .
Small fish . . .
Look, we have a lot of good relations with people
Interview with Milan Sapina, May 2007.
    For more on Carolina Salgado, see Salgado, Carolina, and Maria Fernanda Freitas. *Eu, Carolina – A História Verdadeira.* 14th ed. Lisbon: Don Quixote, 2006.

"Compared with what I saw and experienced at No Calor da Noite . . ."
Staff writer. "Portugal Ups Ante in Match-fixing Probe." Agence France Presse. December 15, 2006.
    For more on da Costa and the general corruption of Portuguese league, see Marinho, Neves. *Golpe de Estadio.* Lisbon: Terramar, 1998. Also available online at www.anti-corrupcao.150m.com.
    See also Staff writer. "Police Raid HQ of European Champions Porto." Agence France Presse. December 3, 2004.
    "João Vale e Azevedo, the former president of the top club Benfica . . ."
Broadbent, Rick. "Philosophy of the Bullfight Places Supporters on Horns of a Dilemma." *The Times* (London). May 8, 2007. 81.

Fixing 1984 semifinal of Cup Winner's Cup
Hatton, Barry. "Porto in a Storm." *Guardian* (London). February 28, 1997. 4.
    Hughes, Rob. "For Corruption Investigators, Soccer Offers a Busy Agenda." *International Herald Tribune.* January 15, 1997. 18.

Portugal woke up on April 20, 2004
Staff writer. "Police Hold 16 in Portuguese Probe." CNN. April 20, 2004.
    Staff writer. "Portugal Ups Ante in Match-fixing Probe." Agence France Presse. December 15, 2006.

"It is time to once and for all to establish . . ."
Lisbon, Eduardo Goncalves and Denis Campbell. "Portuguese Football Champions
Shaken by Corruption Charges." *Observer* (London). December 26, 2004. 16.

CHAPTER 13: THE GUNS ARE FACING THE WRONG WAY

The story of the unsuccessful defence of Malaysia and Singapore might serve as a case
study in organizational mismanagement and ineptitude. Two books that cover it well are
Colin Smith's *Singapore Burning: Heroism and Surrender in World War II* (London:
Penguin, 2005). The quote "better enemy than the Japanese" is on page 54. Also, Warren,
Alan. *Singapore 1942: Britain's Greatest Defeat.* London: Hambledon and London, 2002.

The Japanese side is a case study of good leadership, clarity of purpose, and com-
munication. Masanobu Tsuji, who was one of the Japanese staff officers who both
planned and fought in the campaign, wrote *Singapore 1941–1942: The Japanese Version of
the Malayan Campaign of World War II.* Oxford: Oxford University Press, 1988.

A good fictional account of the entire debacle is J.G. Farrell's 1978 book *The
Singapore Grip*, recently reprinted by the New York Review of Books.

"The growth in this field has been incredible . . ."
Interview with B 16, June 2006.

"The power of this industry [legal and illegal] is mind-boggling . . ."
Interview with David Velazquez, June 2007.

Neteller Case:
Court documents from: United States District Court Southern District of New York:
United States versus Neteller PLC Defendant, July 18, 2007.

Although Neteller did not participate in gambling in any way, as it is merely an
international payment conduit, the two executives pleaded guilty to a charge of criminal
conspiracy in the summer of 2007.

"We are still behind the eight ball with the Internet . . ."
Interview with SO 25, March 2004.

Information that almost every bettor knew . . .
For example, almost any British punter knows that in the third-ranked soccer tournament
in England – the Carling Cup – the big teams would give their younger, less established
players a chance to play. It produced some upsets, as young teams of Manchester United or
Arsenal players were sometimes beaten by regular squads of other lower-ranked teams. It
was a phenomenon that was well known in the U.K. But in China, the market generally did

not know this and would bet as if the regular Arsenal or Manchester United team was playing a much weaker team.

Discussion of gambling markets
Interviews with B 1, 2, 6, 7 13, 14, 16, 21

CHAPTER 14: NO POINT IN GOING OUT THERE

Grobbelaar Case
Grobbelaar v News Group Newspapers Ltd and another. House of Lords, [2002] UKHL 40, [2002] 4 All ER 732, [2002] 1 WLR 3024, 1–4 July, October 24, 2002.
    Grobbelaar v News Group Newspapers Ltd and another. Court of Appeal (Civil Division) [2001] EWCA Civ. 33, [2001] 2 All ER 437, December 4–8, 2000 and January 18, 2001.
    Thomas, David. *Foul Play: The Inside Story of the Biggest Corruption Trial in British Sporting History.* London: Bantam Press, 2003.

"Do you think I went out to Kuala Lumpur on the off chance?
Thomas, 184–185.

"When The Sun *returned from the first trip to the Far East without any solid leads . . ."*
Thomas, 365.

Did the British Police visit southeast Asia?
Interviews with LE 1, 2, 4, 5, 9, 10.

Triad Trial
Booth, Martin. *The Dragon Syndicates: The Global Phenomenon of the Triads.* London: Bantam Books, 2000. 444–79.
    Connett, David. "Triads Victim 'Foiled Murder Attempt'" *Independent* (London). October 15, 1992. 9.
    ——. "Triad 'Hit-man' Had Two Attempts to Shoot Rival," *Independent* (London). October 17, 1992. 4.
    Pallister, David. "Triad Hood Lists Crimes." *Guardian* (London). October 15, 1992. 2.
    Wood, Joe. "Triad Risk Death to Reveal Their Blood Vows." *Evening Standard* (London). October 15, 1992. 18.

Floodlights Case
Thomas, 5–6.
    Bennetto, Jason. "Gambler Guilty of Football Sabotage." *Independent* (London). August 21, 1999. 5.

Chaudhary, Vivek, and Linus Gregoriadis. "Floodlights Scam to Beat Bookies." *Guardian* (London). August 21, 1999. 7.

Peachley, Paul. "Gambling Fanatics Attracted by Glamour of English Game." Press Association, August 20, 1999. 4.

——. "Soccer Match Blackout Plot Men Jailed." Press Association. August 25, 1999.

Gregoriadis, Linus and Vivek Chaudhary. "Syndicate 'sabotaged matches.'" *Guardian* (London). August 18, 1999. 4.

Armstrong, Jeremy. "Triad Behind Football 'Fix'; Plot to Cash in on Abandoned Games." *Scottish Daily Record* (Edinburgh). August 21, 1999. 7.

Frankfurt Trial

"Four Players Approached; Investigators Say Match-fixing Scandal Could Widen." Associated Press. March 13, 2006.

"Eight Men on Trial for Alleged Match Fixing in Germany." Associated Press. January 12, 2007.

"We think he left the country . . ."
Interview with LE 19, July 2007.

"No one wants to know about this case . . ."
Interview with LE 13, June 2006.

"At first, they wanted to help. But as the trial started . . ."
Interview with LE 9, July 2004.

CHAPTER 15: THE STORY OF PAL

In your evidence in the trial-within-a-trial, you told the judge you made millions [from match-fixing]?
[1998] 3 SLR, *Rajendran s/o Kurusamy v Public Prosecutor (Singapore)*

"Any game, anywhere in the world, I could fix it,"
All interviews excerpts in this chapter from interview with Kurusamy, September 2005.

"He is a very dangerous character . . .
Interview LE, June 2005.

"I believe they let Vana go . . ."
Interview with SO, May 2005.

"Pal? He is a chicken gangster..."
Interview with C 2, June 2005.

Lutz Pfannenstiel case and attack with field hockey stick
Banks, Tony. "Football: German Faced Worldwide Ban after FIFA Chief Put Boot In."
Express (London). December 29, 2003. 53.

Players threatened...
Desira, Peter. "Striker Confident of Beating Charge." *Herald Sun* (Melbourne). October 11, 2000. 78.
    Staff writer. "15 Players, Six Clubs Linked to Singapore Match-fixing." Agence France Presse. August 30, 2000.

"It was because people were grateful to me...
[1998] 3 SLR, *Rajendran s/o Kurusamy v Public Prosecutor (Singapore).*

"I am not stupid. I knew the game was fixed..."
Interview with R 2, May 2005

Pal contacted me. He was speaking Tamil.
Malaysian police confession, 1994–1995.

"At night there were people being raped..."
Banks, 53.

"One week before the game, Uncle Jimmie would contact me..."
Malaysian police confession, 1994–1995.

"I was walking around in Kuala Lumpur..."
Malaysian police confession, 1994–1995.

The Blind Man
Williams, 120–132.
    Interview with J 3, May 2005.

Racecourse fixers
Interviews with B 2; J 18, 19; O 6; C 3, April to May, December 2005.

A fight inside the dressing room of Selangor . . .
Interview with P2, May 2005.

"Here a runner can also be a bookie . . ."
Interview with C 2, December 2005.

Alleged Cameroon Fix in 1982 World Cup
Beha, Oliviero, and Roberto Chiodi. *Mundialgate*. Rome: Avagliana Editore, 2005.

10 December 1994, I contacted my fixer
Malaysian Police confession, 1994–1995.

Kurusamy and Jagannathan trial and "Soccer is a sport with a wide following . . ."
[1998] 3 SLR, *Rajendran s/o Kurusamy & Ors v Public Prosecutor*, (Yong Pung How CJ), High Court, Magistrate's Appeal, Nos. 237/97/01–05, March 19 and July 8, 1998.

"Pal continued to match-fix . . ."
Interview with LE 4, May 2005.

"We had agents working the Asian market, they were swamped . . ."
Interview with Mike Saunders, January 2008.

CHAPTER 16: BEHIND THE DOOR
"Look, these things are not coincidences . . ."
Boock, Richard, and Stephen Fleming. *Balance of Power*. Auckland: Hodder Moa Beckett, 2004. 178.

Fixing at the SEA Games
Staff writer. "The Stench from Hanoi." *Manila Standard* (Manila). November 18, 2005. Available at www.manilastandardtoday.com/?page=editorial_nov18_2005.
    Staff writer. "Medal-fixing Allegations Tarnish South East Asian Games." Agence France Presse. November 30, 2005.

"Funny you should mention that game, because it was very odd . . ."
Interview with B 6, April 2006.

CHAPTER 18: A SMALL TOWN IN GERMANY

"FIFA dismisses . . ."
Bond, David, and David and Raoul Simons. "Football: FIFA Gamble over Far East Betting Rings." *The Evening Standard* (London). May 27, 2002. 77.

"Years have gone by and I've finally learned to accept myself . . ."
Galeano, Eduardo. *Soccer in Sun and Shadow.* Trans. Mark Fried. London: Verso, 1999. 1.

"FIFA had not established any specific rules to limit . . ."
Bond, David, and Raoul Simons. "Football: FIFA Gamble over Far East Betting Rings." *Evening Standard* (London). May 27, 2002. 77.

"The best moment I have had with Ghanaian football . . ."
Interview with Sam Arday and Cecil Jones Attuquayefio, June 2006.

"This is the problem in the whole of Africa . . ."
Interview with Sam Arday and Cecil Jones Attuquayefio, June 2006.

At the senior level, close to one hundred Ghanaian players are playing . . .
Figure of just under a hundred Ghanaian footballers from
www.eufo.de/football/div/africa/gha.htm.

Bochum Disaster story
Interview with Michael Oti Adjei, June 2006.

"We have to defend very well . . ."
Interview with Stephen Appiah, June 2006.

Togo problems
Copnall, James. "Bonus Row Haunts Failed Togo Bid." *BBC Online.* June 19, 2006. Available at http://news.bbc.co.uk/2/hi/africa/5096054.stm.
　　Doyle, Paul. "Togo 0 Switzerland 2." *Guardian* (London). Online edition. June 19, 2006. Available at http://football.guardian.co.uk/worldcup2006/minbymin/0,,1788338,00.html.

Nigeria and Ghana banquet
"Nigeria: Aftermath of Odili's Gift . . ." *Africa News.* November 24, 2001.

CHAPTER 19: THE GOLD COAST

Links between politics and football in Ghana
Interview with Craig Waite, an Indiana University scholar, who is studying the connections between Ghanaian politics and football, Accra, February 2008.

See also Bediako, Ken. *The National Soccer League of Ghana: The Full Story, 1956–1995.* Accra: published by the author, 1996.

Coaching in a famine story
Interview with Coach Frederick Osam Duodu, July 2007.

Ghanaian poverty levels
Figures for poverty given in "EarthTrends: The Environmental Information Portal" at http://earthtrends.wri.org/povlinks/country/ghana.php.

Abédi Pelé match-fixing scandal
For a selection of typical newspaper articles see:
- "Probe This Football Scandal." March 29, 2007. www.myjoyonline.com/archives/sports/200703/2943.asp
- Quaye, Michael. "Soccer Fraud." March 30, 2007.
- "Maestro of Disgrace." April 3, 2007. Available at www.ghanaweb.com/ghanahomepage/sportsarchive/artikel.php?ID=121841.
- The Ghana Football Association has produced a variety of press releases on the affair, and the president of the Ghana Football Association, Kwesi Nyantakyi, mentioned it in his own blog at www.ghanafa.org/blogs/president/default.asp.
- Press release of the Ghana Football Association. "Four charged with match-fixing." April 2, 2007. Also "FA demotes, bans and fines clubs." April 11, 2007.
- http://www.ghanafa.org/news/archiveread.asp?contentid=2114
- An Internet discussion forum that discussed Abédi Pelé and the game can be found at http://discussions.ghanaweb.com/viewtopic.php?t=52096.

In fact, there were so many goals scored that various newspapers covering the story could not agree on *exactly* how many goals had been scored with various newspapers reporting the scores as 26–0, 27–0 or even 29–0.

For some of the details of the previous alleged match-fixing scandals see Agyepong, Kofi. "Hearts Threaten FA with Legal Action." Available at www.ghanafa.org/news/200511/344.asp.

"Kotoko Emerge Ghana Champions, Hearts Protest." *Pan African News Agency (PANA).* November 11, 2005.

"*I'm surprised that people are lambasting those 4 teams . . .*"
www.myjoyonline.com/archives/sports/200703/2943.asp

Abédi Pelé Press Release
Thomas, Durosimi. "Abedi Pele Fights to Clear Name." *BBC Sport Africa.* April 17, 2007.

"*You are not the people who deserve the money . . .*"
and details of the fight over money, were confirmed in interviews with the president of GFA, two other GFA executives who were in the room, and three players.

FA denies report on WC finances. Available at www.ghanafa.org/blackstars/200701/1718.asp.

CHAPTER 20: "I SWEAR, I'M INNOCENT"

"*I Swear, I'm Innocent . . .*"
Kwaitto, Samuel Ebo. "Alleged Bribery Scandal in Iran." *Graphic Weekend Edition Sports* (Accra). July 6–9, 2007. 1.

"*In every competition you find gamblers around . . .*"
"*I would not rule out the possibility of gamblers approaching our players . . .*"
"*They may not necessarily have to come to the hotels. Some have agents who establish links and then they do their business.*"
"*Even last week when we played Iran in a friendly match . . .*"
Interview with Kwesi Nyantakyi, July 2007.

"*One of our coaches got involved with some people . . .*"
"*The coach came to my room and knelt . . .*"
Interview with Randy Abbey, July 2007.

Kofi Boakye case
The case became a *cause célèbre* in Ghana, with numerous newspaper and magazine articles written about it. An account of the judge's final summation is found in:

Baneseh, Mabel Aku. "Cocaine Trial Tagor, Abass Jailed 15 Years Each." *Daily Graphic* (Accra). November 29, 2007. Available at www.modernghana.com/news/148843/1/Cocaine-Trial-Tagor-Abass-Jailed-15-Years-Each.

Meeting after the Iran trip
Minutes of the Administrative Enquiry into Allegations of Bribery Levelled Against Abubakari Damba, held on July 3, 2007.

CHAPTER 21: WHO GUARDS THE GUARDIANS?

1869 Harvard versus Oxford Rowing Race

Millers, Bill. "The Great International Boat Race." Friends of Rowing History Web site, 2006. www.rowinghistory.net/1869.htm.

Drinkwater, G.C. *The Boat Race.* London: Blackie and Son, 1939. 56–58. In his book, Drinkwater claims that the Oxford team had, by the final stretch, easily won the race, but had to slow down because a sightseeing boat got in their way.

For further exploration of the general history of professional rowing and the divisions between the amateur – usually upper-class – rowers and the professionals see:

Dodd, Christopher. *The Story of World Rowing.* London: Stanley Paul, 1992.

Halladay, Eric. *Rowing in History: A Social History – The Amateur Debate.* Manchester: Manchester University Press, 1990.

Wigglesworth, Neil. *The Social History of English Rowing.* London: Frank Cass, 1992.

Dickens, Charles. "The Oxford and Harvard Boat Race." Speech at Sydenham. August 30, 1869. www.underthesun.cc/Classics/Dickens/speeches/speeches41.html.

Professional pedestrianism

See Lile, Emma. "Professional Pedestrianism in South Wales During the Nineteenth Century." *Sports Historian.* No. 20 (2000). 94–1005, which outlines some of the culture around professional walking in the nineteenth century. For a good fictional account, "The Loss of Sammy Crockett" by Arthur Morrison (1894) features one of the great detectives of late Victorian literature, Martin Hewitt, who investigates the world of professional pedestrianism.

Horst Dassler and Joao Havelange

The letter that Havelange wrote for de Andrade was first published by Claudio Renato in "Havelange e Avalista Moral de Castor." *O Globo* (São Paulo). April 9, 1994. 12. The article also featured a photo of Havelange, de Andrade, and Havelange's son-in-law, who is the president of the Brazilian Confederation of Football, celebrating at de Andrade's daughter's wedding.

For a description of Havelange's views on de Andrade and visit to him in prison see Rodrigue, Ernesto. *Jogo Duro, a História de João Havelange.* Rio de Janeiro: Editora Record, 2007. 284–85. Rodrigue's biography was essentially authorized by Havelange and in it, Rodrigue reports Havelange speaking of de Andrade in the following way:

"I am not a judge to judge anyone. One thing I know is that he is my friend and I am not going to judge Castor."

See also De Souza, Roberto Pereira. *João Havelange: O Poderoso Chefao. Playboy Brazil* (Rio de Janeiro). May 1994. 124–41.

For a superb account of the international intrigue and financial soap opera of Dassler's world, see Smit, Barbara. *Pitch Invasion: Adidas, Puma, and the Making of Modern Sport.* London: Penguin, 2007.

Yallop, David. *How They Stole the Game.* London: Poetic Publishing, 1999.

Allegations of corruption at FIFA
For a largely critical view of FIFA administration, see: Jennings, Andrew. *Foul! The Secret World of FIFA: Bribes, Vote Rigging and Ticket Scandals.* London: HarperSport, 2006.

Sugden, Alan, and John Tomlinson. *Badfellas: FIFA Family at War.* London: Mainstream Sport Publishing, 2003.

For a pro-FIFA view, see Lanfranchi, Pierre, Christiane Eisenberg, Tony Mason, and Alfred Wahl. *100 Years of Football: The FIFA Centennial Book.* London: Weidenfeld & Nicolson, 2004 (written with FIFA support and guidance).

Recent financial controversies at FIFA
Ledsom, Mark. "Former Boss of FIFA's Ex-marketing Agency Faces Trial." Reuters. November 21, 2007.

"While the FIFA witnesses at trial boldly characterized their breaches . . ."
United States District Court Southern District of New York: MasterCard International Incorporated v. Federation Internationale de Football Association, Amended Findings of Fact and Conclusions of Law, Judge Loretta A. Preska. December 7, 2006.

"Life is made up of bad news . . ."
"Our societies are trying to evade taxation . . ."
"No one talks about that . . ."
Interview with Jerome Champagne, December 2007.

"I was a striker. I was number nine . . ."
"My recollection [of the game] was a wonderful atmosphere . . ."
"I think it is not true . . ."
"I have spent over thirty years working at FIFA . . ."
Interview with Sepp Blatter, February, 2008.

Sepp Blatter had said that the women playing soccer . . .
Staff writer. "Sexy Shorts Good Idea for Women's Soccer: Blatter." *CBC Sports.* January 16, 2004. Available at www.cbc.ca/sports/story/2004/01/16/blatter010416.html.

Two men filming Danish team talk
Interviews with J 20; SO 36, 41, December 2007.

"We don't have to give details on how we conduct an investigation . . ."
Interview at FIFA, February 2008.

See also "Football: Outraged Denmark Vows to Pursue China 'Spy' Case." Agence France Presse. September 16, 2007; and Zeigler, Mark. "World Cup Has Spying Scandal to Call its Own." *San Diego Union Tribune* (San Diego). September 19, 2007. D2.

"Tactical spying by a Chinese television station . . ."
Interview with Sepp Blatter, February 2008.

The FIFA case reference number is 070449 for this case.

Ghana Women Approached to Fix Matches
"Some of the officials listened in on the conversation . . ."
"There was no evidence they had done anything wrong . . ."
Interviews, December 2008

EPILOGUE: THE SALVATION OF SOCCER
"Kenya: Some of the Victims of Violent Attacks That Have Left Many Families Heart-Broken." AllAfrica News. February 3, 2007.
　　"Aid Women Killed in Nairobi Were Presbyterian Missionaries."
Available at www.spcm.org/Journal/spip.php?article6177.
　　Mathare has 500,000 people (www.matharevalley.org/about_mathare_valley.htm).
Kibera has between 600,000 and 1.2 million
(www.economist.com/surveys/displaystory.cfm?story_id=9070714).

"Anywhere in the world that you have some people with lots of money . . ."
"The flying toilets . . ."
"When I play football, I forget about my companies at home . . ."
"Some girls just go for prostitution . . ."
Interviews with Rosemary Njiru, Joyce Motio, and Patricia Ktem, January 2007.

"I got back pictures that were so shocking . . ."
Interview with Clare O'Brien, February 2007.

"So I made this deal with them . . ."
"We looked at a variety of things . . ."
"We had three problems . . ."
Interview with Bob Munro, January 2007.

"Since those early days, MYSA has expanded to other programs . . ."
I spent ten days in around MYSA in January 2007, checking on the existence of the programs mentioned; interviewing over twenty people connected or formerly connected with MYSA, some of whom were quite bitter because of various personal situations with MYSA. However, no one said anything that affected the essential credibility of the organization.

Background on the various mafia groups in Nairobi
Interviews with diplomats, journalists, and a number of Mathare residents, at least one of whom had good connections within the Taliban, January 2007.
    Also Kenya National Association of Social Workers. *Rapid Assessment on Mathare Slum Clashes.* UN Habitat. January 2, 2007.

"They outnumbered him. They just stopped the car."
Interview with Rosemary Njiru, January 2007.

Situation in Mathare, June 2007
Interviews with residents of Mathare and Nairobi, June 2007.
    "Kenya Police Shoot Sect Suspects." *BBC News.* June 7, 2007.

Battles between KFF, FIFA, and Munro
Interviews with Gordon Olouch (Sports Commissioner for Kenya), Peter Lisamula, Mark Ageng on the "Probe into Bob Munro's activities," the acting chair of the KFF, and various journalists and referees.

"People would come to me and say . . ."
Interview with Bob Munro, January 2008.

"Having heard all of this . . .
Wilberforce, William. For a complete text of the speech delivered in the House of Commons, May 12, 1789, see
http://64.233.167.104/search?q=cache:yvHrX_c6EWUJ:abolition.e2bn.org/file_download.php.
    See also Pollock, John. *Wilberforce.* Tring, Hertfordshire:Lion Pubishing, 1982. 87–91.

BIBLIOGRAPHY

BOOKS

Aquinas, Thomas. *Summa Theologica of St. Thomas Aquinas.* Trans. Fathers of the English Dominican Province. Second and Revised ed. London: Online edition, 1920. Available at www.newadvent.org/summa.

Arthur, Max. *The Manchester United Aircrash: 25th Anniversary Tribute to the Busby Babes.* London: Aquarius Design and Print, 1982.

Asinof, Eliot. *Eight Men Out: The Black Sox and the 1919 World Series.* New York: Henry Holt, 1987.

Ball, Phil. *Morbo: The Story of Spanish Football.* London: WSC Books, 2001.

——. *White Storm: 100 Years of Real Madrid.* Edinburgh and London: Mainstream, 2002.

Banks, Simon. *Going Down: Football in Crisis, How the Game Went from Boom to Bust.* Edinburgh and London: Mainstream Publishing, 2002.

Bartholomew, James. *The Welfare State We're In.* London: Politico, 2005.

Beha, Oliviero and Chiodi, Roberto. *Mundialgate.* Rome: Avagliana Editore, 2005.

Bellos, Alex. *Futebol: The Brazilian Way of Life.* London: Bloomsbury, 2002.

Bernès, Jean-Pierre, with Bernard Pascuito. *Je Dis Tout: Les secrets de l'OM sous Tapie.* Paris: Albin Michel, 1995.

Blythe, C.M. Wilfred. *The Impact of Chinese Secret Societies in Malaya.* London: Oxford University Press, 1969.

Boli, Basile, with Claude Askalovitch. *Black Boli.* Paris: Bernard Brasset, 1994.

Boock, Richard, and Stephen Fleming. *Balance of Power.* Auckland: Hodder Moa Beckett, 2004.

Booth, Martin. *The Dragon Syndicates: The Global Phenomenon of the Triads.* London: Bantam Books, 2000.

Bose, Mihir. *Manchester Unlimited the Rise and Rise of the World's Premier Football Club.* London: Orion Business Books, 1999.

Bower, Tom. *Broken Dreams: Vanity, Greed and the Souring of British Football.* 1ˢᵗ ed. London: Simon & Schuster, 2003.

Bresler, Fenton. *The Chinese Mafia.* New York: Stein and Day, 1980.

Clough, Brian, and John Sadler. *Cloughie: Walking on Water – My Life.* London: Headline Book Publishing, 2003.

Coakley, Jay and Eric Dunning, eds. *Handbook of Sports Studies.* London: Sage Publishing, 2000.

Comber, L.F. *Chinese Secret Societies in Malaysia.* Locust Valley, New York: J.J. Augustin, 1959.

Conn, David. *The Football Business: Fair Game in the 90s?* London: Mainstream, 1997.

Connor, Jeff. *The Lost Babes: Manchester United and the Forgotten Victims of Munich.* London: HarperSport, 2006.

Corrupt Practices Investigation Bureau. *Swift and Sure Action: Four Decades of Anti-Corruption Work.* Singapore: CPIB, 2000.

Crick, Michael and David Smith. *Manchester United: The Betrayal of a Legend.* London: Pan Books, 1990.

Dempsey, Paul and Kevan Reilly. *Big Money, Beautiful Game: Saving Soccer from Itself.* London: Nicholas Brealey Publishing, 1998.

Desailly, Marcel, with Philippe Broussard. *Capitaine.* Paris: Stock, 2002.

Dobson, Stephen and John Goddard. *The Economics of Football.* Cambrdge: Cambridge University Press, 2001.

Dodd, Christopher. *The Story of World Rowing.* London: Stanley Paul, 1992.

Dubro, James. *Dragons of Crime.* Toronto: McClleland and Stewart, 1992.

Elleray, David. *The Man in the Middle.* London: Time Warner, 2004.

Eydelie, Jean-Jacques, and Michel Biet. *Je Ne Joue Plus! Un Footballeur Brise L'Omerta.* Paris: L'Archipel, 2006.

Farrell, J.G. *The Singapore Grip.* New York: New York Review of Books, 1978.

Ferguson, Alex with Hugh McIlvanney. *Managing My Life: My Autobiography.* London: Coronet Books, 2000.

Foer, Franklin. *How Soccer Explains the World: An Unlikely Theory of Globalization.* New York: HarperCollins, 2004.

Follorou, Jacques and Vincent Nouzille. *Les Parrains Corses: Leur Histoire, Leurs Réseaux, Leurs Protections.* Paris: Documents, 2004.

Foot, John. *Calcio: A History of Italian Football.* London: Fourth Estate, 2006.

Ford, Trevor. *I Lead the Attack.* London: Stanley Paul, 1957.

Freeman, Simon. *Own Goal! How Egotism and Greed Are Destroying Football.* London: Orion, 2000.

Friedman, Robert I. *Red Mafiya: How the Russian Mob Has Invaded America.* Boston: Little Brown, 2000.

Fynn, Alex, and Lynton Guest. *For Love or Money: Manchester United and England – the Business of Winning?* London: Boxtree, 1998.

Galeano, Eduardo. *Soccer in Sun and Shadow.* Trans. Mark Fried. English ed. London: Verso, 1999.

Giulianotti, Richard. *Football: A Sociology of the Game.* Cambridge: Polity Press, 1999.

Glanville, Brian. *Champions of Europe: The History, Romance and Intrigue of the European Cup.* Enfield: Guinness Publishing, 1991.

———. *The Story of the World Cup.* Rev. ed. London: Faber and Faber, 1997.

Gregg, Harry and Roger Anderson. *Harry's Game: The Autobiography.* London: Mainstream, 2002.

Halladay, Eric. *Rowing in History: a Social History – The Amateur Debate.* Manchester: Manchester University Press, 1990.

Hamil, Sean, Jonathan Michie, Christine Oughton, and Steven Warby, eds. *Football in the Digital Age: Whose Game Is It Anyway?* London: Mainstream, 2000.

Handelman, Stephen. *Comrade Criminal: The Theft of the Second Russian Revolution.* London: Michael Joseph, 1994.

Hardaker, Alan and Byron Butler. *Hardaker of the League.* London: Pelham Books, 1977.

Hersh, Seymour. *The Dark Side of Camelot.* London: HarperCollins, 1997.

Holt, Richard, and Tony Mason. *Sport in Britain 1945–2000. Making Contemporary Britain.* Ed. Anthony Seldon. London: Blackwell, 2000.

Hill, Peter B. E. *The Japanese Mafia: Yakuza, Law, and the State.* Oxford: Oxford University Press, 2003.

Huxley, Aldous. *The Devils of Loudon.* London: Chatto and Windus, 1952.

Imlach, Gary. *My Father and Other Working-class Heroes.* London: Yellow Jersey, 2005.

Inglis, Simon. *Soccer in the Dock: A History of British Football Scandals, 1900–1965.* London: Willow Books, 1985.

Jackson, Jon. *On Edge: Backroom Dealing, Cocktail Scheming, Triple Axels, and How Top Skaters Get Screwed.* New York: Thunder's Mouth Press, 2005.

Jacoby, Neil H, Peter Nehemkis, and Richard Eells. *Bribery and Extortion in World Business: A Study of Corporate Political Payments Abroad.* Studies of the Modern Corporation. Ed. Columbia University Graduate School of Business. New York: MacMillan, 1977.

Jennings, Andrew. *Foul! The Secret World of FIFA: Bribes, Vote Rigging, and Ticket Scandals.* London: HarperSport, 2006.

Jennings, Andrew and Simson, Vyv. *The Lords of the Rings: Power, Money, and Drugs in the Modern Olympics.* London: Simon and Schuster, 1992.

Johnson, Graham. *Football and Gangsters.* London: Mainstream, 2006.

Johnson, Tim, and Stuart Sprake. *Careless Hands: The Forgotten Truth of Gary Sprake.* Stroud: Tempus Publishing, 2006.

Kelly, Robert J. "The Upperworld and the Underworld: Case Studies of Racketeering and Business Infiltrations in the United States." *Criminal Justice and Public Safety.* Ed. Philip John Stead. New York: Kluwer Academic/Plenum Publishers, 1999.

Konick, Michael. *Smart Money: How the World's Best Sports Bettors Beat the Bookies out of Millions.* New York: Simon and Schuster, 2006.

Kuper, Simon. *Football against the Enemy.* London: Orion, 1994.

Lambsdorff, Johann Graf. *The Institutional Economics of Corruption and Reform: Theory, Evidence and Policy.* Cambridge: Cambridge University Press, 2007.

Lanfranchi, Pierre, Christiane Eisenberg, Tony Mason, and Alfred Wahl. *100 Years of Football: The FIFA Centennial Book.* London: Weidenfeld & Nicolson, 2004.

Lansley, Peter. *Running with Wolves.* Newport: Thomas Publications, 2004.

Lecasble, Valérie, and Airy Routier. *Le Flambeur: La Vraie Vie de Bernard Tapie.* Paris: Bernard Grasset, 1994.

Lintner, Bertil. *Blood Brothers: Crime, Business, and Politics in Asia.* Sydney: Allen and Unwin, 2002.

McGinnis, Joe. *The Miracle of Castel di Sangro.* London: Little, Brown and Co, 1999.

McIlvanney, Hugh. *McIlvanney on Football.* London: Mainstream, 1994.

McLintock, Frank, and Rob Bagchi. *True Grit: The Frank McLintock Autobiography.* London: Headline Publishing, 2005.

Millman, Chad. *The Odds: One Season, Three Gamblers and the Death of Their Las Vegas.* Cambridge, Massachusetts: DaCapo Press, 2001.

Moldea, Dan. *Interference: How Organized Crime Influences Professional Football.* New York: William Murrow, 1989.

Moore, Douglas, and Joe Dorai. *That's the Goal! How to Win at Football.* Singapore: Landmark Books, 1999.

Morrison, Ian. *The World Cup: A Complete Record.* London: Breedon Books Sport, 1990.

Mortensen, Chris. *Playing for Keeps: How One Man Kept the Mob from Sinking Its Hooks into Pro Football.* New York: Simon and Schuster, 1991.

Murray, Dian H. *The Origins of the Tiandihui: The Chinese Triads in Legend and History.* Stanford, California: Stanford University Press, 1994.

Neves, Marinho. *Golpe de Estadio.* Lisbon: Terramar, 1998. Available online at www.anti-corrupcao.150m.com.

Padovani, Marcelle, and Giovanni Falcone. *Men of Honour: The Truth about the Mafia.* Trans. Edward Farrelly. London: Warner, 1992.

Pallo, Jackie. *You Grunt, I'll Groan: The Inside Story of Wrestling.* London: Macdonald Queen Anne, 1985.

Park, Stanley. *FIFA 192: The True Story Behind the Legend of the Brunei Darussalam National Football Team.* Boca Raton, Florida: Universal Publisher, 2004.

Pausanias. *Description of Greece.* Trans. W.H.S. Jones. Internet Ancient History Source. London: Harvard University Press and William Heinemann Ltd., 1918.

Peraldi, Michel, and Michel Samson. *Gouverner Marseille: Enquete sur les mondes politiques marseillais.* Paris: La Decouverte/Poche, 2005.

Petrini, Carlo. *Nel Fango Del Dio Pallone.* Sixth ed. Milan: Kaos Edizione, 2000.

Phongpaichit, Pasuk, Sungsidh Priyarangsan, and Nualnoi Treerat. *Guns, Girls, Gambling, Ganja: Thailand's Illegal Economy and Public Policy.* Chiang Mai: Silkworm, 1998.

Pollock, John. *Wilberforce.* Tring, Herts. Lion Publishing, 1982.

Posner, Gerald. *Warlords of Crime.* New York: McGraw Hill, 1988.

Punch, Maurice. *Dirty Business: Exploring Corporate Misconduct – Analysis and Cases.* Second ed. London: Sage, 1999.

Putnam, Robert D. *Bowling Alone: The Collapse and Revival of American Community.* New York: Simon and Schuster, 2000.

Pycroft, James. *The Cricket Field.* (1851). London: St. James's Press, 1922.

Quirk, James and Rodney D. Foot. *Hard Ball: The Abuse of Power in Pro-Team Sports.* Princeton, New Jersey: Princeton University Press, 1999.

Rae, Simon. *It's Not Cricket: A History of Skulduggery, Sharp Practice and Downright Cheating in the Noble Game.* London: Faber and Faber, 2002.

Rodrigue, Ernesto. *Jogo Duro, a História de João Havelange.* Rio de Janeiro: Editora Record, 2007.

Russo, Gus. *The Outfit: The Role of Chicago's Underworld in the Shaping of Modern America.* Third ed. London: Bloomsbury, 2004.

Salgado, Carolina, and Maria Fernanda Freitas. *Eu, Carolina – A História Verdadeira.* Fourteenth ed. Lisbon: Dom Quixote, 2006.

Sanders, Teela. *Sex Work: A Risky Business.* Portland, Oregon: Willan Publishing, 2005.

Seneviratne, Percy. *History of Football in Malaysia.* Kuala Lumpur: PNS, 2000.

Sharpe, Graham. *Free the Manchester United One: The Inside Story of Football's Greatest Scam.* London: Robson Books, 1993.

——. *Coups and Cons.* London: Aesculus Press, 1991.

——. *The Essential Gambler.* London: Robert Hale, 1995.

——. *Gambling on Goals: A Century of Football Betting.* Edinburgh: Mainstream, 1997.

——. *The Book of Bizarre Football: Freaky Forwards, Strange Strikers, Dodgy Defenders and Other Soccer Sensations.* London: Robson Books, 2000.

Short, Anthony. *The Communist Insurrection in Malaya: 1948–1960.* London: Frederick Muller Limited, 1975.

Smit, Barbara. *Pitch Invasion, Three Stripes, Two Brothers, One Feud: Adidas, Puma and the Making of Modern Sport.* London: Penguin, 2007.

Smith, Colin. *Singapore Burning, Heroism and Surrender in World War II*. London: Penguin, 2005.

St. John, Ian. *The Saint: My Autobiography*. London: Hodder and Stoughton, 2006.

Stille, Alexander. *Excellent Cadavers: The Mafia and the Death of the First Italian Republic*. London: Jonathan Cape, 1996.

Stott, Richard. *Dogs and Lampposts*. London: Metro Publishing, 2002.

Sugden, Alan, and John Tomlinson. *Badfellas: FIFA Family at War*. London: Mainstream Sport Publishing, 2003.

——. *FIFA and the Contest for World Football: Who Rules the People's Game?* Cambridge: Polity Press, 1998.

——. *Great Balls of Fire: How Big Money Is Hijacking World Football*. Edinburgh: Mainstream, 1999.

——. *Power Games: A Critical Sociology of Sport*. London: Routledge, 2002.

Swan, Peter with Nick Johnson. *Peter Swan: Setting the Record Straight*. Stroud, Gloucestershire: Stadia, 2006.

Szymanski, Stefan and Tim Kuypers. *Winners and Losers: The Business Strategy of Football*. Harmondsworth, Middlesex: Penguin Books, 1999.

Tsuji, Masanobu. *Singapore 1941–1942: The Japanese Version of the Malayan Campaign of World War II*. Oxford: Oxford University Press, 1988.

Taylor, Chris. *The Beautiful Game: A Journey through Latin American Football*. London: Phoenix Books, 1998.

Thomas, David. *Foul Play: The Inside Story of the Biggest Corruption Trial in British Sporting History*. London: Bantam, 2003.

Vamplew, Wray. *Pay Up and Play the Game: Professional Sport in Britain, 1875–1914*. Cambridge: Cambridge University Press, 1988.

Van Laeken, Frank. *Blunderboek Van Het Belgisch Voetball*. Trans. Kess t'Hooft and Stefan De Wachter. Brussels: Icarus, 1997.

Waldron, Arthur. *The Great Wall of China: From History to Myth*. Cambridge: Canto, 1992.

Warren, Alan. *Singapore 1942: Britain's Greatest Defeat*. London: Hambledon and London, 2002.

Westcott, Chris. *Joker in the Pack: The Ernie Hunt Story*. Stroud, Gloucestershire: Tempus Publishing, 2004.

Whelan, David C. *Organized Crime, Sports Gambling, and Role Conflict: Victimization and Point-Shaving in College Basketball*. New York: Unpublished Ph.D thesis, City University, 1992.

Whyte, Willian Foote. *Street Corner Society: The Social Structure of an Italian Slum*. Fourth ed. Chicago: University of Chicago Press, 1993.

Weiland, Matt, and Sean Wilsey, eds. *The Thinking Fan's Guide to the World Cup*. London: Abacus, 2006.

Wigglesworth, Neil. *The Social History of English Rowing*. London: Frank Cass, 1992.

Williams, Russ. *Football Babylon*. London: Virgin, 1996.

——. *Football Babylon 2*. London: Virgin, 1998.

Wilson, Johnathan. *Behind the Curtain: Travels in Eastern European Football*. London: Orion Publishing, 2006.

Yallop, David. *How They Stole the Game*. 1999 ed. London: Poetic Publishing, 1999.

COURT CASES

Chan Wing Seng vs. Public Prosecutor, Singapore Law Reports [1997]. Singapore High Court, Magistrate's Appeal, 1997.

Cheong Ah Cheow vs. Public Prosecutor A. Cr. J. (Chan J.). Kuala Lumpur Federal Territory Criminal Appeal, 1985.

Grobbelaar vs. News Group Newspapers Ltd. Judge Simon Brown. U.K. Court of Appeal, 2001.

Grobbelaar vs. News Group Newspapers Ltd and Another. Lord Bingham of Cornhill, Lord Steyn, Lord Hobhouse of Woodborough, Lord Millett, and Lord Scott of Foscote. U.K. House of Lords, 2002.

Kannan S/O Kunjiraman & Anor vs. Public Prosecutor. Magistrate's Appeal 96/95/01–02. Singapore High Court, 1995.

Kannan S/O Kunjiraman vs. Public Prosecutor. Singapore Law Report 3 SLR Cheung Phei Chiet, 1995.

Mastercard International Incorporated vs. Federation Internationale De Football Association, Judge Loretta A. Preska Amended Findings of Fact and Conclusions of Law. United States District Court Southern District of New York, 2006.

Manap Bin Hamat and Anor vs. Public Prosecutor. Singapore Surbordinate Court, 1997.

Mathan Jagannathan, et al. vs. Public Prosecutor. Singapore High Court, 1996.

Ong, et al. vs. Public Prosecutor. Singapore Subordinate Court, 1994.

Ong Smith Bernal vs. R. U.K. Court of Appeal, (Criminal Division) 2000.

Rajamanickam Thirujnanasammathan vs. Public Prosecutor. Singapore Subordinate Courts, 1994.

Rajendran S/O Kurusamy & Ors vs. Public Prosecutor. Magistrate's Appeal. Singapore High Court, Nos 237/97/01–05, 1998.

Teo Tiang Hoe vs. Public Prosecutor. Criminal Case no 8, 1995 Rubin, J. High Court of the Republic of Singapore, 1995.

Testo Della Decisione Relativa Al Commm. Uff. N1/C Riunione Del 29 Giugno, 3–7 Luglio 2007. Prcoura Federale Della F.I.G.C. Rome: Italian Football Federation, 2006. 154. 1 vols.

United States of America vs. Alimzhan Tokhtakhtunov Aka Taiwanchuk. Southern District of New York, 2002.

United States of America vs. Vyacheslav Kiriovich Ivankov. United States District Court. Eastern District of New York (Brooklyn), 1997.

United States of America vs. Neteller PLC. United States District Court. Southern District of New York, 2007.

Zainal, Mohamed, Mohamed Ali, and Ali Lomri, – Disciplinary Hearing. no 1–3/2003, p. 6. Disciplinary Committee, Football Association of Singapore, 2003.

FILMS AND TV PROGRAMS

Docherty, Neil, and Linden McIntyre. "Mafia Power Play." PBS *Frontline.* Boston. October 12, 1999.

Ford, Trevor. *Trevor Ford in Conversation with Ron Jones.* Rec. November 3, 2000. Wales Video Archives, in conjunction with the National Library of Wales, Cardiff, 2000.

Kerner, Johannes B. "Interview with Robert Hoyzer." ZDF – Kulissen, Germany. February 9, 2005.

McKeown, Bob. "The Fix Is In." *The Fifth Estate.* Canadian Broadcasting Corporation, Toronto. 1989.

Rocksen, Andreas, and Soren Steen Jespersen. "Dream Catchers." *The Beautiful Game.* TV 2 Danish Television, Denmark-Sweden co-production. June 2004.

Sayles, John. *Eight Men Out.* Orion Pictures Distributor, USA. 1988.

Van den Abeele, Chris, Eric Dupain, Wim Straemans, Tom van de Weghe, and Kris Dechamps. "Tackling the Mafia." *Panorama.* Brussels. *VRT* Belgium. 5 February, 2006.

JOURNAL AND MAGAZINE ARTICLES

Blair, Dale James. "Did the Dons Play Dead." *Australian SSH.* June 30, 1999. 3–15.

Boles, J. and A.P. Garbin. "The Strip Club and Customer-Stripper Patterns of Interaction." *Sociology and Social Research.* 58 (1984): 136–44.

"'Brise de Mer,' Grand Banditisme, Milieu du Football Politique et la Mort de Dominique Rutily." *L'investigateur* (Paris), 2001. Available at www.investigateur.info/affaires/corse/articles/rutily.html.

Dasgupta, Partha. "Trust as a Commodity." *Trust: Making and Breaking Co-operative Relations.* Ed. Diego Gambetta. Electronic ed. Oxford: Department of Sociology, University of Oxford, 2000. 49–72.

De Souza, Roberto Pereira. "Joao Havelange: O Poderoso Chefao." *Playboy Brazil.* May 1994. 124–141.

Duke, V. "Perestroika in Progress? The Case of Spectator Sports in Czechoslovakia." *British Journal of Sociology.* 41 (1990): 41: 145–56.

Enck, G.E. and J.D. Preston. "Counterfeit Intimacy: A Dramaturgical Analysis of an Erotic Performance." *Deviant Behavior.* Vol. 9:4 (1988): 369–81.

Levitt, M. and S. Duggan, "Winning Isn't Everything: Corruption in Sumo Wrestling." *American Economic Review.* 92:5 (2002): 594–605.

Levitt, Steven D. "How Do Markets Function? An Empricial Analysis of Gambling on the National Football League." National Bureau of Economics working paper, available at www.nber.org/papers/w9422 (2002).

Lile, Emma. "Professional Pedestrianism in South Wales During the Nineteenth Century." *The Sports Historian* (became *Sport in History* in 2003). No. 2 (2000): 94–105.

Meyer, Gerhard, et al. "Neuroendocrine response to casino gambling in problem gamblers." *Psychoneuroendocrinology.* 29 (2004). 1272–80.

Moul, Charles C., and John V. Nye. "Did the Soviets Collude? A Statistical Analysis of Championship Chess 1940–64." (2006). Available at http://papers.ssrn.com/s013/papers_cfm?abstract_id=905612.

Nti, Kofi O. "Comparative Statics of Contests and Rent-Seeking Games." *International Economic Review.* 38.1 (1997): 43–59.

Preston, Ian, and Stefan Szymanski. "Cheating in Contests." *Oxford Review of Economic Policy.* 19:4 (2003). 612–624.

Riordan, Jim. "Playing to New Rules: Soviet Sport and Perestroika." *Soviet Studies.* 42.1 (January 1990): 133–45.

Rizek, André, and Thais Oyama. "A Máfia Do Apito." *Veja.* September 28, 2005: 72–80.

Salutin, M. "Stripper Morality." *Transitions.* 8 (1971): 12–22.

Shinohara, K., et al, "Physiological Changes in Pachinko Players; Beta-endorphin, Catecholamines, Immune System Substances, and Heart Rate." *Applied Human Science – Journal of Physiological Anthropology.* 18:2 (1999): 37–42.

Skipper, James K., and Charles McCaghy. "Stripteasers: The Anatomy and Career Contingencies of a Deviant Occupation." *Social Problems.* 17 (1970): 391–405.

Taylor, Beck, and J. Trogdon. "Losing to Win: Tournament Incentives in the National Basketball Association." *Journal of Labour Economics.* 20.1 (2002).

Thompson, William E., and Jackie L. Harred. "Topless Dancers: Managing Stigma in a Deviant Occupation." *Deviant Behavior.* 13 (1992): 291–311.

Wolfers, Justin. "Exposing Cheating and Corruption: Point Shaving in Basketball." *AEA Papers and Proceedings.* 96:2 (2006): 279–83.

Wonders, Nancy A., and Raymond Michalowski. "Bodies, Borders, and Sex Tourism in a Globalized World: A Tale of Two Cities – Amsterdam and Havana." *Social Problems.* 48:4 (2001): 545–71.

NEWSPAPER ARTICLES

For background, I used articles from newspapers and wire services in Australia, Belgium, Brazil, Bulgaria, Canada, China, Colombia, the Czech Republic, Denmark, England, Finland, France, Germany, Ghana, Ireland, Israel, Italy, Kenya, Lithuania, Malaysia, Poland, Russia, Scotland, Singapore, Slovakia, Spain, South Africa, Thailand, Turkey, the United States, and Vietnam. For brevity's sake, I have listed only the articles that were used directly, in the Notes section.

REPORTS

Bruckert, Chris, Colette Parent, and Pascale Robitaille. *Erotic Service, Erotic Dance Establishments: Two Types of Marginalized Labour.* Ottawa: Department of Criminology, University of Ottawa, 2003.

Condon QPM, Sir Paul. *Report on Corruption in International Cricket.* London: International Cricket Council, 2001.

Cronje, Hansie. "Hansie Cronje's Statement before the Edwin King Commission of Inquiry into Cricket Match-Fixing and Related Matters, Capetown, South Africa, June 2000." Audio and video at www.rediff.com/cricket/betting.htm.

Dowd, John M. *Report to the Commissioner, In the Matter of Peter Edward Rose, Manager Cincinnati Reds Baseball Club.* Office of the Commissioner of Baseball. May 9, 1989.

Fassotte, Laurent, appearing before the Union Royale Belge des Sociétés de Football Association Commission d'Enquête. March 8, 2006.

Hussock, Howard. *Soccer Betting in Hong Kong: A Challenge for Home Affairs.* Boston: Harvard University, John F. Kennedy School of Government Affairs, 2002.

Institut de Criminologie de Paris Département de Recherche sur les Menaces Criminelles Contemporaines. Tapie, Courbis, Filippedu, le Belge, mafia(s), foot, argent sale et coups tordus. Paris: Université Panthéon-Assas (Paris II), 2005.

Kenya National Association of Social Workers. *Rapid Assessment on Mathare Slum Clashes.* UN Habitat. January 2, 2007.

King, Judge El. *Commission of Inquiry into Cricket Match-fixing and Related Matters, 2nd Interim Report.* Cape Town, South Africa: Republic of South Africa, 2000.

Mony, Paul Samuel. *M League: A Brief Outline and Report 1998.* Kuala Lumpur: Football Association of Malaysia, 1998.

Prosecutors Report. Hoyzer Case. Berlin: Staatsanwaltschaft Berlin, 2005.

Qayyun, M.M. *Reports of the Judicial Commission.* Lahore: Pakistan Cricket Board, 1998.

Smith, Sir John. *Game at Risk.* London: English Football Association, 1997.

Supdt, Sd/– M.A. Ganapathy. *Report on Cricket Match-Fixing and Related Malpractices.* New Delhi: CBI Special Crimes Branch – Central Bureau of Investigation, 2000.

Touche, Deloitte. *The Investors' Guide to European Football 2000.* London, 2000.

United States Senate. Hearings before the Permanent sub-committee on investigations of the Committee on Governmental Affairs. The New International Criminal and Asian Organized Crime. Washington, DC: United States Senate, 1992.

United States Senate. Permanent sub-committee on investigations of the Committee on Governmental Affairs. The New International Criminal and Asian Organized Crime. Washington, DC: United States Senate, 1992.

INDEX

national teams, 245, 260; sponsorship
deals, 290, 293
Filippeddu, André-Noël "Mr. Christmas,"
156-57
Filippeddu, Jules-Philippe, 157
Finney, Sir Tom, 104, 111
Finland soccer league, 29, 95
Fisher, Steve, 253
Flemming, Stephen, 218
"floodlights swindles," 184-85
"footballerati," 83
Ford, Trevor, 105-8, 111
Foreign Policy, 55
Forselv, Gunhild, 352, 363
Fort Siloso, 173
forwards, role in match-fixing of, 31-32
Foulkes, Bill, 103
Foul Play (Thomas), 181
France: France national team, 211; Ligue
de Football Professionel (French
premier league), 120, 151; match-fixing
investigation, 151-58, 165
Franzese, John "Sonny," 137
Franzese, Michael, 137-39, 142, 146, 188
Friedman, Robert, 3, 126
Frontline (PBS), 2, 122, 126, 138, 174
FSB (Federal Security Service of the
Russian Federation), 115, 124
Fulham FC, 60
Futures Markets Applied to Prediction
(FutureMAP), 71

G-14 (elite European soccer clubs), 159
Gabbert, Michael, 108-9
Galeano, Eduardo, 233-34
Gattuso, Gennaro, 80
Gazprom, 117
Genoa CFC, 27-28
Germany: German Bundesliga, 41, 185,

167, 190, 220; German Football
Association, 166, 179, 185, 189
response to match-fixing scandal,
187
Germany national team, 233-34, 242
West German national team, 43
match-fixing in, 41, 220, 223 (*See also*
Hoyzer, Robert); women's national
team, 298. *See also* World Cup
Germany 2006
Ghana: Ghana national team, 228-32,
235-37, 239, 241-250, 253-54, 256-57,
259-65, 267-69, 271-72, 276-77, 283,
285, 300-1
importance to Ghanaians of, 256
match against Iran, 272, 274-75,
280-82
GFA hearings on bribery before
Iran game, 280-81
vs. Brazil, 243-244, 248-249, 253,
261, 267, 283-84, 290
vs. Czech Republic, 238, 243, 268
vs. Italy, 235-37, 238
vs. South Korea, 235
vs. U.S.A., 238, 243, 261
World Cup camp, 238-49 *passim*,
254, 259, 261, 275, 277
Ghana Premier League, 257-58;
Ghanaian Football Association (GFA),
231, 246, 257-59, 273-74, 277, 280-81;
social conditions in, 237, 255-56,
262, 267
Gil, Jesús, 160
Giner, Vadim, 123
Giner, Yevgeny, 117, 123-24
Girondins de Bordeaux FC, 152
Glanville, Brian, 107, 152
goalkeepers, role in match-fixing of, 23,
29-32, 262